HIDDEN ALLY

Recent Titles in
Contributions in Military Studies

HIDDEN ALLY

The French Resistance,
Special Operations,
and the
Landings in Southern France, 1944

ARTHUR LAYTON FUNK

Contributions in Military Studies, Number 122

GREENWOOD PRESS
New York • Westport, Connecticut • London

Library of Congress Cataloging-in-Publication Data

Funk, Arthur Layton.
    Hidden ally : the French resistance, special operations, and the
landings in southern France, 1944 / Arthur Layton Funk.
        p.   cm.—(Contributions in military studies, ISSN 0883-6884
; no. 122)
    Includes bibliographical references and index.
    ISBN 0-313-27995-0 (alk. paper)
    1. Operation Dragoon, 1944.   2. World War, 1939-1945—Underground
movements—France, Southern.   3. United States. Army. Army, 7th—
History.   4. Great Britain. Special Operations Executive—History.
I. Title.   II. Series.
D762.S68F86   1992
940.54'214—dc20   91-30600

British Library Cataloguing in Publication Data is available.

Library of Congress Catalog Card Number: 91-30600
ISBN: 0-313-27995-0
ISSN: 0883-6884

First published in 1992

Greenwood Press, 88 Post Road West, Westport, CT 06881
An imprint of Greenwood Publishing Group, Inc.

Printed in the United States of America

The paper used in this book complies with the
Permanent Paper Standard issued by the National
Information Standards Organization (Z39.48-1984).

10 9 8 7 6 5 4 3 2 1

Acknowledgments

The author and publisher gratefully acknowledge the following for permission to use quoted material and photographs:

Richard J. Sommers and the U.S. Army Military History Institute at Carlisle Barracks, Carlisle, Pennsylvania, for the oral history of General Paul Adams.

General Michael S. Davison, for his own oral history interview.

Colonel H. A. Meyer, for letters from Meyer to his wife and for other passages from the "Meyer Papers," located in the 45th Infantry Division Museum Library in Oklahoma City, Oklahoma.

Geoffrey M. T. Jones, for an unpublished magazine article and for communications with the author.

Gervase Cowell and the SOE/Foreign & Commonwealth Office, London, for the reports located in the SOE archives.

Jean Favier and the French National Archives, for the Cochet papers.

Francis Cammaerts

Louis Constans

Henri Faure

Geoffrey M. T. Jones

J.-P. de Lassus St.-Geniès

Jacques Lécuyer

Alain Le Ray

André Pecquet

Thomas Piddington

Sir Brooks Richards

John Roper

Claude Vistel

Paul Zeller

La Fédération des Unités Combattantes de la Résistance et des F.F.I. de la Drôme

National Archives

La Sociéte d'Etudes des Hautes-Alpes

Secrétariat d'Etat chargé des Anciens Combattants et des Victimes de Guerre. Mission Permanente aux Commémorations et à l'Information Historique

U.S. Signal Corps

Dedicated to the Memory of

HENRI MICHEL
Dean of French Historians of the Second World War
Colleague, Friend, Adviser

Contents

Illustrations

MAPS

Maps were prepared by the author, who expresses thanks to Anthony Brooks (of SOE Circuit PIMENTO) for suggestions regarding conditions in 1944.

PHOTOGRAPHS   Following page 175

Preface

On August 15, 1944, the American Seventh Army, which included important French elements, implemented Operation DRAGOON (formerly ANVIL) by landing along the French Riviera with the aim of reaching Lyon, France's third largest city 300 miles away, within three months. In less than three weeks, the army had passed Lyon and was pressing forward toward the Rhine.

In preparation for the landings, many agents—French, British, and American—had maintained continual contact with the French Resistance in southeastern France. The agents slipped in, as Jedburghs, as Operational Groups, and as special teams, all directed from London or from the Special Project Operations Center in Algiers. Their activities were coordinated with the Mediterranean Theater Command and with Seventh Army planners in Naples.

Representatives of the British SOE (Special Operations Executive), with a few Americans from OSS (Office of Strategic Services), had worked with the Resistance from the war's early days, and their exploits have been admirably recounted, notably in M. R. D. Foot's official history, *SOE in France*. However, Foot's study, and others covering the French Resistance, concentrate on missions and preparations; they accord minimum space to the military campaigns that succeeded the landings.

In this book, I endeavor to present both preparations and aftermath. The first part deals with the Resistance and with special operations from the beginning of 1944 to the date of the landings. The remainder covers the collaboration of Resistance military units with the regular army until September 3, 1944 when, with Grenoble and Lyon liberated, the first phase of DRAGOON came to an end. I describe some military actions but only insofar as they relate to the French Resistance and to Allied missions. The reader who seeks more details on the

American, French, and German armies should consult such books as Russell Weigley's *Eisenhower's Lieutenants*, Alan Wilt's *French Riviera Campaign*, and the official army history by Jeffrey Clarke, *From the Riviera to the Rhine*.

Admittedly, this work concentrates on a small area—the southeastern corner of France. It would certainly be worthwhile to examine the whole country and to analyze all of the *départements* and all of the missions, as related not only to DRAGOON but also to OVERLORD, the Normandy assault. Such a project, however, would entail inquiries into all 90 French departments and into 118 missions. The present book reduces such monumental coverage into a microcosm: 11 departments, 37 missions, and a military operation far less complex than the northern one. Nevertheless, the pattern of missions and exploits of the FFI (French Forces of the Interior, popularly dubbed the Maquis) had sufficient similarities throughout France, so that conclusions regarding one area throw useful light on the total picture.

The role of the Resistance has not been adequately covered because French writers generally describe only what the French did, and American military historians deal essentially with the American army. This is not to say that writers of either nationality ignore the fact of mutual cooperation. American historians refer to "French Resistance groups," "French Partisans," "the FFI," "the Maquis," but their books rarely present enough detail for a proper evaluation of French support. Most French writers, for their part, refer simply to "les Américains," neither identifying them nor presenting much detail about their contribution to the liberation.

Such egocentrism is understandable. We are confronted with diverse cultures and attitudes, but, more to the point, with diverse wartime objectives as well. The Allied regular armies accepted their mission as destruction of enemy forces and a rapid thrust toward the German border. Members of the French Resistance, on the other hand, dedicated themselves to driving the occupiers from their cities and villages; they thought largely in terms of departments rather than the country as a whole, even though the top echelon of Resistance leaders had tirelessly worked to unify the country's disparate movements. As for the *military* resistance, it had not proved possible, in spite of strenuous efforts, to weld the FFI into a homogeneous army, with a clear hierarchy of command and an unambiguous relationship with French, British, and American headquarters in London and Algiers.

Neither French nor American (nor British) historians can be completely impartial, but it is worth the effort, employing reasonable objectivity, to try to describe the activities of preinvasion special missions, the harassment of the Maquis, and the operations of the regular armies, in order to produce a viable blend that does some justice to all the elements. To clarify events, which by their nature were secret, deceptive, clandestine, and confused, is not easy. I can only hope that from this study will emerge a better understanding of the hardships, the sacrifices, and the heroism of those who struggled through the dark months of 1944 in their efforts to fuse the missions, Maquis, and regulars into an effective instrument for the liberation of France.

Records in the National Archives in Washington, D.C., the British Public Record Office at Kew, and the Archives Nationales in Paris provided most of the sources for this study. At the National Archives I am especially indebted to Robert Wolfe and John Taylor, as well as to Larry McDonald for his efforts in making accessible many of the newly acquired OSS documents. I express thanks to Richard Sommers of the U.S. Army Military Institute at Carlisle Barracks, and to Christopher Woods, adviser for SOE records in London, whose services far exceeded those normally expected of an archivist. For assistance with French records, I thank in particular Gen. Jean Delmas, former head of the French Army Historical Service; Madame Bonazzi of the Archives Nationales; François Bédarida, director of the Institut d'Histoire du Temps Présent; and Guy Reymond, archivist of Digne—among many others.

I am very much in debt to many who, having read all or part of the manuscript, made innumerable helpful suggestions. In the United States: Geoffrey Jones, on mission in southern France in 1944 and later as president of the Veterans of OSS, provided insights and helped me get in touch with former agents; Gen. Michael Davison, in 1944 a battalion commander; Gen. William Quinn, Seventh Army G-2; Col. Thomas Piddington, in 1944 a troop commander with Task Force Butler; and Martin Blumenson, expert historian of the Resistance and wartime campaigns in France.

In England: Sir Brooks Richards, in 1944 French country desk officer in Algiers, and Francis Cammaerts, principal SOE agent in southeastern France, have been extraordinarily helpful and have studied the text and provided me with reams of invaluable comments; John Roper, who was dropped by parachute into the French Alps; Sir Douglas Dodds-Parker, wartime commander of SOE headquarters in Algiers; Anthony Brooks, head of PIMENTO; and Michael R. D. Foot, expert historian of SOE and the French Resistance.

In France: I gratefully acknowledge the help of many. Maguey McCullough and Raymonde Boix, members of the Resistance, directed me to contacts I otherwise might not have been able to make. I have had extremely valuable conversations and correspondence with Resistance leaders, especially Gen. Jean Constans (SAINT SAUVEUR, FFI chief in Region 2); Gen. J. P. de Lassus-Saint-Geniès (LEGRAND, FFI chief in the Drôme Department); Gen. Jacques

Lécuyer (SAPIN, head of the Organization of Army Resistance in Region 2, FFI chief in the Alpes-Maritimes Department); and Gen. Alain Le Ray (BASTIDE, FFI chief in the Isère Department).

Historians of the Resistance have in recent years obtained many insights from the work of local historians who have identified and described Maquis activities at the departmental level. Most of the departmental histories for southeastern France have appeared in the last fifteen years—for example: Ain: Yves Martin (1989); Alpes-Maritimes: Panicacci (1989); Ardèche: Ducros (1982); Basses-Alpes (now Alpes de Haute-Provence): Garcin (1983); Drôme: Abonnenc (1989); Hautes-Alpes: Duchamblo (1951), Béraud (1990); Isère: Silvestre (1978); Var: Masson (1983), Guillon (1990); Vaucluse: Arnoux (1974); city of Lyon: Rude (1974), Ruby (1979). (For complete titles, see "Documents, Memoirs, and Special Studies" in the Selected Bibliography.)

For broader and interpretive studies, all students of the French Resistance are especially indebted to the scholarship of M.R.D. Foot, Hillary Footit, Charles-Louis Foulon, René Hostache, H. R. Kedward, Henri Michel, Henri Noguères, John Simmonds, and John Sweets.

For preliminary research, I acknowledge the work of my students, Mary Lynn Aimone and Bruce Thompson. For keyboard and other assistance, I thank Phyllis Durell, Annick Munier, Ann McDaniels, Nancy Waters, Elaine Meade, and especially Terry Hall of AlphaGraphix in Gainesville, Florida.

I   Preparations: Resistance and Special Operations

1

Introduction

Although the landings in southern France have never received the same attention as that given to OVERLORD, the Normandy assault, it should not be forgotten that in the mind of Gen. Dwight D. Eisenhower, Supreme Commander of the Allied forces, two thrusts into France were considered as integral parts of the overall Allied Grand Strategy. Eisenhower's concept of a broad front, reaching from Switzerland to the channel, imposed on him the need for filling the most eastern segments of the line with forces not logistically dependent on supplies from the Normandy beachhead.

Eisenhower and the American chief of staff, Gen. George Marshall, firmly believed in this strategy, but Prime Minister Winston Churchill and many others, mostly British, vigorously opposed Operation ANVIL, the southern landings. The prime minister used every argument known—and Churchill knew them all—to persuade President Roosevelt, General Marshall, the Anglo-American Combined Chiefs of Staff, and Eisenhower to abandon the project. The British argued that pulling divisions from the Italian Theater would doom an advance into the Po Valley, and with that failure would evaporate all prospects of exploring the Ljubljana route to Vienna. On the American side, neither Roosevelt nor the Joint Chiefs of Staff cared to support British "adventures" northeast of Italy, and they brought forth a variety of arguments: word given to Stalin at Teheran, de Gaulle's reluctance to leave French divisions in Italy, the need for Mediterranean ports—all of which affirmed that ANVIL, even though delayed, must become operational.[1]

At the Quebec Conference, in August 1943, neither Churchill nor the British chief of staff, Gen. Sir Alan Brooke, registered strong opposition to a southern France operation. While he expressed some hesitancy about ANVIL, the prime minister "wanted it definitely understood he was not committed to an advance in northern Italy beyond the Pisa-Ancona line." Brooke approved a southern France landing if the Germans had withdrawn a number of divisions from the area. In the final report, approved by both Churchill and Roosevelt, the planners affirmed that Mediterranean operations should support OVERLORD by gaining airfields around Rome, obtaining Sardinia and Corsica, placing pressure on northern Italy, and entering southern France. Regarding the latter, the report specified: "Offensive operations against southern France (to include the use of trained and equipped French forces) should be undertaken to establish a lodgement in the Toulon-Marseilles area and exploit northward to create a diversion in connection with OVERLORD." With a gesture toward one of the prime minister's suggestions, the report added: "Air-nourished guerrilla operations in the southern Alps will, if possible, be initiated." AFHQ (Allied Force Headquarters) at Algiers, then under Eisenhower, was instructed to begin planning for the southern France assault. By December 16, 1943, Eisenhower's staff had drafted a plan for a Seventh Army assault on southern France with three American divisions, plus a follow-up of seven French divisions. To implement the draft plan, members of the Seventh Army staff flew at once to Algiers, where they started work as "Force 163."

After the Teheran Conference, in December 1943, Roosevelt and Churchill agreed that Eisenhower should leave Algiers to assume the duties of Supreme Allied Commander in London. They also concurred that a British general should succeed to the Mediterranean command, and they named to this post "Jumbo" Wilson—Gen. Sir Henry Maitland Wilson—who had served capably as Commander in Chief in the Middle East. The position of deputy commander went to an American general, the well-liked and genial Jacob "Jake" Devers. Devers was also Commanding General of American forces in the North African Theater, and ultimately, when the ANVIL contingents should build up to two armies, he would take charge of them as commander of Sixth Army Group. He had, therefore, a strong and personal interest in the naming of the ANVIL assault commander.

Shortly after taking up his new responsibilities, Devers learned that the U.S. IV Corps, commanded by Maj. Gen. Alexander M. Patch, Jr., had been assigned to the Mediterranean Theater. Devers had long known and admired Patch, a dependable and experienced officer who had acquired some knowledge of Free French intransigence in New Caledonia, and who had built up a reputation as commander in Guadalcanal. Devers strongly recommended to Washington that Patch be given the Seventh Army. In February 1944, Patch, having been briefed in Washington, flew into Algiers at the end of the month with a handful of staff officers. After intensive talks with Wilson and Devers, he became Seventh Army commander early in March. Although ANVIL was at the time in a state of suspended animation, Patch found no lapse of enthusiasm for it in Washington and no suggestion that cancellation was even under consideration.[2]

It was no wonder that Frenchmen who had been working with the Allies were somewhat bewildered. While the announcement that Patch had been appointed to command the Seventh Army seemed to confirm the fact that ANVIL would take place, there had not yet been any definite decisions concerning the exact role that the French were to play. Allied planning assumed that French divisions would land in France and that inside France the Resistance would be ready to help, but a myriad of how's and when's and where's remained to be spelled out.

THE FRENCH STAKE IN ANVIL

Since June 1943, Gen. Charles de Gaulle, leader of the Free French, and Gen. Henri Giraud, Commander in Chief of the non-Gaullist French troops in North Africa, had served as co-presidents of the FCNL (French Committee of National Liberation), which met in Algiers. The United States had mostly supported Giraud, a conservative, unimaginative career officer who wanted to fight Germans but who lacked the political insights and administrative capacity required of a top-level executive. De Gaulle found him uncooperative and a serious impediment to his own ambitions. In November, after disputes emanating from Giraud's unilateral actions in Corsica, de Gaulle forced his rival to surrender his seat in the FCNL, and thereafter emerged as undisputed single president. Giraud remained as Commander in Chief of the armed forces, however, and a power struggle developed between Giraud and the FCNL over the incorporation and equipping of Gaullist divisions into the rearmament plan that Giraud, at the Casablanca Conference, had negotiated with President Roosevelt. Accordingly, just as the Americans were approaching the French with concrete plans for the use of their troops, Eisenhower was confronted with a French political imbroglio that threatened to upset the orderly planning of ANVIL.

Out of the turmoil, with that inherent and undeniable flair for the right move in a political impasse, de Gaulle emerged with new prestige. When American staff officers outlined the ANVIL plan to him on December 27, 1943, de Gaulle revealed such a grasp of the overall problem (which Giraud had never demonstrated) that an agreement on the use of French troops under Allied control quickly evolved. On December 30, the day he left Algiers to assume his new command at SHAEF (Supreme Headquarters, Allied Expeditionary Force), Eisenhower sat down for a personal conversation with de Gaulle, and each gained a new respect and understanding of the other. Eisenhower seemed to comprehend the sensitivity and pride of the French leader in a way that President Roosevelt never could.

De Gaulle possessed a comprehensive view of Allied strategy and keenly appreciated his own need to work with the great powers at the same time that he made sure he would be accepted as leader within France. In November 1943, the same month that he ousted Giraud from the FCNL, de Gaulle summoned a "consultative assembly" to Algiers and brought into his provisional government three Resistance leaders, Henri Frenay, Emmanuel d'Astier de la Vigerie, and Fernand Grenier, a Communist. These were first steps leading to measures that would ensure that a Gaullist government would prevail after liberation and that the French military (Resistance forces as well as the rearmed French army) would be subordinated to de Gaulle's control. From the beginning, de Gaulle had maintained contacts with the Resistance within France, but finding out what was really going on in the Vichy-dominated Metropole was difficult and dangerous.[3]

THE RESISTANCE

The French Resistance had come into being in 1940—virtually as soon as the Armistice with Germany brought Marshal Philippe Pétain's collaborationist regime, with its capital at Vichy, into existence. However, most activities of the Resistance until 1944 had consisted of developing underground networks, stockpiling arms, publishing clandestine newspapers, forming escape chains, and sabotaging Nazi installations. After June 1941, when Hitler threw his undefeated armies against the Soviet Union, the French Communist Party finally recognized Germany as the ultimate enemy. With its long experience in clandestine operations, it brought its formidable machinery to the Resistance. In 1942, after the Allied invasion of North Africa, Hitler sent occupying troops into the southern zone and forced Vichy to disband the 100,000-man token Armistice Army. Many officers and men, however, continued to keep in touch with each other and set up an underground hierarchy that came to be known as ORA (the Organization of Resistance of the Army).[4]

On the nonmilitary side, many French citizens who were simple civilians began to band together secretly in order to resist the Nazi occupiers. In the South, an energetic journalist of leftist leanings, Emmanuel d'Astier de la Vigerie, united some groups under the title Libération. Another important group, Combat, was headed by the dynamic Henri Frenay, whose energy was largely responsible for the formation of a Gaullist military wing, the Secret

Army, or AS (Armée Secrète). When Combat, Libération, and another group, Franc-Tireur, came together in early 1943 as the MUR (*Mouvements Unis de la Résistance*), they recognized de Gaulle's leadership and accepted, at least in theory, that the military arm would help to impose de Gaulle's FCNL as the provisional government on the French people. In general, the professed policy of the Secret Army was to organize itself so that it could mobilize in force when the Allied invasion occurred but meanwhile was not to engage in premature uprisings that could provoke German reprisals. Under the MUR were listed many *Groupes Francs*, originally oriented toward sabotage but in any case filled with young enthusiasts who wanted action as soon as possible.[5]

Unification was complicated by those companies organized as FTP (*Francs-Tireurs et Partisans*). With its leadership largely Communist-oriented, the FTP strode along its own political and military path. Since many of its chiefs detested both the decadence of the Third Republic and the fascism of Pétain, they looked with suspicion at military Resistance groups headed by officers who had been trained in the pre-1939 tradition and who had served in the suspect Armistice Army. Nor were they necessarily partial to de Gaulle, who was identified by some FTP leaders as the tool of the British and who, in any case, exemplified a political tradition that was anti-Communist. Unwilling to take its orders directly from de Gaulle's provisional government in Algiers, the FTP looked for political and military leadership to the Communist Party or to the CNR (National Council of the Resistance), formed at the insistence of de Gaulle in early 1943 by the great Resistance leader Jean Moulin in an effort to bring all the clandestine movements together.[6]

From the very early days, many Resistance leaders kept in touch with de Gaulle's Free French in London and with representatives of the American and British governments. To administer and maintain the contacts, de Gaulle established the BCRA (*Bureau Central de Renseignements et d'Action*) directed by André Dewavrin (Colonel Passy), which did its utmost to nurture and organize the various Resistance movements in France.[7]

However, the French, almost entirely dependent on British subsidies, had to rely on British planes, weapons, and radio in order to keep in touch with their occupied country. This clandestine support, a unique phenomenon of World War II, came from a unique organization, SOE (Special Operations Executive), with which sections of its American counterpart, OSS (Office of Strategic Services), later became associated. What SOE was, and what it did, must be understood if one is to acquire some sense of the preliminary work and sacrifice that paved the way for ANVIL.

THE SPECIAL OPERATIONS EXECUTIVE

SOE was a secret organization formed after France fell in 1940.[8] It had the mission of holding together, aiding, and providing leadership for those stalwart individuals in Europe who could not accept Nazi domination and who wished to fight on with whatever meager resources they had. Attached to Lord Selborne's Ministry of Economic Warfare, headed after 1943 by Maj. Gen. Colin Gubbins, SOE from its London headquarters in Baker Street, enlarged itself octopus-like so that its tentacles touched ultimately on multitudinous problems: ferrying and parachuting agents into the European mainland, providing machine guns and explosives, and developing elaborate codes and radio communications, all with the purpose of hampering and interfering with the German occupiers. In 1942, for example, SOE's stated mission was to build up and equip paramilitary organizations, which would disrupt enemy transport, communications, and equipment by various methods, but with "particular care to avoid premature large-scale rising of patriots." In general, SOE never believed that widespread, universal risings would be effective: With their superior weapons and trained soldiers, the Germans would inflict unnecessary losses and undoubtedly wreak vicious reprisals against civilians.

Many British plans were developed with the Gaullist BCRA, and SOE maintained a separate section, RF, to provide services for the Gaullists. Using British planes, weapons, and radio equipment, the Free French were gradually able to send in agents and supplies to those who would form the nucleus of the Gaullist military organ, the AS. By August 1943, these BCRA enterprises had led to the formation in France of the BOA (*Bureau d'Opérations Aeriennes*) and in the South, previously unoccupied, SAP (*Section d'Atterrissage et de Parachutage*, or Landings and Parachute Section), responsible for selecting places for drops and for organizing the reception, storing, and distribution of weapons and explosives. Set up along a regional and departmental structure, SAP controlled hundreds of localities where agents and supplies could be landed or dropped.

SOE ran its own French operation, in F section, with French and British agents who built networks, arranged for air drops, and cooperated with Gaullist and non-Gaullist elements of the French Resistance. Headed by Maj. Maurice Buckmaster, this section was the largest unit within SOE concerned with France. For southeastern France, where ANVIL would be operative, F section ran a single circuit, JOCKEY, headed by a remarkable and dedicated agent, Francis Cammaerts (code name ROGER), whose contacts south of Grenoble and east of the Rhône provided him with a rare understanding of the region's possibilities.

The job of such agents as Cammaerts was to identify local Resistance leaders, and to enable them to receive the containers of arms and explosives, parachuted on moonlit nights at prearranged spots. Just as SAP made plans for Gaullist drops, so the F section agents made sure that supplies for their own people would reach the proper destination. The agents could do little without the cooperation of the French underground.

Nor could SOE "set Europe ablaze," as Churchill had urged them, unless they received the planes and weapons that were always in short supply. Even though the prime minister had backed SOE through many lean months, even his prestigious influence could not affect priorities set by the Combined Chiefs of Staff. In early 1944, however, he seriously took up the cudgels on behalf of increased air drops.

After the Teheran Conference, where operation ANVIL had been once more affirmed, Churchill had fallen ill with pneumonia. Then shortly after Christmas 1943, he had taken himself to Marrakesh for a period of convalescence. During the two weeks he spent there, the prime minister received generals and admirals, political hopefuls such as General de Gaulle, and lesser dignitaries such as Emmanuel d'Astier, who urged him to send more aid to the Resistance. Churchill promised d'Astier he would help, and he invited the Frenchman to come visit him in London.

Churchill was as good as his word. When he returned to London, he did convene a high-level meeting of ministers on January 17, which included Brigadier E. E. Mockler-Ferryman, head of SOE's "London Group" (Northern Europe), his superior Lord Selborne, minister of economic warfare, as well as d'Astier. The prime minister vigorously emphasized that he wanted increased arms deliveries especially to that area lying between the Rhône and the Italian border, from the Mediterranean to Geneva.

On January 31, Lord Selborne produced for the prime minister a not-too-optimistic summary of the situation in southeastern France, as well as plans for increased sorties. During the next week, six sorties flew into southeastern France. Churchill was ecstatic, sensing perhaps that a beefed-up Resistance army could replace ANVIL—in which case no divisions would have to be transferred from Italy. He sent a memorandum to Selborne: "I want March deliveries to double those planned for February."[9]

EISENHOWER AND THE FRENCH

Churchill's new policy, conceived and executed unilaterally, raised serious questions regarding Eisenhower's control over issues related to the land the

Supreme Allied Commander was charged to invade. When the prime minister convoked his special committee, he had not invited any Americans even though some agents from SO, the Special Operations section of Maj. Gen. William "Wild Bill" Donovan's OSS, had already joined SOE units in London and were rapidly learning about the French Resistance. In fact, the group that was advising the Supreme Commander had the official designation SOE/SO, although the OSS people never numbered as much as a third of the total personnel. When Eisenhower released to the French, on March 17, a statement about his plans for the Resistance, he was simply reflecting the standard policies of SOE, that guerrillas could best be used in sabotage, in blocking roads and communications, together with hit-and-run attacks over a widespread area. He also saw the need to bring SOE/SO closer to his own planning staffs and a week later absorbed the unit, not serving on the headquarters staff but "consulting, as if attached." Later these SOE/SO components especially involved in OVER-LORD were given a new name, SFHQ (Special Force Headquarters), with joint Anglo-American direction: Brigadier Mockler-Ferryman, head of SOE's Northern Europe section, for the British, and Col. Joseph F. Haskell, in charge of SO's London branch, for the Americans. SHAEF decided that overall control of the French Resistance should be exercised from London, which meant abolishing the line of demarcation in France that had given SHAEF the northern side and Gen. Maitland Wilson's AFHQ in Algiers the southern part.[10]

Eisenhower's vague statement about the use of the Resistance did not in any way satisfy de Gaulle, who saw nothing different from what had been the relationship between BCRA and SOE's RF section. What he hoped for was inclusion in Eisenhower's planning, with concrete tasks for the French in cooperation with the Anglo-American allies. Disappointed with the progress made by his representatives in London, de Gaulle named Gen. Pierre Koenig as his new military delegate. Having distinguished himself as commander of the Gaullist forces fighting with Montgomery in North Africa, Koenig, then 46 years old, brought great experience and prestige to his appointment. He took up his duties in London on April 1, but he was not certain exactly where he stood in the Allied Command hierarchy. He at once began negotiations with Eisenhower in order to resolve this difficulty.[11]

On his side, Eisenhower faced an almost insuperable problem because he himself had never received clear-cut instructions delineating exactly the line he should follow with the FCNL, even though a draft directive had been sent by Roosevelt to Churchill in March. Eisenhower was authorized to talk to Koenig on military matters—on this he had President Roosevelt's approval—but, as he advised the Combined Chiefs, if circumstances required him to reach agreement with the French on other matters, he would need additional authority.

It was clear to Koenig that, if he were to exercise command over the French Forces of the Interior, he would have to control not only the Gaullist BCRA, but also SFHQ. The French general established a London headquarters and began his campaign. He obtained the services of the "Action" section of BCRA, with Col. Henri Ziegler (code name VERNON) as his chief of staff. Because of BCRA's close relations with RF section of SOE, this move served notice that, if OVERLORD called for people or machinery controlled by de Gaulle, an understanding would necessarily have to be reached with the French military delegate. On May 24, Koenig officially requested that all Resistance forces be brought under SHAEF and that a French commander be appointed. A week later, Eisenhower agreed to confirm Koenig as commander in chief of the French Forces of the Interior, but with Normandy D Day set (unknown to the French) for early June, there was no possibility for the French commander to exercise a command that would materially help the landings.

After the beachhead had been established, SFHQ personnel hammered out a working agreement that evolved into a rather awkward administrative structure: Koenig would have two deputies, Mockler-Ferryman and Haskell, with a tripartite Franco-Anglo-American staff (EMFFI, or *Etat Major des Forces Françaises de l'Intérieur*) that would consist of Colonel Ziegler for the French, Maj. Maurice Buckmaster (head of SOE's F section) for the British, and Lt. Col. Paul van der Stricht (head of SO's French section) for the Americans. Significantly, the new organization did not become officially established until June 23, even though an enormous number of crucial decisions were being made on an *ad hoc* basis. Only gradually, well into August, did Koenig obtain real authority, by which time ANVIL had already been launched and Paris stood on the verge of liberation. Had this awkward situation—caused largely by Roosevelt's distrust of de Gaulle—been resolved earlier, some of the ambiguities and misunderstandings that plagued ANVIL might have been avoided.[12]

2

Resistance in Southeastern France

The French Resistance, because of its many confusing and contradicting aspects, almost defies analysis. Some resisters concentrated on politics, some on propaganda, others on helping Allied fliers to escape, and considerable groups devoted their energies to sabotage and fighting. They spanned political and social categories—from Communists to members of the old aristocracy: professors, lawyers, and physicians, as well as peasants. Beginning with small intimate groups of school or business associates, they ended up with literally hundreds of organizations, which far-sighted leaders tried to unify for more effective action. The hierarchy of command, with a duality of political and military leadership, was further complicated because organizations outside of France—ultimately de Gaulle and the FCNL—attempted to control those inside the Metropole. The FCNL had counterparts in local Departmental Committees of Liberation, while the military delegate—General Koenig—theoretically would command all those ragged poorly armed guerrillas who, after the Normandy D Day, comprised the FFI.[1]

In popular usage, all of the guerrillas, the insurgents, the terrorists (as the Germans called them), the Resistance fighters, the FFI, came to be known as the Maquis. Properly speaking, a Maquis (from a Corsican word for the "Bush") refers to a group of young people from five to several hundred, who had taken refuge together, living as best they could in the wilderness. An individual member was a *maquisard*. The number of *maquisards* increased greatly in 1943 by reason of German labor requirements, no longer met by volunteers. In France, the "Forced Labor Service" (STO, or *Service du Travail Obligatoire*) imposed on those selected a grave choice: working for the enemy or going underground. As more and more youths fled to the hills and forests, French citizens whose sons were drafted felt the conqueror's heavy hand more acutely than ever before, and many of them, shifting from a position of acquiescence to Vichy, became active in the Resistance.

Maquis groups were not necessarily military units, but since many of them had some arms and a consuming hate for the occupiers, they tended to develop guerrilla operations. In the plural, the Maquis (*les Maquis*) came to imply the military arm of the Resistance, sometimes small local groups with no affiliations at all, or, at the other extreme military companies and battalions.

The G.I.s of the Seventh Army, when they landed in southern France, used the term Maquis indiscriminately, singular or plural, to refer to all local French fighters they encountered. The Americans may have thought that all of the insurgent warriors belonged to one single command but, while such unity existed in theory, the actuality was quite different. Those French leaders who could view the totality of Resistance effort exerted great pains to unify the fighting elements in the Maquis so that they could strike together, in a coordinated plan, rather than leaving isolated units to harass the Nazi occupiers as they saw fit. However, the difficulties challenged the patience and capacities of everyone, French, English, and American, who confronted the problem.

By their very definition, the Maquis could not easily exist on the plains, along the open highways, or in the garrison cities. The *maquisards* were encamped in forests and, especially in the southeast, in the Alpine high country, where the winding roads and rocky escarpments discouraged too frequent German patrols. Here and there, in huts and tents, bivouacked on a plateau, these tough young patriots grouped together in a common cause to escape forced labor or German reprisals, ready to strike at the Nazi occupation troops with whatever means came to hand.

For the most part, a Maquis contained local people, and many Maquis were identified simply by the town from which the *maquisards* came. Others, especially if the leader were popular, might recruit from a wider area. Take as an example, the 142 members of the 6th company, commanded by Captain Brentrup, in the central part of the Drôme Department. About two-thirds came from Crest and other towns in the area, with about 25 from neighboring departments, such as Ain and Vaucluse, but included in the roster were three North Africans, one Pole, one Spaniard, two Germans, two Belgians, one Italian, one Russian, and one American—Pierre Bettager, from Madison, Pennsylvania.[2] It was not unusual, especially after the Normandy invasion, to find Slavic contingents (Poles, Ukrainians, Cossacks) who, having been forcibly inducted into the German army, had deserted and joined the Resistance.

Many of the French *maquisards* were farm workers—peasants—and members of the laboring classes, who might be in their teens or early twenties. Because there had been very little military training (at the enlisted men's level)

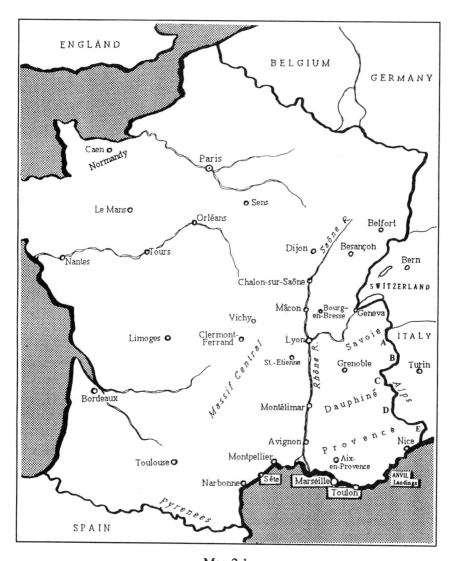

Map 2.1
FRANCE—1944
Passes between France and Italy: A = Little St. Bernard; B =
Modane (railway tunnel), Mont-Cenis; C = Montgenèvre; D =
Larche; E = Tende.

since 1940, most of the recruits knew nothing about tactics or the handling of fire arms. They had to improvise, and indeed, obtain their weapons and training as best they could.

How many were there? How well prepared were they? This was exactly what the Anglo-Americans, before the Normandy invasion, wished to know. How difficult the tasks of making estimates could be can readily be demonstrated by looking at a specific area—about 30 miles east and west, 40 miles north and south—encompassing plain, forest, and mountain, which could be the central part of the Drôme Department, a reasonable choice because later it became heavily involved in the southern campaign and served as the bloody terrain where the German Nineteenth Army came close to annihilation.

THE DRÔME

From a geographic point of view, the region enjoys considerable variety.[3] Along the banks of the Rhône east of Valence, spreads a rolling plain, dotted with farms and clusters of woods, about ten miles wide, then rising gradually 1500 feet to a plateau. From ledges along the plateau, one can see the plain spread out for miles, and once started downhill, an automobile can coast the ten miles from Léoncel to Chabeuil, where the German occupiers guarded the area's most important airport. Behind the plateau, another ten miles to the east, rise the formidable cliffs of the Vercors, a plateau so high, so well protected, and so inaccessible that the Resistance commander for the southeast maintained in this remote locality his regional headquarters. The great Vercors Plateau's southern escarpment descends to the Drôme Valley, with the principal road zigzagging down from the Rousset pass to the little town of Die, famous among Frenchmen for its sparkling wine. Moving westward along the Drôme Valley toward the Rhône, one leaves the protected gorges and emerges on the plain at Crest, whose great cube-like fortress overlooking the town provides a reminder that medieval strategists identified the site as guardian of the route eastward into the old province of Dauphiné. Continuing on toward the Rhône, one reaches the most important north-south highway, National Route No. 7 (N 7), together with the Marseille-Lyon railway, both of which span the Drôme river between Loriol on the south and Livron on the north.

South of the Drôme River, the region is mountainous and wooded. The plain along the Rhône narrows to a mile or two, hedged in between Loriol and Montélimar by the hilly Marsanne forest, some of whose western slopes come close to the river and whose eastern ridges command the great Marsanne plain, almost ten miles across, hemmed in by wooded slopes to the north, toward Crest

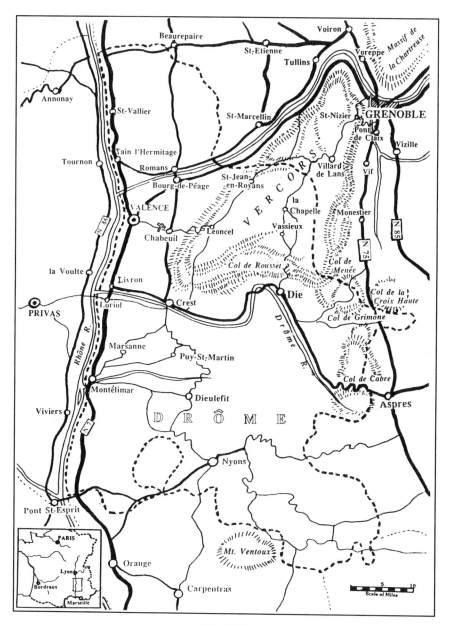

Map 2.2
THE DRÔME DEPARTMENT

and to the east at Puy-St.-Martin and Manas. (Here, in August 1944, would be fought the battle of Montélimar.)

In early 1944, the military Resistance groups of the region, which by this time had all accepted de Gaulle's leadership, came under the orders of Commandant L'HERMINE, the Drôme departmental military chief. L'HERMINE, whose real name was Drouot, had been mobilized as a sergeant in 1939, and soon thereafter became a cadet at the French air academy. After the French defeat, he continued to serve as an officer under Vichy, for a while at the Uriage *Ecole des Cadres*, that unique leadership school near Grenoble, sponsored by Pétain, which became a breeding ground for Resistance. Forced underground when the school was shut down, L'HERMINE remained active with the Secret Army in and around Lyon. One of the more flamboyant characters in the Resistance, he gloried in a black magisterial cape with a coat of arms and L'HERMINE embroidered on it. Surrounded by an admiring retinue, he enjoyed his role as a modern Robin Hood—some said bandit chief—and he played it with gusto and flair. All who knew him remember him as a colorful personality, but unfortunately there were many whom he antagonized.[4]

After February 1944, L'HERMINE received as deputy commander a young graduate of St.-Cyr (the French West Point), Commandant LEGRAND, the *nom-de-guerre* for Jean-Pierre de Lassus Saint-Geniès, who since his escape from a German prison camp in 1941 had served with the Secret Army in the departments of Ain and Savoie.

At that time, there were fewer than 500 *maquisards* in the department. De Lassus estimated that about 150 supported the Gaullist Secret Army, while the rest served with the pro-Communist FTP. However, there were others who, like the Minute Men of Colonial Massachusetts, could be called upon to leave their homes, get what weapons were available, and serve with already organized groups. These were the *sédentaires* (sedentary reserve), of whom there were perhaps 1,500 in the department. The extent to which they could be called up, and their reliability, depended more or less on the arms they might receive. The gathering of these parachuted arms continually preoccupied the Resistance leaders.[5]

To describe the situation at any one moment is difficult because of fluid conditions prevailing before the Normandy landings. The numbers of *sédentaires* changed constantly, as did the numbers and places of Maquis already in the field. Leaders were arrested and executed, and there were conflicts among those who arrogated to themselves authority over the lower echelons of the Resistance. Some Maquis recognized no higher command at all, and others wanted to have orders but remained confused regarding the chain of command.

Although difficult to maintain in occupied France, a clandestine military and political hierarchy connected the various departments and regions. Since the Drôme Department lay within a military region (R-1, with administrative center at Lyon), L'HERMINE and de Lassus irregularly kept in touch with Col. Marcel Descour, known in the Resistance as BAYARD, head of the Drôme-Vercors subregion, and with Col. Henri Zeller (FAISCEAU), responsible for the entire southeast. The regular army officers, especially those in the ORA, indoctrinated to accept a chain of command, did their best to make the system work, although the very nature of guerrilla units, with their disparate political views, their youthful untrained cadres, and their lack of telecommunications, made the task almost insuperable.

No account of Resistance organization is complete without a commentary on a principal concern: sabotage. In his memoirs, General de Gaulle singled out the Drôme Department, pointing out that the Maquis took action against the railroads in particular: "In December [1943], a train of German soldiers on leave was blown up at Portes-les-Valence; the wagons stopped or overturned were machine-gunned by our men, who killed or wounded two hundred soldiers."[6]

Individual acts like this occurred hundreds of times, all over France: There is no space to recount in detail each incident, such as one finds described in twenty-five pages of the Drôme official history; yet tables hardly reflect the heroism of the guerrillas, or the psychological effect on the occupiers. Nevertheless, let the record show that in the Drôme, there were:

17	major railway bridges destroyed, Oct. '43–Aug. '44.
248	attacks and sabotage of railway lines, locomotives, cars, and railway equipment, Feb.'43–Aug. '44.
25	road bridges destroyed, June–Aug. '44.
1	hydroelectric plant sabotaged, July '44.
25	high-tension lines and towers destroyed, Nov. 21, '43–Aug. '44.
15	ruptures of long-distance telephone cables, from June to the end of Aug. '44
2	large-scale attacks against trains of German soldiers on leave, Dec. '43, Feb. '44.
333	Total actions of the Drôme Resistance.[7]

While the work of sabotage never prevented the German occupiers from controlling the country, it produced delays, inconveniences, a need for constant patrols, and an increasing apprehension about the role they played. As General Eisenhower put it, the resistance forces had "by their ceaseless harassing activities, surrounded the Germans with a terrible atmosphere of danger and hatred which ate into the confidence of the leaders and the courage of the soldiers."[8]

INTER-ALLIED MISSIONS

London needed to know more about the work of the Maquis in southeast France, especially since operation ANVIL had been confirmed at the Teheran Conference. SFHQ deemed it advisable, in the interests of Allied-French unity, to send in to France what came to be known as inter-allied missions, teams representing England, the United States, and France, or more specifically: SOE, OSS, and the BCRA. One of the first teams, ordered to inquire about conditions east and south of Lyon (departments of Savoie, Isère, and Drôme) was Mission UNION, dispatched to the field in January 1944 and headed by an indomitable Gaullist of the first hour, Pierre Fourcaud. Fourcaud, then 45 years old, had served in World War I, joined the Free French in 1940, had been arrested and imprisoned while on mission in France, but had been able to escape and get back to London in 1943. With him as members of UNION were the British agent, a former schoolmaster, H. H. A. Thackthwaite, and an American who had served in the French Foreign Legion, Marine Capt. Peter Ortiz. The mission spent four months visiting Maquis groups and conferring with Resistance leaders, especially with those who commanded armed contingents. Ortiz, known as "Jean-Pierre," had responsibility for the Drôme where, with L'HERMINE and de Lassus, he arranged for dropping zones.

UNION completed its mission in May 1944, a month in which the Gestapo decimated the southeastern Resistance by an unprecedented series of arrests, deportations, and executions. Thackthwaite and Ortiz returned safely to England, where they reported on the size and capabilities of the guerrillas, but Fourcaud was arrested and held for two months by the Gestapo before he was released.[9]

Although missions like UNION were temporary affairs, sent out for a specific purpose, SOE had its own agents, in F section, who reported constantly on conditions. It so happened that southeastern France, where Operation ANVIL would be carried out, fell within the compass of a single F-section circuit, JOCKEY, developed by an extraordinary Englishman of Anglo-Belgian descent, Francis Cammaerts. What Cammaerts did and how he organized his units reveal much about the importance of SOE and the status of the Maquis prior to the invasion.

CIRCUIT JOCKEY

Francis Cammaerts was known to Resistance leaders throughout the southeast as Major ROGER, or sometimes more familiarly as *grands pieds* (big feet), a reference to the means of locomotion appropriate to a large-framed six-footer.[10] By June 1944, Cammaerts had spent a total of twelve months in France, eight in 1943 and the remainder in 1944, covering by car, foot, and motorcycle an area almost as large as South Carolina. Within this region, he had organized over 100 "minuteman" teams averaging around fifteen men, each with codes, communications, and drop zones, prepared for sabotage, harassment, and hit-and-run tactics.

To be sure, JOCKEY was only one of about forty SOE F-section circuits operating in France during 1943 and 1944, but it was nevertheless one of the most extensive. Also, while there were other nearby circuits, such as R. H. Heslop's MARKSMAN to the north, Anthony Brook's PIMENTO around Lyon, and Boiteux's GARDENER in the Marseille area, JOCKEY especially held a strategic significance for ANVIL. Cammaerts possessed furthermore unusual perceptions of the region because his personality with its unassuming modesty, combined with an intense moral commitment to his mission, engendered in his contacts a degree of faith and confidence—indeed of affection—that was remarkable.

Because his mother was British and his father Belgian, Cammaerts knew both English and French from childhood. Nevertheless, Cammaerts' education had been essentially British, and after Cambridge, he went into teaching, a profession that became, after the war, a lifelong preoccupation. In 1942, at the age of twenty-six, he joined SOE and went through its various schools— parachuting, sabotage—set up to train recruits in an enterprise calling for skills unheard of in any ordinary curriculum.

Not until March 1943, however, was Cammaerts dispatched to the field with the mission of reconstructing infiltrated circuits and of building new ones. Cammaerts soon concluded that efforts to resuscitate the older circuits might prove self-defeating, and he consequently moved south to the Mediterranean coast, where he made contact with a small resistance group at Cannes. Obtaining a forged identification card that described him as Jacques Thibault, a manager born in Morocco, he began to circulate through a wide area: to Avignon in the Vaucluse, where he met the dental surgeon Louis Malarte; north to Beaurepaire, between Grenoble and Lyon, where he arranged for the first container drop in August; to Montélimar on the Rhône; into the lower Alps, at Digne, where Dr. Paul Jouve, a respected physician and fierce patriot, made use of his wide contacts to assist Cammaerts immensely; to Marseille, where his

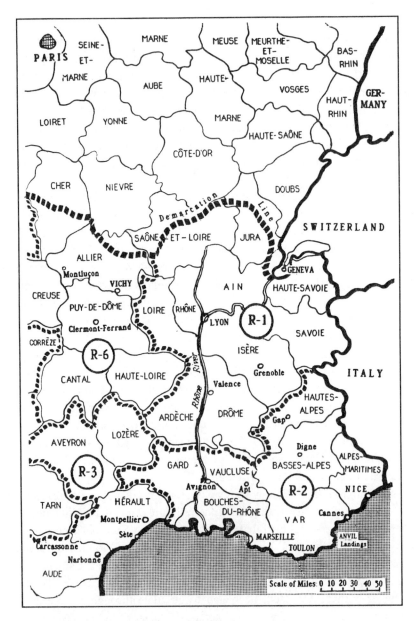

Map 2.3

SOUTHEASTERN FRANCE

Shown are Resistance areas south of the Demarcation Line, which divided Occupied from Unoccupied France, 1940 to 1942. This study concentrates on R-2 and R-1, the ANVIL/DRAGOON invasion area.

principal contact was a Communist, Jacques Méker; to Seyne-les-Alpes, where Cammaerts established one of his more permanent headquarters, with the Turrel family, and where many drops in 1944 brought in agents and weapons.

Cammaerts was able to maintain excellent contacts with SOE's Baker Street headquarters in London. In large part, this was accomplished through his wireless operator, Auguste Floiras, known in the Resistance as ALBERT, a navy veteran from Marseille, who was so expert and conscientious that he transmitted over 400 messages without detection from German direction-finding devices. While the two agents differed in stature—ALBERT's short, wiry body contrasted markedly with Cammaerts' height and build—they found common ground in security and in the affection tendered them by the insurgents.

Cammaerts was joined, in June 1943, by another F-section agent, known in the field as ALAIN, but whose real name was Pierre J. L. Raynaud. A native Frenchman, he had helped the Allies, in November 1942, land in Algeria, where he had been recruited by SOE and sent to England for training in sabotage operations. Raynaud helped Cammaerts by recruiting and establishing drop zones in the southern half of the Drôme department. Paul Pons, a Resistance leader in the Drôme river valley, recalls his first contacts with Raynaud, whom he met during the 1943 Bastille Day—14 July—celebrations:[11]

> We were contacted by an agent of the Intelligence Service [sic]. This officer, "Alain," was one of those rare Frenchmen officially affiliated with a very important Allied service. . . .
>
> Next day, after a long conversation, I conducted him on a tour of the areas I had checked as possibly suitable for parachute drops. These satisfied him, and back at the house, we arranged for a future drop and the code messages to precede it. I was really happy: finally I was going to get what we wanted most: arms, ammunition, explosives.

The foregoing scenario was repeated all over the JOCKEY area, with anywhere from two to ten groups recruited in each department.[12]

In October 1943, SOE ordered Cammaerts to report back in London. He remained in England during November, December, and January, those months in which Eisenhower left Algiers to take up command of SHAEF. He had the opportunity of reporting to SOE officials, arguing for increased drops of supplies (already strongly advocated by the prime minister), and emphasizing the idea of holding the Valensole plateau, the Vercors, and reinforcement with airborne troops.

After one false start, Cammaerts flew back to France on February 9, 1944, in a Lancaster bomber that, having been attacked by German fighters, had to be abandoned. Cammaerts and the crew successfully parachuted to the ground near Beaurepaire, west of Grenoble. Carrying several million francs and some false ration cards with him, Cammaerts would have been in trouble had he been apprehended by Germans or by the French *milice*. Fortunately, he and the crew fell in with patriots. At once he began to reestablish his old contacts.

He was especially successful in the Hautes-Alpes (Upper Alps), the department whose pleasant rounded hills in the west become more rugged and convoluted as the terrain rises toward the Italian frontier at Briançon, where 300 years earlier Vauban and his successors erected impregnable fortresses for Louis XIV. People in this area are mountaineers from childhood, and such was Paul Héraud, a chair-maker in the Hautes-Alpes' principal town of Gap, who in the underground had become, at the age of 37, the most adventurous and dynamic Resistance leader in the area.

Known simply as Paul, or in the Maquis as Commandant DUMONT, Héraud had served in the 1939 French army as a sergeant of engineers, and after the Armistice had become involved in the *Groupes Francs*, the activist arm of Combat, along with his good friend and deputy, Etienne Moreaud. With the welding of various groups into the MUR in 1943, Héraud became departmental chief, universally accepted by reason of his natural leadership qualities. His ability to obtain the devoted allegiance of his followers and his unique capacity to get along with people—politicians, career military officers, peasants, and mountaineers—brought him naturally to the center of Resistance activities in his department, where in 1944 he became not only *Chef FFI* but also a member of the Departmental Committee of Liberation. In the latter part of 1943, in conformance with the BCRA "Plan BLEU" (sabotage of power lines), he had successfully blown up transmission towers, for example in December, when the pylons near Pertuis were dumped into the Durance River.[13]

When Cammaerts finally met Héraud, they immediately struck up a firm friendship that lasted until Héraud's untimely death at German hands just before the ANVIL landings. Cammaerts has written:

> From my first meeting with Paul, I knew that I was dealing with the greatest Resistance leader I had ever met in France. From the first moment I had complete confidence in him, and the result is well known. Supplies began to arrive in important quantities throughout the department. . . . Paul remains for me the greatest friend, the most pure and sure that I have ever known in all my life.[14]

The four months between Cammaert's return in February until the Normandy landings in June saw increasing clandestine activity in the southeast and all over France. No one knew, of course, when or where the Allies would land, but everyone, whether in England, North Africa, Italy, or in France itself, intuitively felt that the great event must come in the spring of 1944. In spite of bad weather, the British and American bombers dropped more and more supplies, although never reaching those amounts that Prime Minister Churchill had hoped for. These figures give some idea of the materials the JOCKEY area was receiving:[15]

1944	Operations	Containers	Packages
March	8	156	133
April	8	117	93
May	18	418	278
June	16	466	343

Even so, Cammaerts was sometimes irritated at sloppy packing in Algiers, which meant a loss of perhaps 20 percent of the contents.[16]

What Cammaerts and SOE were doing must always be viewed against the backdrop of other happenings in London and Algiers, especially as the Normandy D Day approached. Cammaerts had a good deal of leeway in his actions, but he was constrained by the basic SOE directive that emphasized that Allied clandestine operations should support the overall Allied strategy for defeating the German *Wehrmacht*. His responsibility was

> for coordinating sabotage and other subversive activities including the organization of Resistance Groups, and for providing advice and liaison on all matters in connection with Patriot Forces up to the time of their embodiment into the regular forces. . . . Sabotage of communications and other targets, must be carefully regulated and integrated with our operational plans.

Clearly he was to mold and direct the units he armed so that they would give maximum aid to the Allied invasion; nothing in his instructions suggested, at least until June 1944, that he should support purely French internal objectives.[17]

THE FRENCH IN ALGIERS

Meanwhile, the French in Algiers were undergoing a crisis. For months, de Gaulle had been trying to obtain a clarification of the FCNL's relationship with the two western Allies. If he could obtain recognition, and if his French military commanders could be incorporated into the SHAEF structure, he would know with reasonable clarity how he would be able to move within metropolitan France. It was rumored that President Roosevelt was mulling over a directive to General Eisenhower. If this draft evolved into an Allied policy that recognized the FCNL as the provisional government and that brought the French into the exclusive top-secret planning staffs of OVERLORD and ANVIL, then de Gaulle could resist Communist pressures and develop procedures with the Anglo-Americans to apply to liberated areas.

The month of March 1944, however, had brought frustration on all issues to the French. It was learned that Roosevelt was not prepared to recognize de Gaulle. The farthest he would go was to authorize Eisenhower to deal with any group on a purely military basis as the Supreme Allied Commander believed necessary. Thus, he could deal with General Koenig, but not reveal to him top-secret information: The French did not know when the anticipated assault would strike, they did not know what cooperation with the interior Resistance was envisaged, and they did not know whether they would be faced, like the Italians, with an AMGOT (Allied Military Government of Occupied Territory). They were concerned that the Anglo-American command would overlook the political future of France, and make invasion plans without adequately considering either the interior or exterior Resistance.

Thwarted by the Allies' lack of cooperation, de Gaulle took unilateral steps. He eliminated Gen. Henri Giraud, the French Commander-in-Chief, by assigning him to a meaningless inspectorship; he took firm control of the military hierarchy, placing both regular forces and Resistance forces (with Koenig as military delegate outside France) under the FCNL; he invited cooperation with leftists by accepting two Communists into the National Committee, which he now began openly to refer to as the provisional government. Within France, he invited the Resistance to form Departmental Committees of Liberation and he undertook, by dispatching or naming military delegates (national, zonal, regional) to bring all guerrilla groups under a unified structure: the French Forces of the Interior. For his military and political delegates, de Gaulle tried to select individuals who, comprehending the policies and needs of his Algiers government, would control communications and ensure that the policies of the Liberation Committees, together with their military components, would conform to the decisions of his provisional government.

Although de Gaulle imposed his plans all over France, only the arrangements in the southeast, where the Allied troops of ANVIL came in contact with the local French, need concern us here. We have already mentioned the Departmental Liberation Committee in the Drôme. By early 1944, there were similar committees in all twelve departments of the southeast.[18]

De Gaulle also sent "military delegates" into France whose function was to serve as liaison between his provisional government and local military chiefs. For all France, he had named Jacques Chaban-Delmas, and for the southern zone, Col. Maurice Bourgès-Maunoury, with headquarters near Lyon. The latter, code named POLYGONE, 30 years old, had graduated from the prestigious *Ecole Polytechnique* in Paris and had served as an artillery officer before the French defeat in 1940. Continuing in politics after the war, Bourgès would hold a number of cabinet posts and, in 1956, as minister of defense, would attain international prominence during the Suez crisis.[19]

Bourgès-Maunoury and other high-level Resistance leaders, assuming the Allies would land along the Riviera, realized there should be a military commander who could unify action within the possible target area. For this post they chose Col. Henri Zeller, a career officer who had served on the Armistice Army staff at Vichy until it was dissolved in late 1942. Thereafter, Zeller had operated clandestinely within the ORA, especially in the south, where he had contacts at Lyon, Grenoble, Marseille, and Nice. In late 1943, during a secret mission to Algiers, he had seen both Generals Giraud and de Gaulle. From Algeria, Zeller flew to London, where he made contact with Buckmaster but not with the Gaullists in BCRA who may have been suspicious of his Vichy/Giraudist connections. Returning to France, he worked for cooperation and unification of the Secret Army and the MUR, with the professional soldiers of ORA providing the chiefs of staff.[20]

Long before the Allies landed, Zeller had organized a clandestine chain of command that established hierarchies of officers: regional, subregional, and departmental. Southeastern France had two administrative regions: R-1, with its seat at Lyon, included eight departments: Ardèche, Drôme, Isère, Savoie, Haute-Savoie, Ain, Rhône, Loire, and parts of two others; R-2, headquartered at Marseille, was composed of seven: Gard, Bouches-du-Rhône, Var, Alpes-Maritimes, Vaucluse, Hautes-Alpes, and Basses-Alpes (later renamed Alpes de Haute-Provence). Under Bourgès-Maunoury, there were regional military delegates, and under Zeller, regional, subregional, and departmental military commanders (referred to after the French Forces of the Interior were established, as *chefs, FFI*).

Not the least of Zeller's concern was coordination with SOE and BCRA, the source of supplies and orders from the Allies. Technically speaking, by the time of the Normandy invasion, the French sections of SFHQ should have been consolidated under General Koenig's FFI headquarters in London, and in the field, all separate military groups theoretically should have lost their separate identities. However, Regions 1 and 2, which comprised Zeller's command, lay much closer to Algiers than to London. Zeller had reason to suppose that most of his supplies and orders would come from Algiers, directly from de Gaulle, or from the FCNL's special services unit, which had a subcommittee supervising action in France. Yet the transmitters and planes reaching into France remained in Allied hands. De Gaulle could not act unilaterally; he had to coordinate action through the appropriate Allied agencies, SOE and OSS.

The French also had to coordinate the policies and actions of the Gaullists outside France—in Algiers and London—with those of the Resistance leaders inside France, many of whom did not consider, with some justification, that the exterior French, who acted as legislators, really understood what conditions in France were like. Many insurgents believed that the clandestine CNR (*Conseil National de la Résistance*), created by Jean Moulin with de Gaulle's approval, better represented the true aspirations of the French underground, not only of the major Resistance groups, but of the labor unions and political parties.[21]

Aware of the CNR's rival claim to authority, the Algiers government appointed regional and departmental prefects to replace Vichy officials as soon as possible. With primary allegiance to de Gaulle rather than to the CNR, they would strengthen de Gaulle's administrative hold over the entire country.

In southeastern France, there were two regional prefectures, one with its capital at Marseille covering approximately the Resistance area R-2, and the other, centered at Lyon, with its region corresponding to R-1. De Gaulle called the regional prefects *Commissaires de la République*, and months before the ANVIL landings had named his candidates for the southeast: Raymond Aubrac for Marseille and Yves Farge for Lyon.[22]

An engineer educated at M.I.T. and Harvard, 30-year-old Aubrac had been arrested in Lyon with Jean Moulin, but had been able to escape and make his way to Algiers. He would come ashore with the ANVIL troops and take up his responsibilities a few days later when Marseille was liberated.

Farge, on the other hand, was already residing in France. Journalist by profession, leftist in orientation, he had been editor of the *Progrès de Lyon* before the German occupation forced him underground. Although not a Communist, he had been a director of the Communist-dominated *Front National*.

At the departmental level, de Gaulle named Resistance prefects, some of whom had already participated in local underground activity. Altogether, there were a great many political and military chiefs, some self-appointed, some designated by Algiers, others approved by the CNR, who would serve as hidden allies when Patch's Seventh Army came ashore in August 1944.

3

Special Operations
in Southeastern France

Shortly after the successful Allied landing in North Africa, in November 1942, the British inaugurated an SOE operation at the Club des Pins, a group of villas in a secluded area about 15 miles west of Algiers, under the code name MASSINGHAM. In January 1943, Lt. Col. Douglas Dodds-Parker became MASSINGHAM's commander after a meeting in Algiers with Eisenhower, attended by Col. William ("Wild Bill") Donovan, director of OSS, Maj. Gen. Colin Gubbins, executive director of SOE, and Lt. Col. William Eddy, heading OSS-Algiers. Dodds-Parker recalled the discussion:

> Eisenhower said the OSS and SOE should work closely together; that Eddy was to be the head and I was to be his second-in-command. Clasping his hands, he said to us all, "You must work together like this. You must have no secrets from each other." We all agreed. Eisenhower, like Alexander later, inspired devoted loyalty.[1]

Since SOE had already been operating out of Cairo and Gibraltar, it had a considerable head start in planes, ships, containers, and contacts within Europe. Thus, while on paper the Americans were supposed to be equal, they were far behind in organization and equipment. As late as mid-1943, OSS could provide only a plane or two for dropping supplies from Algiers. Up to April 1944, SOE had 18 Halifax bombers available to the Americans' three Flying Fortresses (B-17). There were in fact very few Americans among the many missions, mostly despatched from London, working with the French Maquis.

In North Africa, Donovan sought to gain more freedom of action than he had achieved in England. Consequently, the OSS operation out of Algiers, although ostensibly cooperating with the British, embarked on a number of independent enterprises. OSS differed from SOE in that it contained an Intelligence component (SI) as well as an Operations section (SO). In England, the SI activity had been curtailed because British Intelligence was unwilling to accept a parallel operation by what they considered Donovan's naive newcomers. In French North Africa, however, especially with the American Eisenhower holding the Mediterranean command (AFHQ), an SI operation began to develop.

For France, the OSS Intelligence branch fell under the guidance of a capable New Yorker, Henry B. Hyde, who by the time of the ANVIL landings controlled fifteen to twenty networks in Metropolitan France. Educated in France, Switzerland, England, and Germany, speaking idiomatic French, Hyde exercised a cosmopolitan charm, unusual among Americans, which ingratiated him into many of the diverse circles of intrigue-ridden Algiers. Although his first agents did not reach France until July 1943, ultimately they accumulated significant amounts of information about roads, bridges, German installations, and enemy troop movements, all of which became available to the ANVIL planners. In time, the SI branch recruited a large staff that, attached to the Seventh Army's G-2, moved to Naples when General Patch transferred his headquarters there in July 1944. It should be made clear that the SI unit attached to Seventh Army, although part of OSS, was completely separate from the OSS/SO unit in Algiers. It would not be SI's function to develop liaison with French guerrillas or to serve as interpreters as the advance forces moved through the countryside. This function would devolve on SOE and OSS's SO section.[2]

Throughout 1943, SOE and OSS expanded their activities in the Mediterranean, not so much in France as in Italy, Yugoslavia, and the Balkans. Once the OVERLORD and ANVIL decisions had been made, however, late in the year, the planners focussed their eyes on France. In January 1944, an agreement reached at Algiers among British, French, and American representatives established for special operations three target areas: the Eastern Mediterranean, Italy, and France. Thereafter, MASSINGHAM would concentrate on southern France, would cooperate more closely with the SO section of OSS, and would work with the appropriate agency in de Gaulle's provisional government.[3]

To establish exactly what this agency would be posed a considerable problem for the French because two separate services, one Giraudist and one Gaullist, made rival claims. When de Gaulle eliminated Giraud from active duty in March 1944, he opened the way for integration of the two agencies. The difficult task of consolidation fell to Jacques Soustelle, a brilliant young anthropologist who from the early days had thrown in his lot with de Gaulle. Soustelle's DGSS (*Direction Générale des Services Spéciaux*) became the Algerian counterpart of the London BCRA and, with de Gaulle once established in North Africa, the senior intelligence and operational agency. The London office became a branch, thereafter technically BRAL (*Bureau de Renseignements et d'Action de Londres*).[4]

Under DGSS, there existed an implementing body, the *Direction Technique*, that supervised a small group, the "Action" Service, concerned especially with operations (as opposed to Intelligence) within France. When Commandant Clipet, the Giraudist officer who headed this service, was relieved, Soustelle concluded that an officer close to General de Lattre (who would be commanding the French forces destined for ANVIL) would provide a satisfactory liaison. De Lattre concurred and released his aide, Lt. Col. Jean Constans, for this position.

Constans, a tall, heavy-set officer (code named SAINT SAUVEUR), had since 1941 served as *chef de cabinet* to de Lattre, who having been imprisoned in France, had escaped to London, and finally reached Algiers in December 1943. Constans, coming to Algiers with the general, remained as his aide until May 15, 1944, when he assumed his new position as *"Chef, Service Action"* under Soustelle. One of his major tasks, to develop good relations with MASSINGHAM and especially with the French section head, Lt. Cdr. Brooks Richards, was facilitated by the fact that Capt. Guillaume Widmer, already on the "Action" staff, became automatically a member of Constans' team.[5]

"Willy" Widmer, a French Protestant, outdoorsman, and good horseman, was well accepted by the British officers at MASSINGHAM's Club des Pins, where in fact he was already living. Trained in law and banking, the 36-year-old Widmer, a cousin of André Gide, had worked for the Banque d'Indochine in Shanghai before coming to Algiers by way of Indochina as a lieutenant in the Colonial Infantry. Widmer's Gaullist leanings did not endear him to his superior, Clipet. Widmer went to London with Brooks Richards in February 1944, and during their stay, the two developed a mutual admiration. They were endeavoring to seek better means of coordination between London and Algiers. Widmer also impressed the Gaullist BRAL officers, and back in Algiers, when Constans replaced Clipet, Widmer's influence became increasingly significant. Later, sent into France, Widmer would receive an on-the-spot promotion to colonel. After the war, Widmer distinguished himself in government service, first as governor-general of Württemburg during the occupation of Germany and thereafter as *directeur de cabinet* for several defense ministers.

ESTABLISHMENT OF SPOC—SPECIAL
PROJECT OPERATIONS CENTER

In the spring of 1944, with training for the cross-channel invasion in process, there developed imperative needs for MASSINGHAM (to say nothing of OSS) to obtain a directive from Eisenhower so that the southern French Resistance would give maximum support to the invasion plans. It took some time for SHAEF to enunciate a definite policy. Meanwhile in April, SOE and OSS representatives began to consult on ways by which OSS and MASSINGHAM— also possibly French officers—could achieve better coordination. Out of these discussions emerged a decision to integrate MASSINGHAM with those OSS officers (of SO section) who were especially concerned with France, following somewhat the pattern of the London-based SFHQ.

Once the decision was made in May, the awesome technical capacities of the armed forces in Algiers quickly permitted construction of a new facility, made up of nine Quonset (British: Nissen) huts, over twenty-five tents, and a wooden mess hall, built across from the Villa Magnol (one of the OSS-North Africa installations), which was given the name Special Project Operations Center, or, as it was generally called, SPOC. The Center opened officially on May 23, 1944, scarcely two weeks before the cross-channel attack.[6]

The staffing of SPOC continued the inter-allied procedure of British and American officers sharing responsibilities. The command went jointly to the British Lt. Col. John Anstey, commanding officer of MASSINGHAM, and to the American Lt. Col. William P. Davis, SO director in Algiers. Under Anstey and Davis (who with their staffs occupied the Control Hut), there were four basic sections: French, Air, Jedburgh and OGs, and Intelligence, linked together and with the field by a complex signals operation.

The French section was headed by the British Lt. Cdr. Brooks Richards, who carried on with the same general responsibilities he had shouldered at MAS-SINGHAM, maintaining contact with all the agents and missions in southern France. Francis Brooks Richards (he did not use his first name), a yachting enthusiast and yacht designer, had begun his studies at Cambridge when the war broke out in 1939. At age 21, he received a reserve commission in the Royal Navy, and later assumed command of a small minesweeper that was sunk in 1940. Thereafter, as a member of SOE's Naval Section, he became engrossed with the possibility of making contact with France by sea. In October 1942, on a special mission to Gibraltar, he tried to get arms to Algerian resisters. After the North African landings, he participated in SOE missions to Tunisia and, from December until February 1943, commanded a pro-Gaullist, SOE-trained group of young Frenchmen, holding a position at Cap Serrat. Relieved by regular troops, Richards then carried out SOE missions in Malta and Corsica when, in October 1943, at age 25, he replaced Jacques de Guélis as French desk officer at MASSINGHAM. (De Guélis had to be replaced because neither de Gaulle, who had just eliminated Giraud as rival president of the French Committee of National Liberation, nor Jacques Soustelle, charged with reorganizing French Special Services, would cooperate with one of SOE's F-section officers.) An energetic and capable officer, Brooks Richards went to the British Embassy in Paris after SPOC closed in October 1944. After the war, he would serve with distinction in government posts at home and abroad including, in the 1970s, appointments as ambassador in Saigon and in Athens.[7]

Richard's American opposite number was Capt. Gerard (Gerry) de Piolenc, an engaging and enthusiastic young OSS officer. De Piolenc was actually of French origin, a member of an aristocratic French family. The training section included Lt. Geoffrey Jones, an American who had spent part of his youth in the Fréjus area in southern France and knew French.

With the OSS people being mostly newcomers, the operations at first were maintained as they had been at MASSINGHAM although now modified to conform with directives from SHAEF, AFHQ, and Seventh Army Planners. SPOC was not a policy-making agency (although it recommended policy), but rather a vehicle to carry out and coordinate all orders from higher levels with the end of building up the French Resistance, giving it guidance, and making it capable of assisting Allied regular forces.

To accomplish this, SPOC had responsibility for the 30-odd missions that ultimately operated in southern France. In some instances, however, agents were run from London, in which case SFHQ would coordinate their control with SPOC; intelligence agents in general also had separate arrangements, although SI and SO, within OSS, were not always distinguishable. Altogether, SPOC was involved in six types of missions:

1. British SOE missions, such as the JOCKEY Circuit of Francis Cammaerts.
2. French missions, coordinated with Soustelle's DGSS.
3. Inter-allied missions, made up of British, French, and American representatives.
4. Jedburghs. This was a special type of inter-allied mission. "Jedburgh" was the code name given to teams of three men, at least one of whom would come from continental Europe, the others British or American.[8]
5. Operational Groups. The OGs constituted an elite OSS mission. They were paratroopers organized into squads of thirty who generally fought in component parts, for example, a half: thirteen men and two officers,

all of them American volunteers for "extra hazardous duty" and assigned
to OSS for special missions.[9]

6. Counterscorch. These consisted of French naval personnel sent to the
    ports of Marseille, Toulon, and Sète to keep the Germans from sabotag-
    ing the docks or blocking the channels.

In order to direct and to supply its missions, SPOC kept up a steady volume
of communications with the field. One hut was devoted to writing and receiving
field messages, at first handled almost entirely by SOE. Another hut, using the
MASSINGHAM ciphers, encoded and decoded the messages that, via a teletype
system, were relayed to and from the MASSINGHAM wireless transmitting
and receiving station west of Algiers. The volume of messages, constantly
increasing, and the diversity of situations strained both equipment and personnel. There were over 50 radio operators in southern France, together with
various missions and circuits with their own operators. Each agent might
transmit once or twice a day and receive an equal number of messages from
Algiers. The messages coming to Algiers had to be decoded, copied, and
distributed—hundreds per day—some of which were relayed to or from London.

When SPOC began operations in late May, control of the Resistance, as far
as the Allies were concerned, remained vested with SHAEF, so that actions
within France could be coordinated with OVERLORD. On the other hand,
General de Gaulle, through the French Committee's Special Services, also
communicated with the Resistance. In London, this service had been rendered
by SOE's RF section; in Algiers, it went from Soustelle's DGSS via Brooks
Richards' desk in MASSINGHAM, and after May 23, via the French country
section desk (Brooks Richards and de Piolenc) at SPOC. These complexities
sometimes meant a delay of three or four days before a message reached all of
the French addressees. Within SPOC, decipherment and routing were much
more rapid.[10]

Coordinated with overall control and with the French country section stood
the operations hut, with its maps detailing all of the agents in the field together
with the many drop zones. Operations had to keep track of the equipment being
packed in containers, loaded on planes, and ready for parachuting into southern
France. It worked closely with the air operations section, ensuring what planes
and pilots were available, and whether meteorological conditions would permit
sorties.

The number of planes available to SPOC had increased from twenty at the
beginning of 1944 to over thirty. The basic contingent of eighteen Halifax
bombers (RAF 624th Squadron) was augmented when Roosevelt and Secretary

of State Hull, piqued by de Gaulle's April statement that most of his help came from the British, pressured the Joint Chiefs of Staff to have more American bombers made available for bringing aid to the French Resistance. Consolidated with the three B-17s already serving OSS/SO, the 885th Bomb Squadron ultimately provided SPOC with a total of eleven four-engine Flying Fortresses and Liberators (B-17s, B-24s), together with seven two-engine B-25s capable of handling containers, paratroopers, and pamphlets. The American crews, new to Special Operations, took some time to learn the techniques of communicating with the ground and making pinpoint deliveries on the drop zones. At first they could not match the skill of the Royal Air Force pilots, but they rapidly gained in experience. In May, the month that SPOC was established, the Americans made forty-five successful sorties into southern France and thereafter made an increasing contribution to the task of getting supplies to the Maquis. By September, when SPOC completed its mission, the number of successful sorties into southern France (over 1,000) and the tons dropped (over 3,000) were about evenly divided between the Royal Air Force and the United States Air Force. The British, however, took more than double the number of personnel into the field (411 to 198).

While SPOC controlled the planes assigned to it, the overall command of aircraft remained vested in General Eaker's Mediterranean Air Force, which could alter the allocation or supplement it according to overall strategic requirements. With northwestern Europe under SHAEF, the Mediterranean command gave its highest priority not to France, but to the Balkans and Italy. In 1944, there were over 13,000 successful sorties into Yugoslavia, Albania, Greece, and northern Italy, compared to 1,129 into southern France. Nevertheless, the Mediterranean command did assist SPOC from time to time, making available Wellington and Dakota bombers, and some Lysanders for special missions when agents had to be landed or evacuated.[11]

At SPOC, several huts were devoted to air operations, of which one housed the personnel responsible for those unique types of operations: the inter-allied Jedburghs and the American OSS Operational Groups. The Jeds and the OGs posed additional problems for SPOC, which already administered or had to keep track of SOE circuits, French missions, and inter-allied missions, to say nothing of coordinating all these operations with the needs of General Patch's Seventh Army. How to use the Jedburghs most effectively raised problems among Operations, the Country section, and the Jedburgh section, headed by the British Major Champion. Coordination proved difficult but was eased when Maj. Neil Marten replaced Champion in early August. A Jedburgh himself, Marten had parachuted into the Drôme as a member of team VEGANINE but had returned to Algiers for consultation. The orders for OSS's Operational Groups, administered in a separate section headed by Maj. Alfred G. Cox, also had to be coordinated with Operations and the Country section.[12]

At the height of its operations in August, SPOC personnel numbered about 150, but if one counts all the people—agents, Jedburghs, OGs—operating in the field, one must add another 400 or 500 to the list. Before examining what SPOC did specifically in preparing the way for Operation ANVIL, one must take at least a glance at the ways in which it coordinated its activities—with de Gaulle's Committee of National Liberation and with General Patch's Seventh Army.

THE FRENCH AND SPOC

Up to June 6, the date of the Normandy landings, the French, for security reasons, had not been privy to top-level planning and decisions. Once the Allies were in France, however, this changed and, with Eisenhower strongly arguing for ANVIL, de Gaulle and the French Committee of National Liberation participated in its planning: General de Lattre would move his headquarters to Naples adjacent to those of General Patch, there would be French liaison officers at various levels, and a French representative would serve in SPOC.

This French representative was to be Lt. Col. Jean Constans (SAINT SAUVEUR), who as head of the "Action" Service within Soustelle's Special Services, was already maintaining liaison with MASSINGHAM. The choice of Constans, a military career officer, signified a shift in Gaullist policies, echoing a realization that the Allies, unwilling to extend political recognition to de Gaulle, nevertheless appreciated the value of French soldiers in the forthcoming campaign. Constans conceived of his new job at SPOC essentially in military terms. "We are at war," he told Brooks Richards, "We will have an operation plan to carry out, under orders and a command—that alone is what counts and is related to reality."[13]

There remained, however, the need for a clarification as to where exactly Constans stood in the hierarchy of command. Part of the problem lay in the fact that, when General Giraud was ousted from his command of French forces in North Africa, de Gaulle insisted that thereafter military liaison should be directed to Gen. Emile Béthouart as his chief of staff for national defense. However, in order to have a counterpart in Algiers to the position General Koenig held in London, de Gaulle had named (at the same time as the Koenig appointment) Gen. Gabriel Cochet as military delegate for southern operations (DMOS, *Délégué militaire Opérations Sud*). Cochet was a capable Air Force officer who, like de Lattre, had been imprisoned by Vichy, escaped, and finally had joined the Gaullists in North Africa. It should be noted at once that "military delegate" did not mean "Commanding General," but referred to an officer who represented de Gaulle's FCNL somewhat ambiguously as liaison with the Allied Command and with the military forces of the Resistance—the FFI.

Thereupon the question had to be posed: Did Cochet have powers (in the south) equivalent to those of Koenig? If SFHQ and BRAL joined together in London, should not SPOC and DGSS be amalgamated, and if so, would they be under Cochet? Constans found himself in a curious predicament, not clear just who his superiors were. Facing this dilemma, he sent his deputy at SPOC, "Willy" Widmer, to London on June 22 to seek clarification. After seeing Koenig, Widmer wired Constans assuring him that he was officially empowered to act as Koenig's representative in dealing with DGSS and with Cochet. There was no mention of amalgamation. This was an unenviable position in which to find oneself while, during the months that followed, Cochet attempted to gain authority already distributed between SPOC and Soustelle. Because SPOC possessed the equipment, the personnel, and the money, its directors were not inclined to give up power they held in practical fact, which, if surrendered, could acerbate French political infighting.[14]

Constans later (in 1962) made some trenchant comments about his role in SPOC, where so far as policy was concerned, he considered that he should be on equal footing with Anstey and Davis.[15] However, facing reality, he noted:

> Apparently attached to the British section, but actually autonomous by reason of his designation "Liaison officer," Lt. Cdr. Brooks Richards maintained within SPOC the position of representative of the Allied command to which the agency was subordinated. This Command never manifested a direct presence, which enhanced the influence and personal role of B. Richards.

Constans recalled the excellent and cordial relations within SPOC's tripartite structure, but he could not avoid a sense of frustration, any more than de Gaulle could, at his enforced second-class citizenship. The SPOC commanders, Anstey and Davis, with their overall responsibilities, were not inclined to take Constans into their circle, while they nevertheless expected the French country officer, Richards, to maintain daily contact with DGSS's "Action" representative. With Richards a grade lower than Constans, this interchange devolved essentially on Widmer, whose congeniality and broad-based attitudes were suited admirably to the task. Brooks Richards was not officially a "liaison officer," nor was he autonomous, but, responsible for operations long before Constans arrived on the scene, he could not readily alter the complex business of running agents into France to suit the concepts of a very military regular French officer. Constans never felt entirely comfortable in a situation where without real authority he had to cope, like a new boy on the block, with operations already in progress.

SPOC, OSS, AND THE SEVENTH ARMY

OSS had run into difficulties in Italy where Gen. Jacob Devers, the senior U.S. Commander in the Mediterranean Theater, had subjected some of its activities to severe criticism. For the ANVIL operation, OSS was determined to coordinate its activities with the army command. Such a move made good sense especially in light of the fact that, once the armies were ashore, they would unite to form the Sixth Army Group, which Devers would command. Incorporation into Seventh Army's G-2 could obviate the kind of misunderstandings that had produced problems in Italy.[16]

In due course, a Strategic Services Section (SSS), under Lt. Col. Edward W. Gamble, became attached to Patch's G-2 and participated in ANVIL planning. Gamble was prepared to send a contingent of about 30 persons, with seven vehicles and drivers, over the beaches alongside the landing troops. This unit would be attached to Seventh Army headquarters. OSS did not wish the SSS unit to work with corps or division staffs who might not understand its function as providers of strategic and tactical Intelligence. SSS believed that one of its primary functions in the field would be to make contact with those many agents and chains that Henry Hyde had already established.[17]

The relationship of SPOC to Seventh Army was somewhat different because, for one thing, SPOC was an international body, operating under Gen. Maitland Wilson's AFHQ. So long as Force 163, the Planning Group for the Seventh Army, remained in Algiers, it was not too difficult for SPOC to maintain contact with the planners, who kept SOE and OSS abreast of high-level strategic thinking. Once Patch decided to transfer his headquarters to Naples, where most of the ANVIL units were training, the problem of liaison became acute. Since the packing units and radio transmitters could not easily be moved, it was not feasible for SPOC, which in any case came under Wilson's overall Mediterranean command, to follow Patch to Italy. Nevertheless, a special unit, almost as large as SPOC itself, was organized for transfer to Naples, where it would be attached to Seventh Army headquarters.

This was 4-SFU, Special Forces Unit No. 4, commanded by American Lt. Col. William G. Bartlett, with British Lt. Col. E. S. N. Head as deputy, assigned by AFHQ to the Seventh Army on June 29 and later moved to Naples. The unit would operate under Patch's G-3 with liaison to G-2, and would "control Resistance groups in southern France in support of ANVIL," would be a source for information about these groups, and would be Seventh Army's "channel for obtaining the assistance of Resistance groups." The unit was large, with 22 officers (10 American, 12 British) and 42 enlisted persons (12 American, 30 British) together with a large all-British detachment—over 50—for radio communications. 4-SFU would be provided with over 20 vehicles so that once landed its teams would be mobile and independent of regular army support. It was planned that there would be officers at the various headquarters, army, corps, and division, and teams to serve as interpreters and liaison, or to organize sabotage missions behind the lines. The teams would have adequate mobile radios and would keep in touch with Algiers, as well as with missions already in the field.[18]

Because the officers of 4-SFU were all French-speaking, they were in a position to assist the commanders, especially at the lower levels, in getting help not only from the FFI, but from French civilians. The Seventh Army had not made any special effort to ensure that interpreters would accompany all its units. As a consequence, once the invasion began, interrogators, translators, SSS, and 4-SFU personnel found themselves providing interpretation services, which did not lie within their principal missions. Possibly, because so many GIs of Italian background enabled the VI Corps to get along in Italy, the planners ignored the fact that no comparable numbers of soldiers had descended from French immigrants.[19]

4

Impact of the Normandy Landings

The invasion of Normandy, on June 6, brought repercussions in southeastern France, where but for the Anzio setback a simultaneous landing might have taken place. Certainly no member of the French Resistance knew when or if the Allies would come across the Riviera beaches, but many of them were excited about rumors that action would soon come their way. In fact, plans did exist for operations in the south, but since ANVIL was temporarily "on hold," they remained undeveloped and uncertain.

Eisenhower had already received from General Wilson a summary of SOE, OSS, and French plans for coordinating Resistance activity that might help OVERLORD. Wilson told Eisenhower that a mass uprising was inevitable and that it would be better to direct such an uprising than to try to suppress it. He believed British relations with the French would be better if they supported Resistance groups, and he spoke of sending in some French commando-type forces to stiffen large-scale Maquis operations. The Supreme Allied Commander replied to Wilson that "overt action is to be delayed until it can be helpful to tactical operations." Resistance action "is intended to delay enemy forces moving by rail and road, to sabotage enemy telecommunications, and to carry out general guerrilla tasks." Five days later, on May 21, SHAEF sent Wilson a directive, "Role of Resistance groups in the South of France," which called only for cutting significant north–south railways and roads.[1]

Eisenhower had in mind using Resistance forces essentially to keep German troops stationed in the south from reinforcing the Normandy defenses. He knew from intelligence sources the routes principally used by the occupation forces; it was those he wanted cut, and SFHQ sent out appropriate alert messages to the guerrillas in France.

However, the French Resistance had its own ideas as to what should be done in case an Allied landing paved the way for liberation. Granted that the Maquis along the strategic routes did their best to hinder German movements, there existed no overall plan to integrate Resistance forces into OVERLORD. As a consequence, many French insurrectional plans had been formulated that, while possibly known to the Gaullist military delegates, had not been analyzed or approved by British or American commanders. These Maquis uprisings, and the German reprisals, affected the entire area for which ANVIL was planned.

For southeastern France, French plans had been drawn up to gain control of the great Vercors Plateau southwest of Grenoble and a number of other areas in the mountains. The Vercors, guarded by precipitous escarpments, served as a base of operations for Colonel Zeller, the FFI commander for the southeast, and for Col. Marcel Descour, known as BAYARD, FFI chief for the Alps section of R-1.[2]

In May 1944, Eugene Chavant (CLEMENT), civilian Resistance leader in the Vercors, had come to Algiers where he obtained firm Gaullist support for establishing a strong point on the plateau—Operation MONTAGNARDS. Although Colonel Constans (the French representative to SPOC) knew of the plan, SPOC itself was not involved.

Another plan, to hold the Larche pass approaches, had been developed over a period of several months before June 6. Barcelonnette, a quaint Alpine village, the principal town of the picturesque Ubaye Valley, lies in the center of mountain ranges, and holds the key to the pass over the Alps into Italy. Because of the mountains, there are only five roads providing approaches, each of which winds over high passes or through gorges, ideal for ambush and defense by small mobile forces. If the German garrison at Barcelonnette were neutralized, relief expeditions would have to come from the Larche pass itself or down from Guillestre to the north.

While the Vercors served as an almost impregnable base in R-1, the Ubaye Valley ran through the Basses-Alpes Department, administratively within R-2. Therefore, while Colonel Zeller commanded in both R-1 and R-2, he had a different group to work with in the southern region—and more problems. The principal problem related to overall regional military command: whether the dominant officer should be Robert Rossi, pro-Communist regional chief of the MUR, or Jacques Lécuyer, regional head of the ORA. Both men were highly qualified: young (neither had reached 35), handsome, energetic, Rossi a graduate (like Bourgès-Maunoury) of the *Ecole Polytechnique* and a captain in the Air Force, Lécuyer a graduate of St.-Cyr (the French West Point).[3]

Rossi, known in the Resistance as LEVALLOIS, had grown up in Marseille and joined the AS after the German occupation. Arrested and imprisoned in 1943, he escaped in January 1944 to become active in the MUR. In May 1944, he was appointed FFI chief for R-2 by the regional military delegate. Rossi conformed to the FTP position that Resistance forces should be reserved for urban insurrection, where they might help in establishing leftist controls after liberation.

Lécuyer, stationed in Syria with the regular French army, had tried after the fall of France in 1940 to respond to de Gaulle's appeal by getting to British-controlled Palestine. Imprisoned for this attempt, he was released in 1941 when the British took over Syria. The French army then assigned Lécuyer as an instructor in the *Ecole Spéciale Militaire de St.-Cyr*, set up in Aix-en-Provence. While the school was nominally under Vichy, Lécuyer used his position to rally a number of student officers to resistance. With the code name SAPIN he became, under Colonel Zeller, ORA leader in the R-2 region. He did not believe that Resistance forces should be used for political ends but should be reserved strictly for action against the German occupiers.

The political aspects of Resistance rivalry found emphasis with the arrival of the MICHEL mission, which reached southern France in the spring of 1944. This was an inter-allied mission, sent to the field by MASSINGHAM, under the command of French Capt. Henri Chanay, of the Colonial Infantry, whose code name, MICHEL, has been applied to this group. The mission included a British officer, Capt. Alistair Hay (EDGARD), a French deputy, Lieutenant Lancesseur, and several others.[4]

Helped by the MICHEL mission, and inspired by the conviction that the Allies would soon be disembarking in France, Lécuyer and his colleagues developed a plan to seize and hold a defensible area that, supplied by air, could serve as a sort of redoubt from which further operations could develop. Out of conferences with other military officers had evolved a "Plan Rouge," the aim of which was to gain control of the Ubaye Valley and to establish a "free zone" into which could be parachuted arms, equipment, and reinforcements.

Through April and May of 1944, the local and regional leaders worked out details in meetings held at Barcelonnette and other nearby places. A crucial problem of the plan remained unsolved: to what extent could the planners be assured of reinforcements and supplies to be parachuted from London or, more reasonably, from Algiers. The Ubaye Resistance had not been a recipient of air drops arranged through SOE, and it is noteworthy that neither SPOC nor Cammaerts, in spite of the latter's ubiquitous contacts, was aware of the plans.

It could have been, if there had been no signal from London, that the Vercors and Ubaye plans would have remained unimplemented. Every local command had already been supplied with alert and action codes for insurrection—phrases to be broadcast as personal messages over the BBC. For example, the phrase, *"Le gendarme ne dort que d'un oeil"* (The policeman sleeps with one eye open) would establish the alert, while *"Méfiez-vous du toréador"* (Don't trust the toreador), sent later, would call for action.[5]

On the eve of the Normandy invasion, Eisenhower authorized action messages to be sent to the Maquis throughout France. Whether or not a specific message reached all Maquis groups, in R-2, on the eve of D Day, the BBC pronouncement, *"Méfiez-vous du toréador,"* came through loud and clear.[6]

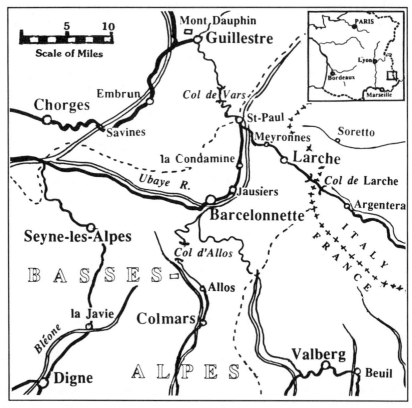

Map 4.1
BARCELONNETTE, UBAYE VALLEY, LARCHE PASS

ACTION AT BARCELONNETTE

To Commandant Michel Bureau, the ORA officer commanding the Maquis of the Ubaye valley, the message definitely meant: "Put Plan Rouge into effect." With his men insufficiently armed, he could only hope that aid would be forthcoming. Next morning, June 6, Bureau met with local civilian leaders and with the officers commanding subsections of his ill-armed forces. He ordered

Phase 1: "Capture the German garrison at Barcelonnette."[7] On this day, the higher-ranking FFI officers were not in the Ubaye area. Colonel Zeller was at Lyon conferring with Colonel Descour, who shortly afterward proceeded to the Vercors. Zeller then went south to Marseille on the 7th and talked briefly with Lécuyer, who, with Captain Chanay (MICHEL), was just leaving for Barcelonnette. The day before, Lécuyer had been through a stormy session with Rossi. Rossi argued that the ORA plans developed by Lécuyer were only valid if an underlying assumption was met—that Allied supplies and reinforcements would be coming. Staunchly military, Lécuyer undertook to go personally to Barcelonnette and overview the situation. His brief conference with Zeller reinforced his determination to follow orders. Arriving at Barcelonnette from the south, he set up his headquarters in the area.[8]

The next day, June 8, Zeller conferred with Rossi at Aix-en-Provence and then continued on to Barcelonnette. Enroute he noted the Maquis in arms but no great reaction from the Germans who kept to their barracks. On June 10, Zeller reached Barcelonnette, where Captain Hay of the MICHEL mission had also arrived and unaccountably had assured the FFI officers that an Allied landing in the south could be shortly expected.

Meanwhile, Cammaerts learned of the new organization brought about by the establishment of the FFI staff under General Koenig. He understood that he would become deputy to Colonel Zeller as senior liaison officer, part of a vast although confusing underground military hierarchy. Cammaerts was at this time not far from Barcelonnette and was invited by Zeller, whom he did not know personally, to review the situation with him. They met on June 10.

The date has interest because by this time Generals Koenig and Eisenhower had concluded that the guerrilla attacks no longer served the purpose of deceiving the Germans about the Normandy landings. The FFI command therefore sent messages to the Maquis to restrain their offensive actions and revert back to the regular tasks of harassment and sabotage.

This order of June 10 reached Barcelonnette at a crucial juncture of the operations. The German garrison in the immediate vicinity (it had been housed in a mountain resort hotel nearby) had been overcome, and a German relief column marching from Gap had been stopped about twenty-five miles west of Barcelonnette. However, word had come in that a more formidable task force would be coming down from Guillestre to the north. Unless help was forthcoming, there was no way that the poorly armed Maquis could hold the passes.

It was at this point that Cammaerts met with Zeller, Lécuyer, the Ubaye commanders, and members of the MICHEL mission. Cammaerts was astonished to learn of "Plan Rouge," which did not conform to any SOE instructions under which he was operating. Nor could he comprehend how

Captain Hay could have implied that landings and reinforcements would be forthcoming. The French were understandably agitated; the British were frustrated and embarrassed to have fallen into such a mire of misunderstandings.

Koening's order to diminish offensive actions held a curious irony. German forces from the north threatened Barcelonnette in the early afternoon of June 11. The French leaders decided to try to hold a series of road-blocks and to intensify their appeals for assistance. Cammaerts cooperated by endeavoring to get some *maquisards* to attack the German right flank. Urgent messages to Algiers finally brought planes that dropped over 100 containers of arms and equipment. Volunteers poured in to get the guns, and took their places along with the footsore and weary fighters who had been without sleep for two days.

However, by this time, the situation was hopeless. The Germans quickly reached a roadblock only seven miles from Barcelonnette. After a desperate defense, in which Captain Hay was killed, the FFI command ordered a withdrawal at nightfall. During the next few days, the *maquisards* scattered into the hills, some into Italy, some to the south where they began to reorganize. Lécuyer moved his ORA headquarters down to Colmars, in mountain country about fifteen miles south of Barcelonnette.

THE VERCORS

While the Maquis effort in the Ubaye was heroic, it was a small affair compared to the Resistance uprising in the Vercors. Ultimately some 4,000 guerrilla fighters, many untrained and unarmed, rallied to the great plateau southwest of Grenoble, where the leaders proclaimed the area—300 square miles of woods and rolling farmland—an independent republic. This they were willing to do because they had faith not only that the rocky approaches were impregnable, but that their small band would soon be augmented by heavy weapons and a battalion of paratroopers from Algiers. They could not believe that the Germans, fighting to hold the Normandy beachheads and fearful of a landing on the Riviera coast, would spare enough troops to launch a serious offensive against them.

Colonels Zeller and Descour, commanding the Alpine section of Region 1, both used the rugged Vercors plateau as their headquarters, keeping in touch from there with their Maquis contingents. Descour had gone directly to the Vercors after meeting Zeller on June 6. Upon receiving word that the Vercors population had begun their insurrection, Zeller, with nothing more to be accomplished at Barcelonnette, hurried to the plateau. With him went Cammaerts, now understanding that his JOCKEY network had been absorbed into the FFI and that he was to serve essentially as Zeller's deputy. The Vercors maintained radio contact with both London and Algiers.[9]

By the middle of June, a crisis situation had developed in the Vercors. Most of the other Normandy-inspired uprisings in the southeast had subsided, either because of Koenig's restraining order or because of German reprisals. Only the Vercors, with its towering walls and hairpin approaches, could defy small-scale enemy efforts to get on top of the plateau, but not forever. By June 15, elements of the Grenoble-based 157th Reserve Division, under Generalleutnant Karl Pflaum, had wrested St.-Nizier from the Maquis. Resting on the northeast road into the Vercors from Grenoble, St.-Nizier provided a gateway to the northern third of the plateau and enabled the Germans to bring in artillery, which the defenders lacked. Furthermore, the Germans could fly in planes from the airfield at Chabeuil, on the western side, and against these the guerrillas had little protection.

Lt. Col. François Huet, code named HERVIEUX, had held the overall Vercors command—a special arrangement because the plateau spread over two departments—since May. He coordinated the defense under Zeller and Descour. He of course consulted with the FFI heads of the departments, L'HERMINE for the Drôme and Commandant Alain Le Ray for Isère, because the approaches to the plateau lay in these departments. An important aspect of the defense was a determination of which Maquis would be on the heights and which around the perimeter. Not all the discussions went smoothly, however, because of personality differences and the basic logistical problems in clandestine warfare.

Amidst these commanders stood Francis Cammaerts, now entwined in the FFI hierarchy as Zeller's deputy and liaison officer. Cammaerts had two radio operators with him in the Vercors, but he was hampered for lack of staff. Nor was he entirely clear as to his position in the chain of command or what was his role related to missions sent in by SPOC.

While SPOC could only authorize actions under its specific control (and Operation MONTAGNARDS was not one of them), it did send the embattled Vercors *maquisards* from time to time encouragement, which gave the Resistance leaders reason to believe they had not been completely abandoned. On the plateau, the leaders recorded innumerable hopeful messages coming in from London and Algiers, and occasionally they gathered up containers with machine guns and ammunition, but few of the mortars and heavy weapons they desperately needed.

A spectacular drop of 420 containers in daylight reached the plateau on June 25, a Sunday, as if heaven had bestowed a blessing while Colonel Huet officiated at a memorial service. The present of some 70 Bren submachine guns,

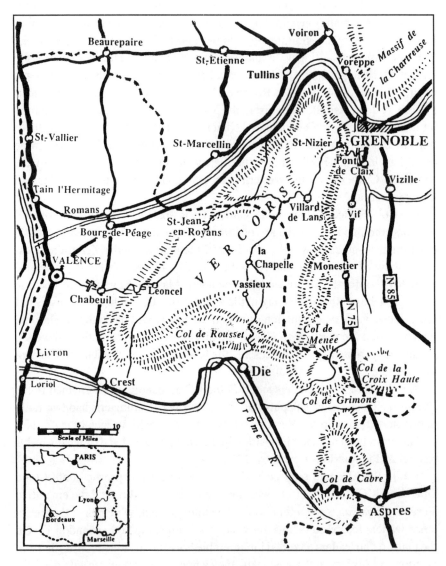

Map 4.2
THE VERCORS

over 1,000 Stens, 648 .30-cal. rifles, and most-prized, 34 Bazookas came, interestingly enough, from the Americans.[10]

Certainly the drop of arms gave some comfort to the Maquis on the Vercors, who, with recruits coming in every day, had good reason to believe that the Germans, constantly probing the Vercors defenses, would not leave the defiant gesture of the French unchallenged. There was always hope that the promised paratroopers would materialize, and this hope had been nourished before the end of June by SPOC's dispatch of special forces to the area: an American OG, JUSTINE; an inter-allied mission, EUCALYPTUS; and two Jedburgh teams, VEGANINE and CHLOROFORM.[11]

MISSIONS TO THE VERCORS

JUSTINE, made up of fifteen men, commanded by two officers, 1st Lt. Vernon G. Hoppers and 1st Lt. Chester L. Myers, landed at Drop Zone "Taille Crayon" near Vassieux in the small hours of June 29. They reported to Colonel Huet and at once began to work with the *maquisards*, especially to train them how to use the American and British weapons they were receiving.

Landing at the same time, the inter-allied mission (EUCALYPTUS) consisted of two British officers, Maj. Desmond Longe and Capt. John Houseman. With them were two radio operators, one of them an American, Lt. André Pecquet (PARAY), who, being bilingual, served also as an interpreter. To the Vercors inhabitants, these commandos in full uniform had to be precursors of an army of paratroopers, and they were greeted with enthusiasm by an ecstatic populace.

The CHLOROFORM Jedburgh team had been alerted to go into the Drôme department right after Normandy D Day, but poor weather postponed their mission until June 30, when they were dropped a few miles northeast of Dieulefit. This group included a Frenchman, Capt. Jacques Martin, an American, Henry McIntosh, a tall, southern paratrooper who had been recruited at Fort Bragg ten months earlier, and a French radio operator, Jean Sassi.

The team had been given the unusual mission of looking into the command relationships that appeared to keep the southern Drôme department from being well integrated into L'HERMINE's overall control. SPOC had reports intimating that Pierre Raynaud (ALAIN), one of Cammaert's assistants, was having difficulty in cooperating with the FTP, which was especially strong in the southern part of the department. Furthermore, the FTP leaders appeared to have joined forces with members of the Departmental Committee of Liberation in demanding L'HERMINE's removal.

All these conditions had been under the scrutiny of Zeller and Cammaerts, who agreed that a transfer of L'HERMINE to another area, where his forthright personality might promote recruiting but grate on fewer nerves, would help the overall Resistance effort. Zeller therefore had the controversial L'HERMINE promoted to lieutenant colonel and gave him a regional command over the "Central Alps."

L'HERMINE was in the process of moving to his new headquarters north of Gap, in the Hautes-Alpes Department, when the CHLOROFORM Jeds arrived on the scene. They were impressed by L'HERMINE's leadership qualities, and when he asked them to go with him, they enthusiastically agreed. They believed that, with other Allied missions in the Drôme area, they would be more useful in some locality where the Allied presence had been less apparent. Although SPOC did not oppose the transfer, it left Cammaerts somewhat in a quandary regarding the disposition of Allied missions. He would have preferred that CHLOROFORM remain in the Drôme.

The other Jedburgh team, VEGANINE, included two British members, Maj. Neil Marten and the radio operator, Sgt. D. Gardner, who was killed when the team jumped into the Drôme department near Beaurepaire on June 9. The third member was French, Commandant Vuchot, generally known by his *nom-de-guerre*: NOIR. They had orders to work with the Maquis to hinder German transport along Route 7, the principal highway paralleling the Rhône River. They joined the Bozambo company, stationed in the northern part of the Drôme department, about halfway between the Rhône and the Vercors. Since this position guarded the northwestern approach to the plateau, NOIR and Marten came under the orders of Colonel Huet, the Vercors commander.

The appearance of so many military personnel in the JUSTINE, EUCALYP-TUS, CHLOROFORM, and VEGANINE missions foreshadowed a significant change in Resistance and Allied relations. Such agents as Cammaerts had indeed been in touch with some professional soldiers, generally officers of the ORA, but he, like many in SOE, believed that a firmer and longer-ranged base would emerge from relations with the civilian Resistance and with those who would be the future prefects or parliamentary representatives. SOE believed furthermore that sabotage, together with hit-and-run harassment, served as the most effective use of force, not a head-on confrontation of the *Wehrmacht*.

Cammaerts found himself in a trying situation. He had been informed that he was officially senior Allied liaison officer, deputy to Colonel Zeller, and that the RF and F circuit distinction had dissolved in favor of a single FFI, but he had no clear instructions as to where he stood in the overall hierarchy of command.

Cammaerts gave vent to his feelings in a long message carried to Algiers on

July 11 by Major Marten, the VEGANINE Jedburgh whose colleague NOIR remained in the Drôme. He pointed out that he had organized small groups of saboteurs that could harass German lines of communication until such time as he knew definitely that an invasion was imminent. He commented on the premature risings right after the Normandy D-Day, emphasizing that FFI leaders assumed that, when they embarked on open warfare, no more than two or three weeks would elapse before Allied reinforcements would pour in. He complained that his appointment as Zeller's liaison officer came much too late: "The result was chaos."

Cammaerts concluded his letter by mentioning that R-1 was better organized than R-2, but "R-2 can be rallied. Coupled with the Italians, they may be able to hold the frontier Alp valleys." "In spite of everything," he added, "I believe there will be a great and general uprising when a serious attack is made in the southeast."[12]

In the field, such officers as Cammaerts, together with hundreds of guerrilla leaders, could scarcely imagine the political and logistical complexities at high levels outside France that affected their struggles and sacrifices. They would not know, for example, how fervently Prime Minister Churchill had opposed the idea of a landing in southern France, with the result that only on July 2 did Patch receive a directive from the Combined Chiefs of Staff giving a green light for ANVIL. Nor would they know that the target date had been set six weeks into the future, longer than any guerrilla group, without reinforcements, even in a natural bastion such as the Vercors, could hold off an organized German attack.

CAMMAERTS AND THE JOCKEY AREA

Although plans for ANVIL were now moving ahead with increased intensity, no definite word could be sent to the field so far in advance. Cammaerts and the Resistance leaders could assume that the main highways from the Riviera beaches northward would become invasion arteries, but they could only continue to prepare for the landings by ambushes, road-blocks, sabotage, and bridge-blowing along possible German supply routes. Cammaerts needed to check on contacts throughout his JOCKEY area and not restrict his liaison duties to the Vercors, which, while looming up as a great sacrificial symbol of French defiance, did not coincide with the SOE guerrilla warfare principles he believed it was his mission to implement. Cammaerts therefore continued to travel around the southeast, returning regularly to his center of operations headquarters, Seyne, in the Basses-Alpes between Digne and Gap.

The department of Basses-Alpes had been hard hit by German reprisal actions after the uprisings on June 6. Not only had the Germans attacked the Ubaye area, but they had carried out raids throughout the department with investigations, arrests, massacres, and executions. Furthermore, echoes of the Lécuyer–Rossi dispute reverberated at the departmental level, with ORA officers accused of noncooperation by the local Liberation Committee. This meant that no one held undisputed command, and there was danger that the FTP, the Secret Army, and the ORA would go their separate ways.[13]

Cammaerts also kept in touch with leaders of the Hautes-Alpes department. No comparable command problem existed there, because Paul Héraud, the wiry carpenter and mountaineer whom Cammaerts held in the highest respect, clearly commanded the allegiance of all the Resistance groups, civil and military.[14]

Francis Cammaerts had developed a close friendship with Héraud, to whom he had entrusted the effort of making contact with Italian partisans so that a combined Resistance effort could hamper German use of the passes—especially the Larche and the Montgenèvre. Cammaerts undertook to have more supplies sent in and was himself designated by Héraud as landing-zone officer (SAP) for the Hautes-Alpes department. Cammaerts writes:

> Paul Héraud was quite simply the greatest man I have ever met. For two years the Germans knew that he controlled resistance in the Hautes Alpes and did not dare touch him. When I slept at his flat we simply booby-trapped everything before going to sleep. It was well known that entry to his flat would blow him and everyone else up.[15]

Satisfied that he had done what he could to the east, Cammaerts did not remain long away from the Vercors and hastened back to his headquarters on the plateau. He learned that in his absence SPOC, having arranged for the assistance he had long since requested, had dispatched a new mission that was dropped by parachute in the small hours of July 7. The assistant was Christine Granville (with the code name PAULINE), a petite attractive Polish woman, then 29 years old. She came in with Mission PAQUEBOT, the leader of which, Captain Tournissa, an engineer, had been sent to the Vercors to supervise construction of an airstrip near Vassieux.

Christine, whose real name was Krystina Skarbek, was of an aristocratic Polish family, had been recruited early as an agent for SOE, had operated in central Europe, and had come to Cairo early in 1944. With her knowledge of languages, she seemed a perfect candidate for operations in Italy or France, or with Poles, many of whom, forcibly recruited for the *Wehrmacht*, sought some opportunity to desert.[16]

Transferred to Algiers, she was assigned to SPOC, where Brooks Richards believed she could serve usefully in various capacities, helping Cammaerts but also in making contacts with Poles and Italians. As soon as she could walk comfortably (she had bruised her hip on landing), she accompanied Cammaerts as he visited in the nearby areas.

COLLAPSE OF THE VERCORS

July 14—Bastille Day and France's national holiday—ushered in a short, exuberant period where those in the Vercors Resistance, rejoicing in the summer sunshine, celebrated their defiance of the Nazi occupiers. Although ominous storm clouds may have loomed on the horizon, they must have felt that indeed London and Algiers, attentive to their plight, were putting out every effort to bring assistance. Why else would Algiers have sent Captain Tournissa to build an airstrip unless planes would follow? Only four days earlier, the American OG team led by Captain Hoppers and the French had fought side by side, fourteen Americans, fourteen *maquisards*, in ambushing a German column on the Grenoble road east of the Vercors near the Col de la Croix Haute. If one commando had been dispatched to the Vercors, should there not be more to follow? Then, at 9:30 in the morning of July 14, two groups of American bombers flew over the Vercors and released hundreds of containers suspended (to indicate their contents) by red, white, and blue parachutes.

The Bastille Day container drop, Operation CADILLAC, doubled the June 25 operation in numbers of aircraft and in tons of weapons. It was the largest daylight drop of the war, an operation that many OSS officers stationed in London recall as their greatest effort to aid the Maquis. With impressive verve, OSS and Gen. Curtis LeMay's 3rd Bombardment Division had massed 320 Flying Fortresses, which, taking off from nine English airfields, delivered almost 4,000 containers to seven Maquis groups. The Vercors received the largest allotment: 72 aircraft dropped 862 containers in the open fields east of Vassieux.

There is no doubt that the American gesture served as a psychological fillip to the Vercors populace, but unfortunately German planes, taking off from the nearby airfield at Chabeuil, appeared overhead just as the Maquis trucks, completely without cover, tried to cart the containers off to safety. Not only did the planes prevent immediate recovery of the weapons, but they continued all day strafing and bombing the principal towns, breaking up the parades and ceremonies scheduled for Bastille Day.[17]

However, in spite of token demonstrations of Allied concern, the Vercors defenders received no further meaningful support. The German bombings of July 14 simply gave warning that General Pflaum, who had been deploying heavily armed units at all approaches to the plateau, would soon unleash his troops, some 14,000 in number, against the ragged companies, perhaps 4,000 in all, which now defended the heights. These 4,000 defenders, it should be borne in mind, were made up of *maquisard* companies scattered over an area twenty-five miles long and about ten miles wide. In some places, there were impassable cliffs and gorges, easy to defend, but on the top, the rolling meadows provided little cover. Considering that the perimeter extended over 100 miles, in no way could the Maquis, with only a few mortars and bazookas, carry out more than a delaying action.

On the 19th and 20th of July, the German forces on the east, west, and south of the plateau began sending reconnaissance patrols along the approaches, and one day later, on July 21, they carried out a maneuver with which the defenders could not cope: They landed a force of over 200 commandos by glider on the meadows near Vassieux. Valiantly the *maquisards* tried to break up this airborne invasion, but with inferior weapons, they could not dislodge the attackers. The son of Colonel Descour was killed while manning a machine gun.

The American commandos of OG JUSTINE could provide only an infinitesimal fraction of the total fire power required. The group had also lost Lieutenant Myers, invalided after an emergency appendectomy, leaving Lieutenant Hoppers in sole command of the thirteen team members.

Meanwhile, the Germans were breaking through all of the defenses. While the special glider troops forced the *maquisards* into isolated positions within the protective forests, enemy reinforcements were preparing to advance up the southern road from Die. The situation on the plateau was now hopeless. Germans were everywhere, destroying the towns, and shooting both *maquisards* and civilians, inflicting atrocities on helpless women, invalids, and wounded.

There was no alternative to dispersal, reluctantly ordered by Colonel Huet. Some would try to break through the German lines, others would attempt to hide in the rough country that dominates the southwestern part of the plateau. Huet tried to develop some sporadic counterattacks, but he agreed that there was no good reason for those not specifically involved in the defense to remain. In particular, Zeller, Cammaerts, and Christine, with their radio operators, all possessed area-wide responsibilities, and would have jeopardized their prime missions if they stayed in the midst of the increasingly bitter and confused combat. Since the Germans had not yet broken through the road from Die, the little party was able to drive to the Col de Rousset, and then find back roads and trails that enabled them to leave the plateau. Obtaining a car from some FTP *maquisards*, they set off for Seyne-les-Alpes, one of Cammaert's principal headquarters, which they reached by the 24th.

The OG team JUSTINE, like the Maquis, underwent a trying ordeal. Lieutenant Myers, recovering from his appendix operation, saw the wounded *maquisards* around him killed without mercy. He became a prisoner, finally ending the war in Poland. Lieutenant Hoppers led his remaining commandos north. He learned that the entire Isère Valley stretching along the northwestern slopes was guarded by one man every fifty meters. For eleven days, he and his men hid in the woods above the town of Saint-Marcellin. As he later reported:

> German patrols scoured the woods and fired into the underbrush trying to scare the Maquis into the Isère valley, where many were shot trying to escape. For 11 days we ate nothing but raw potatoes and occasionally a little cheese. . . . On the night of 6 August we received word from a Maquis that the bridge outside of Saint-Marcellin was no longer guarded. We immediately moved down from the plateau and marched 40 kilometers into the region across the Isère.

Three days later, after marching north, carefully avoiding German patrols, the men of OG JUSTINE struggled into the mountain north of Grenoble, where the FFI leader, Commandant Reynier (VAUBAN), gave them food and blankets. The section, recalled Hopper, arrived in the mountains in very poor shape. "I had lost 37 pounds myself, three of the men were not able to walk for almost two weeks and some of the men had dysentery which lasted for a month."[18]

The fate of Hopper's group was duplicated by many of the defenders. The British EUCALYPTUS team, Longe and Houseman, escaped with some *maquisards* into the woods near Saint-Martin, where they barely escaped German patrols and starvation. Lacking water, they would painstakingly squeeze clumps of moss to obtain the moisture. The team had lost contact with their wireless operator, the American André Pecquet, who had remained with Huet. Ultimately, unable to locate either Pecquet or Huet, the two Englishmen made their way to Switzerland.

Hunted down by German patrols, the Maquis took serious losses, but many of the groups were able to reorganize and revert to the guerrilla hit-and-run tactics for which they were best suited. However, they had suffered a serious setback. German reprisals against the civilians and *maquisards* on the Vercors compare with the worst of Nazi atrocities. The towns of Vassieux and La Chapelle-en-Vercors were practically destroyed, and of the 4,000 *maquisards* who resisted the attack, 640—about 16 percent—lost their lives. In addition to reprisals against people, the Germans pillaged the plateau, making off with over 4,000 head of livestock and large quantities of grain, hay, and potatoes.[19]

The German occupation forces, struck by the realization that France might be lost, now moved to unprecedented activity. On July 25 their barriers holding back the Allied onslaught in Normandy had broken, leaving all of northern France vulnerable to further pressure. At about the same time that General Pflaum's 157th Reserve Division occupied the Vercors Plateau, the German southern command—that is, General Blaskowitz's Army Group G with head-quarters at Toulouse and General Wiese's Nineteenth Army headquartered near Avignon—had to anticipate the possibility of a southern Allied landing and stepped-up guerrilla attacks. For weeks, increased Allied bombing raids had given notice of a possible invasion in the south, especially vulnerable since two of the three Panzer divisions—2nd SS Panzer (*Das Reich*) and 9th Panzer—had been ordered to the Normandy front in June and July. This left only the 11th Panzer, commanded by General von Wietersheim, which, stationed 200 miles west of the Rhône near Toulouse, could move to the Atlantic coast or to the east, depending on where an Allied attack materialized.

Since June, there had been such continual sabotage and ambushing that the Germans were hard pressed to maintain their supply routes. They had to keep the main roads and railways intact, but on some lines they would find forty and fifty exploded rails a day, to say nothing of destroyed locomotives and broken telephone and telegraph cables. On July 28, General Blaskowitz noted: "The activity of bands in the rear of the Army Task Force has been allowed gradually to reach the point that control over a greater part of the area can no longer be assumed."[20]

In July, the Germans began a series of operations designed to make sure that they controlled the principal links between major cities and also to diminish the number of strongholds from which guerrillas (or "terrorists," as the Germans preferred to call them) could launch attacks on their convoys. The Germans, with many divisions spread across the French Mediterranean coast from Spain to Italy, were not simply sitting in the countryside waiting for the Allies to come. They were in fact skirmishing constantly with the FFI who, working with Allied agents, kept the German commanders off balance, unable to coordinate their defenses with any degree of efficiency or reliability.

5

Preparations for
ANVIL/DRAGOON

In March, 1944, because of the deadlock at Anzio, ANVIL had been placed on the shelf, postponed indefinitely. Nevertheless, General Patch never stopped planning, and both in Algiers and in Naples, where Seventh Army transferred its headquarters in July, American officers worked on details with members of General de Lattre's staff. General de Lattre de Tassigny had been confirmed by de Gaulle as commander of Army B, the French troops in ANVIL. Although there had been no French participation in OVERLORD planning, where security restrictions had immensely irritated General de Gaulle, this was not the case with ANVIL, but the partnership lacked complete equality because control of transport and supplies, almost completely in American hands, gave the American commander a privileged position regarding final decisions. If the Americans seemed to be unduly taciturn regarding the landing date of the operation, it must be recognized, that before July 1944, no one, not even the Combined Chiefs, knew when ANVIL would take place. They did not even know *if* it would take place.[1]

Obviously the planners in Algiers, London, and Washington were anxious to reach new decisions once OVERLORD had been launched and Rome had fallen. Four days after D Day in Normandy the Combined Chiefs debated the issue and on June 14 announced: The Italian advance should proceed no farther than the Pisa-Rimini Line, and four American divisions, currently in Italy, should be withdrawn progressively to start training for an amphibious operation. On June 23, Eisenhower, backed strongly by the American Joint Chiefs, had come out strongly for ANVIL no later than August 15. He had a firm ally in General de Gaulle. On his return to Algiers, after a triumphant visit to Normandy, de Gaulle told Wilson that French forces would not serve beyond the Pisa-Rimini Line and would not be available in Italy after July 25.

Map 5.1

THE ANVIL/DRAGOON LANDING AREA

A: 36th Division   B: 45th Division   C: 3rd Division

D: French Commandos   E: First Special Service Force

Blue Line: ●●●●●●●●●

First Airborne Task Force Drop Area: le Muy

The last two weeks of June bore witness to an assiduous Churchillian effort to obtain a decision that would enable General Alexander to preserve his Italian armies. However, the prime minister's arguments persuaded no one in Washington, and Roosevelt's decisive letter of July 2 forced the prime minister to agree reluctantly that the Combined Chiefs should issue the ANVIL directive.

The seven weeks prior to D Day, fixed definitely for August 15, saw intensive training and perfecting of plans. General Patch had not waited for an official directive to initiate this final phase of preparation. On June 23, Eisenhower had dispatched a powerful memorandum recommending to the Combined Chiefs that their directive of June 14 be implemented with ANVIL. This was good enough for Patch, who at once began to shift Seventh Army personnel to Naples, near the training areas. Thus, although Wilson's official directive was dated July 8, intensive final preparations had already begun.

In Naples, the various responsible officers, for ground, sea, and air, worked out the myriad details of this complicated operation, now identified by a new code name: DRAGOON. Together with Patch, Vice Adm. H. K. Hewitt (Naval Commander Western Task Force), and Brig. Gen. G. P. Saville (Commander XII U.S. Army Air Force) coordinated naval and aerial problems, working closely with General de Lattre and Contre-amiral Lemonnier, chief of staff of the French navy. Maj. Gen. Lucian K. Truscott, commanding the U.S. VI Corps, which would lead the assault, brought the experience of his campaigns in Italy to the planning group.

By July 13, an outline plan was ready. It called for a beachhead to be established on fifteen miles of the French Riviera coast between Cavalaire and St.-Raphael, with rapid expansion to a "blue line" about fifteen miles inland. The first wave would comprise three infantry divisions of Truscott's VI Corps: Maj. Gen. John W. O'Daniel's 3rd, Maj. Gen. John E. Dahlquist's 36th, and Maj. Gen. William W. Eagle's 45th. Just beyond the landing beaches, the First Airborne Task Force, commanded by Brig. Gen. Robert T. Frederick, would bring in troops by parachute and glider to seize airfields in the vicinity of Le Muy and Draguignan. The small river Argens provides a valley of easy access from St.-Raphael to Draguignan, fifteen miles to the northwest. Once in possession of that corridor, troops would control a major railroad junction and would find relatively level highways west to the ports of Toulon and Marseille, the first objectives, and northwest to the Rhône Valley. While responsibility for establishing the beachhead would be Truscott's, de Lattre's Army B, consisting of five divisions, would land later to thrust along the coast westward to Toulon. The ultimate objective was Lyon and Vichy, 400 miles away.

That Patch and de Lattre maintained headquarters in Naples made for good coordination between them, but it made communications with Algiers difficult.

Gen. Maitland Wilson commanded the Mediterranean Theater from Algiers, which was also the seat of de Gaulle's provisional government. Thus, while de Lattre's headquarters were at Caivano, near Naples, the French minister of war, Diethelm, and the chief of staff, Gen. Emile Béthouart, remained at Algiers, which also housed the headquarters of Gen. Gabriel Cochet, military delegate for the zone of operations (defined as the Mediterranean coast and about 100 miles inland).[2] Also in Algiers was SPOC, which coordinated most contacts with the French Resistance and with Allied missions sent into southern France.

GENERAL COCHET AND COMMAND OF THE FFI

It should not be difficult to imagine the general confusion that distance and a multitude of command levels engendered. One element that proved overlong in resolution related to overall command. During the landings in Normandy, all relations with metropolitan France remained logically enough in the hands of the Supreme Allied Commander in London, General Eisenhower. Thus, it was he who determined how the Resistance should act to support OVERLORD and, properly, orders to the FFI went out officially from General Koenig, but in practice through the machinery of the SOE/SO office: SFHQ. Thus, none of the Mediterranean elements, Wilson, Gen. Ira Eaker for the air force, or SPOC, were supposed to initiate operations, but only to implement those that in Eisenhower's view would contribute to expanding the Normandy beachhead. Officially, London made policy regarding the Vercors.

The concentration of command made it difficult for General Cochet to exercise any real authority over the FFI in the south, even though de Gaulle had named him back in March as military delegate for the southern zone. In the latter part of June, Cochet, assuming he was authorized by de Gaulle to act on behalf of the FFI, addressed himself to General Wilson with the intention of coordinating Resistance actions and Allied operations. He argued that, just as Koenig's EMFFI had an integrated staff of British, Americans, and French, he should operate in a comparable fashion—that is, in control of SPOC. Furthermore, if he were to become Commanding General FFI, Southern Zone, he would require a reservation (so he wrote) that he could "submit to the French High Command any question which seems to him to raise a conflict with the instructions received from the latter." In reacting to Cochet's request, General Noce (deputy chief of staff for Special Operations, G-3) pointed out that Eisenhower's SHAEF still controlled all FFI operations in France, that Wilson's G-3/Special Operations supervised SPOC (which now had six French officers on its staff), and that there were daily conferences with Cochet. Furthermore,

Wilson's chief of staff, Gen. Sir James Gammell, considered the principle of appealing to French higher authority "totally and absolutely unacceptable."[3]

Within the next few weeks (during which de Gaulle, visiting President Roosevelt in the White House, was absent from Algiers), many organizational problems were resolved. After July 15, when the SACMED (Supreme Commander Mediterranean Theater) obtained authority for operations in southern France as far north as Lyon, Wilson could officially give Patch and his planning staff orders to proceed with ANVIL. Furthermore, he was empowered to oversee what the French were doing, both with their regular armies under Allied command and with their interior forces under Koenig's command. It also gave him supervisory authority over SPOC's southern France operations, and it implied that Algiers could deal directly with the Vercors problem.

Even before Wilson had received the technical authorization regarding French operations, he had on July 7 issued a preliminary directive regarding Cochet's spheres of action. It stated that Cochet would command (a) the FFI in southern France; (b) SPOC, but not technical control of communications, supplies, and aircraft; (c) OSS/SOE groups with the Seventh Army. The directive pointed out that Cochet would have to provide his own staff, although SPOC's staff would be maintained.[4]

When Wilson gave orders to Cochet as "Commanding General, FFI, Southern Zone," many of the higher-ranking Allied officers simply assumed that Cochet could give orders to the French Resistance just as de Lattre could give orders to the French First Army. General Patch, for example, appreciating the convenience of having de Lattre's headquarters adjacent to his own, assumed that Cochet would also come to Naples. But for the French there was a significant distinction between the liaison function of "military delegate" and the authority of "Commanding General," who could give direct orders.

Just returned from his visit with Roosevelt, de Gaulle tried to clarify the distinction when he saw Wilson on July 20. He explained that the FFI covered a complex set of units, intermingled with the civilian population. His provisional government, he pointed out, could undertake to recruit, organize, and administer the FFI, and this the military delegates were empowered to do, but the actual deployment of forces had to be left to commanders in the field. The delegates were go-betweens; they transmitted orders corresponding to the demands formulated by the Allied commanders. Consequently, de Gaulle emphasized that only Koenig could be considered the FFI commander; Cochet could exercise these functions once ANVIL was launched but meanwhile should be considered simply as *"délégué militaire."*

Following the conversation, Wilson modified the basic orders to Cochet on July 29: His "operational control" was defined as "issuing orders and executing orders from Allied Force Headquarters," and his mission was defined as giving "the maximum possible assistance to ANVIL." Such assistance could be no more than what SPOC was doing: working on directives from the Seventh Army planners, with whom Cochet had no direct contact except by liaison. When Cochet's chief of staff, Col. Boutaud de Lavilléon, asked that he be informed three days in advance the exact time of H Hour, his request was denied.[5]

In General Cochet's personal file can be found an organizational chart drawn up by himself, almost pathetically trying to delineate the flow of command. The chart is a spider-web, with himself, DMOS, at the center, and lines radiating in all directions, solid for command relations, dotted for liaison. They go to SACMED, AFHQ, SPOC, DGSS, FCNL, Seventh Army, French First Army, and to the field, zonal and regional military delegates, Committees of Liberation, and *Chefs, FFI*. There is no clear-cut line of military command. Cochet penned a succinct comment: *"Mes pouvoirs et les moyens d'accomplir ma mission ne sont pas à la hauteur de mes responsabilités."* (My powers and the means to accomplish my mission are not at the level of my responsibilities.)[6]

Nevertheless, General Patch liked the idea of working through a French military officer to the French Resistance and, with Wilson's approval, directed General Cochet to embark with him from Naples so that he could have close personal contact at the time of the landings. Patch may have assumed that Cochet, having the title, also possessed the means of communicating directly with the FFI leaders in France, whereas in fact all the facilities and codes were controlled by SPOC. Nor had Patch taken de Gaulle's wishes into account. When the Free French leader learned of Patch's desire, he categorically refused to release Cochet, insisting that he remain in Algiers. While it is true that Cochet could better communicate with the FFI from Algiers, de Gaulle's abrupt decision irritated the Allied officers, who had assumed that Cochet, as part of the military hierarchy, took orders from Wilson and Patch. Cochet himself agonized over the situation, apologizing to Wilson on August 7 that he had to obey de Gaulle, and adding rather lamely that in any case "practically all instructions to the FFI in the southern zone have been given without reference to me."[7]

It is interesting to note that a new directive on plans for the Resistance, similar to SPOC's plan of July 15, bears the date August 8 and was issued over Cochet's name. General Cochet did not, in fact, reach France until August 21, when much of the south had already been liberated. He still had a large responsibility ahead of him, when thousands of FFI troops wished to become incorporated into the regular French army. But at the time of the landings, his voice was scarcely heard or even recognized among the Maquis.

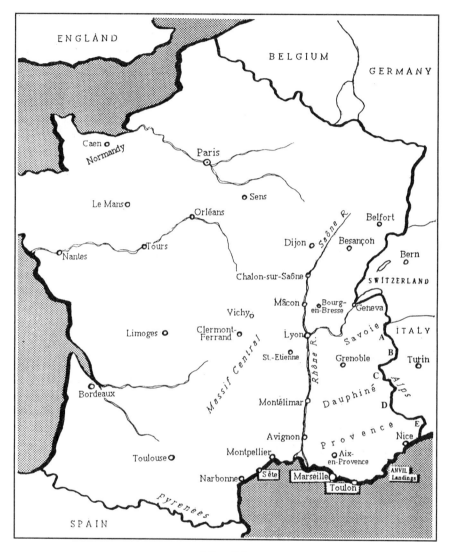

Map 5.2
FRANCE—1944

Passes between France and Italy: A = Little St. Bernard; B =
Modane (railway tunnel), Mont-Cenis; C = Montgenèvre; D =
Larche; E = Tende.

PLANNING AND ACTION AT SPOC

While Seventh Army planners sweated through the hot summer in Naples organizing an amphibious operation involving a force of 50,000, the people in SPOC, a thousand miles away in Algiers, labored on plans to coordinate the regular army's assault with actions of the Maquis. SPOC received the first directives on what Patch expected from the FFI on July 4: a list of railway lines and roads, the cutting or controlling of which would obstruct German efforts to bring its southern occupation forces to focus on Marseille, Toulon, and the beachhead. The planners listed three routes as highest priority—first the roads and railways on both sides of the Rhône as far as Lyon; second, the roads and railways stretching east and west across France from Bordeaux on the Atlantic to Narbonne on the Mediterranean; third, the major road from Milan and Turin into France via the Mt. Cenis tunnel. Next in priority came two north–south arteries, first, the highway running southeast from Lyon to Grenoble and on to Nice through the Alpine foothills, known as the Route Napoléon because the Emperor had followed it after his escape from Elba; second, the road south from Clermont-Ferrand, skirting the western edge of the Massif Central, and then splitting fan-like, southwest to Toulouse, south toward Montpellier, and southeast to the Rhône. Next, the Seventh Army listed the roads through the remaining Franco-Italian passes—Little St. Bernard, Montgenèvre, Larche, Mende—together with the highway running west from Nice, to Marseille and Aix-en-Provence.

Using this directive as a guide, SPOC made plans to alert the Resistance, to deploy the Jedburgh, Operational Group, and inter-allied teams, and to increase drops of arms and equipment. To meet the August 1 deadline given them by Patch, SPOC officials modified their existing directives and by July 15 had produced Draft No. 2, a twenty-three-page document (plus five appendices): "Plan for the Use of Resistance in Support of Operation ANVIL." With a few later modifications, this plan remained the basic order under which SPOC operated.[8] In the event, SPOC followed this plan fairly closely, although the vicissitudes of war, politics, and the weather kept the schedule from being precisely followed.[9] Several factors inserted themselves into the smooth scheduling of missions.

One of these factors involved the need to build on past experience and to fulfill commitments already made. SPOC made out a list of high-priority areas where supplies and individuals should be sent in, even though the areas did not necessarily feature as vital regions for ANVIL strategy. For instance, the Vercors held the No. 1 priority, as well it might have when the draft plan was drawn up. The 2nd and 4th priorities were the Drôme and Ardèche departments—quite properly since they held the Rhône Valley between them. However, the No. 3 priority lay far to the northeast of Grenoble, in the area just south of Switzerland, guarding the road to the Little St. Bernard Pass. While this remote area had minor significance for the early stages of ANVIL, it was important to SOE, which since 1942 had supported a Haute-Savoie circuit, MARKSMAN, headed by an indomitable agent, R. H. Heslop, who as Colonel XAVIER, had functioned with conspicuous success.

The No. 5 priority was the Vaucluse, important for communications with Algiers because, on the plateau southeast of Mont Ventoux, the Maquis had constructed landing strip Spitfire, where small planes such as Dakotas and Lysanders could land.[10]

The 6th priority lay in the Hautes-Alpes region, where Paul Héraud was providing strong support for operations against the occupiers. Cammaerts had made his headquarters, after he left the Vercors, at Seyne-les-Alpes, and it was into the undulating hills of this picture-postcard landscape that many paratroopers and containers were dropped.

ARRANGEMENTS IN R-2

All of the people concerned with the Resistance—the British and Americans in SPOC, the French in Soustelle's Special Services, the G-2s of Patch's Seventh Army and de Lattre's French First Army—had to be disturbed about the organization, or rather the lack of it, in military region R-2, where the ANVIL landings would be made. In particular, planners had to scrutinize the department of Var, along whose coasts the initial onslaught was scheduled, as well as Basses-Alpes to the north and Vaucluse to the northwest.

The disturbing factors were several: The arrest of the French regional military delegate, Louis Burdet, on June 28, meant that no representative of the French provisional government could officially communicate de Gaulle's orders to the FFI commanders, and these commanders were not coordinating their actions because of friction between ORA and other organizations such as the Secret Army or the pro-Communist FTP. The lack of coordination focused in the dispute between Robert Rossi, the pro-Communist regional FFI chief, and Capt. Jacques Lécuyer, head of the ORA in the region.

Then, in mid-July, an unfortunate event grievously ruptured all well-intended efforts to straighten out the situation in R-2. Through betrayals, the German Gestapo had been able to identify a number of Marseille Resistance leaders. They then learned that the Basses-Alpes Liberation Committee planned to meet at Oraison on July 16. The local *Milice*, working with the occupiers, broke in on the gathering and arrested eight, including one of the *"héros de la Résistance,"* Louis Martin-Bret. The next day, in Marseille, the Gestapo located Rossi and arrested him with several others, including the leader of Mission MICHEL, Captain Chanay. The prisoners, 26 in all, were taken to a secluded spot about 15 miles north of Toulon, four miles from the tiny hamlet of Signes. There, on July 18, in a natural hollow encircled by grubby shrubs and rocky outcroppings, all of them were shot and buried in shallow graves. The lonely grove, seldom visited, has been identified since as a melancholy memorial: the *Charnier de Signes* (Sepulcher of Signes).

Less than a week later, a SPOC-sponsored sea communication system between St.-Tropez and Corsica, run by a French officer, François Pelletier, was penetrated. An agent sent out in good faith by SPOC had sold information to the Germans. Pelletier was in the process of arranging transportation for an American OSS officer, Muthular d'Errecalde. Both men were arrested, interrogated, and later, on August 12, shot with eight others at the same isolated spot near Signes already rendered infamous by the twenty-six graves of earlier victims.[11]

Although Burdet was released on July 8, the arrest had so compromised him that he could no longer function as delegate.[12] With Rossi dead and Burdet relieved of his authority, R-2 lacked both a delegate and a military commander.

Meanwhile the German occupiers redoubled their efforts to penetrate the Resistance structure and wipe out Maquis companies when they could locate them. They had successfully gained control of the Valensole plateau, they maintained an occupation garrison of about 400 at Digne, and during the last two weeks of July (the same period in which they attacked the Vercors), they launched patrols north from N85 (the Route Napoléon) between Castellane and Digne, and further north up the Var, Verdon, and Bléone valleys. Against them scattered companies of FFI and FTP blocked roads, set up ambushes, and pulled back fighting to the high Alps. From there, they struck with hit-and-run tactics that made the occupiers reluctant to rely on the Route Napoléon and other major highways.[13]

Concerned about the deteriorating situation, on August 4 Cammaerts met with Lécuyer and other local leaders in an effort to reestablish a logical and workable command structure. The discussions, stormy and prolonged, parallelled in micro-form the divisions of French society, right against left, politicians versus soldiers, and among the latter, divergent views of strategy and tactics. Some of the assembled leaders turned on Lécuyer. Many still held him accountable for the unsuccessful attack on the Germans at Barcelonnette, and they accused him of misappropriating the mission MICHEL for ORA purposes alone. Members of the Departmental Liberation Committee believed that, just as in normal times, the military should be subordinate to political control; on the other hand, many regular officers like Lécuyer viewed the committees as representing the same quarreling political factions that had enfeebled the Third Republic.

Lécuyer had no intention of relinquishing his regional command of the ORA, but he was willing to eliminate himself from the regional FFI staff in exchange for departmental authority. He would become FFI chief in that farthest east department—Alpes-Maritimes—and retain his authority as ORA chief in R-2. This arrangement would have to be confirmed by the military delegate and FFI chief when, as expected, they would be named and begin exercising authority in France. In fact, they had already been named and the military delegate, "Willy" Widmer (to be known in the field as Colonel CLOITRE), had arrived in the Vaucluse three days before the meeting near Seyne.

WIDMER TO FRANCE; ZELLER TO ALGIERS AND NAPLES

In mid-July, General Koenig in London, and Generals de Gaulle and Cochet in Algiers, together with the officials at SPOC, had agreed that the two principal French officers responsible for SPOC liaison with the French provisional government—Widmer and Constans—should be named respectively as regional military delegate and FFI regional chief in R-2. De Gaulle, having conferred with them both, signed their orders of mission on July 29 and told them to get to mainland France as soon as possible.[14] Not trained as paratroopers, they had to be flown in, which meant landing in the Vaucluse Plateau north of Apt, where landing strip Spitfire could handle small bombers. Widmer was the first to leave, reaching Corsica with his staff on August 2. There, two members of the Jedburgh team GRAHAM,[15] Maj. M. G. M. "Bing" Crosby, a Scottish officer wearing a kilt, and Captain Gouvet, found themselves "bumped" to make room for Widmer and his party in three Lysanders. (Widmer's party was not large, since a Lysander generally carried no more than two passengers.) The planes reached zone Spitfire in the early hours of August 2. At the airfield the group ran into Zeller, recently promoted to general, who had been waiting anxiously for transport to Algiers.

Since his departure from the Vercors, Zeller had remained at Seyne, seeking to find some way whereby he could ascertain why the people at Algiers had neglected the valiant Resistance fighters on the plateau and trying to sort out the confused command relationships among the FFI in the coastal areas where unity of command would be most needed. He radioed Algiers for authorization to go there in person.

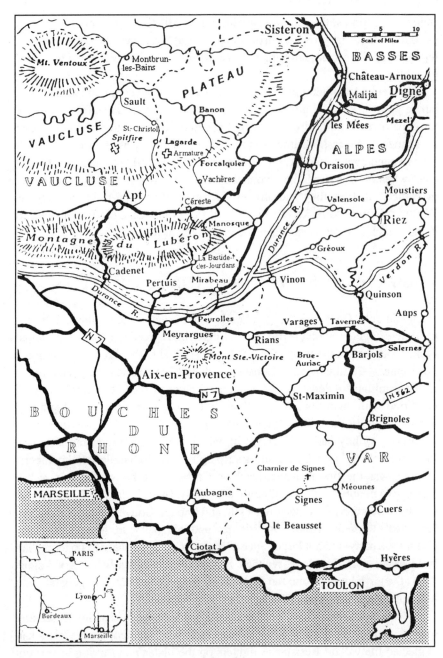

Map 5.3
CENTRAL SECTION OF R-2
Toulon, Marseille, the Vaucluse Plateau, and the Durance Valley.

On July 26, having received approval to visit Algiers, Zeller hurried to Apt, where ARCHIDUC (Camille Rayon), the capable R-2 SAP officer, assured him that he expected a Lysander shortly. With a few days to wait, Zeller had time to reflect on the deplorable catastrophe in the Vercors and gradually came to realize that the Vercors did not represent a true picture of the occupation. In traveling through the southeast, he recorded:[16]

> My black mood evaporated: no train had run since 15 June on the two Alpine lines, Grenoble to Aix-en-Provence, and Briançon to Livron. No isolated German car, no courier could travel the highways, no enemy roadblocks, no control existed outside the garrison towns. No traces of military works or mine fields. The Germans are practically prisoners in their garrisons, from which they only emerge in force for supplies or on a reprisal expedition—and these convoys, these columns are attacked, one out of every two times, by an uncatchable enemy.
>
> After two months of this situation, the German soldier is bewildered, demoralized, fooled—we know him, we steal his mail. He looks with fear on these mountains, these forests, these crags, these narrow valleys from which at any moment a thunderbolt can crash.
>
> He awaits the arrival of "regulars," the Allied soldiers, like a deliverance.
>
> If one excepts the high Alpine valleys (Durance, Ubaye, Var, Verdon, Tinée and Vésubie) where fighting is still going on, as well as the highways along the Rhône valley and around Grenoble, the center of the massif is ours.

Such was the message that Zeller hoped he could convey to the Algiers authorities. Anxious to be on his way, the newly promoted general could spare only a few moments with Widmer at the airfield before the Lysanders took off.

Zeller proceeded no farther than Corsica the first night, but finally arrived in Algiers on August 3. His aim was, of course, to prod the services at SPOC and elsewhere into better support of his guerrilla fighters, but the labyrinthine bureaucracy of wartime Algiers prevented him from seeing anyone at a high level until the afternoon of the fourth, when he was ushered into the office of Jacques Soustelle. What Zeller had to say persuaded a reluctant Soustelle to arrange an appointment with de Gaulle for the following morning. D Day for ANVIL was now only ten days away, but Zeller did not know it.

When he saw de Gaulle on August 5, Zeller was filled with indignation and bitterness that Algiers had neglected the guerrillas on the Vercors. He poured out his grievances to his impassive chief and then expounded on the possibilities that the Resistance provided.

When Zeller finished his eloquent harangue, de Gaulle told him something he did not know: "In a few days we're going to land in Provence." The Free French leader then handed him a copy of the top-secret ANVIL/DRAGOON Operations Plan. The plan envisaged obtaining a beachhead on the French Riviera, taking Toulon and Marseille, and then striking northward up the Rhône Valley; small forces would protect the Franco-Italian Alpine passes, but nowhere in the scheme could he find an effort to exploit the routes, halfway between the Rhône and the Alps, leading up to Grenoble. Zeller noticed that Grenoble's estimated capture was placed at D+90. "By that time," he expostulated, "the FFI will have been massacred, when in fact, if the Allies can hold a beachhead as far inland as a line from Brignoles to Aix [about thirty miles from the coast] they could be in Grenoble in forty-eight hours."

De Gaulle was impressed by Zeller's arguments. It might not be too late, he believed, to get this opinion to Patch and de Lattre. The French leader took immediate steps to put Zeller on a plane to Naples.

Zeller arrived in Naples on August 6 and saw Patch very early the next morning. He was accompanied by Lt. Cdr. Brooks Richards from SPOC who served as interpreter. As Zeller recounted it:

> Patch had summoned his Chief of Staff together with his G2 and G3. Before a large map of the future operations, I repeated my conversation with General de Gaulle, emphasizing my deep conviction of a rapid success in the Alpine massif. I detailed the support which could be provided by the FFI. I concluded: general direction—the Route Napoléon. But, for the love of God, charge! [foncez.]
>
> There followed a long question period on the Maquis, the terrain, the routes. Asked about the dangers which could develop on the right flank, I gave them the assurance of FFI support in the frontier area. They insisted that I take steps to bring about blocking the roads from the frontier passes. The instructions in this regard went out from Naples by radio that very afternoon.
>
> Then there was a long discussion among the Americans in English which unfortunately I do not speak. Finally General Patch vigorously shook my hand, thanked me. Going out the young English captain said with a broad smile: "Mon Colonel, je crois que vous avez gagné." [I think you've won.][17]

During the three days he remained in Naples, Zeller set forth his views, experiences, and arguments to various other groups: especially to the staff and commanders of General de Lattre's Army B. He was surprised and disappointed that the questions asked him revealed a rather widespread misunderstanding of what the FFI had done and were capable of doing.

ORIGINS OF TASK FORCE BUTLER

Meanwhile, General Truscott, whose VI Corps would bear the brunt of establishing a beachhead, had begun to think about his need for a fast-moving cavalry-type force to exploit opportunities as they arose.[18]   He had his eye on a French unit, Combat Command 1, under Maj. Gen. Aimé Sudre, which was then training in the Oran area of Algeria.

It was this Combat Command, referred to in reports generally as CC Sudre, that bore an interesting relationship to the development of Truscott's plans. A problem for Truscott lay in the fact that, while his divisions had tank battalions, the landing schedule provided for only one armored division, but that was French. What Truscott wanted was a motorized armored unit, capable of moving rapidly to exploit an opportunity or available to support other units when needed. CC Sudre was admirable for this purpose. It consisted of a reconnaissance squadron, medium tanks, a battalion of infantry, a group of motorized artillery, a squad of tank destroyers, engineers, and others—over four thousand men and a thousand vehicles.

Truscott obtained from Patch the assurance that Sudre's armored force would remain with the VI Corps, but he could never find out from his superior for how long, nor could he get approval for an American armored command. His request to keep CC Sudre was turned down "as being impracticable for political and other reasons." De Lattre later wrote that he would have liked Sudre and other French troops to be available for a dashing thrust toward Grenoble, but he claims in his memoirs that Patch vetoed the idea:

> General Patch seemed to see in my wish the unspoken anxiety to spare my troops the attacks on Toulon and Marseilles. I then had with him, for the first time, a fairly lively dispute, for it was painful to me that anyone should doubt the offensive will of the French after the proofs they had given.[19]

Feeling strongly his need for a mobile armored force and doubtful about his ability to keep Sudre, Truscott decided on his own to fashion a cavalry-type task force from elements of his VI Corps. In his own words:

> On August 1st . . . I called a meeting of my planning staff, informing them of my decision to organize a provisional armored group to be commanded by Brigadier General Fred W. Butler, my assistant Corps commander, and to be designated Task Force Butler. His staff, and essential communications, were to be provided by the Corps Headquarters. The group was to consist of the Corps Cavalry Squadron, the 117th Reconnaissance Squadron, one armored field artillery battalion, one tank battalion less one

company, one tank destroyer company, one infantry battalion in motors, an engineer battalion and the necessary service troops. It was to be ready to mass in the vicinity of Le Muy on Corps' order at any time after D-Day.

Zeller's explanations may have helped convince General Patch that Truscott's idea of a special task force had considerable merit. Perhaps Patch saw that by giving his support he solved several problems: He satisfied Truscott's wish for a fast-moving contingent of motorized armor, he resolved the question of CC Sudre, and he made a gesture toward cooperation with the FFI. However, Zeller would not be available as liaison. Having learned about the ANVIL plan, the French general had become a security risk and could not return to France. Now the highest-ranking FFI French officer in the landing area would be Colonel Constans, who had left Algiers for France at the same time that Zeller departed for Naples. Constans could only learn about Task Force Butler by radio or from officers who would follow him into France.

On August 11, four days after Zeller conferred with Patch, General Wilson approved a new directive essentially repeating the basic objectives of the ANVIL/DRAGOON plan. There was, however, an addition:

> You should also be prepared to thrust with light forces northward up the Durance River Valley towards Sisteron, with a view to gaining touch with and stimulating the Maquis in the Vaucluse area. Such action will have the additional advantage of providing a large measure of protection to your right flank.[20]

Although Brooks Richards believed that Zeller "had won" his argument, and although SPOC and General Cochet had long advocated a thrust up the Durance Valley, SPOC did not learn immediately of the new possibilities. On August 11, SPOC queried Wilson's G-3 whether indeed Cochet's plan, envisaging "a large effort to hold the Route Napoléon," had Seventh Army's approval. SPOC soon obtained copies of the modified directive, but ironically only four days before the scheduled landings and at a time when Colonel Constans had already left for France.[21]

6

Eve of the Landings

Hampered by uncooperative weather and a variety of problems, SPOC had been able to mount fewer sorties than normal into southeastern France during July. With the full moon coming on August 4, the officers at SPOC knew they had to make maximum use of good flying weather during the first two weeks of August if they were to dispatch into the field the OGs, the Jedburghs, and the members of special missions—over 100 individuals—who had been forced to train in the back regions around Algiers. Most of them had been ordered to Algiers before Normandy D Day, expecting to fulfil missions coordinated with Operation OVERLORD, but week followed week while, with a few exceptions, the teams tested their equipment, practiced parachute jumps, and interspersed their training with occasional forays into the white hillside city of Algiers.

With some fifteen additional Jedburgh teams and ten OGs waiting in the Algiers area since June, the question may be posed: Why were not more of them sent in earlier? In after-action reports, the OGs and Jeds were unanimous in affirming that they should have been dispatched several months before D Day so that they could have begun training programs. Neil Marten, a Jedburgh himself, sent back from the field to take charge of the Jed operation at SPOC, poses the question in his final report and adds: "I have searched for, but cannot find, the reason for this delay." He suggests some possibilities—lack of requests from the field, insufficient air lift, poor coordination—all of which were factors but do not provide a satisfactory explanation.[1]

The basic reasons are complex, and responsibility in a sense goes to the highest echelons because no clear-cut policy regarding aid to the Resistance had ever been formulated. This unfortunate gap followed from President Roosevelt's unwillingness to approve full cooperation with de Gaulle, but Allied nonrecognition was coupled also with military attitudes: a conviction that the French lacked security and a vast ignorance of French guerrilla capacity.

The wisdom of Allied attitudes can be debated, but certain facts cannot. General Eisenhower, charged with making a successful landing on the Normandy beaches, had to plan without a directive regarding his relations with de Gaulle until, on May 13, Roosevelt finally agreed that the Supreme Allied Commander could talk with the FCNL on purely military matters. Y Day, June 1, was now scarcely two weeks away—no time to formulate a large-scale consistent plan that would involve the Resistance. Then, with concern for security, Eisenhower directed the Mediterranean command on May 21 that no Jedburgh should be dropped earlier than Y minus 10, and no OG before Y minus 3. Furthermore, since all control of contacts with the Resistance lay with SHAEF, SPOC had to clear its operations into southern France with London. The resulting bureaucratic snarl was considerable.

After the Normandy landings, and after ANVIL was approved, General Wilson, the Mediterranean commander, requested authority for his command to develop contacts with the Resistance in support of ANVIL. He did not obtain such approval until July 15, after which SPOC could begin implementation of programs long since drawn up. At this point, bad weather became a factor: After the middle of the month, only the nights of July 17, 18, 25, 29, and 31 were suitable, and in the entire month, as General Wilson explained to de Gaulle, only nine nights had permitted sorties. As late as July 28, SPOC was not certain that SHAEF had relinquished control over Jedburghs and that SPOC could dispatch them without clearance from London.[2]

In considering explanations for the delay, Marten mentioned poor coordination, which, after all, follows inevitably from unclear policy. If the chain of command was Wilson (SACMED) to Patch (Seventh Army) to Truscott (VI Corps) and de Lattre (French Army B), where stood SPOC, with its dual Anglo-American command, attached to SACMED's G-3 but with only liaison to Seventh Army? People then at SPOC point out that with three separate desks—French country, Jedburghs, and OGs—and with no single commander designating priorities, there developed internal competition for the available aircraft. No useful purpose is served by dwelling on in-house rivalries; let it simply be noted that obvious sources of friction existed: national and personal differences, resupply responsibility for missions already in the field, and, as D Day approached, increasing pressure on limited facilities. Coalition warfare has never been a breeder of harmony; the miracle is that so many difficulties were coped with and surmounted.[3]

Whatever the reasons for delays before August 1, SPOC bent every effort to make up for the relatively quiet action that in June and July had brought only seven Jedburghs and three OGs into France. Three of the Jedburghs (QUININE,

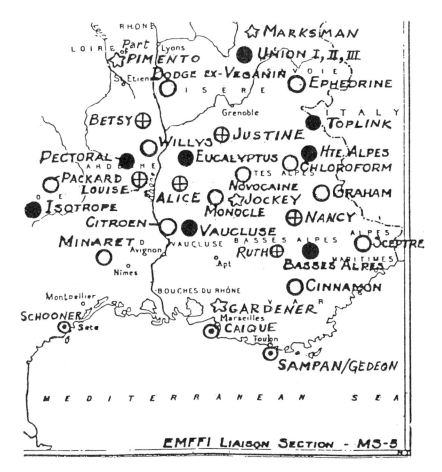

Map 6.1

SPECIAL OPERATIONS IN SOUTHEASTERN FRANCE

In August 1944, the staff of the French Forces of the Interior in London produced a map showing all 118 "Military Support Missions" in France as of August 18, 1944. Thirty-seven of these inter-allied, Jedburgh, OG, SOE, and counterscorch missions operated in southeastern France, the area earmarked for Operation ANVIL/DRAGOON. This map has been adapted from the official EMFFI map. Personnel of these missions are listed in the Appendix.

● Inter-allied (Maquis) missions ○ Jedburgh teams ☆ SOE circuits
⊕ Operational Groups (OGs) ⊙ Counterscorch (anti-sabotage teams)

AMMONIA, BUGATTI) were operating too far west to have any significant immediate impact on the ANVIL landings. Of the remaining four, two were actually combined into one (VEGANINE and DODGE), but because Manierre of DODGE, sent to assist Commandant NOIR of VEGANINE, had been captured, this left only the latter to carry on in the northern Drôme department. One of the OGs, JUSTINE, dispatched to the Vercors, had disintegrated when the Germans overran the plateau. Across the Rhône to the west, in the Ardèche Department, was Jedburgh team WILLYS, which continued to work with OGs LOUISE and BETSY. The seventh Jedburgh team was CHLOROFORM (two Frenchmen, Captain Martin and Lieutenant Sassi, and the American Captain Henry McIntosh), which had followed L'HERMINE from the Drôme department to his new assignment northeast of Gap.

MORE MISSIONS TO THE FIELD

If operations in July had been slow, SPOC made up for it in August. In the first fortnight, with the benefit of long-awaited moonlight and exceptional efforts from packers, schedulers, and pilots, British and American bombers carried five OGs, ten Jedburgh teams, innumerable French officials, and a dozen BLOs (British Liaison Officers), whose special efforts would focus on the Alpine passes.

First, a Jedburgh team, PACKARD, was dropped into the Gard department on August 1. This mission consisted of an American, Capt. Aaron Bank, and two French officers.

Although Bank had been instructed to coordinate his activities with the inter-allied ISOTROPE mission, he did not work closely with that primarily Anglo-French group. In his memoirs, Bank makes only one brief reference to a "two-man SOE team" and has written the writer that they "made contact with us infrequently. They did their thing and we did ours."

Whatever his relations with ISOTROPE may have been, Bank obtained great satisfaction from his initiation to guerrilla warfare, and his enthusiasm increased after the war. Remaining in the American army, he was later instrumental in developing paratroopers and guerrilla commandos within the military forces; indeed, he has been called the Father of the Green Berets.[4]

It should not be overlooked that heads of SOE circuits, like Cammaerts of JOCKEY, theoretically integrated into the FFI, continued to be active in the area. These circuits included several north of Lyon, but most important were Anthony Brooks' PIMENTO, sabotaging railways in the Rhône Valley and to the west, and in the Marseille region, Robert Boiteux's GARDENER.

During the first week of August, three OGs flew to southern France from North Africa. One, PAT, landed near Toulouse, far to the west of the anticipated ANVIL beachhead, but the other two, RUTH and ALICE, parachuted into areas directly ahead of a possible breakout.

RUTH consisted of 15 OSS commandos, led by two first lieutenants, Mills C. Brandes and Carl O. Strand, Jr. The group's mission was originally, along the lines of "Plan Vert," to prevent German use of railroads in the southern part of the Basses-Alpes department and northern section of the Var, roughly a triangle Sisteron–Meyrargues–Draguignan, which comprised a crucial area for operations along the Route Napoléon and the Durance valley, such as Colonel Zeller was at the very moment proposing in Algiers. The RUTH team was dropped in the early hours of August 4—night of the full moon—between Grasse and Castellane, to the zone where only containers were expected by a small contingent of FTP *maquisards*. After three arduous night marches, loaded with heavy equipment, the group reached the Maquis camp at St.-Jurs, in the mountains about twenty-five miles south of Digne. For the next few days, until the ANVIL landings on August 15, Brandes, Strand, and their men blew four bridges in the area. A *maquisard* at St.-Jurs, Oxent Miesseroff, later wrote memoirs that described, not too kindly, the OG's operation: "As the Americans had nothing to do, everything which was worth blowing up having been destroyed long since, they pitched their tents about 500 meters from us, a little vacation camp."[5]

Apparently realizing that more blowing of bridges might be counterproductive, SPOC ordered the group to concentrate on ambushes. Lieutenant Strand, therefore, moved with four men into the Les Mées area, about fifteen miles west of Digne, while Brandes, with the remainder, set up ambushes along the Route Napoléon. They had seen no action, however, when the first U.S. Army elements reached them after the ANVIL landings.

One of RUTH's men, T5 James E. Dyas, injured his knee on landing. Unable to move out with his teammates, he remained in a secure hideout in the Montagne de Malay, where the OG had landed. Just before the ANVIL forces came ashore, he joined forces with OSS agent Geoffrey Jones, a paratrooper whose activities with General Frederick's Airborne Task Force will be recounted further on.

The other OG, ALICE, led by Lts. Ralph N. Barnard and Donald J. Meeks, was sent to the Drôme department "to organize and strengthen the resistance forces," "to reconnoiter National Highway No. 7 [along the Rhône and] to destroy enemy communication lines." The parachute drop of the 15-man section took place without incident, near Dieulefit, shortly after midnight on August 7.[6]

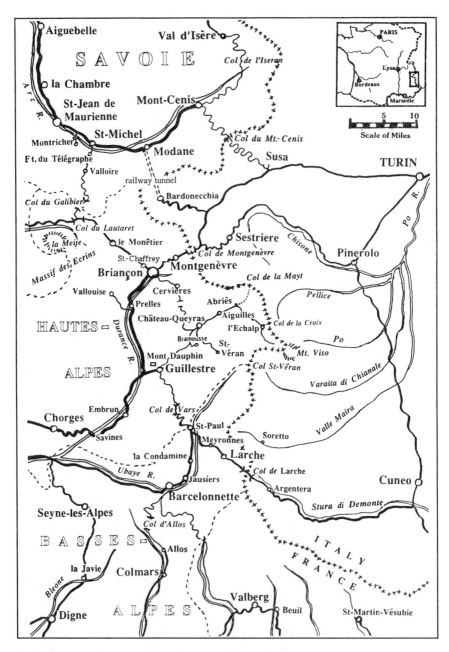

Map 6.2
THE FRANCO-ITALIAN BORDER
The Dauphiné Alps, Larche Pass and Barcelonnette. Montgenèvre
Pass and Briançon.

It so happened that Commandant de Lassus, the Drôme FFI chief, was in the south, near Nyons, when OG ALICE landed nearby. He assigned the section to Captain Kirsch, in charge of the company located on the Combovin plateau about ten miles southeast of the German airfield at Chabeuil. The group set up headquarters there on August 12 and organized its first sabotage operation, blowing two high tension towers on the plain south of Chabeuil.

De Lassus, like many French Resistance leaders, believed that, when American paratroopers with their bazookas and heavy weapons came in, they should preferably attack Germans rather than carry out sabotage, which the *maquisards*, as long as they had plastic explosives, could effectively do. In defense of ALICE's leaders, it should be pointed out that SPOC had ordered them, as essential to the mission, to destroy communication lines. When Jedburgh team MONOCLE reached de Lassus' headquarters, the French leader requested the American member, Lt. Ray H. Foster, to talk the OG into attacking German convoys rather than pylons and isolated bridges.[7]

The ALICE team arrived in the area at a moment not conducive toward pro-Americanism, at least not toward the U.S. Air Force, which was bombing far and wide in anticipation of ANVIL. On August 13, attempting to knock out the bridge across the Drôme at Crest, American planes missed the bridge but destroyed much of the town. Asked to assuage the townspeople's misery, Lieutenants Barnard and Meeks, with three paratroopers, went down to Crest.

Upon arriving they were greeted by a very downhearted and somewhat belligerent group of people. The damage consisted of destruction of about one-fourth of the town, thirty-eight killed, one hundred wounded. Lt. Barnard and Lt. Meeks talked with the people, visited the hospital and encouraged the people that the bombing was a mistake and would not occur again.[8]

BRITISH LIAISON OFFICERS

Besides the Jedburghs, OGs, SOE Circuits, intelligence agents, and inter-allied missions, there was another special group of agents sent into France, sometimes characterized as BLOs: British Liaison Officers. Generally speaking, these officers were transferred from British PWE (Political Warfare Executive) programs, which had been mounted mostly in Greece. With the Balkan actions tapering off after the Big Three, at Teheran late in 1943, had approved the major onslaught to be directed at France, some PWE and SOE agents in Cairo sought a transfer to that area where they believed they would see more action.

Among these officers was Major Havard Gunn, of Scottish origin, who
before the war had joined the reserve of the Seaforth Highlanders. An artist of
considerable talent, he became enamored of the Provençal countryside, like
Cézanne and Van Gogh before him, and when the war broke out was living and
painting near St.-Tropez, where he had purchased a cottage. Joining his
regiment after Hitler invaded Poland, he made good use of his French as a
member of the Spears mission in 1941, when de Gaulle's Free French battled
the Vichy forces in Syria. Later on, transferred to PWE in Italy, he sought an
opportunity to go into southern France to further political warfare objectives.[9]

The concept of British officers going into France appealed to SOE, which
was already helping Italian partisans in northern Italy. If French and Italian
guerrillas could harass German forces in the Alps, the passes might be closed
to Axis troops attacking ANVIL's flank or, conversely, open for Allied troops
crossing from France into the Po Valley, thus reinforcing General Alexander
once he broke through the defenses along the Pisa–Florence–Ancona line.
Furthermore, guerrillas could sabotage the railway from Lyon to Turin, Aosta,
and Cuneo.

THE FRANCO-ITALIAN BORDER

Early in 1944, SOE in Italy (No. 1 Special Force) proposed an operation
known as TOPLINK, which would endeavor to join Italian and French *maquisards* together for a cooperative venture in the high Alps. Later, the overall
SPOC plan affirmed that "an Italian-speaking liaison officer is being dispatched
to the French side, to be followed by two Jedburghs with Italian-speaking
members, and one or more Italian OG's. On the Italian side, British Liaison
Officers are to be dispatched to Maquis area near Aosta and Cuneo."[10]

To implement this essentially British initiative, four majors, ten captains,
and one sergeant began training in Algiers; they, like the Jedburghs and OGs,
expected that they would soon parachute into southern France for coordination
with the Normandy campaign. However, week followed week with no orders,
until finally, at the beginning of August, SPOC began to send them in, accom-
panying French officers with whom they had trained, mostly to work under
Francis Cammaerts in that part of southeastern France that lies between the
Durance River and the Italian frontier. The first team to go in had specific orders
to get in touch with the Italian Resistance north of the Larche pass, in accord
with the concepts of Operation TOPLINK.

Should enemy forces undertake an offensive across the Larche pass, they
would have to descend on the French side down to the crossroads at the Ubaye

River, where the left (southern) road leads to Barcelonnette, and the right, or northern route, runs toward St.-Paul, then over another pass—the Col de Vars—and ultimately to Guillestre and the wide, gently sloping Durance valley. The Maquis, in small groups of fifteen to fifty, were scattered among the crags and slopes, harassing German convoys that ventured along the winding and vulnerable mountain roads.

Guillestre provided another key position in relation to Italy. Traveling northeast from Gap, along the level and fertile Durance Valley, about ten miles beyond Embrun, one reaches a key junction: The right road leads to Guillestre and up through the magnificently forested Queyras to alpine passes navigable only by foot; the left continues along the Durance to Briançon beyond which winds the ascending passage to the Montgenèvre pass. Back at the junction stands Mont-Dauphin, a singular butte that, fortified, could in days before air power, dominate the roads north, south, and east. Indeed, Vauban had built a citadel there in the 1690s when Louis XIV campaigned against the House of Savoy. However, in 1944, the fortress housed only a small German garrison, mostly consisting of about one hundred administrative personnel not given to interfering with the FFI, whose members regularly rode past the fort with impunity.

The chief in this area was the French patriot Gilbert Galetti, a good friend of Cammaerts and Christine, who operated east of Guillestre into the Queyras, with headquarters at a group of chalets above Bramousse. Farther to the east stands another ancient fortress, Chateau Queyras, and beyond, as the road rises and the pine and larch forest thickens, the impassive range of high Alps appears as a formidable barrier, its crests delineating the frontier between France and Italy. Indeed, no road crosses the Alps at this point, but Galetti's people regularly took trails from Abriès or l'Echalp, over the Col de la Mayt or the Col de la Croix, to maintain contact with Italian partisans under Marcellin, who tried to harass German convoys shuttling toward the Montgenèvre Pass from Pinerolo and Turin.

The TOPLINK mission parachuted into Savournon, an isolated spot ringed with hills about eighty miles west of Seyne, on August 1.[11] The group included six persons: two British, one French, and three Italians. The British members were Maj. L.G.M.J. Hamilton and Capt. P.W.R.H. ("Pat") O'Regan. "Hamilton" was a *nom-de-guerre*; he was actually not British but Belgian. Forty-four-year-old Leon Blanchaert had joined the British army, served in North Africa, been captured, imprisoned in Italy, and escaped back to North Africa. The French representative (and wireless operator) was Lieutenant Simon Kalifa, while the Italians, provided by SOE's No. 1 Special Force, included Lieutenants Ruscelli and Renato, with a radio operator named Gino. In order to obtain specific information for Hamilton's mission, Cammaerts had assigned Christine Granville the difficult mission of making preliminary contacts with the Italians.

Unfortunately for the whole TOPLINK concept, the moment was hardly propitious for the Italian partisans. Just as the Germans had wreaked heavy damage on the French Resistance after the Normandy landings, so in Italy, as the Allies forged past Rome, the German forces in northern Italy needed to safeguard the passes—especially those of Tende, Larche, and Montgenèvre—to make certain no flank attack moved against them across the French–Italian frontier. To mention but two of many forays, German mountain troops forced the Rosselli brigade to escape over the mountains from the Stura di Demonte south into France, and they struck hard at Marcellin's partisans, farther north in the Pellice Valley just across the border from the Queyras.

Scarcely rested up from her ordeal in the Vercors, Christine moved from Seyne to Gilbert Galetti's headquarters near Bramousse. From there a helpful ski instructor, Gilbert Tavernier, took her on the back seat of his motorcycle up the Guil Valley to l'Echalp, from which point she proceeded on foot across the 7,000-foot Col de la Croix into Italy. There she met the hard-pressed Marcellin, who was in the process of reestablishing his base in another valley farther north.

Although he had not yet received information from Christine, Cammaerts sent Hamilton and his team (except for O'Regan, who was ill) along the same route to Italy. Unfortunately, Hamilton did not meet Christine and therefore failed to learn about the German attack that had provoked Marcellin's evacuation plans. Finding the Italian partisans scattered and in retreat, Hamilton returned to France, only to learn then from Cammaerts and Christine, around August 5, that the Italians had regrouped, with their command post in an old barracks at the Col de la Mayt.

Disappointed, Hamilton's team returned to Galetti's headquarters where, now joined by an American OSS radio operator, Lt. Mario Volpe, they continued their efforts to help Marcellin and his dispirited partisans by packing supplies on muleback up to the pass. The mission's effectiveness became handicapped soon after, when Hamilton, injured in a car accident, had to be brought to a hospital in Aiguilles. The resourceful O'Regan, an able and broad-gauged officer, carried on in the high Alps where, in September, the mission was joined by two OGs. In spite of these reinforcements, the Germans soon captured the Col de la Mayt barracks, forcing the guerrillas to withdraw farther south, to the Col St.-Véran area. Ultimately, when regular French troops arrived, they pursued the Germans into Italy as far as Cuneo. The Cuneo incident, which required decisions at the de Gaulle-Truman level, provides an intriguing epilogue to the TOPLINK concept, worth examining but beyond the scope of the present study.

THE OTHER BLOs ARRIVE

During the first ten days of August, the rest of the British group, including some French officers but no Americans, came in by parachute mostly to the drop zone in the rolling pastures just south of Seyne. The members of these and other groups were frequently identifiable by their ecclesiastical code names, such as (in English) Holy Savior, Confessional, Cathedral, and the like. Among those so designated can be counted the two highest-ranking French representatives in SPOC, Colonel Constans (SAINT SAUVEUR) and Willy Widmer (CLOITRE); Hamilton was CROSSE and O'Regan CHAPE. Gunn was an exception among the "religious" agents, for he had chosen his *nom-de-guerre*, BAMBUS, from a clump of bamboos he and Christine Granville had come across when they were training at MASSINGHAM.

The group with which Gunn was associated, scheduled to go in on August 1 with Hamilton and O'Regan, was delayed three days, but landed south of Seyne on the fourth and immediately came into contact with Cammaerts.[12] Besides Gunn and two British agents, the mission included two Frenchmen.

The senior French officer, Cdt. Christian Sorensen (code named CHASUBLE and head of the mission), whose name evinced his forebears' Swedish origins, belonged to a wealthy wine-producing family of Algeria. He had served in the Tunisian campaign and later, like Constans, became affiliated with the "Service Action" section of Soustelle's DGSS. He had undergone the same sort of paratrooper training at Massingham's Club des Pins as the British officers.

The other French officer, Capt. Jean Fournier (CALICE), also from "Service Action," had completed similar training. He was a graduate of St.-Cyr, had served with the French army during the 1940 debacle, and later in Africa.

Of the two British team members, one, Sgt-Maj. A. Campbell, was responsible for radio communications, while the other, Capt. John A. Halsey (LUTRIN), would be assigned to the Larche pass area. Halsey, sometimes referred to in the records as Kerdrel-Halsey, possessed dual citizenship through his father, the Comte de Kerdrel, the London representative of the French Railroads, who had married an English woman named Halsey. Captain Halsey had fought with the French army in 1939–40, subsequently served in the British army, and finally joined SOE.

Sorensen had injured his leg on landing, but was sufficiently well to meet a member of the Liberation Committee, who made arrangements for him to see the Basses-Alpes FFI Chief, Georges Bonnaire, on August 7. Their conversation at Seyne gave Bonnaire, a Communist, an opportunity to express a principal FTP grievance, that when the FFI commands were organized on orders from

London, the FTP leadership was kept on the sidelines.

After the Sorensen–Bonnaire discussion, Cammaerts introduced the other members of the mission—Gunn, Halsey, and Fournier—and a general discussion ensued. In general, Sorensen handled French political questions, while the British officers devoted themselves to purely military affairs. The Frenchman pointed out that the mission's purpose was to help bring assistance to the Resistance in the Basses-Alpes–Alpes-Maritimes–Var area, and to coordinate its actions with those of the Allies. When the question of a regional FFI chief for R-2 came up, Cammaerts was able to inform the group that Constans had been named by Algiers and was expected to arrive any day.

Because Hamilton and O'Regan, the Alpine section, were already on their way toward Italy, Gunn and Sorensen were anxious to set up a command post farther south and close to the Route Napoléon. With Lécuyer's help, they decided that Halsey would go to Barcelonnette, while Gunn would go farther south to Colmars, where Lécuyer had previously maintained a headquarters. Sorensen, because of his injured leg, would for the time being remain at Seyne.

Before Gunn left Seyne, the second section of the mission, together with Jedburgh team NOVOCAINE, parachuted into the area in the small hours of August 7. The mission group consisted of six men, led by a French officer, Cdt. Jacques Pelletier (CONFESSIONAL), two British officers, Maj. R.W.B. Purvis and Capt. John Roper, an American radio operator, Lt. Mario Volpe, and two men to serve as liaison with the Italians. Jacques Pelletier was pursued by bad luck, for two weeks later he was accidentally shot in the shoulder by an immature recruit. He survived but could no longer continue with the mission.[13]

The Pelletier segment, scheduled to work with Paul Héraud in the Hautes-Alpes and with Hamilton's Italian mission, landed near Savournon, where they were received by a dedicated resistor, René Guérin. The ring of hills near Savournon, relatively isolated, provided a focal point for clandestine operations. Héraud greeted the mission and arranged for them to meet the next day with the Hautes-Alpes Resistance leaders. On that day, August 8, Cammaerts and Christine drove over to Savournon, west of Seyne, and conducted the team to a forest hideaway east of Gap for the meeting. Christine had just completed an arduous two-week reconnaissance expedition in the area and into Italy; she had undertaken to recruit some Poles out of the *Wehrmacht* and reported that thousands of Italian partisans might join in cooperative ventures with the French.[14]

Héraud's short notice for the August 8 meeting had not prevented all the Resistance chiefs, traveling by car and bicycle or on foot, from reaching the rendezvous site near Gap. There Héraud outlined his plans for guerrilla attacks and for cooperation with the Allied missions. Cammaerts proposed a vote of confidence for Héraud's leadership.[15] The CONFESSIONAL group agreed and proceeded to Savournon in preparation for a move to the eastern Alps. Cammaerts and Christine returned to Seyne. Héraud and Moreaud went to Gap, while the other leaders walked or rode to their homes and command posts.[16]

On the next morning, August 9, Héraud came to Moreaud's house in some agitation. He had learned that Baret, the pro-Resistance deputy prefect, had been arrested; he needed a vehicle to get to Savournon as soon as possible. Moreaud had gone out, but Héraud was able to find a motorcycle on which, with a friend, the Gendarme Meyere, he started south on the Route Napoléon toward Tallard. He never reached Savournon. A short distance above Tallard, the two men were stopped by a German patrol, and alongside a bush-bordered stream they were summarily shot.

Héraud's death, along with that of so many others, brought havoc and grief in its wake. In a Resistance sewn with internecine antagonisms and rivalries, Paul Héraud had virtually single-handed wrought a fabric in the Hautes-Alpes where ORA could talk to FTP and where career military officers would consult with Socialist politicians. And a towering irony lay in the fact that in ten days the Allied army would have thrust its way to the threshold of Gap and Paul would not be there to see it.

One can only imagine the shock to Cammaerts, back in Seyne, on learning of the unexpected and brutal execution of Paul Héraud, whom he not only respected as a personal friend, but viewed as unique, a person who could bring some degree of unity to the continually squabbling Resistance factions. In addition to the shock, Héraud's death came at a time when Action messages from SPOC were beginning to come in and when the number of parachute drops, both containers and agents, increased daily. Clearly, the invasion was imminent, yet a multitude of problems cried for solution.

When he returned to Seyne, Cammaerts found that another Jedburgh team had arrived: NOVOCAINE, commanded by an American, Lt. Charles Gennerich, one of the group with whom McIntosh (still with L'HERMINE northeast of Gap) had trained.[17] The two remaining members of the team were a Frenchman, Lt. Jean Yves LeLann, and another American, Sgt. W. Thompson. Cammaerts gave them the same assignment as the Pelletier–Purvis–Roper mission: proceed to Guillestre, get in touch with Gilbert Galetti in the Queyras, and move on to a Maquis post at Vallouise from where they could carry out guerrilla actions along the roads to Briançon and the Montgenèvre pass. The two teams shortly moved out by gazogene trucks that Cammaerts arranged for, and they reached their destination by August 13. Thereafter, they cooperated with Capt. Jean Frison, the Sector commander, who with his deputies Capt. Lucien Nortier and Capt. François Ambrosi, had over 150 hardy *maquisards* under his command. Many were mountaineers, wearing the floppy berets of the celebrated *chasseurs alpins,* and some of the paratroopers, well trained as they may have been, could not always keep pace with them.

Meanwhile, after the meeting with Bonnaire, and leaving Commandant Sorensen to recuperate at Seyne, Major Gunn had moved south with Lécuyer to Valberg on August 8. In his official report, Gunn writes: "Difficulty of movement, area surrounded by German garrisons; made first recce area BAR-CELONNETTE-LARCHE, had to travel as Gendarme, uniform hidden." Gunn's uniform, of course, consisted of the kilts of the Seaforth Highlanders, difficult to conceal under any circumstances, but, wishing to let it be known that Allied support had arrived, Gunn and the other British officers (as well as Jedburghs and OGs) wore their uniforms as frequently as feasible.

Already, Capt. John Halsey, having co-opted a sergeant of Spanish origin, Fernandez (RUDOLPH), already in the field, had established a base of operations at a ski resort just south of Barcelonnette, where he was able to begin reconnaissance in the Larche pass area. He was in touch with Christine Granville, who, with her ability to speak Polish, was making efforts to persuade the 50-odd Poles in the Larche garrison to desert the leaders outrageously inflicted upon them. This effort of Christine's embodied one part of her mission, and since coming down from the Vercors, she had already reached a number of Polish soldiers, who maintained a clandestine organization centered at Mont-Dauphin. While at Valberg, Gunn kept in constant touch with SPOC and with the various field missions, awaiting the "Action" messages they all knew would soon be transmitted.[18] On August 11, Cammaerts learned that Constans had finally arrived, and he concluded that he should go see him at once.

CONSTANS AND CAMMAERTS

Because Constans was not qualified for jumping by parachute, arrangements had been made for him to come in by Dakota (DC 3) along with Jedburgh GRAHAM and half a dozen important Gaullists, including Charles Luizet, slated to become de Gaulle's chief of police in Paris. But incredible obstacles kept delaying this flight. First of all, the Lysander pilots who had flown to the Vaucluse on August 2 maintained that the runway was too short for a Dakota. In spite of the fact that Colonel Zeller, who had accompanied them, tried to persuade them that the 2000-yard strip at Spitfire had been half camouflaged with lavender bushes, the RAF would not approve the Dakota mission until the runway's suitability had been verified.[19]

In any case, the delay provided Constans with an opportunity to obtain a final briefing from de Gaulle. His orders, dated July 29, had been signed by the general himself, and read as follows:

1. Colonel Constans is named Commandant of the French Forces of the Interior of Region 2. In this regard, he is qualified to give all necessary orders concerning the constitution and staffing of the FFI. He will direct their action and ensure coordination with operations planned by the High Command.
2. The limits of R-2 are fixed as follows: Course of the Isère River from the Rhône to Grenoble; course of the Romanche River, border of the Hautes-Alpes department to the French-Italian frontier.
3. Colonel Constans will report to his post as soon as possible.

ALGIERS, 29 July 1944
/s/ C. de Gaulle

Constans met with General de Gaulle on August 5, shortly after the French leader had seen Zeller. However, for Constans, the briefing session with de Gaulle, which lasted only fifteen minutes, had not been inspiring. When he returned to his office, Constans jotted down the elements of the conversation: "Don't spill any French blood except for good reason. Unify all movements that have military forces which submit to military discipline. The fighting will be hard and the outcome perhaps less rapid than one thinks. In any case, see you soon." The farewell had been cordial, but the general may have had his mind focused on matters of higher import: With the Allied breakthrough in Normandy, de Gaulle's need for a political, military, and economic understanding with Roosevelt and Churchill became increasingly urgent. Northern France was becoming more interesting than the south. (In two weeks, de Gaulle would leave Algiers for good.)[20]

A few days after his interview, Constans, the other passengers, and the two Jedburghs who had been replaced by Widmer on Corsica (Major "Bing" Crosby of the Gordon Highlanders and Captain Gouvet) flew to an airfield at Cecina, south of Livorno in Italy. There on August 9, they were picked up by a Dakota captained by Flying Officer Rostron, but forced to return because of bad weather. A day later, the Dakota took off again and this time, in the early hours of August 11, after circling for over an hour, landed at Spitfire, to be taken in charge by the ever-vigilant ARCHIDUC.

The takeoff for the plane's return trip turned out to be a nightmare. The pilots learned that indeed the runway had been covered with lavender bushes, but these had been *planted*, 1200 yards from the beginning of the strip, not simply laid on. There was also a potato patch farther down the runway.

Furthermore, thirty passengers, mostly American airmen from downed Flying Fortresses, had crammed into the plane. When the takeoff began, the plane had not gained flying speed when it hit the lavender bushes and ground to a stop. The pilot tried again, having reduced his passengers to twenty-two, and this time became airborne, his tail wheel scarcely clearing the potatoes.[21]

Back on the ground, ARCHIDUC escorted Constans and the rest of the group along a few miles of foothills to Drop Zone Armature, near the hamlet of Lagarde, about fifteen miles up a curving road from Apt. Reuniting with Widmer, Constans set up his headquarters and sent word to Resistance leaders in R-2 (and part of R-1) to meet with him as soon as possible. D Day was now but four days away, though neither Constans, nor Cammaerts, nor others in France knew the exact date or place.[22]

At the same time that Constans landed in the Vaucluse, another segment of the BLOs parachuted into the hills around Seyne. This group consisted of Maj. Xan Fielding (CATHEDRAL), who had worked previously in Greece, and a personable South African, Capt. Julian Lezzard, who, having injured his back on landing, was unable to participate in further activities.

In his memoirs, Fielding provides colorful details of his brief mission, which lasted for only a few days before being overrun by the ANVIL landing forces. On the morning of August 11, Fielding obtained medical aid for his companion and soon located Cammaerts and Christine at the Turells. He had not anticipated Cammaerts' youth and size:

> I was faced with a smiling young giant whose coltish appearance was exaggerated by sloping shoulders and an easy resilient poise. These features, to begin with, obscured the contradictory qualities of leadership and modesty with which he subsequently impressed me. It was only later I realized that for him resistance was tantamount to a new religion, which he had been preaching and practicing with remarkable success for over three years.

During the day, while the containers dropped along with Fielding were recovered, Cammaerts explained the local situation to the newcomer and prepared to drive to Apt for the meeting with Widmer and Constans.[23]

Of the problems to be resolved, the most urgent related to commands and command relationships, especially in those departments where the landings might take place and along the Route Napoléon. In the previous month or so, since the Normandy landings, Cammaerts had witnessed a significant evolution from an essentially civilian "waiting" Resistance, with its not-yet-mobilized *sédentaires* and its stockpiling of material, to a Resistance of active and structured military forces, receiving more and more arms, and captained in many instances by self-promoted natural leaders, as much brigand as patriot, or a handful of St.-Cyr graduates. Now the untimely deaths of Martin-Bret, Robert Rossi, and Paul Héraud automatically established Constans' agenda: What should be done with Lécuyer? Who should replace Héraud? With Zeller absent, did Constans fulfill the role of FFI commander? What was his relationship with Bourgès-Maunoury? To what extent would Constans, a regular army officer, presumably therefore sympathetic to the ORA, find broad acceptance?

Cammaerts planned to travel the 75 miles to Apt in a Red Cross truck, driven by Claude Renoir (a son of the painter), which had already provided him with safe cover during trips in his area. Still at Seyne was Commandant Sorensen, who, because of his injured leg, had not accompanied Gunn to the south, as well as the recently arrived Major Fielding. Cammaerts undoubtedly weighed the advisability of leaving them at Seyne or of having them accompany him. Because Fielding's French was somewhat rusty, travel on open roads risked a possible interception, but in the end Cammaerts decided to bring the two officers along with him.

The trip began on August 12. Fielding has described it:

It was full of confidence, then, that I started out on my first journey through enemy-occupied France, my only worry being the baggy Charlie Chaplin trousers I was wearing. In these flapping garments, I felt almost like a freak beside Roger [Cammaerts] and the dapper Chasuble [Sorensen], a suave, silent man with greying hair, neat dark features and a tired, urban manner.

Our drive was so uneventful and enjoyable that I had to keep reminding myself that I was not on holiday but on active service—a fact which escaped me at each of the delightful villages where, while Roger conferred with the local leaders, I drank a glass of wine outside the cafe under the palm trees.

When Cammaerts met Constans, it was not in Apt, but at the Maquis near Lagarde, where ARCHIDUC controlled Drop Zone Armature. In the locality as well, "Bing" Crosby and his French partner of Jedburgh team GRAHAM, Captain Gouvet, fumed at Constans' debates, which they considered unnecessarily prolonged. Eight American airmen, who could not be carried in the Dakota, stood by, hoping for another air lift. Also, in the small hours of August 13, an OSS Operational Group, "NANCY," led by Capt. Arnold Lorbeer, came in by parachute.[24]

Cammaerts discussed the general situation in the area with Constans, agreeing with the absent Zeller's recommendation that Lécuyer, who had many contacts in the eastern part of R-2, should be continued as FFI chief for the

Alpes-Maritimes Department. In this department, the German 148th Division maintained control of the principal cities, like Nice and Cannes, as well as the main towns along N85, the Route Napoléon: Grasse and Castellane. Lécuyer had been coordinating operations just north of the boundary between Alpes-Maritimes and Basses-Alpes. SPOC was not inclined to support leftist efforts to remove Lécuyer altogether; indeed, SPOC continued to send him arms, money, and reinforcements.

The succession to Héraud, in Hautes-Alpes, proved more complicated. (L'HERMINE was not under consideration, since he held a "regional" command in the Central Alps, theoretically making him senior to the departmental hierarchy.) The possibilities included Etienne Moreaud (DUMAS), Héraud's deputy; Colonel Daviron (RICARD), the departmental ORA chief; and Captain Bertrand (O'HERNE) of the Gendarmerie. Of these, Cammaerts favored Bertrand because Moreaud possessed no military background and Daviron, while a career officer, had demonstrated little initiative. Constans took Cammaerts' recommendations into consideration, but postponed decisions until he obtained more information. In the event, Constans chose Moreaud over Bertrand.[25]

Having concluded his discussions with Constans by the morning of August 13, Cammaerts, along with Sorensen and Fielding, and with Claude Renoir at the wheel, began the journey back to Seyne. On leaving Digne, scarcely an hour's drive from their destination, they were arrested. They remained in custody until two days after the landings.

This untimely arrest, after months of extreme care, threatened to end Cammaerts' career at the very threshold of southern France's liberation. That he and his colleagues came through the ordeal unscathed resulted from the enormously resourceful efforts of Christine Granville.

Learning of Cammaerts' capture, Christine, back in Seyne, immediately informed SPOC and consulted with Cammaerts' long-time ally Dr. Jouve about what might be done. Following the doctor's advice, she bicycled the hilly twenty-five miles to Digne and got in touch with a gendarme—an Alsatian named Schenk—who served as go-between in her negotiations with the Gestapo agent Max Waem, a Belgian in the Germans' employ. Christine was able to get over a million francs parachuted to her from SPOC. With the funds as bribe and the Allied landings as threat, she persuaded Waem, after ten hours of arguing, that it would serve his best interests to accept an Allied safe-conduct and release his prisoners. Schenk, not Waem, ultimately obtained the money but, because he was murdered a short time later, never made use of it. (The money disappeared.) Waem, quite aware by August 17 that no substantial German elements stood between Digne and Allied forces in Draguignan, fifty miles to the south, ushered his prisoners out of the prison, started them on the road to Seyne, and placed himself at their disposition. His trust was not betrayed. In time, Waem obtained a safe-conduct to Italy and, after the war, repatriation to Belgium.[26]

On returning to Seyne, Christine and the three released agents were greeted by John Roper at the Turrels. Undismayed after his ordeal but euphoric at his release, Cammaerts faced a great backlog of information to digest. Half a dozen new teams—Jedburghs and OGs—had been dropped into his area, and American troops now controlled a great semi-circular beachhead, fifty miles east and west of St.-Tropez, extending fifty miles into the interior.

II ANVIL/DRAGOON:
The Main Thrust to Grenoble and the Rhône Valley

7

The Landings

The landings of Truscott's VI Corps—the 3rd, 36th, and 45th Divisions—would be made along French Riviera beaches stretching some thirty miles from Cavalaire-sur-Mer in the south to the pleasant bay of Agay to the north. All of these landing sites, together with the first major objective, Toulon, lay within limits of the Var Department. It might have been thought that SPOC would have concentrated on the Var, with agents as heavily dispersed as they were in the Ardèche, the Vaucluse, and the Alps. If there was not an unusual number of contacts, it was not because the Var lacked a vigorous Resistance movement.

In fact, the Var possessed much hilly, forested land suitable for Maquis encampments; indeed, with one-half of its stony terrain covered with woods, it ranks first among all French departments in timbered acreage. Furthermore, with Resistance developing since the early days, the Var had begun to unify its movements in 1943 and was the first to organize a Committee of Liberation. Its military components registered the same disputes and rivalries already noted in the other departments. The FTP, the largest and most widely spread, maintained its companies throughout the Var. One of them, the 4th company, had established a camp in the Montagne de Malay, northeast of Draguignan, where Sergeant Dyas of OG RUTH was recovering from the knee injury he received on landing.

The ORA, under Lieutenant Colonel Lelaquet, was especially strong in the northwest part of the department, with sectors centered at Méounes, Brignoles, Brue-Auriac, and Varages. At the latter town, Colonel Gouzy, who would be one of the first to cooperate with the Allies, maintained his command post.

The Gaullist Secret Army had organized itself principally in the Toulon area and around the department's administrative center, Draguignan, in which Pierre Barrème and Captain Fontes had activated their clandestine headquarters. At nearby Les Arcs, where the railway from Toulon joined the line from St.-Raphael, Cdt. Jean Blanc was in charge. By the time of the ANVIL/DRAGOON landings, the AS had banded together with the *Groupes Francs* and the MUR to form the CFL (*Corps Francs de la Libération*). With the formation of the FFI in June, Commandant Salvatori, located in the Toulon area, attempted as chief of the FFI to persuade all the diverse heterogeneous units to cooperate in the common effort.[1]

The most successful unification effort had brought into existence the *Brigade des Maures*. Stretching parallel to the coast behind St.-Tropez, the Massif des Maures comprises some fifty miles of low-lying hills, covered with pines, chestnuts and cork trees, in some places isolated and stark, belying the nearby activity along the coast. In this area, a handsome young architect, Marc Rainaud, had forged a unit that contained elements of the FTP, the ORA, and the AS, with Maquis cantonments throughout the massif as well as on the St.-Tropez Peninsula itself. While the Brigade had been alerted for several days before D Day, Rainaud did not know that the beaches south of St.-Tropez had been earmarked for "Iron Mike" O'Daniel's 3rd Division.[2]

Unfortunately, the *Brigade des Maures* had not been well served by SPOC. Some 26 Drop Zones had been confirmed in the Var Department, but a series of failed missions plagued the effort to drop containers and packages. After Normandy D Day, only eight deliveries were successful, and of these, two occurred after August 15, scarcely providing time for recuperation and distribution. While the Var might be considered to be within the limits of Cammaerts's JOCKEY circuit, or part of GARDENER, run by Robert Boiteux out of Marseille, neither Cammaerts nor Boiteux had circulated much in the Var.[3]

There were good reasons why, even though ANVIL/DRAGOON's first assaults would be made along the Var beaches, widespread contacts with the Resistance were lacking. Simply because the department faced the Mediterranean and included the French naval base at Toulon, German defenses and counterespionage were especially effective. Cammaerts, who had maintained contacts with a group at Nice (in the Alpes-Maritimes Department, adjoining the Var), had undergone the unhappy experience in April 1944 of learning that the ring had been penetrated. An entire network had been arrested with loss of codes and transmitters.

From August 10 on, SPOC feverishly attempted to increase its drops, and to send in agents and teams that had been training for months in the hills and deserts around Algiers. The plan called for teams to drop into all regions just beyond the "blue-line" semicircle, which ANVIL planners hoped to achieve as a bridgehead from which thrusts would fan out, chiefly to the north and west. SPOC wished to reinforce the antisabotage teams in Toulon, Marseille, and

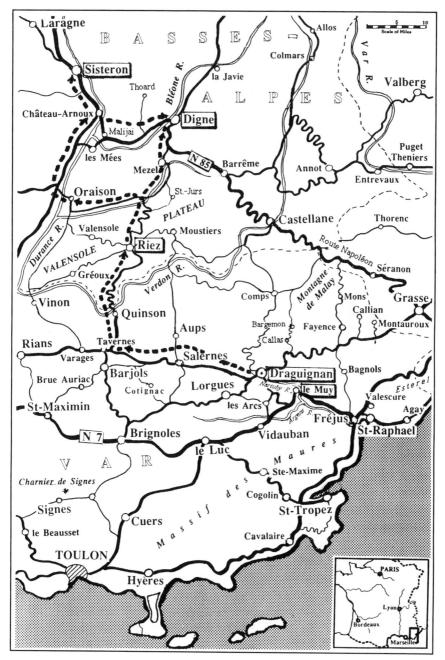

Map 7.1
THE LANDING AREA
First Airborne Task Force Drop Zones: Le Muy and Draguignan.
Task Force Butler to Riez, Digne, and Sisteron ▪▬▬▬▬▬▬▶

Sète, and also to have an agent on the spot to help Maj. Gen. Robert T. Frederick's FABTF (First Airborne Task Force) when its 7,000 paratroopers landed on D Day near Le Muy and Draguignan.

THE AIRBORNE LANDINGS

Farmers who trudged to their fields around Le Muy were startled, in the dark predawn haze of August 15 to find that thousands of parachutes had floated through the fog from squadrons of Allied C-47s. They were observing the first units of the FABTF, which had taken off from Italy several hours before.[4]

The drops encircled Le Muy, a small town about 15 miles from the coastal beaches where the 36th and 45th Divisions would land. Between Le Muy and the coast flows the Argens River, separating the two rugged outcroppings of the Massif des Maures on the south, and the picturesque Esterel on the north. Because few good roads penetrate the pine-covered slopes and ravines, the Argens Valley provides an easy access to the principal east–west highway, N7, and ten miles beyond, proceeding along the Nartuby River to a junction at Draguignan, to those roads that connect Grasse on the east with the Durance Valley to the west. If the paratroopers could hold a circle around Le Muy and Draguignan, and if the landing forces could quickly join up, then Patch would control key strong points on the three major east–west arteries.

The German Nineteenth Army commander, Gen. Friedrich Wiese, had correctly assessed the Allied need to gain control, farther west, of the major ports Toulon and Marseille, together with command of the Rhône Valley. His major defenses against an invasion, other than coastal batteries and block houses, consisted of seven divisions, four of which protected the coast between the Rhône and Spain. His only armored division, the 11th Panzer, had been stationed near Toulouse, over 200 miles from the landing beaches. East of the Rhône, Wiese had deployed his three remaining divisions, the 244th protecting Marseille, the 242nd defending a stretch from Toulon to the landing area, and the understrength 148th covering the Riviera resorts, Cannes and Nice, eastward to the Italian border. The 242nd and 148th Divisions made up the LXII Corps, under command of Generalleutnant Ferdinand Neuling, with headquarters at Draguignan. Under the Occupation Forces Command, Generalmajor Ludwig Bieringer held responsibility for control and defense of the Var Department, of which Draguignan served as the administrative seat.

It should be recognized that in the hilly, forested regions of southeastern France, Maquis irregulars had so terrorized the German troops that, except in convoys or antiguerrilla missions, they rarely moved out of their defensive positions in the towns. Non-German traffic could move relatively easily over the highway if the drivers by-passed urban areas. Thus patrols of the FFI, or of the Seventh Army after the landings, could penetrate 50 to 100 miles beyond the military "front lines." No lines as such existed; the ANVIL operation consisted of reducing road-blocks or village defensive positions. Other than the major cities, such as Marseille or Nice, no town boasted a garrison of more than 1,000, and many of them had less than 100. Most small villages hosted no permanent occupation troops at all.

With excellent intelligence about LXII Corps headquarters, and with reports on the strength of German garrisons in the Draguignan–Le Muy area, Seventh Army planners had good reason to believe that a vigorous airborne attack could seize this strategic inland communications center. They knew also that Maquis groups had been harassing the German occupiers and that their cooperation could be enormously helpful to the paratroopers.

SPOC AND THE FIRST AIRBORNE ATTACK

Responsibility for getting in touch with the Resistance fell, of course, to SPOC. A preinvasion plan had called for Muthular d'Errecalde, the agent who had operated in the Var Department with the MICHEL mission in June, to rally the area FFI and organize them to support an airborne operation. However, d'Errecalde had been betrayed and arrested at the end of July. (He was shot later, but SPOC did not learn this until after the invasion.) For a replacement, SPOC fixed on Lt. Geoffrey M. T. Jones, the 24-year-old OSS training officer, who had been instructing recruits at Blida airfield near Algiers since June.

In his youth, Jones had lived in southern France, spoke French, and before he joined OSS, had been attached to an airborne field artillery unit. Resourceful and aggressive, he would prove an ideal choice for the mission. SPOC arranged for him to be dropped as soon as weather and facilities would permit. Shortly before he left for France, Jones received a promotion to captain.[5]

With him, SPOC sent a French naval officer, Capitaine de Corvette Léon Pierre Auguste Allain (LOUGRE), who was in charge of a counterscorch mission for Toulon, where agents would try to prevent German demolitions of ships and docking facilities. (It is curious that Allain should have been sent with Jones into the northern Var Department 50 miles from Toulon, when one of his deputies, Ensign Ayral, was dropped at the same time only a few miles from the French naval base.)[6]

Although every effort was made by SPOC to infiltrate the two officers ten days before the invasion, weather and administrative snarls delayed the departure until August 10. Jones and Allain dropped into rocky terrain, Drop Zone Prisoner, on the Montagne de Malay, about 15 miles (as the crow flies) northeast of Draguignan. Unfortunately, Allain injured his leg in landing, a handicap that did not however greatly impair his subsequent activities. The two officers quickly made contact with an FTP Maquis group, led by Joseph, an able and enthusiastic Communist at Mons, a picturesque medieval "perched village" overlooking the plain below. They were joined by Sgt. James Dyas, a member of OG RUTH, which had parachuted into the area a week earlier. Injured in landing, Dyas had been cared for by local *maquisards*.

In the seventy-two hours now remaining before D Day, Jones and Allain were able to reach key Maquis leaders, Captain Fontes at Draguignan, Lieutenant Silvani at Montauroux, Cdt. Jean Blanc at Les Arcs, who, together with Joseph, could muster some 200 *maquisards*. They all met together near Mons during the afternoon of August 14, and that night at 8:00 they received the BBC messages warning that the invasion was imminent. They laid out a plan of action: First, Joseph, under the guidance of the two Allied officers, would undertake to knock out the German radar installation at Fayence, about twenty descending miles south of Mons.[7]

If the Fayence radar could be put out of commission, it would leave Generals Neuling and Bierenger with incomplete intelligence on Allied intentions. The radar station was located at an abandoned reservoir on the heights above Fayence, with its antenna perched atop an immense boulder—La Roque—from which it could survey the invasion landing beaches at St.-Raphael, fifteen miles away. Jones remembers having had instructions regarding the radar before he left Algiers and needed only a BBC message for execution. Brooks Richards recalls that, when he learned the place and time of the invasion, he immediately realized how vital the installation was. However, having been given highly classified information about the landings shortly before D Day, he was classified BIGOT, a code term that for security reasons prevented such officers from taking any steps that might jeopardize military secrets. In spite of this, Richards instructed his deputy, under no such restrictions, to get off a message to the RABELAIS (that is, Allain and Jones) team. With the message received, the Resistance group crawled up the old reservoir water mains, placed explosives underneath the German installation, and blew it up, rendering it entirely unusable.[8]

Meanwhile, in the early hours of August 14, Jedburgh team SCEPTRE had dropped on to the Montagne de Malay, at Zone Prisoner. The American member, Lt. Walter C. Hanna, had trained with McIntosh (CHLOROFORM), Gennerich (NOVOCAINE), and Swank (EPHEDRINE). The steep, rocky slope brought disaster to the French member of the team, Lt. François T.

Tévenac, who broke his foot, and to the American radio operator, Master Sgt. Howard Palmer, who sprained a knee. They encountered Jones and Allain on the mountain, but, with Tévenac requiring a doctor, they remained near Mons while the others went down the mountain toward the designated parachute areas.[9]

Because Allain could not possibly get to Toulon at once, he cooperated with Jones in the American's immediate missions, first, to knock out the radar and next, to locate the airborne landing area, where he would coordinate Maquis assistance and, in particular, tear down the antiglider stakes—known as Rommel's asparagus—in those fields designated for the gliders to come in. According to the plan, the Maquis leaders, together with the Allied team, would descend in the dark toward the Le Muy landing area. Seven *gendarmes* from the various districts involved would accompany the party in the hopes that, if stopped by a German patrol, the Allied officers could be identified as prisoners.

Jones, Allain, and Dyas, with the *gendarmes,* began the descent in the small hours of August 15. As they went down toward the plain, their greatest peril came not from enemy patrols, but from an attack by an Allied plane whose bombs exploded so close they stalled the engine. By dawn, as they approached the Le Muy area, the first paratroopers had already come to ground.[10]

General Frederick's First Airborne Task Force consisted of over 5,000 American paratroopers to which had been added almost 2,000 members of the British Second Independent Brigade. The plan called for the British together with the U.S. 509th Parachute Battalion (reinforced by the 463rd Parachute Field Artillery) and the 517th Parachute Infantry Regimental Combat Team, to drop into a 15-square-mile area centered at Le Muy beginning at 4:30 AM on D Day, August 15. These forces would immediately attempt to gain control of Le Muy, establish road-blocks, and safeguard the flat area just south of Le Muy where gliders of the 550th Infantry Battalion would land late in the afternoon.

Jones and Allain, descending from the mountains, first encountered some men of the 463rd Parachute Field Artillery who had landed about five miles off target into the zone assigned to Col. Rupert D. Graves' 517th Regiment. In the confusion of the gray haze, Jones was able to identify himself to the paratroopers and help establish a command post for Graves at the Château near Ste.-Roseline, just northeast of Les Arcs, one of Graves' objectives.

Between dawn and 9:00 most of Frederick's troops had come in except for two battalions scheduled for the afternoon, and two groups that through pilot error had parachuted far from their objectives. Since these two groups benefited from contact with the Maquis, let us examine their adventures (and misadventures) before turning to the principal exploits of the Airborne Task Force.

By an unanticipated error in navigation, five plane loads of troops—company A of the 509th Battalion, and elements of the 463rd Field Artillery—were dropped a few minutes too soon and found themselves deployed in the hills just south of St.-Tropez, twenty miles from their objective. Almost at once Capt. Jess Walls of the American paratroopers met detachments of Marc Rainaud's *Brigade des Maures*, which had taken up positions in the peninsula since the 14th. The Americans were able to assemble five guns, and before dawn, the paratroopers and the FFI decided to attack the St.-Tropez German garrison, which had withdrawn to several pillboxes and to the ancient citadel. By 9:00 most of the town had been occupied by Rainaud's men.

Also, in the same area, coming in by sea, the U.S. 15th Infantry Regiment (3rd Division) under Col. Richard Thomas had landed along the stretch of beach known to sunbathers as Tahiti and Pampelonne, and by noon had occupied the high points of the peninsula. In the afternoon, elements of the 2nd Battalion joined the FFI and the paratroopers, bringing about a German surrender late in the afternoon. With its harbor cleared and good facilities for communication, St.-Tropez appeared ideal to Seventh Army staff officers seeking a shore-based command post for General Patch. They chose the Hotel Latitude 43 at St.-Tropez on D + 1, and the Commanding General moved in during the morning of August 17. Learning how the *Brigade des Maures* had assisted his American forces, Patch took time out from a pressing schedule to review these irregulars and to award the Silver Star to their leader, Marc Rainaud, with letters of commendation to seven others, two posthumously. Rainaud subsequently joined 4-SFU (SPOC's Special Forces Unit) and was assigned to Task Force Butler.[11]

The other error in navigation brought three groups of Lt. Col. Melvin Zais' 3rd Battalion (of the 517th Parachute Regiment) to ground near Callian and Montauroux, small "perched villages" about halfway between Grasse and Draguignan, and 25 miles east of their objective. These villages, old fortified towns built on precipitous slopes, command the wooded valley road to Grasse some fifteen to twenty miles inland from the coast. Even as villagers protected themselves from Arab attacks in the Middle Ages, so now in 1944 small contingents of Germans could hold off attackers from the main road below. As the FABTF gained control of its target area, groups of fleeing Germans holed up in the little towns, attacked by the FFI before the Americans could move in tanks and artillery. It took a day for most of the American paratroopers (and some members of the British Second Brigade) to orient themselves and march west through a region infested by German patrols. Many had joined their units by August 16, but a few remained behind. These included about 35–40 injured men, cared for by their own medical people and the French, at Montauroux and Fayence. They were not molested by the Germans.

Another group, about the same size, organized defenses in the area and along with some FFI, harassed the batches of Germans, pulling back from Le Muy and Draguignan, who were infiltrating the area. About 25 men, led by Captain Hooper of the 517th, withdrew to Montauroux, where they held off attacks until reinforcements rescued them a few days later.

At Fayence, some of the paratroopers, including Sgt. Howard Heckard and Corp. Albert Deshayes (Company G, 517th) joined Hanna's SCEPTRE Jedburgh team and the local Maquis group led by Lieutenant Silvani. They fought intermittently against Germans in the area, but could not dislodge Major Turnov, commanding 200 Germans defending La Roque, the site of the demolished radar installation, just above Fayence. After five days, a patrol of the 517th, probing along the road south of the town, received bursts of 20.-mm. gunfire and called in artillery. This shelling somewhat softened the German will to resist, and Turnov sent word to Hanna that he was prepared to discuss surrender, but only to Americans. Hanna, Heckard, and Deshayes, the only Americans at hand, negotiated with the German for three hours and bluffed him with threats of an imminent attack. Turnov agreed to surrender, provided the shelling stopped. Unknown to Hanna, a paratrooper attack was being prepared, and the bombardment did cease. On the next morning, the 21st, 184 Germans filed out and stacked their arms.[12]

In spite of the two erroneous drops, one south and one north of the designated area, the bulk of Frederick's FABTF landed where they were supposed to, and in the early morning haze of August 15, gathered up equipment and made for the designated assembly points. By noon, Frederick's troops had control of the small villages around Le Muy. Frederick established his command post at Le Mitan, two miles to the north. Geoffrey Jones was able to confer with the general, placing at his disposal the 200 FFI from the neighboring villages. Another OSS agent, Capt. Alan Stuyvesant, representing SI, had parachuted with the Task Force, thereby providing Frederick with two OSS officers who could make radio contact with their respective field headquarters (SSS and 4-SFU), with Patch, as well as with Algiers. Jones and Allain had been handicapped by lack of a radio operator, but Stuyvesant had one, George Pecoraro, who made the jump with other paratroopers. Captain Allain remained with Frederick for a few days until he was joined by members of his team, and then made off for Toulon, his principal objective. Sergeant Dyas, whose knee still bothered him, served as driver and "gunman," "taking officers and agents on reconnaissance and intelligence missions behind and around the enemy lines." For the first few days after the landings, Jones and Stuyvesant helped General Frederick in providing liaison with the Maquis—no clear-cut distinction being made between SO and SI.[13]

In the afternoon of August 15, Frederick organized attacks at Le Muy and Les Arcs, the latter of which had been occupied for a while by the FFI when the German garrison withdrew. In the late afternoon, two more battalions came in, Lt. Col. Wood G. Joerg's 551st, which jumped, and Lt. Col. Edward Sach's 550th, which arrived in gliders.

Jones had organized many of the *maquisards* to pull down the antiglider stakes in the landing area, but in spite of this effort, most of the gliders and many of the pilots became casualties. Of the 407 gliders, only 50 were salvageable; there were 283 jump or crash injuries, less than four percent of the total task force. Over 7,000 men had come in, with 220 vehicles, 213 artillery pieces, and 1,000 tons of equipment.[14]

By dawn of August 16, Frederick resumed the offensive and, by early afternoon, had taken Le Muy. Bitter fighting developed around Les Arcs, as the Germans tried to retake it, but with all three battalions of the 517th engaged, the town was in Allied hands by late afternoon, when advance units of the 45th Division, coming up from the beach, began to arrive. Inside Draguignan, FFI Captain Fontes harassed German positions, especially the Gestapo stronghold, Villa Gladys. While the German garrison tried to destroy vital factories and power installations, Colonel Joerg's battalion, alerted by a courageous member of the Resistance, Mademoiselle Vidal, moved in and by 6:00 had occupied the town.[15]

It so happened that, when the paratroopers and the FFI drove the Germans out of Draguignan, they liberated the prefectural seat of the Var Department, where the new prefect and the Department Liberation Committee should have been installed, prepared to replace the Vichy administrators and to cope with the innumerable civic problems that liberation brought in its wake. The Var, however, was not typical in that Draguignan, with a population of 11,000 was dwarfed in size and importance by the naval-base city of Toulon, ten times as large. Consequently, the Liberation Committee, under the chairmanship of Henri Sarie, generally met at the port, not at the inland town. When Draguignan became free, one of the Committee's members, Henri Michel, went there at once to ensure that Sarie would be recognized as the new prefect until Frank Arnal, designated by de Gaulle's provisional government, could take over. Michel, then a young teacher in charge of press matters for the Committee, would later become France's foremost historian of the Resistance, founder of the French Committee for the History of the Second World War, editor of its *Revue*, and a leading influence in accumulating documents about the Resistance. Without the archives and inquiries that Michel was instrumental in developing, studies of the Resistance (such as the present one) would be immensely more difficult to achieve. This book is dedicated to Henri Michel.[16]

With Draguignan, which had served as an administrative center for the Germans, in Allied hands, the paratroopers quickly destroyed the enemy command. General Bieringer, the departmental commander, was taken prisoner, although General Neuling and his LXII Corps staff escaped to the northwest. On the next day, General Frederick in person brought Bieringer to General Patch's command post at St.-Tropez. On the eighteenth, Colonel Hodge of the 117th Reconnaissance Squadron, now a part of Task Force Butler, routed Neuling and his staff from a cave. He, too, was brought to Patch. Thereafter, the German LXII Corps ceased to exist, leaving its two components on their own: the 242nd Division to defend Toulon and the 148th to protect Cannes and Nice.[17]

GUNN AND LÉCUYER

Jones and Stuyvesant were not the only agents available to the invading forces on Patch's right flank. Farther to the north, at Valberg, Havard Gunn and Capt. Jacques Lécuyer, the ORA commander for R-2, had received alert messages and waited for the imminent Allied invasion. Lécuyer, named FFI chief for Alpes-Maritimes on August 4, had to divide his attention between his ORA regional responsibilities and his departmental FFI concerns. Fortunately, so far as Alpes-Maritimes was concerned, he possessed an able deputy in Lt. Pierre Gautier (MALHERBE), who like Lécuyer had been active in the ORA and had operated throughout the department. He had maintained good relations with the FTP, headed by Jamme (known as JOB), although he was not on close terms with the former FFI leader, Melin (CHATEL). Melin had previously led MUR contingents and, in any case, limited his activities primarily to the city of Nice. Through Gautier and by his own visits as ORA head, Lécuyer had been in continual touch with the Maquis—especially those in the northern mountain part of the department, where Resistance actions were coordinated by Captain de Lestang-Labrousse (RODOLPHE).

Prior to the landings, Lécuyer's contacts with Algiers had been reinforced by the presence of Havard Gunn, who for the most part had remained at Lécuyer's command posts. Through messages from SPOC, Gunn had already learned that an airborne attack would occur, and had orders like Jones to demolish antiglider stakes at possible landing sites.

Gunn found that Cammaerts and Sorensen had been arrested at Digne at the same time (August 14) that he and Lécuyer received the action message from Algiers. Lécuyer recalls:

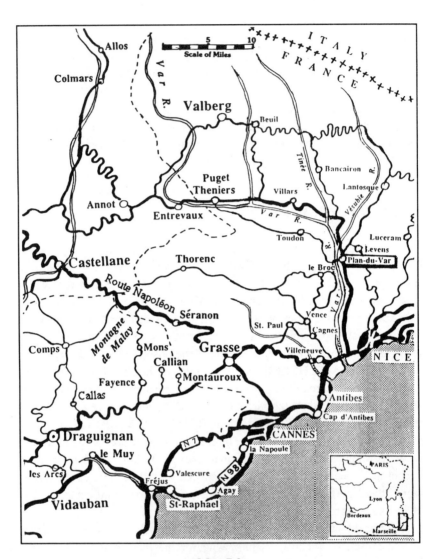

Map 7.2
DRAGUIGNAN TO NICE
East from the Landing Areas toward the Italian Border.
Strategic Bridge at Plan-du-Var

When the message was received, Bamboos (Gunn) looked me up and told me: "The landings are for tonight, we must as soon as possible get in touch with the landing forces in the Draguignan, Le Muy, Les Arcs, Vidauban areas in order to inform them of the situation to the north and east."

Gunn hoped that he could reach some American troops and persuade them to rescue Cammaerts. He, of course, did not know what efforts Christine was already making to obtain his release.

Lécuyer and Gunn, with two FFI scouts, came down from the hills on D Day and after some efforts reached General Frederick at his command post on the sixteenth. The general, sympathetic with the Maquis effort, ordered a detachment of armored jeeps to accompany the two officers up to the Route Napoléon. Gunn soon learned that Cammaerts had been released, and decided therefore to retrace his steps with the idea of obtaining arms and equipment for the Maquis.

Lécuyer moved on beyond the Route Napoléon, persuading the leader of the jeep detachment that by following the hill roads he could reach the Var River a few miles north of Nice without German interference. When they reached the river, they at once encountered machine-gun fire from the other side. The American officer asked Lécuyer how far it was to Nice. "A good twenty kilometers," he replied. The American then said: "You told the General that one could get to within twenty kilometers of Nice without firing a shot, which was true, but now we're being shot at; I'll report by radio and go back." Lécuyer recalls that the detachment spent the night at a Maquis command post, which clearly demonstrated that not the Germans, but the FFI controlled the uplands.[18]

After he took leave of Lécuyer and the Americans, Gunn proceeded along the Route Napoléon to Castellane, which had just been liberated, and then south to Callas, which had been occupied by the FFI and some of Frederick's paratroopers. By this time, most of the Airborne had been relieved by elements of the 142nd Infantry team.

Quickly, members of the patrol escorted Gunn to company, then regimental, and finally to division headquarters at Le Muy where he met General Dahlquist. He dined that night with the general, explaining to him how free the roads were, how few garrisons were left in the mountains, and what opportunities existed for surprise strikes. Dahlquist appreciated the information and, on the next day, authorized a 142nd Regiment patrol up the route Gunn had used, as far as Castellane, some fifty miles north of his command post. On the same day (this was the day Task Force Butler moved through Draguignan and on to the Valensole plateau), Dahlquist enabled Gunn to see General Truscott who, having just conferred with Patch, had reached agreement that Frederick's First Airborne would take over the right flank position from Dahlquist. He found

Gunn's information helpful: Truscott's diary is succinct: "Maj. Gunn (Br of Maquis Forces) in with report that right flank is clear."

Gunn received encouragement from the American officers, who arranged for a convoy of six trucks to bring captured German arms and other supplies to the Resistance groups along the Route Napoléon. With one of his trucks, he returned to Lécuyer's command post at Thorenc early on the 20th. Both Gunn and Lécuyer were prepared to cooperate with the Allied regular forces as they drove eastward toward the Italian border.

But General Patch had other matters to contend with. He had to decide whether Task Force Butler should be launched, he had to find out whether the French troops were landing on schedule, and most of all, he had to determine the best methods of reaching the Rhône valley.

Task Force Butler
and the Liberation of Digne

By D + 1, August 16, General Patch could view with satisfaction the positions of his Seventh Army. In the south, the entire St.-Tropez Peninsula had been cleared, and elements of the 3rd Division were moving inland. They would be joined later by de Lattre's French First Army (Army "B") and together begin the drives westward toward Toulon and the Rhône. With the German 11th Panzer Division still on the far side of the Rhône, German resistance had been sporadic and ineffectual.

North of the 3rd Division sector, General Eagle's 45th Division had landed in the vicinity of Ste.-Maxime and was moving rapidly across the Massif des Maures toward Vidauban, its objective on the "blue line," in the flat country watered by the Argens River. Vidauban lay only a few miles southwest of Les Arcs and Le Muy, now occupied by Frederick's paratroopers.

The 36th Division had run into strong resistance when its landing craft pressed toward the St.-Raphael beach. Instead of a direct assault, Dahlquist's troops came ashore to the east of their objective, then moved on Fréjus by circling St.-Raphael. This maneuver delayed the 36th's thrust up the Argens valley to join the paratroopers fifteen miles away at Le Muy. The VI Corps commander, General Truscott, was furious at Dahlquist's lack of drive but, nevertheless, was sufficiently satisfied with his positions on D + 1 to judge that further consolidation of the beachhead would not be required.

Except for some minor hitches, the ANVIL/DRAGOON landing had been exceptionally successful. With the "blue line" virtually achieved by the second day, General Patch controlled, within that semicircle fifty miles long and twenty miles deep, a well-disciplined, well-equipped combat force of almost 100,000, together with 10,000 vehicles. Also, in his VI Corps commander, General Truscott, he had an able aggressive leader who believed, like the cavalryman he was, in bold moves at the enemy's flank.

During the landings and the day after, Truscott reviewed the situation several times with General Butler. By the end of August 16, he was convinced that the Provisional Task Force could move north as planned, and he gave Butler orders to convene the component elements at Le Muy.[1]

After the talks with Truscott, General Butler came to Le Muy on the 17th to take command of his heterogeneous force—a selective group of fighting units that now, for the first time, came together. In addition to the 117th Cavalry serving as the recon and communication core of Butler's Force, Truscott allocated various other elements to provide the necessary mobility and punch to this unique 20th-century cavalry: a battalion of infantry (the 2nd Battalion, commanded by Lt. Col. Charles J. Denholm, from the 143rd Regiment, 36th Division); two companies of Sherman tanks (from the 753rd Tank Battalion); a battalion of self-propelled 105-mm. howitzers (59th Armored Field Artillery); some Tank-Destroyers (Company C, 636th TD Battalion), together with companies of engineers, trucks, maintenance, and medical corps.

Altogether, the Task Force included some 3,000 troops and 1,000 vehicles, which with its tanks and mobile assault batteries, provided Butler with a formidable armored scouting force, but clearly one that lacked the punch of an armored division. Also, although the Force had a full complement of radio receivers and transmitters, entirely adequate for internal communications, the Task Force could not, in this mountainous country, always rely on contact with Truscott's or Patch's command posts. Light Cub airplanes helped in scouting and communication, but Butler had only one attached to his group.

The 117th Cavalry Reconnaissance Squadron not only spearheaded the Task Force, but provided Butler with some of his staff. Headed by Lt. Col. Charles J. Hodge, the 117th formed part of the celebrated "Essex Troop" from northern New Jersey. When they reached southern France, the troopers, numbering almost 900, had gained some battle experience in Italy. Completely mechanized and mobile, the squadron could, in the tradition of its mounted forebears, probe miles ahead of the main body. The horses had given way to vehicles—about 240 jeeps, command cars, half-tracks, and trucks; the sabers were replaced by 105-mm. assault guns and by light M5 tanks firing 37-mm. guns. The basic fighting units (aside from the headquarters and service companies) consisted of three troops, A, B, and C, about 125 men and five officers each.[2]

ULTRA and DRAGOON

While the Airborne Task Force was consolidating its positions around Le

Muy and Draguignan, while Truscott's divisions were reaching and penetrating the "blue line," and while Task Force Butler was assembling for its march to the north, an intelligence breakthrough brought Patch information of extraordinary significance. This information came to him from the deciphering and analysis of German Enigma coding machine messages that were intercepted and sent to the field from Bletchley Park in England with a top classification: ULTRA.

On D + 1, the British liaison officers and the American ULTRA specialists had begun operations adjacent to General Patch's command post at St.-Tropez. Dissemination of the information was extremely limited—going only to Patch of the commanding generals, but, of course, also to Wilson and Devers. No division commander or any French officer was privy to the ultrasecret messages that, once delivered in the field, were destroyed. Because knowledge of the system remained classified until 1975, no general who may have used ULTRA could admit it in memoirs written before that date. Because both Patch and Truscott had died before the declassification, they left no personal testimony as to ULTRA's influence. On the other hand, the American ULTRA specialist with Seventh Army, Donald S. Bussey, and the G-2, Lt. Col. William Quinn, have been queried about the role these signals played, and they agree that Patch "had been fully persuaded on the value of the ULTRA intelligence."[3]

Late in the afternoon of August 17, Bussey received from Bletchley a deciphered message in which the German high command ordered all forces in southern France to begin a withdrawal except for those defending Marseille and Toulon. On the next day, Patch had available a long message (XL 6919) expanding on details of the Nineteenth Army's withdrawal.[4] The salient features of Hitler's order were:

1. Construction of a defense line Sens–Dijon–Swiss border.
2. Withdrawal of all forces from southern France, with 11th Panzer Division as rear guard of Nineteenth Army in Rhône valley.
3. Defense of Franco-Italian border by LXII Corps, with 148th Division (Cannes area) and 157th Division (Grenoble area) protecting eastern flank of Nineteenth Army.
4. Protection of port cities of Marseille and Toulon "to the last man."

Since the LXII Corps headquarters had already been overrun and the corps commander was a prisoner of war, Patch knew that coordination of German resistance to his north and east would be practically impossible. However, the Seventh Army commander had a number of other factors to consider. He had to ask himself whether Task Force Butler, together with the 36th Division, could provide an adequate flank defense. His decision was also made difficult by the attitude of his French ally, General de Lattre, commanding the five French divisions that comprised over half of the Seventh Army. Patch wished to employ the French, especially their Moroccan mountain troops, to guard the Alpine passes, but there were two problems. First, de Lattre, feeling deeply that French honor needed combat in a major theater, protested vigorously against his troops being tied up in the mountain fastness. "Whatever the cost," he wrote later, "I had to escape from the trap—pull myself out from south of the Alps—and with the least delay, reach as far north as possible." Second, the schedule for unloading French troops meant that the mountain division would not be available for a week.[5]

Into this dilemma, which confronted Patch on August 18, entered his senior, Gen. "Jake" Devers, who conferred with Patch that evening. As commanding general of the Seventh Army, Patch controlled the forces currently in action, but overall command of the entire operation rested with the Supreme Commander of the Mediterranean, Gen. Maitland Wilson, whose deputy was Devers. Furthermore, it was understood that, when de Lattre had two corps ashore, he would become independent of Patch, but would remain subordinate to Devers, who would command a newly formed Sixth Army Group. Therefore, Devers, who liked to remain on friendly terms with the French, was very much involved in decisions relating to commands and overall strategy. Interviewed in 1967, Devers said:

> I happened to come into the headquarters right then and I suggested to Patch, or his chief of staff, Doc [Major General A. A.] White, "Let him go, let him go up the other side. I'll take care of that flank over there because we can keep the airborne in there and some others to protect it."
>
> In other words . . . the airborne group under Frederick took over the job that had been originally assigned to the French. I didn't wire back for authority to do this. . . . I got them to do what they did. . . . Patch issued that order after I told him I'd take the full responsibility.[6]

Taking into account all these factors, Patch issued Field Order No. 2 at noon on August 19. De Lattre's French forces would concentrate on Toulon and Marseille. Truscott's VI Corps would push the Germans toward the Rhône. Frederick's Airborne Task Force, which had passed into reserve, would establish and hold a defensive flank along the general line Fayence–La Napoule and protect the army right flank. Since there is no mention of flank protection north of Fayence or east of Digne, Patch did not, at this time, have any real apprehensions regarding the more northern Alpine passes. As Bussey put it in his postwar report: "there was no indication that the enemy would adopt an attitude other than defensive on the flank. Accordingly it was decided to pursue, and all

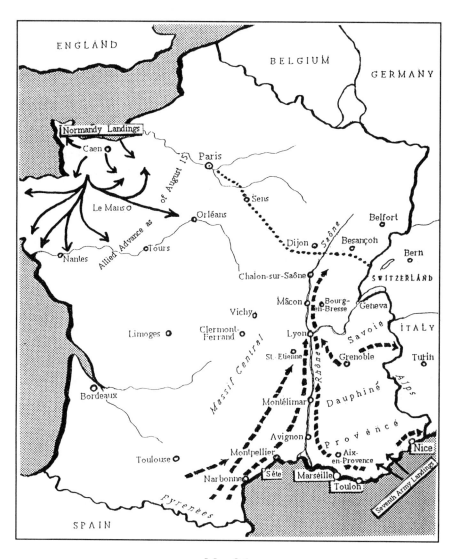

Map 8.1
GERMAN RETREAT FROM SOUTHEASTERN FRANCE

unloading priorities were altered with the whole emphasis given to fuel and vehicles."[7]

Patch now realized from ULTRA that a great opportunity lay before him. With the FABTF relieving the 36th Division on his eastern flank, Patch had at his disposal Dahlquist's division to move on up to Grenoble, take care of the passes into Italy, or reinforce Task Force Butler. What Butler reported could be crucial to the decisions Patch and Truscott would soon have to make.

TASK FORCE BUTLER GETS UNDER WAY

At dawn on August 18, Task Force Butler left its dispositions around Le Muy, and with Capt. William Nugent's Troop C in the van, headed for Draguignan and the Valensole Plateau. Following the 117th Cavalry's lead, the main body was prepared to speed along the paved highways at over 20 miles an hour, stretched out over thirty miles.[8]

General Butler truly faced the unknown. Colonel Zeller had assured Patch that no major German forces existed in the Durance Valley, but Zeller had left the area over two weeks earlier. G-2 had little precise information about enemy concentrations, and local intelligence was sparse. To be sure, 4-SFU, the Special Force Unit attached to Seventh Army, was supposed to provide interpreters and radio contact with the Resistance, but no officers from this unit had yet reported.

As the first units started off on August 18, they had no idea what sort of opposition they might meet, but they assumed that German units remained in the rolling shrub-covered hills. Their first encounter with the enemy occurred only fifteen miles from Draguignan, when C Troop received some shots emanating from one of the numerous grottoes near Aups. One of the Task Force's tanks wheeled around and poured in a few rounds of high-velocity shells. Quickly, there emerged the staff of the German LXII Corps, headed by its commander, Lt. Gen. Ferdinand Neuling, who surrendered his side-arm, a hand-crafted Luger, to platoon leader Lt. Joseph Syms. Syms turned the weapon over to Colonel Hodge, who after the war kept it as a prized memento of the southern France campaign.[9]

Meanwhile, the main column, with Capt. Thomas C. Piddington's A Troop in the lead, moved rapidly through Salernes and then north toward Quinson. Forty miles northwest of Draguignan, around 1:30 P.M., Piddington reached the Verdon River south of the small town of Quinson. To the north lay the day's objective, the vast Valensole Plateau, a large plain twenty miles across, set in among an area of hills, small mountains, and gorges. (A few miles to the east, the Verdon runs through spectacular gorges, which are in peace time a great tourist attraction.) To reach the plateau, it was necessary to cross the river and then mount a zigzag road up several hundred feet to the plain, but the bridge was out. Ironically, it had been the objective of Allied bombers several days before, and when they failed to demolish it the local Maquis had finished the job. What had been meant to hinder German reinforcements or escape had boomeranged.

However, members of the Maquis got to work. Together with the townspeople of Quinson, they pitched in and built a ford at a shallow point of the river. Two tank bulldozers cut trails to the ford, where the French guided the ponderous tanks and self-propelled howitzers across the 16-inch deep stream. Only one 4 x 4 was flooded.[10]

In crossing the Verdon River, at the southern end of the plateau, the American forces entered the French department of Basses-Alpes (now known as Alpes de Haute-Provence), of which Digne, a spa celebrated for its sulfurous waters, is the principal center. To the FFI, it was imperative that Digne, the department's prefectural seat, garrisoned by the largest German contingent in the area, be liberated.

In the department of Basses-Alpes, the FFI came under the military command of Commandant NOEL (Georges Bonnaire) who, while a Communist and head of the FTP, had been accepted by the AS as FFI commander for the department. He had hopes of forcing the German garrison at Digne to surrender and had already alerted the FFI units in the area regarding the plan of action.[11]

The area around Digne was well organized. District I, in the south around Manosque, had Captain Brondi (JANVIER) in command, while the Valensole Plateau was the responsibility of Capt. Justin Boeuf (DECEMBRE). District II, to the west, was under Captain Alain. District III, which included Digne, had Captain Lindenmann in command. To the southeast, covering Barrème and Castellane, was District IV, under Boiteux. Each of the districts contained many Maquis detachments, such as the redoubtable *Maquis de Thoard*, northwest of Digne, and the FTP *Maquis Fort de France* to the southeast.

In the early afternoon of August 18, Captain Boeuf learned from a messenger on bicycle that the Americans were coming up to the Valensole Plateau. Boeuf rushed off on his motorcycle and met an advance unit, which took him in their jeep to Riez. Boeuf helped establish an effective location for the CP and sent a message off to Lindenmann. When Butler arrived, Boeuf argued vehemently for a detachment to move to Digne.[12] The liberation of the departmental *chef-lieu*, while of great significance for the French, did not have any political value for Butler, who had planned to advance up the Durance Valley. He could see, however, that Digne protected his right flank. Set in the midst of mountains, the little resort town held a key strategic position, dominating the Route Napoléon (N85) to the southeast and cutting the road north that led to Cammaerts' headquarters at Seyne. These were the only roads by which the Germans, if they chose to do so, could bring in reinforcements from Italy.

Butler agreed to dispatch part of Hodge's squadron, Troop B, under Capt. John Wood, toward Digne. Thus, while the main force would continue north up the relatively level Durance Valley, Wood, who was already bivouacked five miles north of Butler's command post, would move north on a parallel road about fifteen miles to the east. Unlike the Durance road, however, Troop B's route led into rough mountain country, the narrow highway snaking upward through forested slopes where a few heavy guns could dominate the final eight miles of the approach to Digne.

By late afternoon, Captain Lindenmann had arrived, and he was able to confer with Captain Wood, with Boeuf, and with Lieutenant Brandes in command of OG RUTH, which had parachuted into the area a week earlier. General Butler later recalled his first contacts with the commander of RUTH and a local *maquisard*, whom he described as a "tough bunny—about five feet tall and five feet broad."[13]

Butler gave Brandes the assignment of protecting Troop B's right flank even though only three men (of OG RUTH's original thirteen) could go because "the rest of the men didn't have shoes which could possibly hold up." Brandes augmented his ragged commando with twenty-five *maquisards*, a bazooka, and a mortar.[14]

While Butler bivouacked at Riez, 4-SFU, the group that had been organized to maintain contacts with agents and the FFI, finally set up a headquarters at St.-Tropez. There were, in fact, two groups coming ashore at the same time: 4-SFU and SSS, the latter to serve as liaison with intelligence agents operating in the path of the Seventh Army.[15] Both of them arrived at St.-Tropez on August 16, D + 1, and established command posts on the grounds of Hotel Latitude 43, Patch's headquarters. Col. Edward Gamble commanded the SSS contingent, and Col. William Bartlett was in charge of 4-SFU.

Since vehicles and equipment had been loaded on different ships, the men of 4-SFU and SSS worked under considerable handicaps trying to find transportation from the beach to St.-Tropez. 4-SFU controlled operations—that is, SOE and OSS' SO, both of which were administered by SPOC—while SSS involved OSS' SI, the intelligence unit directed by Henry Hyde, also out of Algiers. (British intelligence operated separately.) Administratively, the two units came under Colonel Gamble, but operationally, they were separate. Nevertheless, since the Americans were all OSS, they frequently knew each other, and indeed some officers were interchangeable. Both units had to be in contact with the

G-2s of army, corps, and division, but at the combat level, distinctions as to whether information came from SO or SI contacts became academic.

Under normal anticipated circumstances—that is, a build-up within the "blue line" leading toward a breakout, possibly weeks later—the delay in obtaining a full complement and sufficient vehicles would not have hindered the missions of 4-SFU or SSS. The planners had arranged for only one-third of the units to come ashore with the assault troops; a second third was to arrive on D + 10, and the final segment on D + 15 (August 30). In the event, however, by the time the third group crossed the beach, Seventh Army had bypassed Lyon and overrun almost all of the agents controlled from Algiers.

Colonels Gamble and Bartlett began, as soon as possible, to establish radio communications with Algiers though Colonel Gamble suffered from a leg injury resulting from a jeep accident, and Henry Hyde had just come down with jaundice. They wasted no time in sending SSS teams to each of the VI Corps divisions: one under Lt. Robert Thompson to the 3rd, one under Capt. Justin Greene to the 36th, and one under Frank Schoonmaker to the 45th.

Similarly, Colonel Bartlett assigned the 4-SFU field representatives who reported to him on August 18 at St.-Tropez: two Americans, Capt. Henry Leger and Donald King; three British, Capt. Ralph Banbury, Sgt.-Mjr. Lloyd, and a driver; and four Frenchmen, Lt. Marc Rainaud (the *Brigade des Maures* leader who had just been decorated by General Patch), Sous/Lt. Comp., Sous/Lt. Fageot, and *Adj./Chef* Maxent. Captain Leger's report explains the situation:

> The vehicles consisted of one motorcycle and two bantams [jeeps] (one of which was ours). We were to join the Task Force Butler.
>
> To the consternation of all present, it was found that TFB had left on the morning of August 18, 1944, at 0545. It was jointly decided by Capt. Banbury and Capt. Leger that the party would start immediately and find TFB. After nine solid hours of riding through friendly and unfriendly territory we caught up with TFB bivouacked in vicinity of Riez. We reported to Major Hansen, G-3 of TFB, who introduced us to General Butler who had us briefed by Lt. Col. Hodge, operations officer, who gave us our assignments as follows:
>
> Capt. Banbury and S/Lt. Comp to B Troop; Mr. Donald King to A Troop; Lt. Rainaud to CIC Hqs troop; Capt. Leger to Hqs troop with order from Gen. Butler to be his liaison with the Maquis and anything and everything French that might come his way.[16]

With the 4-FSU personnel assigned, early on the morning of August 19, Task Force Butler moved off the Valensole Plateau. Captain Wood's Troop B, with the mission of striking at Digne from the south, drove north to the Asse River, which flows southwest ultimately to join the Durance. Besides his own troop, Wood had with him Lieutenant Brandes and three men from OG RUTH, Captains Lindenmann and Boeuf of the Basses-Alpes FFI, together with the 4-SFU representatives, Captain Banbury and Sous-Lieutenant Comp.

Crossing the river, with Maquis fighters in support, Troop B sped up the Asse Valley toward the formidable wooded slopes that provided excellent cover for German machine gun fire. By 8:30 the column had reached Mézel, about ten curving mountainous miles south of Digne. Here the force ran into German opposition. Wood brought up some light tanks, forcing the enemy into the hills, where they were pursued by Léopold Comte's 3rd FTP Company, by FFI under Deromas (FELIX), and units of the Asse Secret Army. Comte would later be the first member of the FFI to enter Digne.[17]

At Mézel another agent joined Wood's staff. This was Capt. Jean Fournier (CALICE), a member of the Sorensen mission. While Sorensen had accompanied Cammaerts on the ill-fated trip to Apt, Fournier had gone south with Gunn and Lécuyer, where he checked out possible landing sites in the Alpes-Maritimes Department. He then struck west to carry out a similar mission on the Valensole Plateau. Moving mostly on foot, Fournier had hiked to Mézel during the night of August 18/19, and met Captain Wood in the morning.[18]

Having broken up the German blocks at Mézel, Troop B worked its way along the winding upgrade and shortly before noon reached the southern outskirts of Digne. The small force had run into mines hanging from trees and had received scattered German fire, but was able to take up positions that threatened German headquarters located on the edge of town in the Ermitage Hotel. Meanwhile the departmental FFI commander, Commandant Bonnaire (NOEL), had sent out orders to all under his command. He ordered them to set up road-blocks on all the roads leading to Digne. If or when feasible, the Maquis elements would move cautiously toward the town, with some units assigned the responsibility of seizing storage depots and fuel dumps.

It soon became clear to the German command that it would not be possible to defend the Ermitage, and Generalmajor Hans Schuberth, commanding the 792nd Liaison Staff (*Verbindungs Stab*), decided to capitulate, as long as he could surrender to the Americans. He had been out of touch with his superiors at Avignon for four days, and had no way of assessing the overall situation.[19]

The capture of Schuberth did not mean, however, that the entire garrison at Digne had surrendered. Captain Wood saw that his small force and light guns would have difficulty in attacking German defensive positions in and around the town. As he moved into the southern part of Digne, Captain Wood sent a series of messages to squadron headquarters reporting heavy opposition. By 3:00 in the afternoon, he had not been able to advance farther.

While Troop B and the FFI attacked Digne, the main columns of Task Force Butler proceeded up the Durance Valley toward Sisteron. Henry Leger, the OSS man from 4-SFU, located a serviceable bridge across the Durance at Oraison. Piddington, leading the advance, crossed the river and moved his A Troop up the west bank toward Château-Arnoux, while Troop B's 3rd Platoon sped north on the opposite bank (where OG RUTH and the FFI had set ambushes), passed the spectacular rock formation called *Les Pénitents* at Les Mées, and continued on to Malijai, a key position that guarded the road branching off toward Digne ten miles to the east.

In this area the Americans met up with more Resistance fighters. During the night of August 18/19, in accordance with Bonnaire's orders, the 16th and 19th FTP companies had moved into the hills around Malijai. From the hills, in the early morning of August 19, the *maquisards* witnessed Germans executing three civilians, but they were not strong enough to intervene.[20]

Actually the Germans were attempting to reinforce the garrison at Digne. From Sisteron, early in the morning of August 19, a company of about 135 men (2nd Battalion, 194th *Sicherungregiment*) marched south with the intention of crossing the Durance at Château-Arnoux to assist the troops on the north bank of the Bléone. Between 2 and 3 A.M., however, the FFI blew the two bridges over the Durance, thus preventing the Germans, who arrived at Château-Arnoux at dawn, from crossing. The German officer-in-charge was apparently reluctant, for fear of Maquis ambushes, to march on to the next bridge, about five miles south. To cross there would in any case have placed him south of the Bléone, in hilly wooded country infested with Maquis. He therefore remained at Château-Arnoux, deploying his forces in the park adjacent to the old castle. Meanwhile the commander of the local gendarmerie had sent a message to the Maquis south of the town to alert them regarding the German presence.

The German commander, with no way of making contact with German headquarters at Digne, insisted to the mayor that he send a French messenger to Digne, under threat of taking hostages and burning the town. He gave the mayor until 1 P.M. to obtain a reply. A gendarme volunteered for the mission. Instead of going to Digne, however, he bicycled to the nearest Maquis command post and turned over the message to the local FFI leader.

By this time, Piddington's Troop A had reached a point about five miles south, and the well-informed Maquis knew that the column would join them in a few minutes. When Piddington arrived, he met with the Maquis leader and the gendarme. Together they opened the German message and, laboriously translating it, learned that the commander, in a quandary, sought instructions from his superior. Knowing the approximate size, armament, and disposition of the German force, Piddington prepared to attack but agreed that the gendarme should return to see if the Germans might surrender. He set 1:15 as the deadline. It was now about noon.

Upon returning to Château-Arnoux, the gendarme found the Germans still in the park, to which the iron grilled gate was locked. Finally the German officer agreed to meet Piddington, who had now moved into Château-Arnoux itself. A few minutes later, the German commander, without cap, jacket, or arms, came out of the park and met Piddington at the gendarmerie, a few yards south of the park. The Germans surrendered, marched out of the park, and stacked their guns. Piddington, loathe as he was to reduce his number of vehicles, loaded approximately 135 Germans onto some trucks and sent them to the rear. Troop A then moved on to Sisteron.[21]

Behind Troop A came the main body of Task Force Butler. When Butler was about ten miles from Château-Arnoux, he became aware of the situation at Digne, where Captain Wood was reporting German resistance. Butler decided to send reinforcements and ordered Maj. James C. Gentle, executive officer of the 143rd Regiment's 2nd Battalion, to form a mini-task force and go to Wood's assistance. Task Force Gentle was made up of an M8 armored car, a tank company of eight Sherman tanks, and a company of infantry. By 2:00 P.M. this force had crossed the Durance at Les Mées and dispersed the Germans, who began to withdraw toward Digne, attempting a vain resistance from foxholes along the road. Gentle moved steadily toward Digne. Around 5:30, he was held up by a fire fight about seven miles west of the town. As he proceeded, he was joined by the *Maquis de Thoard* and shortly reached a munitions dump, defended by a few Germans. After brisk fighting, in which Gentle's radio was knocked out, the munitions dump blew up. An hour later, the Shermans moved onto the Grand-Pont over the Bléone, on the outskirts of Digne. The arrival of the Task Force demonstrated to the beleaguered Germans that they had a new and more formidable enemy to cope with. All of the German points of opposition surrendered. By 7:00 P.M., after two years of occupation, Digne had found freedom. The Americans and the FFI rounded up over 400 Germans.[22]

If the Americans had anticipated that the FFI would now join them in the push northward, they would have been disappointed. Because the resistance forces, whether FFI or FTP, were organized departmentally, they considered their main task to be expelling the Germans from their department. They then sought to occupy the departmental seat, oust the Vichy incumbents, and replace them with officials of their own choosing. This meant a triumphal entry of the Departmental Liberation Committee, representing a variety of political views, but frequently dominated by Communists and Socialists who undertook to play an interim role until the regular councils and administration could take over. At the same time, the Gaullist provisional government, represented by the *Com-*

missaires de la République, would oversee the installation of a new prefect. As for the *maquisards*, after a period of exuberant rejoicing, these warriors tended to return to civilian life or to continue to fight under their old leaders until such time as they became absorbed into the regular French army. In the Basses-Alpes, Germans still threatened Barcelonnette, where Commandant Bureau continued the struggle for control of the Larche pass.

During the liberation celebration at Digne, both Cammaerts and Major Fielding, freed from Gestapo headquarters only three days before, visited the town, trying to locate a 4-SFU representative. Meanwhile, Captain Banbury had gone up to Seyne, where he encountered Cammaerts by chance. He was able to bring him up to date regarding Butler, at Sisteron, where Cammaerts, together with Christine, promptly went to report.

Colonel Constans also learned about Task Force Butler. He had completed his reorganization, and after visiting de Lassus and Descour on August 16, he also sought out General Butler and caught up with him at Sisteron on the twentieth.

Butler himself established his CP just south of the city, and found himself more and more in touch with the FFI. Writing about his experiences a few years later, Butler expresses high praise for the Resistance: "It is only fair to state that without the Maquis our mission would have been far more difficult."[23] The historian of the 117th Cavalry believed, however, that Butler might have made even better use of them. He writes:[24]

We were beginning to meet more and more Maquis. The groups we were meeting were better trained, better disciplined and more heavily armed. Their assistance is invaluable, as they mop up the rough country between the roads up which we advance. Their enthusiasm and sincere desire to be of assistance is most gratifying. Unfortunately the commanding officer of the Task Force lacks confidence in them, with the result that they are not being employed as well as they might be. The information which they give to us as to enemy movements ahead has, up to this time, proved accurate in composition and timely to within six hours.

9

Liberation of Gap and Grenoble

With his Task Force bivouacked in the Sisteron area on August 19, General Butler prepared for further action to the north. In prerevolutionary times, Sisteron guarded the rocky pass between Provence and Dauphiné; in modern times, it serves as a gateway to the Hautes-Alpes Department, with its prefectural seat at Gap, a thriving attractive town of 15,000 set like a gem in a bowl of Alpine hills.[1]

After Paul Héraud, the Hautes-Alpes FFI leader, had been killed, Colonel Constans had resolved the succession problem by naming Etienne Moreaud, Héraud's deputy, to serve as departmental chief. In the four days since the landings, Moreaud scarcely had time to exert real leadership and obtain cooperation from all the other Resistance commanders. On the other hand, the charismatic Colonel L'HERMINE, who had been named "commander of the Central Alps" by General Zeller back in July, believed the time had come for a general uprising against the Germans. As preparation for an onslaught against Gap, he ordered that a strategic bridge to the east should be destroyed, and he gave the mission to the Jedburghs of CHLOROFORM.

This long bridge, on piles, spanned the Durance at Savines, where the road from Gap crosses the river and leads toward Guillestre and the Italian passes. In the 1950s, a large dam greatly enlarged the small lake (Lac de Serre-Ponçon), completely engulfed the old town, and necessitated construction of a new bridge; but in 1944, while the lake was smaller, it still required a long roadway from one side to the other. Algiers approved the mission, and on August 14 L'HERMINE ordered the Jedburghs—McIntosh, Martin, and Sassi—as well as a handful of *maquisards* loaded with explosives, to cross the high pass south of Orcières in order to reach the bridge without being observed.

For the mountain-trained guerrillas, crossing the pass was routine; for

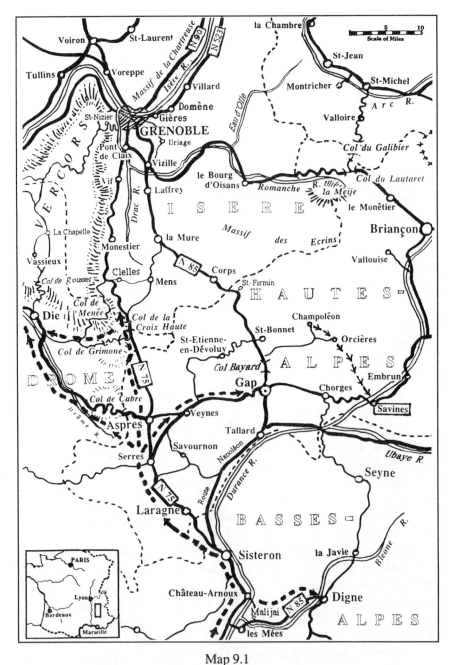

Map 9.1
THE ROUTE NAPOLÉON (N85): SISTERON TO GRENOBLE
Task Force Butler ▪▪▪▪▪▪▪▪▪▪▶ Jed Chloroform →→→→→→

McIntosh it was somewhat more arduous. One of the company recalled the climb:

> This was a tough test for all of us, but especially for the American lieutenant. Untiring leader in flat country, he suffered in the mountains. . . . Every twenty minutes the American asked, "How far to the top?" And we would answer, "In twenty minutes." For him it seemed the climb would never end.

By morning of August 16, the bridge was out. Had the Germans crossed in this direction, they would have found it extremely difficult to progress westward. In the event, the road was never required by them, for the Gap garrison surrendered and the Germans never attempted an offensive over the passes.[2]

When he received word of the landings, L'HERMINE radioed Algiers, "Can we attack Gap?" and told the other Resistance chiefs that he had received an affirmative reply. L'HERMINE hoped that the German commander, with intelligence that the Americans were on French soil, would be ready to surrender. Through the officials in Gap he unofficially communicated this notion to the Germans, while at the same time he consulted with the FFI leaders about the feasibility of an attack. There were more Germans in Gap than in Digne, and they had recently been reinforced by a nearby garrison, bringing the number of troops to over a thousand. Although many of these Germans were noncombatant administrators, they were attached to General Pflaum's 157th Reserve Division, headquartered at Grenoble, which could readily send reinforcements down from the north.

L'HERMINE insisted that the attack should be planned for the morning of Sunday, August 20. Moreaud and other officers continued to have doubts and were in favor of waiting until the Americans actually came into the area. On the 19th, the Hautes-Alpes Prefect went to the German headquarters to obtain a reaction from Captain Hermann, the officer in charge. He obtained a firm reply: the Germans would not surrender to the "irregulars," but he might be prepared to negotiate with officers of a regular army.

This left the Maquis leaders in a quandary, since they were not unanimous in their will to attack. There were conferences by telephone and finally a meeting in the small hours of the morning, wherein it was decided to make contact with the Americans. Word had come in that American advance units were moving up the Durance River Valley.[3]

Moreaud, learning that troops had already been reported about twelve miles north of Sisteron, went down with John Roper to find them. He met some men who conducted him to Butler's CP, just south of Sisteron in the small hours of

August 20. The shivering duty officer made an appointment for the FFI leader to see Butler at 8:00. Moreaud and Roper therefore went back to order the Maquis to hold off the planned attack and on the road encountered the other commanders, L'HERMINE and Colonel Daviron, along with the Jedburghs Martin and McIntosh. Also with them was Lt. Jacques Céard, leader of Sector D, whose 150 *maquisards* guarded N75 north of Aspres. Returning together, they saw Butler at 7:30. The general, quite cognizant of the threat to his right flank, agreed to send aid. He had already concluded that Aspres, rather than Sisteron, would be the key point from which to exercise his expected orders—go north on N75 to Grenoble or west to the Rhône. He therefore planned two moves, one north to guard the pass at La Croix Haute, and the other east to hold Gap. He told the Resistance leaders that one group (Nugent's Troop C) would go toward Grenoble, and the other (Piddington's Troop A) would take the right fork just north of Serres in order to reach Gap by 5:00 that afternoon.

The French leaders, Moreaud, Daviron, and L'HERMINE, with the American McIntosh, then left to order their troops (estimated at about seven hundred) to take positions around Gap. Two officers of the Maquis, Genty and Woussen, would remain with the Americans as guides. The FFI would be deployed on all sides of Gap: Captain Tortel's column would attack by Puymaure, a hill in the northwestern part of Gap where the Germans maintained their radio installation; Dusserre's *maquisards* would block the road from Embrun; Sector K would enter Gap from the south; and L'HERMINE's commandos would come in from the north, through the Col Bayard. The Americans would be approaching Gap from the heights lying to the west. Butler gave orders to form a mini-task force, similar to the one used at Digne, this time to be built around Captain Piddington's A Troop, now heading for the Aspres-Veynes area about fifteen miles west of Gap.

Troop C had already started north. Leaving Sisteron in an American jeep, Lieutenant Céard guided Nugent's vehicles up N75 to the Col de la Croix Haute, where they joined 200 *maquisards*. Nugent sent patrols ten miles farther on, to Mens and Clelles, halfway to Grenoble. They encountered no Germans, but received reports of four hundred Germans to the north. Butler sent a message to Truscott: "My main body control pass at Croix Haute. Partisan support organized and building up."[4]

General Butler remained at his CP at Sisteron, where Colonel Constans found an opportunity to discuss the campaign with him, together with possibilities of deploying the FFI along with the Task Force. Butler felt comfortable talking to regular military men: "Officers of the old French Army were coming in now," he wrote, "and the assistance of these trained officers was invaluable." There is here possibly a hint that military men could speak to other

military men, whereas the threadbare un-uniformed *maquisards* may not have
engendered the same sort of respect that the general accorded Constans, who,
incidentally, is the only French officer referred to by name (the code name, that
is, SAINT SAUVEUR) in Butler's memoirs. It may have been that Butler,
having been in Algiers from time to time before the landings, actually recognized him, and, of course, he had Captain Leger of the 4-SFU team on his staff
as his liaison "with the Maquis and anything and everything French that might
come his way." Leger states in his report

> Following instructions given by Gen. Butler, Col. St. Sauveur [Constans]
> and I worked out a plan whereby a French liaison officer would be attached
> to Task Force Butler as his representative and also that of the Regiment de
> la Drome. . . . Regular radio contacts were established between Task Force
> Butler (through 36th Division) and Col. St. Sauveur's Hqs. and Comman-
> dant Legrand's [De Lassus] Hqs.[5]

On this same day, Cammaerts, in uniform, accompanied by Christine and
the 4-SFU representative Banbury, journeyed from Seyne to Sisteron in order
to pay his respects and offer his assistance to General Butler. The effort proved
disastrous. Perhaps the general felt he had already made adequate contact with
the FFI through Constans, or perhaps within him lingered some anti-British
sentiment; in any case, he made it clear he had no use for Cammaerts' services,
affirming that he was "not the slightest bit interested in private armies."

Queried by the writer many years later, Cammaerts remained at a loss in
trying to explain why Butler literally "threw him out." "Christine and I went to
see Butler twice," he states, "the first time he snapped at us and his GSOI
(Intelligence) had to apologize.... Perhaps Butler simply didn't like our faces....
When you talk about Butler's relations with members of the Resistance these
were nearly all army men."[6]

The historian can only deplore Butler's short-sightedness in ignoring the one
Allied officer who knew more about the terrain and the people in it than anyone
else.   Granted that Constans, Widmer, Leger, and others had competence as
liaison with the Resistance, but none of them had lived in France, like Cammaerts, for most of the previous eighteen months. None had traveled so widely
or knew more French patriots. Clearly Butler preferred to deal with the French
military officers, but he could have done this without losing the counsel and
support offered by one of SOE's most capable agents.

While they were at Butler's command port, Cammaerts and Christine
learned about the imminent move on Gap. With the help of a Task Force officer,
they were able to reach the city before Troop A began its attack. Meanwhile,

Captain Piddington had assembled his force near Veynes, about ten miles north of Sisteron, where he conferred with his FFI guides, and waited for the assault guns and tanks to join up.

The road from Veynes to Gap, covering about fifteen miles, offers no significant obstacles. For the most part, the road runs straight along the Buech Valley floor. The surprise comes about five miles before reaching Gap, when one realizes the highway had lain along a plateau. Reaching the limit of the plateau, one sights the city nestling in a valley eight hundred feet below. Not far above the road stands an orientation table where a 360° disc locates the distant towns and mountains. Just beyond, the road begins to zigzag in sweeping curves down to the town. From the fields and farms, one can readily pick out, slightly to the north of Gap's center, the little round wooded hill called Puymaure. It was there that the German occupation force had located a radio transmitter and a sizeable contingent of troops.

Piddington's miniature armored force reached the *Table d'Orientation* around 4:00. Under his command, he had his own motorized troop, augmented by five 105-mm. assault guns and three light tanks. In addition, he acquired about a hundred *maquisards* who piled on to the armored cars, jeeps, tanks, and other vehicles. When he reached the point overlooking Gap, he learned from local citizens about the location of the German barracks. To the astonishment of the bystanders, he drove his jeep across a field to get a better look. Satisfied with the positioning, he ordered Capt. Omer Brown, in charge of the assault guns, to emplace his howitzers in a meadow from which he could readily hurl shells at the Puymaure position.[7]

Upon his arrival, Piddington, having picked up the information that the Germans might be willing to surrender, gave orders for a show of force. By 4:30 the assault guns had fired forty rounds at German installations. The first shot was particularly impressive, because it knocked over the radio tower at Puymaure. Thereafter, Germans began to come in, their hands high in surrender, to give themselves up to the Americans. Shortly before 5:00, the time designated for the attack, Piddington moved his CP down to the edge of town. With indications that all the Germans might be willing to surrender, Captain Brown volunteered to drive to German headquarters under a flag of truce to see if there was a possibility of avoiding bloodshed. Piddington obtained permission from his own superiors to delay the attack until 6:00. It was, however, difficult to get the word to the FFI groups, which were already beginning to move.

Captain Brown's mission was successful. Around 6:30, he returned to report that the German officer-in-charge had surrendered and had ordered the garrison to the town square, where they began to report in groups of fifty to a hundred.

For the next few hours, Piddington, with the cooperation of the FFI and the prefecture's secretary-general, Baret, tried to establish some sort of order in the midst of a rejoicing population gone wild. Thousands were parading in the streets; some zealous citizens shaved the heads of collaborationist women, and the crowd, identifying three Gestapo agents among the German prisoners, grabbed them and, save for American intervention, might have executed them on the spot. (They were, in fact, shot on the following evening.)[8]

Around 7:30, just as it was beginning to get dark, the final groups of Germans gave up. There had been some confusion in the northern part of the town, when firing was heard at Puymaure. It turned out that elements of L'HERMINE's commandos had moved in and just narrowly missed being fired at by the Americans. The FFI from all sides moved into Gap, and while they rejoiced at the town's liberation, they had tears in their eyes that the great Resistance chief, Paul Héraud, was not there to join them.[9]

Piddington and the Maquis had their hands full. They held over one thousand German prisoners, of whom several hundred were Polish, under guard, but they could imagine no way of sending them to the rear. Piddington saw a logical solution: Use the Poles, who detested their German masters, as guards. He and Christine, who could harangue them in their own language, encouraged them to shed their *Wehrmacht* uniforms and volunteer to fight on the Allied side. However, General Butler would have none of it, even threatening to have Cammaerts and Christine arrested for interfering.

This effort to recruit the Poles brought an unhappy termination of all efforts the two SOE agents had made to rally the Resistance east of the Rhône. They faced no alternative but to leave the area and seek support from higher military authority. With help from a member of the Task Force staff, they ultimately reached Seventh Army headquarters, but General Patch did not send Cammaerts back to the area he knew so well. Instead, he assigned him to de Lattre, whose Army B he later accompanied up the Rhône's western bank. With his knowledge of the French people and language and with his official position as General Zeller's liaison officer, Cammaerts could have been of inestimable value to General Butler, and later to Dahlquist and Truscott, whereas his experience and talents were lost in an area assigned to the French, who could readily establish their own liaison missions.[10]

General Butler, still without specific orders, decided to move his CP from Sisteron to Aspres. Learning that Gap had been liberated, the general decided to drive to his new headquarters by way of Gap. Delighted to see so many German prisoners, he promised Piddington he would send help to take care of them. Colonel Constans also visited Gap that evening, conferred with FFI leaders, and recommended to Butler that reports about German reinforcements coming down from Grenoble should be taken seriously.[11]

The Germans were, in fact, moving down the two roads from Grenoble, one column threatening the pass at La Croix Haute (guarded by Troop C and Céard's Maquis), and the other, marching south along the Route Napoléon, posing the possibility of Gap being reoccupied. Lucien Blache, commander of a Secret Army contingent at St.-Firmin, about twenty miles north of Gap, learned that a sizeable German force, estimated at 800 to 1,000 men, was approaching his sector. He set up road-blocks.

On the morning of August 20, a report had reached the FFI that the Germans had passed Corps and were continuing on toward Gap. The report stated that the enemy had heavy machine guns, mortars, and a 90-mm. field gun. The local Maquis, numbering about one hundred, possessed one machine gun, forty rifles, and a few revolvers. On reaching St.-Firmin, the Germans spread out through the woods to avoid guerrilla ambushes. By nightfall, they had reached a point twelve miles north of Troop A's vulnerable outposts at Col Bayard, where Piddington had positioned his assault guns. Jedburgh CHLOROFORM (McIntosh, Martin, and Sassi), together with a number of L'HERMINE's *maquisards*, stood in support.

Meanwhile, at Aspres, Butler had received orders to proceed west to Loriol, on the Rhône. However, aware of the potentially dangerous situation at the Col Bayard, he ordered Major McNeill (G3 of the 753rd Tank Battalion) to form a small task force of Sherman tanks, tank destroyers, and infantry. This force pulled out of Aspres early on August 21 and within two hours was in position at the Col Bayard.

At 10:00 A.M. the Germans attacked. Piddington radioed his headquarters: "1015: enemy patrols trying to enter Col Bayard but are stopped." The Germans did not press the attack, but turned around and started north. One enemy group, of which half were Polish, broke off from the main body. A platoon of McNeill's tanks, along with Jedburgh McIntosh and the FFI, pursued them and took three hundred prisoners. Later some of these Poles served briefly as guards when the Germans were put in trucks and sent to the rear. Two American officers in a jeep started after the remaining Germans and, although unable to catch up with them, were able to estimate that about a thousand men were retreating toward Grenoble.[12] Later that afternoon, Piddington's Troop A and McNeill's tanks, relieved by elements of General Dahlquist's 36th Division, sped west along the road to Aspres, Die, and Crest, to join up with the main body of Task Force Butler, already taking positions for what would be known as the battle of Montélimar.

THE LIBERATION OF GRENOBLE

If General Patch had any concern by this time that the eastern flank held counteroffensive possibilities, ULTRA certainly had removed them. He had, in fact, before noon of the 20th, authorized Truscott to send Task Force Butler west to the Rhône. As soon as possible thereafter, the 36th Division would follow, with one regiment (143rd less 2nd Battalion already with Butler) alerted for a move on Grenoble and the others following up the Durance. Butler only received his orders at 4 A.M. the next morning (August 21) but, in the course of the day, moved all except a few elements to the Rhône.[13]

Truscott had in mind that the entire 36th Division would follow Task Force Butler to the Rhône, but he did not make this intention entirely clear to General Dahlquist, who understood his mission as also protecting the east flank and moving up to Grenoble. Consequently, on the 22nd, Dahlquist ordered two battalions of Col. Paul Adams' 143rd Regiment to move north. Adams had his 3rd Battalion, under Lt. Col. Theodore Andrews, proceed beyond the Col de la Croix Haute, and sent his 1st Battalion, under Lt. Col. David M. Frazior, over to Gap, where it took the Route Napoléon north beyond the Col Bayard. (The 2nd Battalion was with Butler.)[14]

Grenoble served as headquarters for the German 157th Reserve Division, consisting of three infantry regiments and two artillery battalions, commanded by Generalleutnant Karl Pflaum. Pflaum had fought on the Russian front in 1941 before he was transferred to France. The 157th, having been assigned to antiterrorist duties, had elements scattered around the cities of southeastern France, such as Gap, Embrun, and Chambéry, as well as at Grenoble. Lacking sufficient power, with its communications constantly harassed by Maquis groups, and uncertain how the invasion was progressing, the 157th could muster no concentrated or effective measures of defense.[15]

German intelligence as to the exact position and movement of the Allied forces was meager and delayed. German records complain of the lack of air reconnaissance. The commander at Digne, when captured, admitted that partisans had kept him out of contact with his superiors for four days. On August 20 (with Task Force Butler already in Aspres and Gap, 60 miles from Grenoble), the Nineteenth Army was insisting that elements of the 157th hold Grenoble until August 30. At the same time, the German C-in-C Southwest, Kesselring, assuming that the 157th was now under his command, ordered the division to retire to the Mont Blanc–Montgenèvre pass line, "leaving rear guards in regiment strength at Grenoble and sufficient forces to control roads leading from Grenoble to the passes. Efforts would be made to leave rear guards until about the 30th, depending on Allied advance from the south. To delay this, roads south of Grenoble to be destroyed, beginning immediately."[16]

Clearly, C-in-C Southwest did not realize how harassed General Pflaum had been. In early August, Pflaum had mounted Operation *Hoch-Sommer*, in which he sent detachments southeast, into the valleys of the Romanche, Drac, and Eau d'Olle, to destroy the Maquis of Oisans. He needed to secure the road to Briançon, which guards the Montgenèvre pass to Italy. Pflaum had sent other troops down the two main roads south of Grenoble, but these had been stopped on August 19 and 20 at the Col de la Croix Haute and at the Col Bayard. On the 21st, they also were retreating in the direction of Grenoble, ambushed and attacked by FFI units along the way.[17]

These FFI companies came from both the Isère and the Drôme Departments for, while Grenoble lies in Isère, the boundary between Isère and Drôme extends north and south only a few miles west of N75, the Aspres–Grenoble road. The Drôme FFI chief, de Lassus, had authorized the newly arrived French commandos under Lieutenants Muelle and Beaumont, with several Drôme FFI companies, to harass the Germans near Clelles, north of the Col de la Croix Haute. On the 21st these forces, together with local Maquis companies, moved on Pont de Claix, just south of Grenoble, routed the German garrison, and sent messages to the Americans, still at the Croix Haute pass, that the way was clear. (By this time Colonel Adams, commanding the 36th Division's 143rd Infantry, had relieved the Task Force Butler units holding the pass.)[18]

On August 21, General Pflaum concluded that he should carry out the order to abandon Grenoble so that the 157th Division could guard the Alpine passes. His effort to hold the road to the Montgenèvre pass having failed, he had only one option left—to withdraw to the northeast up the Isère Valley (Route N90) to the Little St.-Bernard, as well as into the Maurienne leading to the Modane tunnel and the Mont-Cenis pass. During the afternoon and evening of the 21st, the German garrison burned documentary records, destroyed installations, and began to pull out. By midnight, the city had been evacuated. Not many elements remained to protect the rear guard, only the companies that, retreating from Oisans, had reached Vizille, and the scattered units retreating from Col de la Croix Haute and the Col Bayard.

All of the German units were hard pressed by the FFI, which did their best, with their limited firepower, to cut off isolated enemy groups, block roads, and occupy key positions. Because Grenoble is surrounded by mountains, the Resistance fighters could control all areas except those where the Germans had become well entrenched. With the German withdrawal, however, elements of the Isère FFI were able to enter the city during the night of August 21/22 and occupy the more important installations. Cdt. Louis Nal (BRUNET) with his *Groupes francs* took over as the enemy departed. Into the city came the *maquisards* from the Chartreuse mountains to the north: Sector II under LE BARBIER (Lyautey de Colombe) along with companies HUGUES (Guyot), PAUL II (Weill), STEPHANE (Etienne Poitau), and many others. Commandant Le Ray set up his CP at the Hotel de la Division, and the newly designated prefect, Albert Reynier (VAUBAN), with members of the Departmental Committee of Liberation, began to take over the administration.[19]

There were still enemy forces at Vizille, and within twenty-five miles of Grenoble along the two roads, N75 and N85, leading into the city from the south, there were groups of Germans. Nor was it impossible that the Germans retreating to the northeast and northwest, finding their ways blocked, would return. From the FFI point of view, it was necessary to get American forces into Grenoble as soon as possible.

The American forces were on the way. Andrew's 3rd Battalion, leaving the Col de la Croix Haute at dawn of the 22nd, encountered no enemy resistance. The first recon units reached Pont-de-Claix, a few miles south of Grenoble, where Routes 75 and 85 converge, around 5 A.M. The town had been occupied the day before by French guerrillas. About two hours later, Adams arrived with an infantry company, a few tanks, and a field artillery battery. However, with scant information about German strength, he was hesitant to proceed into town with his small force.[20]

On the morning of the 22nd, a journalist with the 143rd, Edd Johnson of the Chicago *Sun*, hopped onto a trolley bringing French commuters into Grenoble. He wore a correspondent's khaki, but was soon recognized and hailed as the first American to help liberate the city. He was escorted to a hotel, where he took a bath, and then in the early afternoon reported to Adams what had happened.[21]

The city was exuberantly celebrating its liberation. Crowds swelled into the main thoroughfares, along which proudly marched detachments of the Resistance—from the Vercors, from Chartreuse, from all the mountains around Grenoble.

At 2:00 P.M., most of Andrews' 3rd Battalion had reached the city. Adams conferred with Commandant Le Ray about the possibility of a German counterattack. Adams' resources were pitifully thin, and the *maquisards* were poorly armed, but together they established road-blocks on the main roads out of Grenoble, northwest toward Lyon and northeast where the road led toward the Franco-Italian frontier. Just east of Grenoble, at Gières, Adams placed a platoon reinforced with FFI. He could only hope that his other battalion, coming up the Gap–Grenoble road, would soon appear, but Frazior's 1st Battalion had not made rapid progress. It encountered more German resistance than the 3rd.

The German forces involved were the remnants of those who had participated in Operation *Hoch-Sommer*. Units of the 157th Reserve Division had progressed some thirty miles up the Romanche/Eau d'Olle Valleys, on the eastern side of the 8,000-foot Belledonne chain, when word of the Allied invasion reached them. They had been fighting principally against Sector I of Commandant LANVIN (André Lespiau), who has described the actions in detail in his book *Liberté provisoire*. By the 21st, LANVIN had lost contact with the Germans and assumed that some had continued northeastward over the mountains into the Maurienne, which, since it leads to the Mont-Cenis pass, would permit withdrawal to Italy. The others he assumed would be withdrawing down the Romanche Valley.[22]

As LANVIN and his FFI troops followed down the valley, they were hailed as liberators. Some Germans had, in fact, retreated ahead of them, and in the morning of August 22, were reported moving along N91 between Séchilienne and Péage de Vizille, where the road crosses the Romanche. Shortly after noon, an advance reconnaissance of Frazior's battalion made contact with the enemy. Learning that Germans were up ahead, the 93rd Field Artillery, attached to the battalion, set up batteries at Laffrey and began to shell N91. At this point, between 3 and 4 P.M., LANVIN located the Americans, meeting a lieutenant in charge of a small contingent of tanks and jeeps, about halfway between Séchilienne and the bridge. LANVIN believed that the bombardment was doing more harm to civilians than it was to the Germans and requested a cease-fire. The Americans agreed. LANVIN was impressed by the rapid radio communication between the observation post and the battery.

LANVIN and the Americans planned a coordinated attack, directed against the Germans at the bridge over the Romanche, to commence at 5:00 P.M. One American company would circle around north and west of Vizille, with the other coming up from the south. There was a misunderstanding, however, since the American movement began an hour earlier, and the FFI moved at 5:00. Unfortunately, the *maquisards* came under the fire of the American battery, and there was some wild scrambling before the French were identified. There was more confusion as the Americans moved north into Vizille, mixed up with the Germans, estimated as 500–600, withdrawing into the Chateau and its park. In the end, the Germans surrendered. The American report estimated 150 enemy casualties, and 150 prisoners, who were turned over to the FFI. French reports mention 700 prisoners.[23]

The action at Vizille slowed the advance of the 1st Battalion, which was only able to reach Grenoble between 8:00 and 9:00 that evening, but it had developed real cooperation between the Americans and the FFI. Colonel Adams later testified how helpful the French had been in pointing out areas where Germans still operated. Adams recalled that a lot of *maquisards* attached themselves to

Capt. Zerk O. Robertson's L company. "He is a nice country-type fellow," Adams said, "brave as anything. So, he had a company of Maquis as well . . . . I later got into a little bit of trouble over it, but I didn't mind it . . . because they were real helpful to us and fought alongside Robertson's company."[24]

Just as the 143rd Infantry (minus the 2nd Battalion) was getting organized in the city, with its command post at the Hotel Napoleon, Colonel Adams learned that his units were to move over to the Rhône where the rest of the 36th Division was trying to block the retreat of the main German forces. Since the 45th Division would now control the eastern sector of the American advance, General Eagles ordered the 179th Regiment to move into the Grenoble area as soon as possible.

At dawn on the 23rd, the day following "liberation," the first recon elements of the 179th's 1st Battalion, commanded by Lt. Col. Michael Davison, began entering the Grenoble area. By the afternoon, the 3rd Battalion under Lt. Col. Philip Johnson had arrived, along with Col. Harold Meyer, commander of the 179th, who set up his CP at the Hotel Suisse et de Bordeaux.

Relations between the French and the 179th Regiment, which remained in Grenoble for four days, established a bond that lasted into the postwar years. Colonel Adams had set a good precedent, fighting together with LANVIN's *maquisards* at Vizille and cooperating with Commandant Le Ray, the departmental FFI chief. The exhilaration of the rejoicing populace was shared by the troops, which, to their pleased surprise, had faced no German panzers on their march north.

By the 23rd, when Colonel Meyer relieved Adams, the city had somewhat settled down. Meyer, who had taken over the 179th Regiment at Anzio only five months earlier, was delighted with the French. He wrote his wife:[25]

> Every soldier and officer, to a man, loves the people of southern France. There were throat lumps and tears for all of us from the uncouth, the unlettered, to the cultured as our convoys rolled through the villages, along country roads, and as we were greeted by a happy, courteous, dignified and proud people.

Colonel Meyer was fortunate in the capable staff that supported him: His much-more experienced deputy, Lt. Col. Preston Murphy (who had been acting commanding officer), cooperated with good grace and enthusiasm; his supply officer, Capt. Harlos V. Hatter ("my Jewel, the Mad Hatter," Meyer wrote his wife), supervised the 200-mile truck route to the beach so capably that the regiment never had to "pull its punches for lack of ammunition."[26] The two battalion commanders at Grenoble would be affectionately remembered by the

French: Colonel Davison would later destroy a troop of German panzers at Meximieux, where "Place Davison" now commemorates the town's liberation.

Meyer's other battalion commander, Lt. Col. Philip Johnson, has been especially honored in Grenoble, almost as if he, not Meyer, held the regimental command, and as if he, not Adams, had liberated the city. Johnson stands alone as the only American officer who is mentioned by name in the French accounts of Grenoble's liberation. Johnson soon became acquainted with Colonel Huet, who had held the principal FFI command in the Vercors before the Germans overran the plateau.[27]

After the Vercors dispersal, the various commanders, Huet, Geyer (Thivollet), and Costa de Beauregard, had hidden in the wooded western slopes of the Vercors and then, in early August, had gradually begun to regroup the survivors of the debacle. While Geyer organized his 11th Cuirassiers in the Royans area between the Vercors and Romans, Huet established a command post at Tullins, about ten miles northwest of Grenoble. He kept with him André Pecquet, the American bilingual agent who had served as radio operator for the British EUCALYPTUS team in the Vercors.

When Huet learned that American forces were arriving at Grenoble, he quickly moved, with Pecquet, from Tullins to the city. Pecquet carried with him orders signed by General Caffey (on the staff of General Wilson, Supreme Commander for the Mediterranean), which affirmed in French and English:

> This officer is a fully accredited representative of the Supreme Allied Command. He has been instructed to join forces whenever possible with Resistance units to wage increasing war against the German invader for the liberation of France.

On August 23, Pecquet reported to Meyer's CP in Grenoble and introduced Huet to the 179th Regiment commander. Meyer and Huet became friends and thereafter shared a headquarters office with the sign: "Colonel Meyer—179th and Lieutenant Colonel Hervieux [Huet's code name]—FFI." Pecquet became the official liaison officer. Meyer also kept in contact with new prefect, Albert Reynier.[28]

Although officially "liberated," Grenoble remained vulnerable to possible German counterattacks from the northwest and the east. After consultation with Huet and Le Ray, Meyer reinforced the road-blocks, of which there were six encircling the city. He assigned Colonel Davison's 1st Battalion to look after the west (the road leading along the Isère River toward Romans) and the north, the rugged Chartreuse escarpment, which as Sector II had been the responsibility of Captain Lyautey de Colombe (LE BARBIER), whose command post was located at Voreppe, about eight miles northwest of Grenoble. Davison recalls that LE BARBIER (as he knew him) was wounded on a patrol toward Romans. Davison ordered him into an ambulance, but the FFI leader persuaded the driver to drop him off at his home, rather than a hospital, so he could continue the fight.[29]

An especially vulnerable area, as far as a German counterattack was concerned, lay along N523, the road on the southern bank of the Isère, going east and northeast from Grenoble. With numerous FFI in the slopes overlooking the road, the Germans would find it hard going to continue toward the Little St.-Bernard or into the Maurienne. They might, therefore, try to return and break through the city to the road leading northwest to Lyon. Meyer had posted a road-block, consisting of an American platoon plus several hundred *maquisards*, at Gières. on the eastern outskirts, but it was not strong enough to repel a serious attack.

Indications that the Germans would try to break through developed in the afternoon of August 23, the day following the "liberation," when shells began to fall on Gières. German forces were reported all along the road northeast of Grenoble, and Maquis groups in the mountains began planning ambushes. About midnight the Germans attacked the road-block, overran it, and took a number of prisoners, including Lt. Clarence E. Coggins, commanding company A of the 179th Regiment. Learning of the attack, the Americans rushed artillery to the east of town, and all day long on the 24th, an artillery duel developed between the Americans and the Germans. The Resistance forces could do little to help because their tactics of fighting at close quarters made them too vulnerable to the American barrages. The Germans, with a CP at Domène (about three miles northeast of Gières), were grievously harassed. They could not break through the continuously reinforced American line, yet their escape route to Italy was so heavily obstructed by FFI ambushes that their losses were certain to be heavy if they tried to withdraw.

Lieutenant Coggins later reported that German officers conferred with him several times during the afternoon, each time more courteous than they had been before. Finally, around 5:00 they told him they wanted to discuss surrender terms. Coggins was ready to go along with them, so he, a German officer, the mayor, and a nun, Sister Marie-Françoise of Assisi, drove with a white flag through the French and American lines to the Allied command post. Huet recounts the episode:

> The German officer is very stiff. "Heil Hitler. I've come to discuss terms of surrender. There are too many of you and you are too strong. Our men can do no more. There are 1000 of them. Ammunition is exhausted." He

looks at me with hate. "I surrender to Americans, not to French." Colonel Johnson takes me by the arm, throws his arm around my shoulder and replies: "He and I, it's the same thing, we are one. Take it or leave it."

By nightfall, the surrender had been arranged, and by dawn of the 25th, the thousand Germans were rounded up as prisoners. FFI groups came down from the hills and rounded up stragglers along some twenty miles of highway.[30]

With this surrender the threat of a counterattack from the northeast was ended. It was now a matter of trying to destroy the Germans before they escaped entirely.

10

The 3rd Division to the Rhône

Patch and a few officers on his staff knew from ULTRA that on August 18 Hitler had ordered the withdrawal (except for the two divisions in Toulon and Marseille) of all German units in southern France. Patch certainly realized that de Lattre, responsible for the two port cities, would encounter strong resistance, but he could anticipate that the three American divisions of Truscott's VI Corps would face rear guard defenses rather than a vigorous counteroffensive. In any case, to the extent that ammunition and fuel could service them, Truscott urged O'Daniel and Eagles to drive as rapidly as possible to the west.

There would be three thrusts from the beachhead to the Rhône. De Lattre's French First Army (technically still Army B) would fight its way along the coast, capturing the ports and continuing on to Arles, Montpellier, and Toulouse. At the time, no one could tell whether the *IV Luftwaffenfeldkorps* and the 11th Panzer Division, which occupied the area between the Rhône and the Spanish border, would withdraw or fight.

North of the French, Truscott sent "Mike" O'Daniel's 3rd Division, with its 7th, 15th, and 30th Regiments, along the principal highway, N7, which connects the Riviera resorts of Cannes and Nice with Aix-en-Provence and then follows the Rhône valley northward. Parallel to the 3rd Division thrust, about twenty miles north, run secondary roads through hilly country, which Eagle's 45th Division—157th, 179th, and 180th Regiments—would cover, protecting the 3rd Division's flank. Truscott still controlled the French "cavalry" unit, Combat Command Sudre, which moved rapidly along the secondary roads. Farther north lay the Valensole Plateau, immediate objective of Task Force Butler, behind which followed Dahlquist's 36th Division.

Patch received the German retreat order via ULTRA about the same time, August 18, as General Blaskowitz, commanding the German Army Group G,

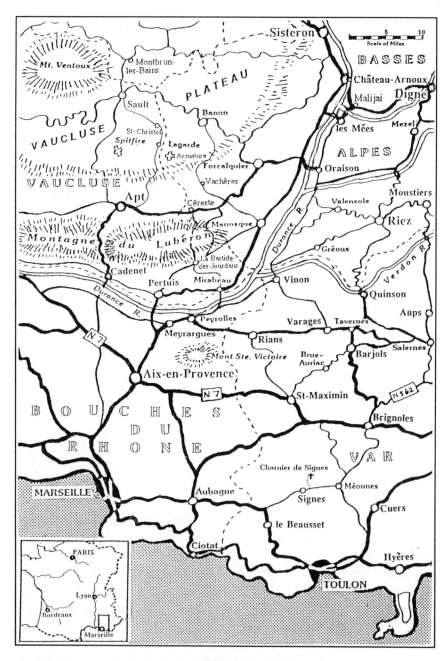

Map 10.1
WEST TOWARD THE RHÔNE
Toulon, Marseille, and the Vaucluse Plateau

and General Wiese, in command of the Nineteenth Army, obtained the message through their own channels. By the 18th, the German high command could assume that the principal Allied thrust would come from the St.-Raphael-St.-Tropez beachhead, headed for the Rhône. Wiese had to form defensive positions hastily along a line hinged on Toulon and running straight north to Brignoles on N7 and to Barjols in the undulating wooded country twelve miles farther north. He assigned Kampfgruppe von Schwerin to be in charge of these defenses at the time of the landings. Wiese's strongest division, the 11th Panzer, stationed in Toulouse, had already started to cross the Rhône and would be joined by the 198th Division, but neither could move rapidly enough to defend Brignoles and Barjols, which were left to Schwerin and to elements of the 242nd Division, already in the area.[1]

Following the basic strategic plan for use of the French Resistance, SPOC might logically have sent agents, Jedburgh teams, and OGs into the highlands north of the bridgehead to do what they could, in cooperation with the local Maquis, to harass German reinforcements of the strongholds.

Only one team, however, was sent to that part of the western Var that might have vitally impeded German defenses. This was Jedburgh team CINNAMON, which included a British officer, Capt. R. Harcourt, and two Frenchmen, Capt. F. L. Ferandon and Sous-Lt. J. G. Maurin. They were dropped on August 13, two days before the invasion, at a point between Barjols and St.-Maximin just west of the anticipated German defense line. This team was to make contact with the British SOE agent, Major Boiteux (FIRMIN), head of the GARDENER circuit, which coordinated Resistance groups in the Marseille area. They were also to work with Colonel Lelaquet, ORA Chief for the Var Department.[2]

The team was plagued with misfortune. Captain Harcourt broke both legs on landing, and the efforts to find a safe house, as well as medical assistance, hampered the team's usefulness. Furthermore, Colonel Lelaquet, pursued by the Gestapo, had gone underground. Captain Ferandon finally made contact with Colonel Gouzy, ORA chief for the western part of the Var Department, and also with Lieutenant Galvain, chief of staff for the Var FFI.

There were few Maquis in western Var, and many members of the Resistance who had suffered reprisals after June 6 were loathe to take arms until they were certain that the landings had taken place. Nevertheless, once word of the fighting at the Riviera beachhead reached the western Var leaders, they rapidly began to organize small groups in order to harass the Germans. Realizing that Brignoles and Barjols held key positions for the German defense, the FFI tried to ambush and interfere with German reinforcements going to those points.

On August 18 O'Daniel's 3rd Divison and Eagles' 45th ran into serious resistance from German artillery and mortars trying to hold Brignoles and

Barjols. The full strength of Col. Lionel McGarr's 30th Infantry Regiment (3rd Division), 3,000 men with tanks and artillery, took up positions around Brignoles.

Farther north, at Barjols, which is surrounded by hills, Colonel Meyer, commanding the 45th Division's 179th Regiment, deployed two battalions. There was genuine cooperation between Americans and Maquis. Reports had reached the 179th that partisans were already engaged with 300 Germans. The guerrillas had made contact with another American regiment (the 157th) of the 45th Division, which coming from Salernes, was by-passing Barjols to the north, and heading toward Varages. The 157th had already sent company C to Aups, five miles north of Salernes, to help an FFI group that was fighting the German garrison. Behind the 179th's positions at Barjols, eight miles to their rear—at Cotignac—enemy mortar fire was threatening their line of communications.

Colonel Gouzy reported on the operation in his area, and recounted a situation that unfortunately sometimes occurred.

> 18 August. Varages. Established Command Post . . . formed a guerrilla group under the command of Lieutenant GALVAIN. 3 P.M. open fire. Germans surprised. 4 P.M. German mortars firing on us. We continue firing with guns and grenades. The enemy breaks off and retreats. We are held down by the American bombardment. Our guerrilla groups retreat covered by the fire of the others.

By evening of the 18th, Colonel Meyer was prepared for an all-out assault on Barjols the next day. The FFI was ready to help. They swarmed around the regimental CP. Captain Dean, S-2, began organizing a combat group, incorporating guerrillas with a 3rd Battalion rifle company, to go back to Cotignac to mop up the German remnants. At Cotignac they took eight prisoners, bringing the total in that area to 204. The FFI had already been harassing the German elements around Barjols, at one point taking as prisoners three Poles who said they had gone without food for three days because of guerrilla ambushes and Allied air raids.

In the course of August 19, the 179th, helped by two battalions from the 157th, overwhelmed the German garrison trying to hold Barjols. The two American regiments then hastened westward, passing through Varages and Rians, with advance units as far as the Durance River by nightfall. Meanwhile, the 180th Regiment, which had been held in reserve, moved up to Rians, about fifteen miles west of Barjols. Thus, in two days, the 45th Division moved its three regiments about 50 miles through the German defensive lines, and now massed the power of some 9,000 men, backed by tanks, tank destroyers, 105-mm. howitzers, and a truck supply system ferrying gasoline, ammunition, and food from the beachhead over 100 miles of roads, some of them winding through very hilly terrain.

Where possible, the Maquis helped the regular troops, and the Allies helped the French guerrillas. With its desire to reach the main body of the German Nineteenth Army at the Rhône, the American force by-passed many German garrisons in smaller towns. Some of these Germans wandered about, trying to surrender; others attempted to rejoin their companions over the back roads; some held fast in the towns. The Maquis did yeoman work in flushing out these isolated units, in guarding prisoners, in establishing road-blocks, and in getting information to the American commanders.

The guerrilla forces under Colonel Gouzy moved to Varages, a few miles north of Barjols, and for the next few days, they mopped up German troops stranded in the area. On August 20, the 179th Regiment picked up a message from Colonel Gouzy:

> I am at Varages. Learned that sizeable detachment of Germans is on road Varages—Brue. They are from Barjols. . . . An officer of the American M.P.'s for Varages is with us.[3]

Because the 179th, after capturing Barjols on the 19th, had assembled just west of the road connecting Barjols and Varages (they are about five miles apart), it was a simple matter for the 179th to send a reinforced company to the area designated. They captured over one hundred enemy stragglers—mostly Poles.

A few miles to the south, on August 19, 30th Infantry (3rd Division) assaulted Brignoles and virtually destroyed those elements of the German 757th Regiment that were trying to hold this key town. Meanwhile, the two members of the CINNAMON team, with two dozen *maquisards*, moved on to St.-Max-imin, still held by the Germans. But in the course of the day, Sudre's First French Combat Command, together with the 30th Regiment, broke the German defenses and moved rapidly on to the west.

By taking Brignoles, St.-Maximin, Barjols, and Rians, the Seventh Army had now gained control of the north–south roads whereby the Germans could reinforce Toulon, the first major objective of de Lattre's Army B. While the French forces would lay siege to Toulon and Marseille, it would be the task of the 3rd and 45th American Divisions to complete protection of the French flank by taking Aix-en-Provence and getting control of the Rhône. By nightfall on August 20, the 30th Regiment had reached the outskirts of Aix, with the 15th in control of route N96, which goes from Aix in a southeasterly direction toward the sea.

THE VAUCLUSE DEPARTMENT

By August 19, the 157th Regimental Combat Team (45th Division) was pressing ahead toward the Durance River, the level valley of which, south of the Luberon mountains, serves as the natural direct route to Avignon and the Rhône. The bridge over the Durance at Mirabeau, though damaged, permitted foot soldiers across, and some patrols of the 1st Battalion, encountering no enemy, reached the north bank during the 20th. In crossing the river, the Americans moved from the Var Department to the Vaucluse, the prefectural seat of which was the celebrated old city of Avignon, resting on the Rhône, dominated by the great 14th-century Palace of the Popes. Within the Vaucluse boundaries, fifty miles north rises majestic Mont Ventoux, surrounded by a vast plateau that harbored innumerable Maquis, well-armed and waiting for American tanks and howitzers to support them.

In this region, about 1,000 Maquis forces aligned themselves under the leadership of Lt. Col. Philippe Beyne, a former tax collector and officer of the Colmar 152nd Infantry, who with his deputy Max Fischer, had organized the Maquis Ventoux into groups that could be counted among the best equipped and best trained of the Vaucluse Department.[4] One of the inter-allied missions, headed by Cdt. Gonzague Corbin de Mangoux and Maj. John Goldsmith, had been dispatched in July to the Vaucluse to improve coordination between Beyne, as head of the Ventoux FFI, and the FTP and *Groupes Francs* in the area. Among the latter was one of Cammaert's units, centered at St.-Christol and led by an able dental surgeon from Avignon, Louis Malarte.[5]

The first member of the mission, the Frenchman Corbin de Mangoux (code named AMICT) had come in by Lysander on July 12, landing at the Spitfire strip south of Sault where he was received by the SAP officer ARCHIDUC (Camille Rayon), known generally among the Resistance as Jean-Pierre, or simply J-P. (This landing strip is the same from which Zeller departed on August 2.)

Goldsmith was parachuted in a week later, on July 19, together with a Canadian officer, Maj. Paul Emile Labelle, and two Frenchmen, Robert Boucart and René Hébert. (A radio operator had been dropped earlier.) The Frenchmen were soon incorporated into Beyne's forces, while Goldsmith remained with ARCHIDUC, whose activities he has described in colorful postwar memoirs.[6]

While the Vaucluse mission worked with Beyne and other Maquis on the plateau, the German Nineteenth Army Command, then operating out of Avignon, scarcely ten miles from the plateau's edge, decided to send a punitive detachment toward Sault, known to be Beyne's command post. The Germans needed supplies, and they had to keep open a route across the plateau north of Mont Ventoux in case the southern roads were lost. A series of attacks along the road north of Apt was carried out starting on August 4 by some 400 Germans of a motorized transmission unit, KNA 485. They were repulsed, dangerously close to the Spitfire landing strip, but reformed on the 7th and, breaking through the Maquis defenses, ultimately occupied Sault and ten miles beyond, Montbrun-les-Bains.

In gaining control of the road from Apt to Sault, German patrols passed within a few hundred yards of Spitfire. With a dangerous situation developing on the plateau, Goldsmith returned to Algiers on August 12, to report on what he had experienced.[7]

About five miles east of Spitfire, ARCHIDUC operated a Drop Zone, Armature, near Lagarde. Although, because of the rocky terrain, Armature should have served only as a reception field for containers, SPOC kept sending teams into that area. True, Commandant Rayon—ARCHIDUC—controlled very efficient crews at both sites, and Colonel Constans, when he first arrived in France, maintained his command post at Lagarde; nevertheless, since the Germans now kept a contingent at Sault, operations on the Vaucluse Plateau had become somewhat precarious. When the Germans threatened nearby St.-Christol, some the *maquisards* felt they should withdraw, and indeed, Constans moved his headquarters a few miles east, to the Maquis of the 10th FTP company, in rugged hills between Céreste and Vachères.[8]

Before he left Lagarde, however, two more Jedburgh teams came in. The first, CITROEN, included two Englishmen, Capt. J. E. Smallwood and Sgt. F. A. Bailey, together with a Frenchman, Capt. René Alcée. During the night of August 13-14, they landed on the rough ground at Armature without mishap, were received by ARCHIDUC, and met Constans and Widmer. Some time later, a second unexpected Jedburgh team, MONOCLE, dropped seemingly out of nowhere. This group was made up of a Frenchman, Capt. J. Tosel, and two Americans, Lt. Ray Foster and Sgt. Robert Anderson, both from Minneapolis. MONOCLE had been ordered to the Drôme, where they would obtain further instructions from the FFI chief, de Lassus. They moved up to Crest on the 16th, the day after the landings took place far to the southeast.[9]

Smallwood's CITROEN group, scheduled to remain in the Vaucluse, shortly met Commandant Beyne and proceeded to his CP at Sault, where they met the Canadian Major Labelle, of the Goldsmith mission, now serving under Beyne as a technical counselor. Beyne assigned the Jedburghs to two *Corps Franc* companies, commanded by Cammaerts' friend Louis Malarte (PAULO), which were to cover the right (northern) bank of the Durance River in the important sector between Manosque and Pertuis. This sector lies between the Montagne Ste.-Victoire, so beloved of the painter Cézanne, on the south and the Luberon mountain chain on the northern side of the river. If the Germans sought to follow the Durance northeast from Aix, they would come this way; if the Allies, landing on the Riviera beaches, wished to drive toward the Rhône, they would logically try to control the Durance Valley. Shortly after word of the landings reached them, CITROEN and the two Maquis companies established a command post at La Bastide-des-Jourdans, in the Luberon hills about ten miles north of the Durance River, and just a few miles from the line separating the Vaucluse and the Var Departments. There they awaited news of the Allied advance.

The departmental boundary held no meaning for the Americans, but it played a part in the actions of GRAHAM and CITROEN, the two Jedburgh teams in the area. Maj. M. G. M. "Bing" Crosby, of the Gordon Highlanders, and his French colleague, Captain Gouvet, of GRAHAM, had landed at Spitfire in the Dakota which had brought in Colonel Constans. Crosby, who like Havard Gunn wore the kilts of his regiment whenever feasible, had been deputy president of the Jedburgh Selection Board in England and a company commander at Milton Hall (where the Jeds trained) before coming to Algiers. It was ironic that a person so involved in the program reached the field only four days before the invasion, and even more ironic that his area should have been overrun within a week. It was also ironic that French departmentalism should have affected his mission.[10]

Crosby and Gouvet (without the third member, who was to join later) had been assigned to the Basses-Alpes, although their orders permitted a wider range if appropriate. Nevertheless, Colonel Constans confirmed the assignment at Spitfire (which is in the Vaucluse), and shortly after landing, the two GRAHAM team members went to a Maquis near Céreste, just over the departmental line. It was understood that they should work in cooperation with the Basses-Alpes FFI chief, Georges Bonnaire (NOEL), who happened to be a Communist and not over-enthusiastic about British missions. Also, like many FTP officers, he was especially interested in liberating the prefectural seat, in this case Digne, in the eastern part of the department. Crosby did not get along with Bonnaire, whom he categorized as hating action, more interested in *"défilés"* (parades and military reviews) than real work. On the 19th, when both Crosby and Bonnaire saw Butler at Sisteron, they reached a mutual agreement that Crosby should devote himself to the western part of the department, which would leave Bonnaire to concentrate on Digne. Because Digne was liberated that same day, Bonnaire could feel that for him the task of departmental FFI chief had been for the most part successfully concluded, since no German forces, except at the Larche pass, remained in the Basses-Alpes.

Crosby, however, received reports that Germans had occupied Apt, in the Vaucluse Department, but only ten miles west of Céreste, where he already had made good contacts with the FFI leaders in the area. Knowing by this time that American forces were pushing west, he alerted the Maquis—numbering about six hundred—to a possible attack on Apt. During the twenty-first, on a reconnaissance around Apt, he ran into several Americans on a jeep patrol, from the 157th Regiment's 1st Battalion, at this time holding positions just south of the Luberon mountains. The battalion commander agreed to coordinate an attack with the FFI and scheduled it for the following morning.

The CITROEN Jedburgh team, Smallwood, Alcée, and Bailey, also made contact with the American contingent. Beyne had sent CITROEN to La Bastide-des-Jourdans just south of the pass through the Luberon chain, where they joined up with several Maquis companies under the general command of Capt. Joseph Juan, known as DUCHENE, operating in the Pertuis area. One of these companies, the independent Buckmaster unit led by Louis Malarte, possessed a good quantity of arms and was eager for action.[11]

Smallwood had met the commander of the American battalion when the Americans crossed the Durance and had accompanied him on a patrol toward Cadenet, where a German rear guard with tanks was blocking the road. A skirmish involving the FFI produced an extraordinary heroic act. Smallwood recalled that the tanks

> came rumbling down the street at us and we beat a hasty retreat. One of these tanks was knocked out of action by a man of the FTP when he came up behind it and slipped a grenade through the visor in front of the driver. The explosion probably killed the entire crew. We caught the tracked vehicles advancing on Pertuis. . . . Gammons [grenades] did the job. The column turned back.

The American colonel unpinned the bar of decorations from his own jacket and awarded them on the spot to the intrepid young *maquisard*.

On August 22, Crosby and the 600 FFI from Céreste moved to the outskirts of Apt and waited for the Americans. Meanwhile, Smallwood and Alcée came up from the south with a heterogenous group made up of the *Gendarmerie Maritime*, some Indochinese troops, two of Malarte's companies, and 200 men of DUCHENE's 8th company. They undertook to block the roads leading out of Apt toward the north and west.

When the American detachment showed up on the morning of the 22nd, the

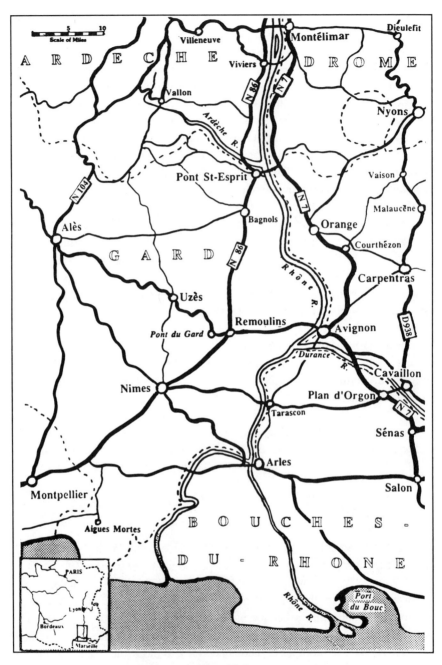

Map 10.2
THE LOWER RHÔNE VALLEY

French (and the Jedburghs) were disappointed at what seemed to them an inordinate delay. The delay emphasized a difference in tactics that marked much American cooperation with the FFI. The French were accustomed to the quick maneuvers of the guerrilla, a rapid attack with small arms and grenades, and a hasty retreat. The Americans preferred, when possible, to bring in artillery, and to do this, they needed time to assess the situation, set up observation posts, and call up the batteries. At Apt, therefore, the attackers lost the element of surprise: The German rear guard, observing they were outnumbered, quietly withdrew, too weak to oppose the Americans but too strong to be cut off by the FFI. What opposition the Germans could provide in the town was quickly overcome, and by late afternoon, Apt had been liberated. Jedburgh teams GRAHAM and CITROEN had contributed to the victory, and had fulfilled a basic aspect of their mission by bringing FFI and Allied regulars together.[12]

The Germans were attempting to hold a circular defense around Avignon as long as they could. On the 22nd, their line stretched from Arles to the Durance along the southern slopes of the Luberon range to Apt. General Wiese hoped especially to hold the strategic gap at Orgon, where the Durance flows toward Avignon, with the Luberon mountains on the east balancing the Chaine des Alpilles to the west. North of Apt rises the vast Vaucluse Plateau, backed by the imposing slopes of Mont Ventoux. Wiese was pulling out the small units in the plateau, hoping to keep control not only of N7, the Rhône Valley road, but also of D938, which, running north through Cavaillon, Carpentras, Vaison, to Nyons, skirts the western slopes.[13]

It was this latter road that Colonel Beyne believed he could block with the Maquis Ventoux, headquartered at Sault, where de Mangoux, Labelle, and Hébert, members of the SPOC Mission (Goldsmith had returned to Algiers), continued to ensure his contacts with the regular forces. On August 20, Beyne had ordered his men down to the plain, where they took up positions around Malaucène, rough country ideal for ambushes, between Carpentras and Vaison. They were successful in blocking the road, forcing the Germans to use the Rhône passage and alternative routes to Nyons.[14]

By the 23rd, both Wiese and Truscott were revising their strategies. For Truscott, the success of Task Force Butler in reaching the Rhône between Montélimar and Loriol presented him with the possibility of cutting off the German retreat. He knew, of course, from ULTRA and tactical intelligence, that the German Nineteenth Army would continue to fall back; he knew also that as more and more of de Lattre's regular French divisions came ashore he could count on them for pursuit of the enemy rear guard. Accordingly, he decided to pull Eagle's 45th Division out of the pursuit and, by sending it north, use it to reinforce or relieve the 36th Division. O'Daniel's 3rd Division, in the process of being relieved by de Lattre, would take over the pursuit north and south of the Luberon mountains, with Avignon as the immediate objective.[15]

General Wiese also appreciated the dangers of being forced to push his entire army through the narrow defile north of Montélimar. In consultation with General Kniess, commanding the LXXXV Corps, he decided to rush his 198th Division from the rear guard defense around Avignon to Montélimar, with his lone armored division, the 11th Panzer, protecting his flank. By August 21, the first formidable Mark III and Mark IV tanks had arrived east of the Rhône, and in the days to come, they would prove themselves a virtually impenetrable barrier along the Nineteenth Army's eastern flank. Von Wietersheim, commanding the armored division, was ordered to guard a line about 25 miles east of the Rhône: Vaison, Nyons, and Crest. The unexpected encounter of a patrol to Crest with Task Force Butler elements surprised both parties.[16]

The U.S. Seventh Army also moved with great rapidity, and the units of the 3rd Division soon swept through the Vaucluse Department. On the 24th, the Germans pulled out of Avignon, the department's administrative center. With the arrival of the American units, the Jedburghs' work came quickly to an end. Crosby, of GRAHAM, assigned to the Basses-Alpes, went back to Barcelonnette, carried out a hazardous patrol in the Larche area, and returned to find that the regulars—Sach's 550th Battalion—had taken over. The CITROEN team, Smallwood and Alcée, with FFI companies under Vincenzini and Malarte, reconnoitered ahead of the 7th RCT's 2nd Battalion, along the road to Avignon, which they entered on August 25 about an hour before the regiment.

The liberation of Avignon, prefectural seat of the Vaucluse, one of the great historical monuments of southern France, called for great rejoicing. The Departmental Liberation Committee took over, and Colonel Beyne, FFI Chief, with Juan as deputy, established his FFI headquarters in the city. There was a sort of symbolic coincidence, because regular French and regular American troops met there on the same day. The French now had the mission of crossing the Rhône (all bridges having been destroyed), wiping up a vast sector between the Pyrenees and the Rhône, and pursuing the Germans up the Rhône's western bank. The American 3rd Division would chase the Nineteenth Army, which was now more concerned with developments at Montélimar than with the pressure in the Vaucluse.

The FFI and the CITROEN team pressed ahead a little too vigorously. Only stopping for lunch in Avignon, they ran into trouble about ten miles north, at Courthézon, not far from the celebrated vineyards of Châteauneuf-du-Pape:

We were trapped in an ambush and badly shot up. The autobus in which our patrol was travelling was fired and blown up with a hit on the 300 kilos of plastic lying in the baggage compartment. The defense of Courthezon was taken over by an American column [2nd Bn, 7th Regiment, 3rd Divison].

Commandant Alcée sent out several patrols and captured three Germans. He was kept busy with the need to maintain peace between the men of the FTP and the FFI who were at each other's throats most of the time over their political differences. His own troops bothered him much more than did those of the enemy.[17]

The Germans were attempting to hold the road between Courthézon and Vaison, guarding one of the ways to Nyons. On the same day that Avignon was liberated, some patrols of the American 7th Infantry came over the Vaucluse Plateau to the north of Mont Ventoux, and others followed the 2nd Battalion toward Orange. On the next day, August 26, the entire 3rd Division controlled a sector from the Rhône at Orange to the hill country twenty miles to the east, and was rushing on, six battalions abreast, to Montélimar and Nyons.

11

Task Force Butler to the Rhône

Five days after the landings, General Patch's strategy was proving to be more effective than anticipated. The primary Allied objective, to seize the ports of Toulon and Marseille, was being achieved by de Lattre's army. The danger of those seaports being reinforced was minimal, a fact that Patch knew from ULTRA and from situation reports. All evidence pointed to the fact that the Germans were withdrawing and pulling back to a defensive line around Avignon. With Truscott's 3rd and 45th Divisions pushing west, with no more than holding actions by the enemy, Patch had to be assured that the French could control the seacoast, and that the 11th Panzer Division, which was crossing the Rhône, would do no more than protect the withdrawal. Intelligence informed him that German units were retreating up the Rhône and beginning to be seriously blocked by the destruction of the bridge at Loriol.

The bridges over the Rhône and its tributaries in the fortnight before D Day became major targets. Allied planes made incessant raids with varying degrees of success. Of great importance for ANVIL were the bridges over the Drôme River between Crest and the confluence, near Loriol and Livron, where it joins the Rhône. Two major bridges span the Drôme in this area, a railway bridge and the vehicular bridge on N7, the major north–south highway vital for enemy reinforcements or, in the case of defeat, the principal line of a German withdrawal.

On August 13, waves of heavy bombers struck at a railway bridge at Crest, but effected more damage to the town than to the bridge. On D + 1, August 16, while the American Seventh Army dug in along the Riviera, bombers flew in again and this time inflicted serious damage to the railway bridge at Livron.[1]

The highway bridge was left to the Resistance. Back in July, Commandant de Lassus had consulted with one of his capable subordinates, Henri Faure, head

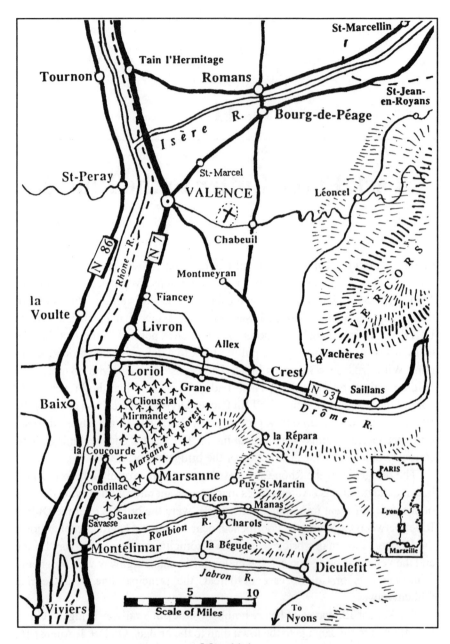

Map 11.1
BATTLES OF MONTÉLIMAR AND VALENCE

of SAP for the Drôme and Ardèche Departments, who was charged with responsibility for blowing the bridge when ordered. On D Day, de Lassus gave Faure the green light; he also ordered Captain Pons to put two smaller bridges near Crest out of action.

Faure sent away to a neighboring Maquis for additional plastic that would be needed to blow the massive stone arches. On the night of August 16, carrying some 400 pounds of plastic, he posted half a dozen men with machine guns at each end of the bridge while the rest of his 20-man commando sneaked past the German guard and silently set their charges under the bridge. Fortunately for the guerrillas, the Germans had posted no sentries but remained inside a shack with the blinds closed.

By one o'clock in the morning, the plastic had been set in place. Faure lit the fuses and quietly led his men away from the bridge. Half an hour later, a violent blast shattered the southern arch, leaving a gap of 100 feet, more than the German engineers could span with temporary girders.[2]

Destruction of the bridge caused an enormous traffic jam of German vehicles that, because of Hitler's retreat order, were beginning to rumble northward on N7. The Germans tried to place planks on the railway bridge, and they began to construct fords in the Drôme, which in summertime sometimes, if rainfall is slight, is quite shallow. Some tanks could cross, but lighter vehicles bogged down. Three days later, when Task Force Butler's first artillery reached Crest, the shells that poured down on the retreating columns turned the bottleneck area into a cauldron of blood and destruction. The damage might have been even heavier—indeed the whole Nineteenth Army might have been destroyed—except for the almost impossible task of ferrying gasoline and ammunition from a beachhead 250 miles away.

WEST TO THE RHÔNE

It was not until the evening of August 20 that Butler received an official command to leave Aspres and proceed along N93 to the Rhône. He immediately ordered the 117th Cavalry move. Anticipating that they would be leading their troops to the Rhône, Capt. John L. Wood, commanding Troop B, and Capt. William E. Nugent of Troop C drove over the winding road along the Drôme Valley from Aspres to Crest on August 20. They found no Germans along this important artery. Butler has left his own impression of the road:[3]

The route lay over a formidable mountain range with a twisting road cut into the side of the cliffs. Movement off the road would have been impossible. Our path could have been blocked in any one of scores of places, but no enemy action developed, nor had demolitions been executed. Whether we have the Maquis to thank for this free open road I do not know, but open it was. . . . I was horror-struck at the grade and nature of the road but all elements had made excellent time and none of the heavy vehicles had succumbed.

At Crest, Wood and Nugent had no trouble in making contact with Captain Pons, whose *maquisards* had been armed over the previous months with the help of Cammaerts. Pons put them in touch with a resident of Crest, M. Hoffète, with whom they spent the night. They were also quickly in touch with the recently promoted Colonel de Lassus, the Drôme commander, who designated one of his officers—actually a priest, Captain XAVIER (Lucien Fraisse)—to serve as liaison with the Americans.[4]

On the next morning, Wood's troopers, having left Aspres at first light, reached Crest around 9:00. With guides provided by de Lassus, two platoons of Troop B headed south to Puy-St.-Martin, then southwest across the Marsanne Plain, another 15 miles to the outskirts of Montélimar. Between the plain and the Rhône River, the protective hills of the Marsanne forest extend to Savasse, about three miles north of the town. As an FFI officer put it, "this is as far as we control things." The FFI patriots in these hills were of the Secret Army; five companies—about 500 lightly armed men—which constituted Captain Bernard's 4th Battalion. Because of casualties among various leaders, Bernard had taken command of the battalion only two days before the landings.[5]

Wood proceeded close enough to Montélimar to note that the perimeter was guarded by German road-blocks too strong for an attack. He withdrew and reported to Butler.

The main body of Task Force Butler had meanwhile followed. General Butler had consulted with FFI leaders, who explained to the Americans the tactics used by the German convoys traveling north on N7. With the forces at his disposal, Butler could harass the German movement, and he could test the possibility of throwing road-blocks across the highway.

Butler established his CP near the small town of Marsanne, nestled in the eastern slope of wooded hills about halfway between Montélimar and the Drôme River. From there, as he waited for the 141st Regiment (36th Division) to reinforce his widely dispersed units, he sought ways and means of accomplishing his mission: denying N7 to the enemy.[6]

To the north, he had Nugent's C Troop carry out a reconnaissance along the north side of the Drôme toward Livron. This was the area assigned to Pons' company, which had been regularly ambushing and attacking German traffic on N7. At this time, several days before the German rear guard reached the Drôme, the retreat was disorganized and erratic—sometimes a car, sometimes a convoy of trucks, horse-drawn wagons, individuals on foot and on bicycles. The curé at St.-Vallier, a few miles to the north, described what he witnessed:[7]

> 21 August. German columns continually passing. They have more and more the appearance of hunted beasts. They pass, guns ready, watching the side of the road and windows. Near Ponsas a tank helps them get through, firing on the Resistance. . . . They get Frenchmen and place them on the hoods of their cars. This afternoon they took some young people in the rue St.-Rambert and used them as a shield.

Knowing that the Americans would soon be coming, Pons and his captains, Fié, Antoine, and Didelet, carried out raids on the 20th, both south and north of the Drôme, destroying trucks and soldiers. At dawn, Didelet, only thirty yards from the road, knocked out three German cars with his machine gun. Luckily he escaped back into the woods with no casualties.

Encouraged by this raid, Pons decided on a daylight attack with several hundred *maquisards* toward Fiancey, about five miles north of the Drôme. By 2 P.M., he had hidden his men in the orchards and small hills facing the town. An hour later, a convoy of twenty German trucks approached, and when within range received a salvo from one bazooka, six machine guns, and an assortment of small-arms fire. The attack played havoc with the Germans, but with their habitual resourcefulness, they quickly counterattacked, driving Pons' men back into whatever shelter they could find. Struggling back to Allex, about five miles from N7, they were reinforced by some of Captain Bentrups' 6th company and Captain Chapoutat's 2nd company of about eighty men—which were in contact with platoons of Nugent's Troop C.

Troop C had reached Crest shortly after 9:00, and Nugent had cautiously started west toward the Rhône, outposting one platoon to the north as protection for his right flank and reaching Allex with the other two. He encountered no Germans. If his actions seemed overly cautious to the French guerrillas, it should be remembered that Nugent was in completely strange country with only that information about the Germans he obtained from the FFI. In describing their contact with the Americans, the French speak of "tanks" and "armor," but Nugent knew that his M8 armored cars, with their 37-mm. guns, were not tanks and would be excruciatingly vulnerable if faced by a German Mark V Panther.

After considerable discussion with the French and checking by radio with Butler, Nugent and the FFI moved west, one platoon toward Livron and the other toward Fiancey. With the earlier raid of Pons and the attack with the guerrillas in the late afternoon, the combined efforts left 50–60 enemy trucks destroyed. However, with his cars and jeeps stretched out over ten miles, Nugent prudently withdrew his units back to Crest for the night, leaving the *maquisards* to trudge back as best they could. He reported to Butler, now at Marsanne, what he had observed.[8]

Meanwhile, Butler had been deploying his forces in order to hamper German traffic on N7. He had the report from Captain Wood, who had patrolled within a few miles of Montélimar, that the city was defended with road-blocks. It would take more than a mechanized cavalry troop and guerrillas to mount a serious attack. With the advice of FFI members, Butler placed his heaviest units, the 143rd Infantry's 2nd Battalion, under Lt. Col. Charles Denholm, and the 49th Field Artillery, at Condillac, about halfway between Marsanne and the Rhône. Condillac, where a venerable chateau served as a convenient command post, lies in a pass surrounded by the hills of the Marsanne forest. From Condillac there is a two-mile descent westward to the Rhône and N7, which runs at this point through the little town of La Coucourde. The Marsanne hills crowd the highway, the railroad, and the river into a passage less than a thousand yards wide, and on the farther, western side, a flat area permits only a mile of passage before hills rise steeply from the valley bottom. The Germans retreating northward had to work their way through this pass or seek an alternate route across the Marsanne plain in the direction of Crest. Butler (or Dahlquist, who took over the command two days later) had to place an effective road-block at La Coucourde and throw a defensive line across the southern part of the Marsanne plain, where the Roubion River, flowing from the eastern hills at Manas, westward to Montélimar, provides a fifteen-mile-long natural barrier.

To the north, Butler kept the 117th Cavalry's Troop C along the Drôme River, and he also heeded the recommendations of Captain Bernard, leader of the south Drôme's 4th Battalion, to deploy the 117th's tanks and artillery in the hills north and east of Cliousclat, a few miles from Loriol. Because the highway bridge over the Drôme had been knocked out, German vehicles were backed up into the flat ground for miles around the bridge, while engineers worked to build fords and to plank the undamaged railroad bridge for vehicular traffic. When the assault guns and tanks of the 117th Cavalry began sighting toward Highway 7, they found targets beyond belief.

On the evening of the 21st, Captain Pons' company had withdrawn to Crest, where the men tried to get some rest after their open fight with the enemy. That night, an American officer took Pons by jeep to see General Butler. A veteran of guerrilla warfare, Pons could hardly believe what he saw at the American CP:[9]

We found ourselves in the midst of a veritable sea of vehicles. The general was not there. Waiting for him to return we admired (the word is not too strong) the vehicles moving around in absolute silence. No bumping, no shouting, absolute silence. Each driver seemed to know to the very inch, just where his station was even though there were on this plain hundreds and hundreds of moving vehicles of all sorts: trucks, tanks, armored cars, assault guns, jeeps, ambulances, mobile artillery, etc. I had known the French army and seen the German army, but what a difference I noted here with my own eyes.

When Butler returned, he told Pons he was aware of the operation the French guerrillas had just carried out, and asked him to attack again the next day at the same place—Fiancey. He promised armored support, and Pons with considerable hesitation agreed to assemble his men next morning at the same positions, ready for an attack by 2:00 that afternoon—the 22nd.

Colonel de Lassus also discussed the situation with Butler that same evening. Since Sisteron, Butler had continued to be in touch with the regional FFI commander, Colonel Constans, who had now established a CP about eighteen miles east of Montélimar at Dieulefit. Butler also had available Captain Leger, the French-speaking OSS representative of 4-SFU, who remained in touch with Constans as well as with Captain XAVIER (Father Lucien Fraise), the Jesuit liaison officer. De Lassus had some doubts regarding FFI collaboration with the Americans, whose reliance on artillery, air strikes, and rapid motorized deployment facilitated by radio communication differed vastly from the hit-and-run guerrilla tactics his men were capable of.

Nevertheless, on the 22nd, Pons deployed his men once more along the approaches of Fiancey, beyond the several wooded hills that might have provided cover. Early in the afternoon, a convoy approached, but this time guarded by tanks—identified by Pons as Tigers—against which the embattled guerrillas had no recourse but to withdraw to the woods halfway back to Allex. About 5:00, a platoon of Wood's Troop C hove into sight and the Germans withdrew. Wood set up defensive road-blocks around Allex but did not believe he had enough power to carry out more than a reconnaissance mission. There is nothing in the American records that suggest he had been ordered to coordinate an attack with Pons' company. Fortunately, Pons was able to return to Crest with no men killed, although seven were seriously wounded.

It was clear to Colonel de Lassus that there should be a better understanding between his forces and the American command. He wrote to Pons:

We are not at the *entire disposition* of the Americans, who have a tendency to engage our troops like the infantry of a regular army. You take orders only from your FFI chiefs. My orders are unchanged. Offensive guerrilla operations toward the west.

I know about the fine combat of your Company near Fiancey. When the time comes for recognition, this will not be forgotten. At the moment, we are engaged in a struggle on which the future of our country depends. In spite of their fatigue, send your men back for ambushes.[10]

De Lassus' criticism of Butler is correct. In all his task force, Butler controlled only one battalion of infantry and he desperately needed more. Learning of the withdrawal at Fiancey, Butler despatched an urgent message to Dahlquist, whose 36th Division was supposed to reinforce him: "French infantry support proving absolutely unsatisfactory. Request one battalion infantry by motor without delay."[11] When one recalls that Butler, with an American battalion and field artillery concentrated on La Coucourde, could not keep a road-block there because of German counterattacks, one has to place his criticism in context. If the super-armed Americans could not stand up against German Mark V Panthers, what could be expected of French guerrillas with Bren guns and an occasional bazooka? So urgent did Butler find the need for infantry, he even brought his engineer company into the line with results so disastrous he was severely criticized (in his postwar memoirs) by Colonel Hodge, commander of the 117th Cavalry, then serving on Butler's staff.[12]

On the previous evening, August 21, having been relieved at Gap, Captain Piddington brought his Troop A into the new battleground. On the next day, reinforced by George McNeill's mini-task force of Shermans and tank destroyers, he was assigned responsibility for guarding the north bank of the Roubion River, a stretch of about eight miles between Manas in the east and Sauzet on the west. For a cavalry troop of 125 men with a handful of armored cars and jeeps, together with six tanks and two tank destroyers, this meant small patrols with large gaps in the line. Piddington had the assistance of several hundred *maquisards* from Captain Bernard's 4th Battalion of FFI.

What neither Butler nor Piddington knew was that General von Wietersheim's formidable 11th Panzer Division, charged with the defense of the Nineteenth Army's flank, was maintaining patrols as much as fifty miles eastward of the main body. These reconnaissance units were probing Allied positions along a 100-mile north–south stretch. The most northern patrols had actually crossed the Roubion and, before Piddington deployed his units, had penetrated beyond Puy-St.-Martin in the direction of Crest. Other units of the 11th Panzer Reconnaissance Battalion had reached La Bégude, about four miles south of the Roubion. Several bridges along Troop A's sector remained intact: at Manas, Charols, and another south of Cléon. A fluid situation existed in which units on either side might surprise the other.[13]

While all units of Task Force Butler had been deployed by August 22, spread thinly from Allex in the north to the Roubion River in the south, the first 36th Division elements did not begin to arrive until that afternoon. Butler remained in charge until Dahlquist, expected on the next day, set up his CP in the battle area. When the 141st Regiment's 2nd Battalion, commanded by Lt. Col. James Critchfield, arrived at Marsanne late in the afternoon, Butler ordered it south to the hills around Savasse, just north of Montélimar, where Nugent's Troop B and several hundred *maquisards* of the Secret Army's 13th and 14th companies were entrenched. For the next two days, Critchfield's men tried to attack toward Montélimar but were thrown back by the 11th Panzer Division's *Kampfgruppe Thieme*, which was powerful enough to pulverize the Americans in their attempts to gain control of the hill road to Condillac. In this hard-hitting duel between tanks and artillery, neither Troop B nor the FFI, trying to hold the eastern flank along the Roubion, could bring much to bear.

Nevertheless, the French guerrillas did their best to flesh out the few infantry troops the Americans had available. This is attested by the records of Bernard's 4th Battalion:[14]

22 Aug.: In Cliousclat area, Corps Franc damages about 10 trucks on N 7. Section of 7th Co. destroys two cars, while the rest of the company, with American elements, destroys considerable material. Commanding officer of 8th Co. wounded and escapes. Contacts Germans, thus giving US reinforcements time to arrive.

13th and 14th Co., with U.S. tank protection, are attacked in the night by Tiger Tanks with German infantry using the password (France Amérique) which had been betrayed to them by a traitor named Chabas, who is to be shot. After hard street combat, Germans withdraw leaving 2 or 3 dead. Allied losses: 13th Co.: 4 dead, four wounded; 14th Co.: 2 dead; U. S.: 3 dead.

Two US tanks destroyed; French car burned. 17th Co. takes position on N 7; 30 men put at deposition of US to protect heavy machine guns.

23 Aug.: CO of 7th Co. executes under heavy fire a reconnaissance on N 7 and brings intelligence from which American tanks can enfilade and destroy numerous vehicles. A second patrol farther north sends information to battalion HQ which, by means of the GIP-radio given to Capt. Bernard, alerts the American artillery which is directed on troop groupings and trucks.

8th Co. carries out several barrages on the Crest-Bourdeaux road, while the company's liaison "side-car" hits an armored column, and is blocked between the enemy and a deep ditch. Personnel escape under protection of FM [*Fusil mitrailleur*: automatic weapon].

13, 14, 17 Cos. take up defensive positions on heights north of Sauzet.

17th Co. dispatches two combat groups to the village, protected by 3 US tanks at the exits. The 30 men who have been here for several days under protection of the US heavy machine guns remain in place at the request of the U.S. Col., addressed to the Chef de Battalion.

By the 23rd, General Dahlquist and the remaining battalions of the 141st Regiment had arrived in the battle zone. He had been given a hard time by Truscott, who hoped that he could cut off the Germans with a superhuman effort to bring superior forces to bear. Truscott's diary for August 21 has the entry: "36th fouled up. Not moving infantry and artillery as ordered. Baehr [VI Corps Artillery officer] back to straighten them out." Also, on the 22nd:

> No news from Butler, 36th or French. Staff meeting. Lt. Col. Rosson [VI Corps Asst. G-3] sent up to Gen. Butler to straighten them out and get picture. . . . [Truscott] works on papers and messages till 1030 and off by Cub to 36th CP at Aspres. Neither 141st nor artillery moved. Gen. Dahlquist not in. Col. Vincent [36th Div. Chief of Staff] catches hell. CG [Truscott] orders Col. Harmony [CO, 141st Regiment] to push 141st with all speed. . . . Letter to Gen. Dahlquist, a roasting. Gen. Dahlquist later on phone—more hell, but given 179th for use at Montélimar. 143rd [which had just moved into Grenoble] to stay in Grenoble area. Col. O'Neill [VI Corps G-4] in to discuss critical gasoline situation, 10,000 gallons from 45th to move rest of 36th.[15]

In actual fact, the 141st Regiment was already moving as fast, considering the availability of trucks and fuel, as possible. Truscott had conferred with Col. John W. Harmony, the capable and highly esteemed commander of the 141st, on the road to Aspres, where he expected to obtain further orders from Dahlquist. In Dahlquist's absence, Truscott ordered the 141st to Montélimar, and Harmony rode with Critchfield to the battle area, where they engaged the enemy that same night.[16]

General Dahlquist personally came into the battle zone in the early hours of August 23, but told General Butler to maintain his dispositions until he became oriented. Dahlquist took over at 3:00 that afternoon, setting up his CP near Marsanne but next day moving back to La Répara about five miles south of Crest. By this time, the plan was for the entire 36th Division to take over the Montélimar battle, while Butler's Task Force would be dissolved but held in reserve. The 141st Regiment, already in place, would try to block highway 7 north of Montélimar, especially at the narrow passage south of La Coucourde. The 142nd, coming in from the southeast, would take over a defensive line along the Roubion River. As to the 143rd, the 2nd Battalion already made up part of

Task Force Butler, while the other two had just occupied Grenoble. Truscott decided *NOT* to send the 179th Regiment (45th Division) over to Montélimar, even though it was closer, but to send it up to Grenoble where it would relieve the 143rd Regiment, which would in turn then come back southwest to the battle area. This caused logistical strains, but had the advantage of enabling the Texas Division to fight together as one unit.

12

Montélimar and Valence

When General Truscott ordered Adams' two battalions to join the rest of the 36th Division, a new attack possibility opened up. The shortest route from Grenoble follows the Isère Valley to the Rhône, and then joins N7 at Valence. Valence, the administrative seat of the Drôme Department and a major objective of the politically minded Resistance, also served, because of the Chabeuil airfield nearby, as a major barrier to Truscott's effort to reach Lyon. Dahlquist wondered whether Adams, cooperating with de Lassus, whose FFI controlled the feeder roads to the east, could take Valence from the Germans and place a block across N7.

A few miles northeast of Valence, on the Isère River's northern bank, lies the town of Romans and, on the south bank, Bourg-de-Péage. Another ten miles to the east, in the Vercors foothills, stretches the "Royans" area where Commandant Geyer (THIVOLLET) had reassembled his 11th Cuirassiers Resistance fighters after the Vercors debacle. From the time of the landings, Geyer had led his forces to several hit-and-run attacks along Route 7. He was now ostensibly under the orders of de Lassus, not Huet, but acted pretty much independently. On the 22nd at his own initiative, attacking Romans with his own and other groups, he was able after some sharp fighting to occupy the town and take over 100 prisoners. This was the same day that the Germans, having evacuated Grenoble the night before, made it possible for Colonel Adams, commanding the 143rd infantry, to move in. Adams sent out patrols from Grenoble, one of which took the road toward St.-Marcellin, fifteen miles from Romans. There was here a vivid possibility: If the Germans had evacuated Grenoble and Romans, might they not be leaving Valence? If Adams' two battalions were ordered to move southwest, might they not join Geyer's and de Lassus' guerrillas in an operation against the Drôme Department's prefectural seat? Such an operation definitely had an attraction for Dahlquist, who wanted to bring all of his division into a concerted move against the Rhône highway.

The plan also appealed to de Lassus and to Colonel Constans, who had accompanied Butler into the combat area and had established his command post at Dieulefit, about fifteen miles from Butler at Marsanne and de Lassus at Vachères. De Lassus drove down to confer with Constans on the 22nd, reporting on the general situation, especially on the anticipated arrival of the American 36th Division into the battle area.

When de Lassus returned to his CP, he learned that FTP leaders, irked that Geyer had occupied Romans without consulting them, had undertaken an attack by 350 *maquisards* on Valence. The Germans had *not* withdrawn from Valence and indeed considered it a key defensive point in their retreat. They repelled the FTP units with artillery and machine-gun fire, killing fifteen and destroying most of their trucks. Butler had reviewed a French report of the 22nd that approximately eight batteries of 88- or 105-mm. antiaircraft guns were protecting the Chabeuil airfield southeast of Valence.[1]

Dahlquist nevertheless thought that Valence could be taken. On August 23, Adams' battalions, relieved by Colonel Meyers' 179th, withdrew from Grenoble and assembled at Bourg-de-Péage, the southern half of Romans. At the same time, Patch sent a Seventh Army operations officer, Col. Clyde E. Steele, to Romans for an interrogation of Geyer's prisoners. While Dahlquist was settling into his new CP south of Crest, Steele, guided by de Lassus, drove up to Romans along the back roads, which wind along the foothill plateau between the Vercors and the plain. De Lassus recalled the mission:

> Wishing to have information from the prisoners taken at Romans, he took me in his jeep by way of Léoncel and Saint-Jean. We did not find Commandant Thivollet [Geyer] there, but left orders to bring all the prisoners next day. Our arrival at Romans caused a fleeting fear, as the citizens did not recognize American uniforms or vehicles, but once we were recognized, an indescribable enthusiasm overtook the town; we could hardly get away.
>
> Passing through Saint-Jean on the return, Colonel Steele gave a speech before the war memorial to the assembled populace: through an interpreter he proclaimed with eloquence that the successors of La Fayette had come to liberate the French people.[2]

On the following day, August 24, General Truscott flew in to the Montélimar battle zone for a conference with Dahlquist, who was still smarting from being dressed down for his alleged slowness in bringing his division to the Rhône. According to Truscott's diary:

CG and Wilson [Capt. James M. Wilson, Truscott's aide] off by Cub to Marsanne, 36th CP and long conference with Gens Dahlquist, Stack, Butler, Col. Vincent, Lt. Col. Slayden. They raked over coals, but now water under bridge. Dahlquist confident of holding position and blocking escape this side of Rhône. CG not so much so. Half-hearted O.K. to taking Valence if feasible. T F Butler is to be assembled in reserve prepared to move out if possible to N. 36th mission same, to be prepared for possible push S. 157th possibly to Die.

With Truscott's unenthusiastic approval, Dahlquist then authorized Colonel Adams, who only reached Romans/Bourg-de-Péage at noon on the 24th, to carry out an attack, together with the FFI, against Valence. By this time, the Germans had withdrawn from Chabeuil, which became the command post for Adams and Colonel Steele, along with Constans and de Lassus.[3]

There were some besides Truscott who had misgivings. The FFI had agents inside Valence, and possessed solid information concerning the German tanks and artillery defending the city. When the Pons company learned of the impending operations, Lieutenant Armand, who had recently verified the German dispositions, sent a message to Pons:

I do not understand why, with the Intelligence I have given, one is going to attempt such an attack, for no artillery piece which I have identified and marked on the map has been moved. I am sure we won't succeed, but I am going with the American tanks.[4]

Another FFI officer in this area also thought that better use of Adams' force could be made. This was Commandant NOIR, sole remaining member of Jed VEGANINE, now commanding ten companies scattered throughout the northern part of the Drôme Department. On August 23, de Lassus had ordered him to follow up Guyer's capture of Romans by taking Tain l'Hermitage, where a gorge formation would permit artillery, if posted on the heights, to make passage along N7 virtually impossible. When Adams came to Romans, NOIR talked to him:

I asked him if he could not come near the banks of the Rhône, and he replied that he had his orders and that he was going to attack Valence. I made the point that it was perhaps not very useful to take Valence, Tain, or any other town on N7, that the Germans would certainly use sufficient strength to force the passage, but that it would be extremely useful to have a few ambush tanks, hull down amongst the hills on the banks firing down N7 and that he would then produce quite different results than with our small arms, and compel the Germans to use minor roads.

Had the Americans held on to Romans, they could have inflicted heavy damage to the Germans as they retreated through the gorge at Tain. In postwar questioning, General Blaskowitz affirmed that he considered failure to do this one of Truscott's major errors.[5]

There was no time to make any changes, and the order to attack Valence remained firm. Learning that Colonel Adams had come to Romans, de Lassus drove there in his blue Buick, and worked out plans during the late afternoon and during the evening meal, which the two commanders shared. Adams agreed to schedule the attack for 10 P.M. which would give de Lassus time to drive to the various FFI company headquarters and give instructions.

The FFI commander planned to move on Valence from the northeast (down the Bourg–St.-Marcel road), from the southeast (starting at Montmeyran), and from the east—the most powerful thrust westward from Chabeuil. In the north, de Lassus assigned four companies (Morin, Sabatier, Chrétien, and Sanglier) that would be supported by two tank destroyers and a Sherman tank. Adams would provide a platoon of riflemen and an interpreter who would rendezvous with the FFI at St.-Marcel. In the south, de Lassus arranged for seven companies under the overall command of Commandant Benezech (ANTOINE) (Roger, Pierre, Wap, Chapoutat, Bentrup, Pons, and Pequiniot [just back from Grenoble]). With them, assembling at Montmeyran, would go two tank destroyers. From Chabeuil, Adams would send Frazior's 1st Battalion in the lead with Andrews' 3rd Battalion one thousand yards behind, supported by tanks, tank destroyers, and field artillery. With this group, de Lassus assigned two companies, Perrin and Kirsch.

The Kirsch company was the group with which OG ALICE, led by Lieutenants Barnard and Meeks, had been operating. (On August 18, a dozen men from the Kirsch and ALICE groups had made a daring raid into Montmeyran, where six German trucks and fifty men had parked. In hard fighting, they destroyed four of the trucks and a command car. As a result, the Germans abandoned Montmeyran to the FFI and did not return.) ALICE did not, however, participate in the Valence attack on August 24. When Task Force Butler entered the area on the 22nd, the group was recalled and, after a few days' rest in Crest, moved on to the area between Grenoble and Lyon.[6]

Colonel Adams established his CP at Chabeuil around 7 P.M. and undertook to obtain confirmation of his orders, since he had received a message from General Dahlquist to be prepared to move on Crest at short notice. He shortly obtained a confirmation: "Seize Valence today. Get assistance from Maquis."

Dahlquist had reason to be apprehensive. He knew that his operations order for August 25 had been captured, and he believed that the Germans, possibly the 198th Division and elements of the 11th Panzer, were assembling for a major attack. The general realized that his southern defense along the Roubion River would be especially weak, since Truscott had ordered the 117th Cavalry's Troop A out of the line for patrol duty on the Italian frontier. Troop B would have to protect this area until Lynch's 142nd Regiment, coming up from Nyons, replaced the motorized cavalrymen. Dahlquist concluded that, needing all the force he could muster, the fighting in the Montélimar area took priority over Valence. At 8:30 P.M., before Adams had deployed his troops, Dahlquist sent a message to the 143rd's commander: "You must have bulk of your force in Crest by daylight 25 Aug. 1944." With Valence about twenty miles from Crest, Adams would have to get his battalions moving before dawn, and he personally would have to leave earlier.

A ware that he might have to break off the attack, Adams nevertheless started moving the 1st Battalion around 10 P.M. according to the plan. De Lassus, with Adams and Constans at the Chabeuil CP, could communicate with his FFI companies via the American radios. How the attack progressed is here described by Stephen Weiss, then an eighteen-year-old private, who went in with the first units:

> We moved cautiously down this road with tank destroyers strung out in a line like beads, keeping a proper interval. In the vicinity of the airfield, we were fired upon by Germans using rifles and machine guns. One American was killed instantly.
>
> We sought cover in the ditches, and then, supported by the tank destroyers, we attacked the enemy's firing positions. . . .
>
> Moments later I manned a machine gun atop one of the tank destroyers, but I missed hitting two Germans fleeing across the flat farmland.

The infantrymen re-formed in the cover of night, working their way along the road covered by the tank destroyers, which in the darkness Weiss could hear

> moving noisily down the road, eliminating any chance of surprising the enemy.
>
> When the Germans heard the tank destroyers, they let loose with a salvo of automatic and self-propelled weapons. Three of the tank destroyers were hit immediately, began to burn, then explode. Tree and shell fragments resulted in heavy casualties.
>
> Out in the field, . . . eight of us moved slowly towards the enemy, watching their gun crews firing, silhouetted by their own gun flashes.
>
> A flare burst above us and all became greenish daylight. We stopped and waited, slowly sinking into the ground. Machine guns blazed at us, pinning us down but hitting no one. We knew we could go no further. At

the same time, the company and few remaining tank destroyers pulled back, sealing our fate in the open field.

Since it was now about midnight, Adams knew he could not continue the assault and still bring the bulk of his two battalions to Crest by dawn. He gave the order to withdraw. (Weiss and his companions were able to escape capture and had the good fortune to find shelter with friendly French citizens. After several days of hiding, taken in charge by Resistance members, they rowed across the Rhône and joined the forces of Colonel Binoche, FFI chief in that part of the Ardèche Department. Later they were attached to an OG operating south of Lyon.)[7]

Back at the Chabeuil command post, Constans and de Lassus were justifiably upset at Adams' refusal to continue the attack. Adams explained his orders and agreed that they could call General Dahlquist to find out if he would rescind them. Dahlquist, reached by radio in a few minutes, agreed that Adams could leave some tanks and artillery to cover the withdrawal, but insisted that Adams continue his move south.[8]

THE MAIN BATTLE

Dahlquist was finding that the Germans not only protected their retreat, but were in a position to attack. On August 25, having captured the American operational order, General Wiese planned a thrust across the Roubion River. Traffic to the north had been virtually stopped as the Nineteenth Army massed for a three-pronged offensive: one, across the Roubion near Cléon where, with Task Force Butler having been withdrawn, a weak corridor would exist until the arrival of Lynch's 142nd Regiment from Nyons; two, thrusts north of Montélimar to dislodge the American forces holding the hills south and west of Condillac; three, an attack eastward from Loriol along the Drôme River toward Allex and Grane, ultimately to Crest. By this time, the full strength of the German 198th Division and Von Wietersheim's 11th Panzer Division, with the 305th Division not far behind, could be thrown against the Americans, who with one division (plus artillery) and a 250-mile supply line were defending three sides of a square with 15-mile edges. General Dahlquist was hard-pressed. He wrote his wife, "Strenuous fighting never developed except in small spots but one afternoon I was fighting on three sides which kind of kept me hopping."[9]

During the afternoon of the 25th, the Germans pushed across the Roubion well up into the Marsanne Plain, but were stopped by Frazior's battalion, which had withdrawn from Valence. The main German attacks by *Kampfgruppe HAX* and *Kampfgruppe WILDE* toward Sauzet and Condillac had the Americans reeling back from their hill positions, but the Germans were not strong enough to press their advantage and clear Dahlquist's men from the Marsanne forest.

Thus far, the Resistance forces had stuck by the Americans even though their arms could not compare with those of the Americans. On the 24th, a service platoon of the Secret Army's 14th company had crossed the Rhône to try to destroy the road on the far side of the river. An FFI officer, Lieutenant Gerard, was taken prisoner but managed to escape, bringing with him information about German artillery emplacements.

August 25 was a grim day for the FFI as well as for the Americans. At the request of the U.S. commanders, the 13th company withdrew to provide protection for the artillery batteries. Lieutenant Apostol's 14th company, having pulled back to a small village in the Marsanne forest, was surprised by a German patrol and lost two men. Later in the day, Commandant Bernard's entire 4th Battalion withdrew eastward for twenty-four hours of much-needed rest.

In the north, from Livron and Loriol, *Kampfgruppe THIEME* launched a thrust with 100 vehicles and tanks toward Allex and Grane. Dahlquist called up Task Force Butler, which had been held in reserve near Puy-St.-Martin, to rush toward Grane, on the south bank of the Drôme. Here Capt. Omer Brown, who had commanded the 117th Cavalry's assault guns at Gap, was killed while trying to insert a grenade into a German tank. On the northern bank of the Drôme, Dahlquist now controlled elements of the 45th Division's 157th Regiment, sent over to hold Crest at all costs. Even then, the German threat forced a rerouting of American supply trucks.

The German offensive continued through the 26th until the 27th when the American lines were restored. In the north, Grane and Allex were retaken as well as the hills along the Rhône; in the south, the Germans had been forced back across the Roubion. The situation had been desperate but not hopeless. On the 26th, Truscott had flown in to Dahlquist's CP south of Crest for a "heart-to-heart" talk prior to Patch's arrival for lunch. Truscott had been prepared to relieve Dahlquist of his command for failing to place an effective road-block across N7. Considering the heavy German attacks, Dahlquist believed he had done as well as could be expected. Although Truscott "did not fully concur," he decided to leave Dahlquist in command.[10]

While the German offensive on August 25-26 failed in opening up an alternate escape route across the Marsanne Plain, it succeeded in its major objective: enabling the 11th Panzer Division to cross the Drôme and forge ahead toward Lyon. Although the vehicular bridge at Livron could not be used, German engineers had fashioned four or five fords that enabled the bulk of the

Panzers to cross. Late on the 26th, torrential rains poured across the battle area resulting in floods, which made the fords unusable for several days. By that time, however, although losses in trucks, cars, mobile artillery, and railroad guns were enormous, most of the Nineteenth Army's troops, and notably the 11th Panzer Division, had escaped the trap and were stretched out on roads beyond Lyon, headed for reorganization along the Rhine.

By August 27, elements of the German 198th Division were fighting rear guard actions around Montélimar, which had now been reached by reconnaissance patrols of General O'Daniel's 3rd Division, pressing up the Rhône Valley from the south. With the Drôme River flooded, the Germans desperately tried to keep N7, where hundreds of motionless vehicles had piled up, from falling under Allied control. Task Force Butler units had reinforced the 36th Division at La Coucourde, where road-blocks were finally thrown across the road and a high-ranking German officer, General Richter, was captured.

Nevertheless, although the Germans had been pushed back across the Roubion, they still held some five miles of ground east of Montélimar on the road leading to Dieulefit. Fighting side by side with elements of Lynch's 142nd Regiment, Jean Abonnenc's FFI 11th company (3rd Battalion) pressed an attack against the perimeter of the German's defensive circle. Abonnenc recalled that, at the moment of giving the order for his guerrillas to advance, an American officer advised him, "Let us do it, pull your company back." Several minutes later, American artillery began firing and destroyed the enemy position.

On the 28th, the 3rd Division occupied Montélimar and from the east poured in the tired guerrilla companies of Bernard's 4th Battalion, Noël's 3rd Battalion, and Girard's FTP regiments, to be met by enthusiastic citizens who, for the first time in weeks, could open their shutters and breathe the heady air of freedom. On September 3, the Resistance forces paraded triumphantly through the city, reviewed by de Lassus and Constans, who awarded decorations and gave due recognition to the commanders.[11]

With the German withdrawal from Montélimar on August 28, the crucial situation lay at Livron and Loriol, where the final German units might be prevented by the Allies from crossing the Drôme. General Wiese, commanding the Nineteenth Army, decided that the 11th Panzer rear guard should hold a ring around the strategic towns until noon of the 29th, while all remaining units would form into small combat groups and get out as best they could.

At the same time, Dahlquist brought everything at his disposal to attack the Livron–Loriol passage. North of the Drôme, he had two battalions of the 157th Regiment (assigned to him from the 45th Division) attacking from Allex toward Livron, and south of the river he brought in the 157th's 3rd Battalion together with elements of Task Force Butler and all the 36th Division regiments.

In spite of this massive assemblage of fire power, the Germans managed to hold the Allied forces at bay long enough to get sizeable numbers of personnel—if not equipment—across the Drôme. By the evening of August 29, the battle that had been waged in the area between Montélimar and the Drôme River was over.

Although the Germans had given up hopes of defending areas south of the Drôme River, they were not by any means defeated. They may have lost over 2,000 vehicles and over 300 pieces of artillery, but by August 30, as they fought rear guard actions south of Valence, General Blaskowitz' Army Group, which still counted 130,000 men, including the almost intact 11th Panzer Division, was digging in around Lyon, with retreating troops stretched over one hundred miles. Advance units had passed Bourg-en-Bresse and were heading for Mâcon. To safeguard the retreat, the 11th Panzer was attempting to hold flank positions about 10–15 miles east of N7.[12]

VALENCE AGAIN

With the Germans withdrawing north, de Lassus planned again to liberate Valence. For the Resistance in the Drôme Department, occupation of the prefectural seat had prime importance: The Committee of Liberation could take over, and the Resistance prefect, Pierre de Saint-Prix, already chosen, would replace the Vichy appointee. For the Americans, however, Valence had lost its strategic significance. If Truscott moved more troops over to N7, they would be closing a trap on only rear guard elements; what the VI Corps commander wanted was for Dahlquist to push his division past Valence, retake Romans, and threaten Lyon. However, by this time, Truscott hoped that the 45th Division, much farther north, would be able to cut across the German retreat. On August 30, elements of Eagles' division were already at Meximieux, northeast of Lyon, skirmishing with tanks of the 11th Panzer.

De Lassus therefore did not plan his attack this time in coordination with the Americans, although he remained in touch with Colonel Steele, who since August 24 had succeeded the wounded Colonel Harmony as commanding officer of the 141st Infantry. De Lassus organized his companies much as he had during the fruitless effort six days earlier, and began moving into Valence about 4 A.M. on August 31. Colonel Steele also sent a reconnaissance company under Major Morrison, with two tank destroyers, into the town, but the patrol was not coordinated with the FFI. It did, however, help de Lassus in a mopping up the operation where a few hundred Germans made a final stand in the park. Resistance ended around noon, with about 600 Germans in FFI custody.[13]

Colonel Steele visited the town briefly in the afternoon of August 31, but he was mostly concerned with pushing his own regiment on to Romans and Beaurepaire, and with ensuring that the 143rd Regiment, now across the Drôme and following the 141st, could move north on N7, right through Valence.

De Lassus, along with Colonel Constans (whose command extended only to the Isère River), kept occupied with liberation celebrations throughout the department and with military reorganization. The celebrations at Montélimar have already been mentioned. It is only appropriate that the final words on Valence should be those of de Lassus:[14]

On 4 September I knew that Lyon had been liberated. As soon as possible I sent a car for my wife, a refugee for six months north of Lyon. . . .

Late in the morning there was a military review in Valence to celebrate the anniversary of the Republic. My troops were fine and made a great impression.

A big dinner ended the day at the Hotel de la Croix d'Or. My wife had just arrived. . . . No one knew her in Valence.

But during the night, as she was exhausted by the car journey, I had to take her to the hospital. . . .

Next day I placed an announcement in the press: "Lt. Col. Legrand, chief of FFI in the Drôme Department, takes pleasure in announcing the birth, on 5 September 1944, of a daughter: Dominique de Lassus Saint-Geniès."

There was general surprise. . . .

This anecdote will complete my memoirs.

On the same day that Valence was liberated, the Germans abandoned St.-Vallier. The curé described the situation:

Night of 30/31 Aug. A terrible storm. But continually the roar of motors, horns sounding, cries of riders, and especially of men on foot, exhausted, soaked through, imploring the vehicles for a lift.

The FFI open fire on the battery and on the columns. Dead and wounded. . . . Officers try to find the mayor; knocking on various doors, they finally find M. Grenier at his mother's house. Rain, thunder. The Germans screaming: "The Mayor—hostages, hostages!" Anguishing minutes. By the time he comes down, they demand 15 hostages tomorrow at 0800 and tell him to stop the FFI fire or they'll burn down the village. The mayor tries to find the FFI, but they have left during the storm.

31 Aug. at dawn, the mayor tells everyone left in St.-Vallier to evacuate, and at 0800 he goes down to the German HQ to offer himself as hostage in place of the fifteen.

As luck would have it, the HQ is empty—German officers have left. But before they left, they mined the bridges. The one over the Rhône blew up at 1140.

The mayor and the curé walk thru the deserted town, debris everywhere, stacks of German equipment; only a few Germans now passing—bare feet, tired, pitiable. They abandon their arms, but pillage anything of value they can find.

With the liberation of Valence, the Drôme Department officials began the work of rehabilitation. However, the pursuit of the Germans continued, to the north toward Lyon, east toward the Alps, and west, across the Rhône, in the Ardèche Department.

Francis Cammaerts (ROGER), SOE's
F Section agent in southeastern France

Paul Héraud (DUMONT), FFI chief in
Hautes-Alpes

Lt. Henry McIntosh, of Jedburgh CHLOROFORM, entering Jap on August 2,
1944, with local *maquisards*, before the Allied landings.

Havard Gunn (BAMBUS), British Liaison Officer, in 1985, in front of one of his paintings of St.-Tropez

Brooks Richards, French Country Section head in SPOC

Geoffrey Jones, OSS officer with SPOC, who joined Frederick's First Airborne Task Force

Jean Constans (SAINT-SAUVEUR), French representative at SPOC who became FFI Chief, in R-2

Conference of three generals: Left to right, Lucian Truscott, VI Corps; Alexander Patch, Seventh Army; and Jacob Devers, Deputy Commander, Mediterranean Theatre. National Archives 111-SC-196331

Shortly after the landings, General Patch reviews FFI troops at Saint-Tropez. National Archives 111-SC-193191

Jacques Lécuyer (SAPIN), ORA Chief in R-2, FFI Departmental Chief in Alpes-Maritimes

Alain Le Ray (BASTIDE), FFI Chief, Isère

The author (left) with Etienne Moreaud (DUMAS), who succeeded Héraud as FFI Chief in Hautes-Alpes. Photo taken in 1984

Lt. André Pecquet (also known as Paray), OSS. Photo taken after he had lost weight during his ordeal in the Vercors.

Henri Zeller (FAISCEAU), FFI Chief, Southeastern France

Drouot (L'HERMINE), FFI Chief, Central Alps.

J.-P. de Lassus St.-Geniès, FFI Chief, Drôme

Marc Rainaud, leader of the *Brigade des Maures*, is decorated by General Patch, August 17, 1944. National Archives 111-SC-193192

General de Lattre de Tassigny, commanding the French First Army, with Alban Vistel, FFI Chief in R-1

John Roper, British Liaison Officer (center), with Gilbert Galetti to his left, with *maquisards* in the Queyras

Destruction on Route N7 after the Battle of Montélimar (August 22-31, 1944). National Archives 111-SC-194368

Captain Thomas Piddington, commander of Troop A, 117th Cavalry Reconnaissance Squadron

Brigadier General Frederic B. Butler, Commander of Task Force Butler. National Archives 111-SC-203996

Jean Constans's false identity card

Livron bridge, spanning the Drôme River between Livron and Loriol, blown August 17, 1944, by Henri Faure and a group of *maquisards*, causing a bottleneck for German Nineteenth Army retreating up Route N7

III The Flanks

13

East: The Dauphiné Alps

Patch, Truscott, and the ANVIL planners had never been too much concerned with the threat of a German attack across the Alps from Italy. From intelligence, they knew that two divisions, the 148th headquartered at Nice and the 157th Reserve Division at Grenoble, might provide some opposition, but they knew that these divisions, without much heavy armor, would be at first confronted by Frederick's Airborne and by the 36th Division, landing farthest to the east.

From his experience with the mountain fighting in Italy, Truscott could well assess the problems the Germans would face in sending reinforcements through the southernmost passes, the Tende, the Larche, and the Montgenèvre. Not only were there formidable gorges and hairpin curves in the French Alps, but on the Italian side, assuming forces were based logistically on Cuneo or Pinerolo, there still remained many miles of mountain roads before reaching the passes.[1]

It did not seem logical or likely, in the early part of the ANVIL campaign, that the Germans would rely on other resources than the two divisions already in place. A Seventh Army intelligence officer commented:

> We were told by the G-2 of the Army several weeks before the invasion that there was no need to put men on the Italian border. As a result, we placed all our agents in other localities. We regretted this later when it became apparent that the situation on that border was dangerous and when we found we had no one covering the strategic points.[2]

To be sure, SPOC, not SSS, had agents in the area—half a dozen British Liaison Officers, several Jedburghs, and an OG—but these were "operations," not primarily gatherers of intelligence. Nevertheless, it is clear enough that neither Patch nor Truscott believed it would be necessary to make an offensive move toward the passes as long as reconnaissance patrols and air observation failed to report evidence of a threatening enemy move. This meant that, except for small scouting expeditions, the Seventh Army was content until regular French troops would come in to leave the Alpine passes to SPOC and the French Resistance.

SPOC had long since included Alpine operations in its plans, especially with Operation TOPLINK and the dispatch of the British officers. There were schedules to send even more agents into the Alps, where they would operate under the general supervision of Francis Cammaerts. Up until August 13, the date that Cammaerts, along with Fielding and Sorenson, fell into Gestapo hands at Digne, SPOC had already placed in the Alpine area two Jedburgh teams and half a dozen British agents. On the day of the ANVIL/DRAGOON landings (while Cammaerts remained in prison), these missions were deployed as follows:

The Jedburghs: CHLOROFORM (McIntosh, Martin, Sassi) had just destroyed the bridge over the Durance River at Savines, and had returned to L'HERMINE's headquarters in the Champoléon Valley northeast of Gap. NOVOCAINE (Gennerich, LeLann, Thompson) had carried out a similar mission, blowing up a bridge at Prelles, south of Briançon, after which they returned to their camp at Vallouise.

The British Liaison Officers: Of the TOPLINK group, Hamilton, injured in an accident, was hospitalized at Aiguilles, while his colleague O'Regan, keeping in touch with Gilbert Galetti in the Queyras, patrolled on the Italian side of the frontier.

Major Purvis and John Roper maintained their CP at Vallouise, in contact with Maquis in the area. John Halsey remained near the Larche pass, with his headquarters near Barcelonnette. He kept in touch with Captain Bureau, commander of the FFI, and also with Christine Granville, who at the time of the landings was doing her utmost to get Cammaerts released. Havard Gunn, working with Lécuyer from their CP at Valberg, had been the first to make contact with Allied troops shortly after the first wave of paratroopers came in.

Cammaerts, imprisoned at Digne from August 13–17, had missed the excitement that followed as news of Allied landings spread to the north. On his return to his headquarters at Seyne, he found that several missions had already arrived and needed instructions. The first to come in were a Jedburgh team, EPHEDRINE, and an inter-allied mission, both of which had orders to go north.

EPHEDRINE was led by the French Capt. L. Rabeau, whose teammate was an American, Lt. Lawrence E. Swank of Washington, D.C., "Larry" to his friends McIntosh, Gennerich, and Bank with whom he had trained in the States and at Milton Hall. The radio operator was French: Corporal J. Bourgoin.[3]

Map 13.1

THE DAUPHINÉ ALPS

Larche, Montgenèvre, and Mont-Cenis Passes to Italy

Shortly after they landed, a few miles west of Seyne in the small hours of August 13, another group from Algiers, the PROGRESSION mission (a continuation of UNION), an Englishman and a Canadian together with five French officers, were parachuted to the Drop Zone. The British officers were Maj. D. E. F. Green and Canadian Maj. C. B. Hunter, whose objective was to get to the Savoie Department, many rugged mountainous miles to the north. Along with the personnel came over fifty containers. The landscape was strewn with unopened cylinders that needed to be stored, together with the broken contents of others that were poorly packed or whose parachutes failed. The reception committee had not been prepared for either the number of men or the number of containers.[4]

Late in the afternoon of the 13th, having learned that Cammaerts had been arrested, the entire group—Green and Hunter, the three Jeds, and the five Frenchmen—decided to move toward Barcelonnette and the Larche pass, but having run into Christine the next morning, they decided on her advice to join those groups already in Vallouise. While Christine embarked on her efforts to get Cammaerts released, the ten men, in a charcoal-burning truck, turned north from Barcelonnette, and started up the road toward Guillestre.

About 9 P.M., near St.-Paul, a tragic accident occurred. One of the French instructors, Lieutenant Hook, had left his loaded gun stacked in the trunk and a sharp turn caused the rifle to discharge. The bullet struck Swank, who died several hours later. He was buried in the local St.-Paul cemetery on August 15—D Day—while the ANVIL forces began their landings many miles to the south. Three days later, the remaining men reached Vallouise, and joined forces with Roper, Purvis, Gennerich, and the other contingents keeping an eye on the Montgenèvre pass.

Among these contingents in the area were the fifteen American paratroopers of OG NANCY, led by Captain Arnold Lorbeer and 1st. Lt. William F. Viviani, who had been dropped the same night as Swank's EPHEDRINE. Although NANCY, as an Italian-speaking group, had been assigned to operate at the Montgenèvre pass, the section was dropped at Armature, the area at Lagarde where Constans had the day before conferred with Cammaerts. Armature was too rocky for personnel drops and over 200 miles from the Italian border, but the group suffered only minor injuries and camped out in the area along with the airmen stranded when the rescuing Dakota had to leave them behind.

The question posed itself: How was NANCY to get from Lagarde to the Montgenèvre pass? The official report best describes this effort:

After a little haggling with the local Maquis, we obtained a good-sized wood-burning truck with three guides. Our sleeping bags and ruck sacks were used to line the sides of the truck, and then men were crowded in the center prepared to fire through cracks. A tarpaulin was placed over the truck and we departed that night [14 August]. 15 August—It was a highly uncomfortable, but at the same time exciting 250 mile trip. At first flat tires and lost guides jinxed us, but the truck continued on, often along main roads under the noses of German patrols and garrisons, without being stopped. At Sisteron, our guides bribed the local gendarmes to let us cross the Durance river. From there to Guillestre it became a parade of wine and roses. It was D-Day, and the radio was calling upon southern France to rise and oust the Germans. The spectacle of 15 Americans traveling this far north a few hours after the invasion of southern France created a tremendous impression.

At Seyne, we unexpectedly contacted Christine, famous secret agent. The stories of her womanly charms had not been exaggerated. At Guillestre we met Lt. Volpe [radio operator] of the Anglo-American mission.

Lorbeer and his men did not go to Vallouise, where the other groups watching the Montgenèvre pass were camped. Instead, he took a road east of the main highway to Briançon, and established a command post at Cervières, set in the mountains just south of the Montgenèvre pass, about ten miles east of Vallouise.[5]

While the British, American, and French agents in the field knew that the invasion was imminent, none of them knew the date or place of the landings. The increased bombing raids provided some indication, but more specific were the warning messages that gave notice of action to follow. For example, on the day of the landing, SPOC ordered the Alpine area:[6]

This is the plan for cutting the roads and principal Alpine passes which are: Mont-Cenis, Montgenèvre, Col de Larche, Petit Saint-Bernard—STOP— Following phrase will indicate temporary obstruction in 24 hours: "Le Vésuve fume" [Vesuvius is smoking]—STOP—Following phrase will indicate destruction prolonged blocking and must be carried out in 48 hours: "Voir Naples et Mourir" [See Naples and die].

On the next day, August 16, not only was the "Naples" message broadcast over the BBC, but SPOC dispatched a specific exhortation: "Operation Col de Larche being primordial, I agree on its rapid execution—STOP—Let us however take all measures to protect the civilian population from reprisals."

In carrying out these orders, Commandant Bureau worked closely with John Halsey and Fernandez, who had been in the Barcelonnette area for over a week, surveying the region and, with their limited supplies of explosives, destroying bridges and roads. Together they had agreed on a demolition plan that, on August 14, ruptured the road to Larche just south of Meyronnes. In the town of Larche (which lies some four miles below the pass at the frontier), there was a small German garrison of 150, of whom about a third were Poles whose hostile attitude toward their German superiors paralleled that of the Resistance. Around August 12 or 13, Christine Granville had gone up to Larche with a *gendarme* to persuade the Poles that, when the time was right, they should sabotage the military installations and join the FFI.[7]

Two developments precipitated action: the Allied landings on the 15th and the decision of the German commander to force the citizens of Meyronnes to repair the road. When work on the road began, Halsey, Commandant Bureau, and the *sous-préfet* Jean-Pierre Cuin, after some deliberation, mustered about 50 *maquisards* to threaten the Germans in charge of the work crews. Shots were fired; a German soldier was wounded.

The German commander faced an impasse: Half his garrison was mutinous; the Resistance had cut his communications to higher command; he had no assurance that reinforcements would come from Italy; he needed a doctor for his wounded soldier. Faced with an ultimatum, he agreed to confer, but only with regular officers, not with the FFI. All parties concurred that they would meet at Meyronnes in the evening of August 19—about the same time that the garrison in nearby Digne was surrendering to Task Force Butler. To this meeting proceeded a firm Allied front: Roper, Fernandez, and *sous-préfet* Cuin in uniform, together with one of Lécuyer's men, Bob Ceccaldi, who for the occasion donned the uniform of a Chasseurs Alpins Captain. John Halsey reported what happened:

> After an hour's talking the German commander refused to surrender so I suggested very forcibly that I, Rudolph [Fernandez] and Bob should dine at Larche as the enemy had plenty of food there. To my surprise the German commander agreed, and we went up by bike. After the meal the commander assembled practically the whole garrison in the hotel and we argued. . . . The Poles deserted with all their arms, and at 0230 hours the German commander accepted my terms and I took him away with his dog which I have kept to this day.

Before they deserted, the fifty-odd Poles, as admonished by Christine, had removed the breech-blocks from the heavy guns, bringing with them some mortars and machine guns. They were incorporated into Bureau's FFI as a heavy-machine-gun company, and fought with the French *maquisards* in their attempt to keep Larche from being reoccupied.[8]

With news of the Allied landing, Bureau's companies increased in number, and he was able to deploy his men in small groups along the road from Meyronnes up to the Larche pass. The Germans still occupied the pass, and began to move in troops and artillery, which they mounted on the ridges overlooking the Ubaye Valley. Bureau did what he could to prevent the reoccupation of Larche and Meyronnes, but he had only meager supplies of guns and ammunition. He had not obtained any materials from Algiers and, while he knew that Allied troops had liberated Digne and Gap, he had received no assurance that an American relief column would be coming to help. John Halsey alone provided a slender link with the Allies.

While Halsey negotiated the surrender of the small German garrison at Larche, John Roper was playing a similar role at Mont-Dauphin.[9] After seeing Butler at Sisteron with the Hautes-Alpes Resistance chiefs, early in the morning of August 20, he and Gilbert Tavernier, on their overworked motorcycle, rode beyond Gap up the road to Guillestre. Just beyond Embrun, they met Gilbert Galetti together with Lieutenant Braillon of the FFI and a German interpreter. As Roper recalled:

> I accompanied these two French officers to Fort Mont Dauphin where we had an interview with the garrison commander who agreed to surrender the next day, which he did. Major Purvis came down for the ceremony on 21st August.

As in all these instances, the Germans, numbering eighty-six, wished to surrender only to authentic Allied officers, not to the Maquis chiefs. Roper insisted that the German officer in charge surrender to the French, and after some hesitation, he agreed to do so. For the surrender of the garrison, not only did Purvis make an appearance, but also Captain Lorbeer with some of his men from OG NANCY. Lorbeer reported:

> The terms were simple. The prisoners were permitted to take all personal belongings and were moved to Chateau Queyras, later to be gathered in by Allied troops. Weapons were left to the Maquis. Except for the officers, the garrison consisted of old customs officials in ill-fitting army uniforms, and they left no doubt about their contentment at this turn of events. It was a Hollywood scene with general handshaking, flag-raising, and conducted tours of the spacious German quarters.[10]

Several days earlier, Lorbeer's group had withdrawn from their camp south of Briançon and, on Major Purvis' advice, were now bivouacked at one of Galetti's posts, the chalets above Bramousse about halfway between Guillestre and Château-Queyras. From this camp, they patrolled down the road that

Germans would have to mount if they came over the Larche pass in force. Although Gap had now been liberated and American road-blocks set up, no evidence had reached the embattled FFI in the high Alps that Allied reinforcements were on the way.

THE AMERICANS AND THE FFI AT LARCHE AND BRIANÇON

While Colonel Adams' 143rd Infantry moved into Grenoble on the 22nd, Col. George E. Lynch's 142nd had assembled in the Gap area. (The remaining regiment of Dahlquist's 36th Division, the 141st, had struck westward to reinforce Task Force Butler.)

Lynch, understanding that he should patrol north and west of Gap, sent elements of his 2nd Battalion, under Lt. Col. David P. Faulkner, east to Embrun. It was there, early on the 22nd, that the regular military forces began to meet up with the irregulars—Gennerich (of Jed NOVOCAINE), McIntosh (of Jed CHLOROFORM), Lorbeer (of OG NANCY), Purvis, Roper, Hamilton, and Halsey of the BLO group, and the Maquis. Unfortunately Cammaerts, who would have been the person most competent to coordinate the actions, had been summarily dismissed by General Butler and was on his way to see General Patch at St.-Tropez.[11]

After participating in the surrender ceremony at Mont-Dauphin, John Roper went along the road to Gap with the intention of locating American troops, which he knew had liberated the town. At Embrun he met Colonel Faulkner, who had been ordered to carry out reconnaissance toward the Alps passes. Faulkner's forces included two tank destroyer companies, three antitank batteries, and three infantry companies, including jeeps with machine-gun mounts. Roper rode with them toward Guillestre, where Faulkner established his CP. From Guillestre he sent patrols up toward Briançon and into the Queyras where, guided by Purvis, his men found Major Hamilton at Aiguilles. Hamilton had injured his leg in an automobile accident and was recovering in a hospital. Another patrol under Lieutenant Frank motored south to check on enemy dispositions in the St.-Paul, Meyronnes, and Larche areas.

At 10 A.M. on August 22, orders came through from Dahlquist: "142 Inf will force and take Briançon and establish road blocks in that vicinity." Faulkner was already getting information from Gennerich, Purvis, and Roper, and was testing the roadbeds and bridges to see if his heavy tank destroyers could proceed north.

Then everything came to a halt. Dahlquist had not perceived, as Truscott had, the great opportunity of cutting off the Germans at the Rhône. He had permitted his 141st Regiment to sit idle, he had sent two battalions up to Grenoble, and he was preparing to throw another battalion at Briançon. New to the command of troops in battle and not privy to ULTRA, Dahlquist had given emphasis to his role of protecting the flank. Truscott was furious and wrote him an angry letter:[12]

> Apparently I failed to make my mission clear to you. The primary mission of the 36th Infantry Division is to block the Rhone Valley in the gap immediately north of the Montelimar. For this purpose you must be prepared to employ the bulk of your Division. If this operation develops as seems probable, all of your Division will be none too much in the Rhone Valley area. . . . The elements of your Division now in Grenoble should be moved without delay to the area now occupied by the Butler force. . . . On the roads in the vicinity of Gap and east thereof, I desire that you employ blocking forces only. Keep in mind that your primary mission is to block the Rhone Valley.

By noon of the 22nd, Dahlquist had ordered: "Due to critical shortage of gasoline the use of motor vehicles will be held to an absolute minimum," and two hours later, the mission to take Briançon was called off. By nightfall, orders directed the 142nd Infantry to move west from their current position, although Faulkner's 2nd Battalion would continue at Guillestre until relieved by elements of the 45th Division.

In spite of the limitations on gasoline, Faulkner did his best during the 23rd to push patrols in all directions. Purvis accompanied one to Briançon, where they made contact with another recon that had come over the Lautaret pass from Grenoble. Gennerich's Jedburgh team with 250 *maquisards* moved toward the town, and Captain Frison with over 1000 FFI took up positions in the area. The appearance of the American armored patrols alarmed the Germans, and around noon, they began to withdraw as the Resistance forces swelled. Although the American attack had been called off, Frison and the FFI decided to attack the town—carefully, because although the Germans may have left, they still occupied the forts above the city and controlled the Montgenèvre pass.[13] Purvis reported:

> The reception was terrific. The Germans had left two hours before. They had blown the road at Fort des Salettes with the town water supply on leaving. . . . Found it very difficult to have any defensive units put out toward Montgenevre as Americans had left for Grenoble. Town was in a very natural state of hysteria and those responsible thought more of wreaths on monuments than any possible return of enemy.

CONFESSIONAL [Pelletier, head of the mission] and Captain Frison arrived late evening. While going to Grand Hotel for night, CONFESSIONAL was accidentally shot in shoulder by a boy with a revolver who had been in F.F.I. one hour. This proved serious and he took no further part in the mission.

Faulkner also sent a recon under Lieutenant Frank to the Larche road to verify whether an enemy column was coming over the Larche pass to threaten the FFI defensive positions. In the small hours of August 23, Frank returned to report that indeed the Germans had broken through several road-blocks and were approaching the Ubaye Valley. Faulkner had promised Roper that he would send a mini-task force to Larche, but having received orders that his division was moving west, had to cancel the mission. Nevertheless, as Roper recalled:[14]

Captain Lorbeer . . . and I took a subaltern of Colonel Faulkner's staff down to the Larche valley and as far up it as Meyronnes where, by close reconnaissance and resulting fire, we convinced him of the presence of Germans who had, in fact, advanced through Larche to Meyronnes that afternoon. The local FFI under Captain Bureau of Condamine were in disorderly retreat.

Although the bulk of the 142nd Regiment had already moved west to the Rhône, Faulkner remained in the Guillestre area until he was relieved by elements of the 180th Infantry under Col. Robert L. Dulaney. Roper and Lorbeer continued their reconnaissance with one of Dulaney's officers, Major Smith, and planned countermoves against the German advance.

Farther to the south, at Barcelonnette, John Halsey was equally concerned that, with Bureau's conservative reluctance to face the Germans, no American help had yet come to the rescue. On the night of August 22/23, he drove off to Embrun to see what he could do. Not having come into contact with the helpful and sympathetic Faulkner at Guillestre, he ran into reluctant cooperation. As Halsey reported:[15] "[at Embrun] the Lt. Col. in question was so disinterested that he would not even get out of his bed and more or less said he did not believe that there were any enemy within a hundred miles of his troops." In any case, the division was moving out, so there was no point in trying to get reinforcements. Halsey had better luck with the units that were coming in:

I contacted one of the [45th] Infantry battalion commanders who was most understanding and introduced me to the divisional [sic. Should be regimental] infantry commander Colonel Dulaney, who promised me all his help.

True to his word, Dulaney sent reconnaissance patrols out on the night of August 23 to St.-Paul ("everything quiet"), to Guillestre (contacted Lorbeer's Operational Group at Bramousse), to Condamine ("Halsey talked to the FFI at Larche on the telephone"), and to Briançon (in touch with Purvis). However, at ten o'clock next morning (August 24), everything once more ground to a halt. A command from Division Headquarters read: "All vehicles in the Division in this area except those necessary for water and LOs [Liaison Officers] are grounded. No rations or gasoline will be drawn until the dumps are moved up."

Clearly the requirements of the battle on the Rhône took priority over operations in the eastern Alps. The lower command echelons would not have known what Patch learned through ULTRA. On August 22, a message had notified him: "157 Division . . . ordered to retire to pass line Mt. Blanc-Montgenevre leaving rearguards in regiment strength at Grenoble and sufficient forces to control roads leading from Grenoble to the passes." On the next day, a signal mentioned that the formidable 11th Panzer Division would be in the area of Nyons,[16] the position to which Faulkner had been ordered. The highest priorities kept supplies shuttling to the Rhône; the Alpine passes would have to wait.

Again, Truscott faced an important decision. All of the 3rd and 36th Divisions were now concentrating their efforts on the German retreat up the Rhône. Truscott had two regiments that were relatively unengaged: Colonel Meyer's 179th in Grenoble and Colonel Dulaney's 180th at Gap. Until the battle at Montélimar was resolved, he could not afford to send these regimental combat teams farther north, yet he would require them for the major task of attacking the main German column if it escaped the trap and proceeded toward Lyon. He did not want the 180th to involve itself too much in the Alps, but he needed reconnaissance in the area. Indeed, Truscott was well aware of the embattled FFI effort to harass the Germans. Under date of August 24, he wrote in his memoirs:[17]

> I stopped at Aspres to see Eagles [Commanding General, 45th Division]. . . . Eagles was having his troubles with the Maquis who were active in all the border towns, and badgering Eagles to send American troops to support them.

To relieve some of this pressure, Truscott decided to send part of Task Force Butler over to the Alps. The unit he chose was Captain Piddington's Troop A of the 117th Cavalry Reconnaissance Squadron.

Although Piddington was already heavily engaged in holding a line on the Roubion River northeast of Montélimar, he disengaged on the 24th and back-tracked to Gap, the town he had liberated only four days before. Here he reported to Dulaney, who ordered him to send one platoon to Barcelonnette, while he with the remaining two platoons would patrol from St.-Paul to Briançon.

At the same time, Halsey learned that Dulaney was unable, because of the orders to ground all his vehicles, to send any assistance. As Halsey recalled the situation:[18]

> Accompanied by Major Fielding who had just arrived, I went to Gap and contacted L'Hermine who let me have 60 maquisards (commando-trained) commanded by Lt. McIntosh [of Jedburgh CHLOROFORM] and then proceeded to 45th Division HQ and demanded an interview with Major-General Eagles to whom I and Major Fielding explained the situation. It is doubtful today even in my mind whether it was an act of the Almighty or whether the General understood the situation but on my return to Colonel Dulaney's HQ there was a message for me to pick up an armoured car reconnaissance patrol and take them to the Larche area.

Of course it was neither the Almighty nor Eagle's wisdom; it simply happened that Piddington and his Troop A, already ordered to patrol to the east, were ready and available.

For the Larche mission, Piddington assigned his second platoon, com-manded by Lt. Kenneth Cronin, who was ordered to make a "show of force" in the Barcelonnette area, to coordinate his activities with McIntosh, and to remain until relieved by the First Airborne Task Force. The platoon, which consisted of three M-8 armored cars, firing 37-mm. cannon, and a half-dozen jeeps, could not, because of bridge demolitions, follow the direct route to Barcelonnette but took all day, traveling about 200 miles from the Rhône, to reach its destination. About five miles west of Barcelonnette, Cronin met McIntosh and Martin of Jed CHLOROFORM, with their company of *maquisards*. Cronin recalls meet-ing McIntosh: "He is a Georgian [actually from Florida] with the most southern accent I have ever heard and who spoke French exactly as he spoke English but the Maquis understood him, and were quick to obey his commands."[19] (With the two other members of CHLOROFORM being French, there was never a communication problem.)

Once in Barcelonnette, Cronin and McIntosh quickly got in touch with John Halsey and Captain Bureau, who now had six companies spread out in the valley facing the German positions in the mountains. For the next few days, the FFI, the American platoon, and John Halsey patrolled the road between Jausiers and Condamine, "moving around," as Cronin put it, "a great deal to give the appearance of more strength than we actually had." The Germans showed no signs of an offensive but, with 110-mm. howitzers in the mountains, could put down a deadly barrage. At one time, Halsey and Cronin together salvaged a jeep that had been abandoned by its driver. With the rescued jeep "going like hell to town," Cronin spotted a little movement up on the mountain—either a machine gun or observation post. "In order to lay the gun on the target," he remembered,

> I had to elevate to maximum elevation since it was so high up on the mountain. I put a couple of rounds into the suspected target and [Halsey] who was sitting next to me and who was supposed to be keeping an eye on the field above the embankment to keep anyone from sneaking up on us, was sitting there watching the gunnery and saying "Lovely, lovely, lovely," as only a Brit can say it.

Meanwhile, John Roper had been cooperating with patrols from the 2nd Battalion of the 180th Regiment, up to Briançon and across the Col de Vars to St.-Paul and to that same road net, St.-Paul-Condamine-Meyronnes, which Halsey, Cronin, McIntosh, and Bureau were keeping under observation. The British officers deplored the caution of the Americans and the Maquis: the former being under orders to carry on reconnaissance but not to attack, and the latter realizing how vulnerable they were to a German barrage. In any case, although the Germans did not mount a serious offensive from the Larche pass, they reoccupied the villages along the Larche road and kept up such intensive shelling that the Allies, without heavy reinforcements, could do nothing except maintain contact.

On August 25, Patch ordered General Frederick to send elements of his Airborne Task Force up to the Larche pass. This meant that, as soon as Lt. Col. Edward Sach could move some of the 550th Glider Infantry Battalion to Barcelonnette, Cronin would rejoin Piddington north of St.-Paul. During the days between the 25th and the 28th, when the first Glider troops came in, the Germans almost closed the road between Jausiers and St.-Paul by their bombardments. To quote Cronin:

> The Germans didn't react until we started to move north . . . then everything hit the fan. The enemy had those roads leading to the pass taped and registered with artillery and really let us have it. We beat a hasty retreat into Condamine and the artillery followed up. We finally had to retreat behind a small mountain spur to the rear of Condamine to get into a defilade position. Luckily no injuries were sustained except to our feelings. One thing was certain; we weren't going to be able to get jeeps through that pass. It would have to be armored cars traveling at high speed to make it and that was problematical.

Cronin did take an armored car up to St.-Paul, where he met Piddington, who told him to have the platoon make a dash for it. Knowing that the airborne forces would possess much more offensive power than a recon platoon, Piddington's superiors believed that the entire troop would be more useful in the Guillestre–Briançon area. Cronin returned to Barcelonnette, bringing with him the regional military delegate, Willy Widmer, who would be conferring with NOEL and Bureau about further actions.[20] On the next day, August 28, Cronin's platoon made a run for it and rejoined the other units of the 117th Reconnaissance Squadron at Voiron, north of Grenoble. That evening, the first elements of Colonel Sachs' battalion moved into bivouac around Barcelonnette.

The historian of these events would like to report that, with tanks and howitzers reinforcing Bureau's FFI, the Allies soon repulsed the Germans and raised a triumphant banner on the Larche pass. This did not happen. Although Bureau's FFI expanded to more than twelve companies with over a thousand *maquisards*, the Germans made ever more vigorous efforts to hold the pass, with artillery emplacements along ten miles of mountain crests. Halsey and Jed CHLOROFORM patrolled and advised, the Airborne battalion did what it could, the Allied air force bombed enemy installations, and beginning on September 6, elements of the French regular forces—the 2nd Moroccan Division—reinforced the line. By the end of September, these French units had relieved the weary *maquisards*, who had fought in the high mountains for two months.[21] Even then this Alpine campaign, possibly the least celebrated of World War II, would continue through the frigid winter and well into the spring of 1945.

TASK FORCE BIBO AND BRIANÇON

Since the Larche area had been assigned to the First Airborne Task Force, VI Corps now had to be concerned more with the passes to the north, the Montgenèvre (controlled by Briançon) and the Modane and Mont-Cenis passes, approached by way of St.-Michel in the Maurienne. Truscott decided to pull the 180th Infantry out of the area, so that it could follow the 179th to Grenoble. The 2nd Battalion of the 180th still had one platoon at Briançon.

On August 27, Truscott ordered Lt. Col. Harold S. Bibo, of the Headquarters staff, to organize a task force to relieve the 2nd and 3rd Battalions of the 180th. The Task Force was to consist of Troop A of the 117th Recon Squadron, already in the area; a Chemical battalion; two platoons from the 180th's Anti-Tank Company; one battery of 105s from the 171st Field Artillery Battalion.[22]

In the evening of August 27, Bibo was briefed at VI Corps headquarters at

Aspres and, around midnight set off toward Chorges, to confer with officers of the 180th Regiment, which his task force, officially designated as PFPF (Provisional Flank Protective Force), was to relieve. Captain Piddington, whose Troop A was operating north of the Col de Vars in the Guillestre/Briançon region, conferred with Bibo on the road to Briançon.[23]

Clearly, Briançon, which guarded the Montgenèvre pass and which had already been occupied by Maquis along with Jedburghs and one platoon of the 180th's 2nd Battalion, was the key point of Bibo's responsibility. Consequently, after a conference with his officers early in the morning of August 28, Bibo drove up to Briançon and set up his command post in the Grand Hotel. There were many Maquis forces in and around Briançon, under the general command of Captain Frison, who had outposts and road-blocks in the mountains near the town, at Cervières, and along the road from Briançon to the German-held pass at Montgenèvre.[24] The members of the NOVOCAINE Jedburgh team, Lieutenant Gennerich and his French colleague, Lieutenant LeLann, were there, together with the British officers Major Purvis and Captain Roper, and an American, Lt. Mario Volpe, the radio operator for the CONFESSIONAL (UNION III) mission.

During the night of August 28/29, German elements occupied strong points around Briançon and in the morning they began shelling the town. With bombs falling in the vicinity of the Grand Hotel, Bibo ordered his headquarters to withdraw, around 11:00, to positions at Le Monêtier, about twelve miles on the Grenoble road. All the American outposts were overrun, and company C of the 83rd Chemical Battalion was surrounded. Its losses were heavy: three officers, fifty men, twelve 4.2 mortars, and about twenty-five vehicles. Some men from the company were able to straggle through and escape the German patrols. The Resistance also suffered. Ten men from Captain Céard's company, driving up to the Fort des Têtes, were intercepted and summarily executed by the Germans. At the fortress, Paul Baldenberger, a member of the local Liberation Committee, was shot.[25]

The Germans had indeed occupied the area and on the next day, August 30, rounded up 250 able-bodied citizens from whom the officer in charge, Major Schneider, chose twelve hostages. Two townspeople, a physician, Dr. Lepoire, and an attorney, former public prosecutor Daurelle, sought to save the hostages by guaranteeing the town's neutrality. For the next few days, terror reigned: German soldiers requisitioned what they chose and destroyed buildings—wantonly it appeared to the citizens. Until the local German forces were reinforced by Afrika Korps elements from the 90th Panzer Grenadier Division, Briançon had no power, no water, no telephones, and little food.[26]

Early in the morning of August 30, Bibo did in fact receive corps orders (issued the previous day) that he would be relieved very shortly by the French. While Bibo's CP was now at Lauteret, Piddington's was about halfway between Lauteret and Briançon, in the shadow of mountains, which showed patches of snow and glacier even in summertime.

That evening, Major Howes, from Seventh Army, turned up at Bibo's CP with a French liaison officer to make preliminary arrangements for the relief by the French. With knowledge that his task force would soon be relieved, Colonel Bibo went to Chambéry, north of Grenoble, to meet with French Colonel Bonjour, whose forces would be taking over the northern sector.[27] While he was away, Troop A patrolled and skirmished around St.-Chaffrey, with the 2nd Platoon generally under fire. Jed NOVOCAINE participated in the patrols.

Bibo returned to his headquarters late in the evening of September 1 with word that everything was ready for the French takeover. All units were to be prepared to leave and rejoin their parent units on the following day.[28]

In Briançon, by September 3, some order had returned: Electricity had been restored, and the hostages had been released. The Germans, although reinforced, did not intend to attack, simply to safeguard the escape routes along which stragglers from the Maurienne were still limping eastward. In any case, elements of the French 4th Regiment of *Tirailleurs Marocains*, forerunners of General Dody's 2nd Moroccan Infantry Division, had now reached the outskirts of the mountain city.

On September 5, the Germans withdrew back to the forts protecting the Montgenèvre pass, leaving only rear guard units that were captured on the next day when the Moroccans, along with Frison's FFI, entered Briançon. For the second time, the townspeople hailed their liberation, this time without fear of reoccupation; but the pass remained in German hands until the following spring.

14

East: Cannes and Nice

Although General Truscott had not been able to cut off the retreating Germans at Montélimar, General Patch could view the accomplishments of his Seventh Army with a certain satisfaction. The move north had been accomplished in record time, far ahead of schedule, and the whole of southern France required only a mopping-up of stragglers. With Toulon and Marseille besieged by de Lattre's Army B, it was simply a matter of time before the ports would fall into Allied hands. Hitler had no way of reinforcing the two divisions that stubbornly carried out a last-ditch defense.

On the other hand, the Germans could, if they chose to do so, reinforce their 157th Division (Pflaum) and their 148th (Fretter-Pico) across the Alpine passes. Patch had good reason however, through air reconnaissance and ULTRA, to believe that the enemy would continue to withdraw, not mount a counteroffensive, in the east.

On August 20, a stream of ULTRA reports from Bletchley had come through. One of these, dated 1:20 P.M. London time, revealed that the German High Command had ordered General Fretter-Pico to pull back toward the Italian border. The part applying to the eastern flank read:

148 Reserve Division to defend area around Grasse as long as possible without running risk of annihilation. Then to withdraw with main forces via Nice, Breil, Cuneo to take over new sector with left boundary coast at Menton, right boundary Embrun, Chianale-Varaita valley. If situation allows, groups to be pulled back fighting into Tinée and Var valleys as far as Larche-Condamine to bar a possible Allied outflanking thrust across Maddalena [Larche] Pass. . . .

At 0900 August 19, leaving strong rearguards in contact with Allies, main body 148 Division to withdraw from evening 19th onward first to east bank of the Var sector and to start from there movement ordered into new sector. In no circumstances to let Allies push them back by outflanking movement to north.

Late in the evening, another long message was deciphered. It mentioned that LXII Corps (whose headquarters had already been overrun) "will gradually be withdrawn to former Franco-Italian frontier and employed in its defense." It continued: "148th Division's task is to defend possible retreat route Grasse to Cannes." The 157th Reserve Division "to withdraw when pressed, behind 19th Army, to line Briançon–Chambéry–Aix-les-Bains. Later task to defend Alpine Sector, left at Embrun, right at Mt. Blanc."[1]

Patch certainly gained reassurance from these messages, but was disturbed that de Lattre had protested vigorously against having his divisions bottled up against the Alps. Patch had however accepted General Devers' suggestion about transforming the First Airborne Task Force into a regular offensive unit. The official orders for the FABTF to relieve Dahlquist and assume responsibility for the eastern flank reached General Frederick late on the 19th. The British Second Brigade would leave the theater, but it would be replaced by the "Black Devils," the First Special Service Force, a Canadian–U.S. Commando of regiment size that had previously served under Frederick's command in Italy. Now under Col. Edwin A. Walker, the Special Service Task Force had reduced off-shore batteries on islands near Toulon and had been held in reserve since D Day. Frederick would "establish and hold defensive flank along the general line Fayence–La Napoule," positions occupied by the 36th Division.[2]

The "general line" must not be thought of as a 1914–1918 length of trenches. Beyond the coast lie valleys and hills, dotted with small villages, served by a labyrinth of winding dirt roads. In some of the hill towns, a German garrison might hold out for days while traffic continued unopposed on nearby roads; elsewhere demoralized Axis troops, preponderantly made up of impressed Poles, Ukrainians, and Cossacks, eagerly surrendered when they had the chance.

The left, or northern limit of Frederick's responsibility, Fayence, had held out until the 21st, when the Germans surrendered to Jedburgh team SCEPTRE. Another stubborn defense took place at Callian. This was a little perched village where some of the wounded paratroopers had been left, and where patrols of the 141st Regiment's 2nd Battalion, under Lt. Col. James Critchfield, had penetrated as early as D + 2. With a French Resistance contingent ready to help, the Americans found themselves faced by a garrison unwilling to surrender. It finally took a mini-task force under the battalion's executive officer, Maj. Herbert Eitt, to subdue the Germans. The 141st, which controlled the Route

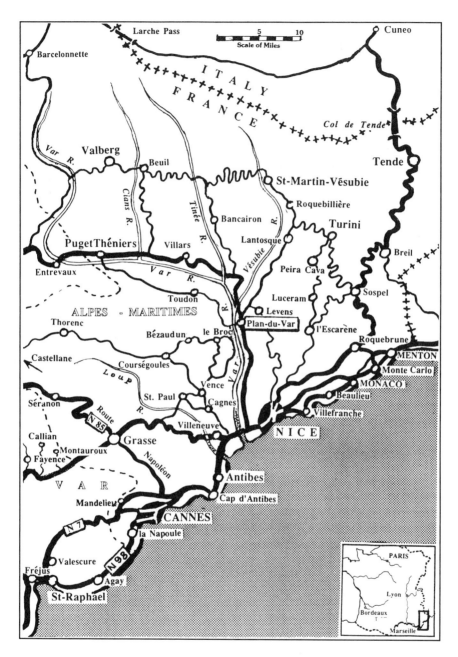

Map 14.1
CANNES, NICE, AND THE ITALIAN BORDER

Napoléon (N85) from a point a few miles northwest of Grasse all the way to Digne, began to move out as the paratroopers took over their positions.[3]

The Airborne Task Force now assumed responsibility for protecting the Seventh Army's eastern flank. General Frederick moved his headquarters to the Hotel Courier in St.-Raphael. Just outside the city limits, at Valescure, the OSS men, Captains Geoffrey Jones and Alan Stuyvesant, set up a headquarters. It was here that Jones joined forces with Pierre Escot, director of a Gaullist intelligence network that possessed wide information sources in the direction of Cannes and Nice. With Frederick now responsible for offensive moves eastward, the association with Escot became extremely valuable, and he was absorbed into a burgeoning SO/SI type of operation attached to Frederick's G-2.[4]

General Frederick now deployed his units along the highways leading to Italy. By the 22nd, the Airborne's line ran just a few miles west of Cannes, extending northwest until it reached N85, the Route Napoléon, several miles south of Castellane. The Germans still held some rear guard units in Grasse, the celebrated perfume center on the winding Cannes–Castellane road. As Frederick's troops moved east, they approached the boundary between the departments of Var and Alpes-Maritimes. The 509th Parachute Battalion, outside Cannes, had already crossed the border.

All this movement seriously affected Commandant Lécuyer, who since early August had been FFI chief for Alpes-Maritimes and who, as ORA regional chief, knew the area extremely well. Many of the mountain towns had been or could be liberated by the FFI, and he realized the strategic significance of the Var River, which meets the Mediterranean just west of Nice, the departmental seat. While the Germans were strongly fortified around Nice, they had only small garrisons in towns beyond a twenty-mile defense line. Lécuyer believed that troops could reach the little town of Plan-du-Var, where a wide flat valley extends to the south with mountains to the north, without encountering serious resistance.

Since the landings, Lécuyer's companies had plagued German garrisons in the Alps, striking at German concentrations toward the Italian border. The French knew, at a time when American plans had scarcely been formulated, that key positions in the high valleys had to be controlled if the Germans were to be forced out of France. The valleys and ridges lie at right angles to the coast, and make a series of potential defensive lines north of that Riviera coastline stretching from Nice to Monte Carlo.

By August 19, Lécuyer could be assured that no German troops remained in the mountain quadrilateral roughly defined by the Italian border in the north, by the Tinée River in the east, and the Var River on the south. (By this time the

U.S. 36th Division occupied the territory to the west.) The last of the German garrisons in the Tinée Valley, those protecting a hydroelectric plant at Bancairon, had just surrendered to three of Lécuyer's companies. Lécuyer himself had gone there to accept the enemy commander's surrender, explaining to the German officer that, while his Maquis uniform was somewhat improvised, he was indeed a legitimate French officer.

East of the Var–Tinée line, a series of ridges running north–south could serve the Germans as defensive bastions. East of the Tinée Valley, the next strategic positions lie along the Vésubie River Valley, marked by the town of Lantosque and farthest north, St.-Martin-Vésubie, ten miles (as the crow flies) from Italy. On August 17, a band of Lécuyer's *maquisards*, Groupe MORGAN (Foata), entered St.-Martin and forced the garrison to surrender. The conquest was short-lived, however, since German plans were being formulated to hold the Tende pass, and elements of the 90th Panzer Division were beginning to take up positions along the border. On the 21st, the Germans reoccupied St.-Martin.[5]

Havard Gunn, now at Thorenc (Lécuyer's CP), understood the implicit strategic import of St.-Martin and did his best to persuade the FFI into another assault. Several Resistance groups responded. (One of these, known as the *Battalion* HOCHCORN from the code name of its leader, Commandant Dormois, included in its heterogeneous makeup a section of navy firemen, *marins pompiers*, from Marseille.)[6] Gunn went to St.-Martin and later succinctly reported:

> Entered town. Tried to organize FFI who were very disordered and very political. Largely FTP. Gained very interesting military information. Entered all villages not occupied by enemy along frontier but position obviously very insecure. Enemy patrols all along parts of Italian frontier and raiding villages, etc. Left St.-Martin for Plan-du-Var.

Both Gunn and Lécuyer believed the Americans should be advised that it might be possible to reach Plan-du-Var from the north.

Organizing a small convoy, Lécuyer, Gunn, and some staff on motorcycles set out for the Allied CP and finally reached General Frederick at his headquarters in St.-Raphael. While he agreed with the possibilities of an attack from the north, General Frederick explained that his orders required a defensive position, with only reconnaissance to Grasse and Cannes.[7]

Frederick told Lécuyer and Gunn that, even though he was supposed only to recon toward Grasse, he was going to attack it the next day. He did also obtain a modification of his orders. The written version (Patch Field Order No. 3, 6 P.M., August 25, 1944) read:

FABTF:
(1) Seize and hold the West bank of the VAR in zone.
(2) Protect the right (East) flank of Seventh Army along the general line:
    LARCHE PASS (incl)--TOUDON--West bank of the VAR river to its
    mouth.
(3) Reconnoiter to NICE.

Patch had of course been able to digest the information, derived from the
ULTRA decrypt of August 20 ordering a German withdrawal. Thus, on the
twenty-third, as Frederick prepared to take Grasse, Patch possessed a reasonably
good assessment of what the enemy might do on the Italo-French frontier.
Knowing that Generalmajor Otto Fretter-Pico, the 148th Division Commander,
would hold the east bank of the Var, he could readily authorize Frederick to go
that far, and then wait and see.

Patch gave Frederick responsibility also for the Larche pass, where
Piddington's Troop A, John Halsey, and Jedburgh team CHLOROFORM had
been giving what support they could to Captain Bureau's embattled FFI.
Frederick detached Colonel Sach's 550th Battalion, which in the next few days
made its way to Barcelonnette and began taking up positions along the roads
leading to the pass.[8]

When Lécuyer and Gunn told General Frederick how free the mountain
roads were, they were somewhat disconcerted when the general told them he
would look into it if the intelligence they brought could be verified. While
Frederick's immediate objectives were Grasse and Cannes, and his orders
limited him to reconnaissance no farther north than thirty miles, Lécuyer and
Gunn were describing a route via Puget-Théniers on the upper Var, more than
fifty miles from the coast. Lécuyer pointed out that over the lower Var no bridge
remained intact except at Plan-du-Var, where the Var Valley mountain road
emerges onto the plain less then twenty miles from Nice.[9]

In the event, General Frederick chose not to take the northern route to the
Var River, which made it more imperative in Gunn's and Lécuyer's view that
the Maquis must at all costs hold the bridge at Plan-du-Var. By this time,
Commandant Sorensen (CHASUBLE) and Xan Fielding, the officers who had
been imprisoned with Cammaerts, had joined them. Ostensibly, Sorensen was
FFI chief, as Constans' deputy, for the eastern part of R-2, and he needed to
develop familiarity with the Alpes-Maritimes.

Meanwhile, the 517th and the First Special Service Force struck at Grasse
on August 24, entered the town without opposition, and moved ahead to the
German defensive positions along the Loup River. On the next day, August 25,
Frederick transferred his Task Force headquarters to Grasse. With this move

went Captain Stuyvesant, the SSS officer responsible for intelligence and contacts with French agents, as well as Capt. Geoffrey Jones, who had been providing various liaison and other services for FABTF since he joined them on D Day.[10]

Along the coast, Yarborough's 509th Regiment, having reduced the German strong points west of Cannes, by-passed that most elegant of Riviera resorts and the nearby resort of Antibes, so that the troops could take a shorter route to Nice and the Italian border. Therefore, while patrols of the 509th probed along the coast road at Mandelieu and La Napoule, others sounded out German defenses away from the coast.

On August 23, a three-jeep party had encountered members of a Cannes Resistance patrol outside the city, where Germans were entrenched with mortars and heavy machine guns. Reinforcements came up, but a sharp fire-fight, in which both Americans and FFI took casualties, enabled the Germans to hold on.

The German group, however, formed no more than a rear guard for the withdrawal from Cannes of the German garrison, under Colonel Schneider, planned for the dawn of the 24th. The Resistance within Cannes had long prepared for this opportunity, with MUR forces under Vahanian in the city's western sector, and those of Miniconi (FTP Commandant JEAN-MARIE) in the east and north. Schneider had orders to destroy the city before he evacuated it, but, either because of Resistance pressure or from repugnance toward such useless and savage destruction, he left the hotels and civic structures intact. On the 24th, the Germans withdrew, leaving the city to a rejoicing population, to the FFI, hailed as liberators, and to the Committee of Liberation, headed by Gabriel Daville, an officer in one of Miniconi's FTP companies. Yarborough's 509th came along without opposition, joined in the parade, and hastened on to their next objective, Nice.[11]

To attack Nice it would be necessary to cross the Var, which, with its bridges blown, provided a nasty obstacle. Ironically, while the ABTF had not yet crossed the Var, Resistance forces planned an attack in a strategic area fifty miles ahead, the value of which the Americans would appreciate three weeks later when they—and the FFI—would face the German decision to hold the ridges north of Monte Carlo. This defense line lies barely five air miles east of the Vésubie Valley, and the leaders of Lécuyer's groups, Foata (Group MORGAN) and Mazier (Group FRANÇOIS), having control of the Vésubie, believed the Germans might be prepared to relinquish positions around Turini. Should these strong points be grasped, the way might be open to Sospel, a key point on the road to Italy. Unfortunately for Foata and Mazier, the Germans saw control of the passes as essential to their defense: They undertook to reoccupy St.-Martin and to reinforce their defenses at Turini. The Maquis attack turned into a disaster. Gunn, then at Plan-du-Var, learned of the effort too late:

> Knew this area heavily defended by German Alpine troops. Tried to change orders but SAPIN [Lécuyer] left no competent staff officer in charge. All his staff moved to Nice. Left to contact US forces. Crossed Var river, found US regimental HQ [presumably Col. Graves' 517th regiment]; colonel commanding promised to give small mixed patrol for dawn next morning for recce of valleys concerned also make enemy think Americans advanced farther than they had. My idea also was to try and support FFI attack on Turini at dawn if I was unable to get troops orders changed. Given jeep. Tried all night to cross river Var to reach Nice, impossible because of mines. Returned lead patrol up valleys. FFI had attacked Turini before my arrival. Complete defeat and ten killed. Operation very rash and badly managed.[12]

For Gunn and Lécuyer, the bridge at Plan-du-Var still offered a great possibility for Frederick's paratroopers. Although in summertime the Var River is no more than a trickle threading its way through a vast pebbly riverbed, the Germans had sown mines that would make a precarious crossing for men and vehicles.

Operational Group RUTH had now joined Lécuyer. Under the leadership of Lieutenants Brandes and Strand, the group had worked with Task Force Butler until Digne was liberated, and was then reassigned to the area in which Gunn and Lécuyer were operating. They never did locate Gunn, but, after a conference with Lécuyer and Sorensen at Thorenc, they joined the Maquis units that were protecting the bridge at Plan-du-Var. Although the Germans held Levens, from where they could fire toward the bridge, FFI units and members of OG RUTH harassed them so effectively that they could neither occupy the bridge nor destroy it.

Meanwhile, although he had not accepted the northern approach, on the 26th, Frederick ordered the 517th Regiment to fan out along the Loup River, crossing it to the north in the direction of Courségoules and Bézaudun, and to the south toward Vence (the picturesque old village where Matisse would later decorate his celebrated chapel). Advance elements reached the Var, where they could fire across the river at the German installations; and on the next day, the three battalions of the 517th occupied Bézaudun and Le Broc.

Lieutenant Gautier (later general) recalls:

> The American command understood that we held Plan-du-Var and maintained contact with the eastern bank. Artillery was placed at my disposal and its accurate fire hit the German positions. On the evening of the 27th

the Americans crossed the Var, and, guided by a number of our people, took Levens and La Roquette [two miles south of Levens]. The crossing of the Var had taken place just as, to the south, another American group reached the river banks. . . . We had succeeded in what we wished, that is to get the Allied forces east of the Var, although their mission at this moment did not extend beyond this line.[13]

The other "American group" was presumably Lieutenant Brandes and OG RUTH, which encountered advance patrols from the 517th parachute regiment on the 27th. When Brandes reported to the Regimental command post in Grasse, Colonel Graves sent an anti-tank company to relieve the OG. By this time, Geoffrey Jones, attached to the Task Force's G-2, had moved his headquarters to Grasse. He found a truck for the well-worn group—they had been in the field for almost a month—which reported back to 4-SFU.[14]

Captain Jones became more and more useful to General Frederick by providing accurate information about enemy dispositions. Although originally trained as an artillery paratrooper, Jones moved readily into the SI (intelligence) sector, where his energy and knowledge of the area enabled him to feed valuable information to Frederick's G-2.

LIBERATION OF NICE

On August 27—as German forces evacuated Nice and an insurrection began—Jones obtained a copy of General Fretter-Pico's field order for the day. Jones recalls the situation:

An SO probe of young agents behind enemy lines in Nice ambushed a German command car and brought back a bloody knapsack full of papers. As we began to sort out this lode with the help of a (I will never know why he was visiting us) British officer, we made an astounding discovery: these "papers" were the just written plans for German forces on the eastern flank to withdraw for the next three days to fortified positions on the Italian frontier—and the Field Order and maps to carry them out! Working all night by candlelight, we translated/processed a complete report that by early morning was ready for me to wake up the General, who immediately gave me his L. S. aircraft and had me flown to General Patch's headquarters.

The order made it clear that the 148th Reserve Division would pull back toward the Italian border, but would hold a line roughly ten miles west of the frontier, blocking the coast to Italy at Monte Carlo, and defending the mountain road leading by way of Sospel to the Tende pass. The order warned: "Watch out—terrorists are everywhere. . . . Do not go singly, only armed and in groups. . . . Skirt the terrorist infested city of Nice."[15]

The liberation of Nice, the largest city on the French Riviera, provoked for the French not only joyous celebrations, but also the beginning of intense political infighting. Whether the new administration would be Gaullist or Communist provided heady grist for the mill of a local power struggle. If Nice had been the same as other liberated cities, then, as the Germans withdrew, Frederick's airborne troops would have made a token parade through the city and then passed rapidly ahead in pursuit, even as Truscott and de Lattre would by-pass Lyon. Happily or unhappily, as the case may be, the Americans became more immersed in Nice than they anticipated.

The protracted mountain stalemate, which kept the First Airborne Task Force in the area until mid-November, meant that Nice, within 25 miles of the front lines, of necessity became Frederick's headquarters and the nearest center for rest and recreation. The attractiveness of this celebrated resort, which even in wartime gushed with enough wine to inspire the term "Champagne campaign," stood in marked contrast with the deadly Alpine conflict so close at hand.

Like all departments, the Alpes-Martimes (of which Nice was the prefectural seat) had produced a Departmental Committee of Liberation (CDL). However, well before the August 15 landings, a split between those who looked for a people's insurrection led by FTP units and those who wished to cooperate with the FFI and Gaullist appointees had developed. As Frederick's Airborne Task Force approached Nice, the department had become divided: pro-Communist political leaders and the FTP dominating Nice, the administrative center; and in the mountains, the FFI structure of Sorensen, Lécuyer, and the latter's deputy, Pierre Gautier (MALHERBE), maintaining control.

It took some time before Nice settled down to something resembling normalcy. On August 27, with the Americans still on the Var's western bank, the CDL called for insurrection. Fortunately (as the Allies knew from Fretter-Pico's captured "Order of the Day"), the Germans were withdrawing. The Nazi departure kept bloodshed at a minimum, and the uprising prevented the Germans from destroying important hotels and other facilities. On the next day, as Maquis and paratroopers paraded in the streets, hysterical Gallic joy poured forth in ecstatic exuberance. Some rioting and vandalism continued for several days.[16]

Sufficient order had been established in Nice by September 5 for General Frederick to move his headquarters from Grasse to the resort city. While the Leftist CDL professed no great affection either for the Americans or for the ORA domination of Maquis units fighting in the Alps, the city administration cooperated to the degree necessary to continue the fight against the Germans.

THE STRUGGLE ON THE FRANCO-ITALIAN FRONTIER

General Frederick, at the beginning of September, now witnessed a third evolution of his troops from, first, a contingent of paratroopers with the mission of seizing a limited strategic objective, second, an infantry division in pursuit, and now a group of mountain fighters holding a line (memories of World War I), with continual patrols and limited offensives. The "line" concentrated on three passages into Italy: along the coast, beyond Monaco as far as Menton, the Tende pass 30 miles north, and finally, northwest, the Larche pass. Between Tende and Larche, along the Italian border, stretch miles and miles of snow-capped roadless Alpine peaks.

By September 6, the disposition of the Task Force covered a front, which would be held for months to come: Based on Menton on the Mediterranean, Frederick's troops controlled l'Escarène, Luceram, Peira Cava, and ultimately Turini. The brunt of fighting developed in the 517th Combat Team area, with efforts to break through German defenses on the road to Sospel.

Alongside the G.I.s, units of the FFI continued to fight. Noteworthy among those was the Hochcorn group, which had chased the German garrison out of St.-Martin de Vésubie a week before the Allies reached Nice. The group worked especially with the Special Service Force and is recognized in the Force's history:[17]

> Shortly after crossing the Var, Lieutenant Colonel Becket received a visit from Major Hochscorn who came to offer the services of his battalion. Hochscorn Battalion was put to work on several reconnaissance missions, the first near l'Escarene and later with Second Regiment on patrols in strength around Mt. Agel [west of Roquebrune]. Veterans of two and three years clandestine resistance against Germans, the Hochscorns performed courageously and well while under Force command. Their main limitations were lack of unified training, lack of uniform ordinance, and lacks in warm clothing and proper supply in the mountains. Both discipline and command were good. The lieutenants were mostly graduates of St. Cyr, and most of the officers and NCO's had gone through the invasion of France with regular regiments.

Appreciating the needs of the FFI, Havard Gunn continued to act as liaison between Lécuyer and the Allied Command. Early in September, he went to Brignoles, where 4-SFU had established its CP, and consulted with Colonel

Head about reorganization in the Alpine area—from the coast to Larche—where the ABTF had responsibility. Although the arrangement arrived at did not change the situation already in existence, 4-SFU established an "Interallied Mission" in which the two British officers, Gunn and Halsey, would continue "operational" liaison, and the American, Geoffrey Jones, would concentrate on intelligence (which he was already doing in cooperation with Frederick's G-2).

Major Gunn developed a staff that included Capt. Yves Hautière (VESTIAIRE, who had been dropped with Major Fielding), Lieutenant Etienne, and others. Halsey was technically part of Gunn's group, but he remained at Barcelonnette in a liaison capacity with the FFI and with the Americans after Colonel Sach's 550th arrived. The Gunn group did its best to provide arms and material to the FFI fighting with the ABTF, remaining in operation until October 10.[18]

Capt. Geoffrey Jones continued to work in coordination with the Airborne Task Force's G-2. He had in fact made his services invaluable. General Frederick, while at first somewhat indifferent, was impressed by Jones providing the German operation order, and also by the expeditious way in which he later obtained information about the port at Nice. As Jones recalled:

> Frederick never really accepted us until after the German defense plans were authenticated. Of course, I never asked him if he was pleased with us because he was a formidable gentleman, but the very fact that he began to use us for something besides translating and running errands showed that he felt that we were a tool he could rely upon.

From modest beginnings at Valescure, where he first became associated with Pierre Escot, Jones built up a considerable organization for providing intelligence to Frederick and to Colonel Blythe's G-2. Again in Jones' words:

> We were able to build up a multinational group of over 120 volunteer men and women from local indigenous and refugee resistants—who served as translators to cooks and couriers to counterintelligence and coup-de-main agents—complete with its own network of clandestine radios (built from local materials) and behind the line infiltration systems by sea and mountain pass. We also had our own ski patrols (with uniforms homemade from sheets) and a small fleet of sail and motor boats which supplied from tactical targets for naval guns to guerilla groups for sabotage actions. And from our first typed notes of August 19th, we eventually provided General Frederick and/or his G-2 with over 500 properly processed (i.e., translated, evaluated, etc.) reports of all types of special operations and intelligence from French, Italian, Polish, Russian and even refugee German informants . . . we were

able to recruit/direct in support of the FABTF.

By mid-September, Jones was setting up chains out of his headquarters at the Manoir Belgrano in Nice to obtain information about enemy positions and intentions in Italy. He also developed special missions, such as JARGNAC into the Po Valley, TALBOT into Monaco, and HENRI to Sospel, and he remained in touch with John Halsey at the Larche pass and with the Hamilton mission farther north. Another group, mission MICHEL, provided intelligence and guides for the 517th's 3rd Battalion under Lt. Col. Melvin Zais. The work done was complex, in Jones' words, "a classic example of how an SO operation can be equally effective in the SI field during its operations."[19]

After September 15, when General Devers, as commanding general, Sixth Army Group, began liquidating OSS operations in southeastern France, Frederick requested that Jones—but not Stuyvesant—be exempted from the recall and transferred to the First Airborne Task Force, as head of the Strategic Services Subsection. "The organization which he has developed," read the request,

> is a coordinated, energetic, dependable group of French and Italian people, many of them working without remuneration for the Allied cause. This headquarters desires to retain this organization and the benefits of its activities. The organization depends entirely upon the energetic leadership of Captain Jones, and it is believed that it will dissolve without his continued presence.

The request was approved, and Jones continued his work on the Italian border, even after the Airborne was relieved, until March 1945.[20]

The month of September 1944, which witnessed the final activities of SPOC and 4-SFU, brought about inevitable changes among the Resistance fighters. With Paris liberated and with the provisional government installed, de Gaulle wasted no time in either liquidating the FFI or bringing them under regular army command. In theory, the FFI ceased to exist after August 27 (before either Lyon or Nice had been liberated), and the Resistance regions, such as R-1 and R-2, became once more traditional military districts. By the middle of September, the government had decided that *maquisards* who wished to continue fighting should be reassigned, after formal agreement to enlist until the end of the war, to regular army units.

It goes without saying that confusion was rampant as old organizations persevered alongside the framework of new ones, and in places the Maquis simply disregarded orders, fighting in the mountains under their old chiefs.

Although all Resistance fighters, AS, *Corps Francs*, FTP, and ORA, came under the government's decrees, clearly the more manageable units, as far as amalgamation was concerned, were those already under regular army officers and, in particular, the ORA.

In eastern R-2, for which Commandant Sorensen held responsibility as representative of Colonel Constans (chief, FFI, R-2, under General Zeller, chief FFI Southeast) and General Cochet (Military Delegate, Operations South), the various FFI units were amalgamated into seven battalions to form a "Southern Alpine Group" (*Groupement Alpin Sud*), attached to de Lattre's French First Army. Assigned to the command was a rigid regular officer, Colonel Lanusse. Commandant Lécuyer served as Lanusse's deputy, and Lieutenant Gautier took charge of several of the newly organized battalions fighting in the Alps with the FABTF. The combat elements remained essentially the same, but their designations changed. Later, the Alpine Group South was absorbed into the 3rd RIA [Alpine Infantry Regiment], under the command of Colonel Lelaquet, former FFI chief in the Var Department. Gradually, French divisions took over the combat in the Alps, but Americans, first the FABTF, then elements of the 19th Armored Division, kept fighting along that "forgotten front" until March of 1945, when the units facing Italy all became French.[21]

15

West: Toulon and Marseille

While O'Daniel's 3rd Division pursued the tag end of the German army to Avignon and beyond, General de Lattre's Army B, landing a few days behind, was organizing its attacks on Toulon, the French Naval Base, and on Marseille, France's second city, whose port facilities were vital to the ANVIL/DRAGOON strategy. The operation against Toulon would take place in the Var Department, whose prefectural seat, Draguignan, lay within the area accorded to Frederick's First Airborne Task Force. Marseille, on the other hand, served not only as administrative center for the Bouches-du-Rhône Department, but also as headquarters for R-2, an area that came under the purvue of the regional prefect, or in liberation terms, the *Commissaire de la République.* Marseille served also as a Gestapo center, from which the German agent Ernst Dünker spun the webs that had entangled Resistance leaders and Allied agents, many of whom had been executed at the notorious *Charnier de Signes.*

SPOC maintained contact with Maj. Robert Boiteux (FIRMIN), whose GARDENER circuit covered the Marseille area and the coast to the east. Cammaerts also had a contact in Jacques Méker, heading a small "Buckmaster" group that worked with some MUR elements. However, Cammaerts did not wish to get heavily involved in providing arms that, because of strong Communist influences in Marseille, might be used for internal political squabbles rather than for fighting Germans.[1]

SPOC supported an essentially French project of trying to save the ports of Toulon, Marseille, and Sète from being destroyed by the departing Germans. The plan originated in the French navy or, more precisely, in the *Aeronavale,* which assigned teams (two officers, four men), one for each port, who would be trained and parachuted by SPOC prior to D Day. The teams would get in touch with the local Resistance, obtain information, and either by radio or by

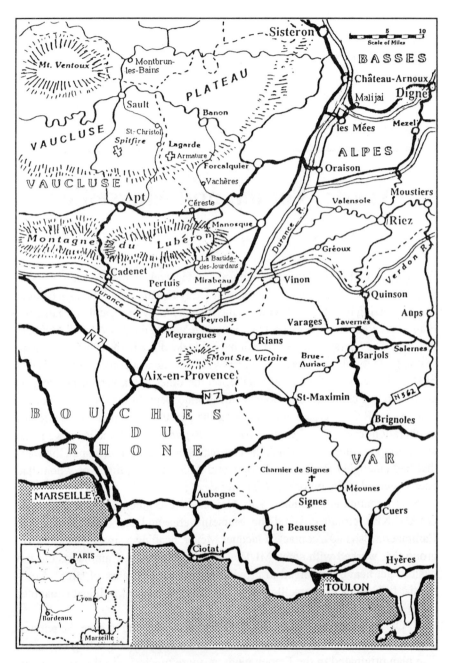

Map 15.1
TOULON AND MARSEILLE

courier, transmit data to Algiers. As part of their "antiscorch" training, which was distinct from other programs, the men studied German techniques of port destruction at Naples, Tunis, and other harbors. Heading this group of Navy paratroopers (*Groupe des parachutistes de la Marine*) was Capitaine de Corvette Allain, who coordinated the project in Algiers. With the attack on Toulon calculated by the planners for D + 28, no one anticipated that Toulon and Marseille would be under siege within five days of the landings.[2]

The first group, destined for Toulon, parachuted into France in the middle of June 1944. It consisted of Lieutenants de la Ménardière (SAMPAN), Midoux, and Sanguinetti, with a radio operator, all of whom soon made contact with FFI regional ORA head Jacques Lécuyer, with the Toulon FFI chief, Salvatori, and with sympathetic French naval officers stationed in the port. Allain remained in Algiers, where he and another member of the Toulon team, Ensign Ayral, stood by, not certain whether they could get to mainland France prior to D Day. Meanwhile, although the team could transmit messages by radio, it had no way of sending maps and photographs, which would be of tremendous value when the Allies attacked Toulon. With such materials, Midoux made his way to ARCHIDUC's CP in the Vaucluse, 100 miles north of Toulon, where he became enrolled among those scheduled for the next flight out. This flight happened to be the Dakota, which almost aborted during its bumpy takeoff before dawn on August 12—the same plane that had brought in Constans. Midoux only reached Algiers to learn that the invasion was under way, and his colleagues Capitaine de Corvette Allain and Ensign Ayral had already been dropped in France.[3]

Both Allain and Ayral had planned, organized, and trained the three antiscorch teams, but after the teams left for the field, their work was essentially done. As Allain put it,

a few days before the landings, as the [French] Navy had no mission planned for the two remaining teams, SPOC organized
   1)   Mission LOUGRE (Allain), advance unit for the Airborne Task Force landing
   2)   Mission GEDEON (Ayral), liaison with the Var Maquis in anticipation of the attack on Toulon.

We have already dealt with Allain in connection with the Airborne Paratroopers, but must comment briefly on team GEDEON, which included, along with Ayral, Sub-Lt. Horace Moore of the British navy, a radio operator and three French quartermasters. They landed north of Toulon on August 12 and, in the next few days, allied themselves with Maquis groups in the area of

Signes (not yet known as a German execution spot) as well as with Ménardière and his SAMPAN team.

Ménardière had developed contacts with the FFI but had not succeeded in getting much cooperation from French naval officers. Even though many of these officers had repudiated Vichy, they nevertheless maintained that they should obey orders only from Admiral Lemonnier, de Gaulle's naval chief of staff. In spite of difficulties, Ménardière and his group successfully hampered some German destruction efforts. They were able to pull barges over the rudders and propellers of two ships, the *Galissonière* and the battleship *Strasbourg*, so that the Germans could not tow them to the principal channel, which remained only partially obstructed. After the port's liberation, Seventh Army engineers, working with French personnel, were able to get the base in operating condition by September 20.

Meanwhile, on July 18, the mission (CAIQUE) destined for Marseille, headed by an engineer, Parayre, was dropped about 75 miles north of the port and soon learned about the arrests that the Gestapo had made. The team managed its clandestine movements with great care, and by the time of D Day, had made contacts with ARCHIDUC for further drops, with the Toulon team, and with sympathetic French naval officers within the Marseille port.

Unfortunately, Parayre did not receive his action messages on time, and after the landings, the Germans increased their security arrangements. Realizing that the Germans, if defeated, would try to sink vessels in the channel entrances, Parayre hoped to scuttle ships that might be available for this purpose. Needing an armed group to protect his engineers, he met Major Boiteux on the 19th and obtained from the SOE agent fifty kilograms of explosives, but by the time he was able to muster the necessary people, he learned that the Marseille Resistance was planning an insurrection. If this took place, the Germans would certainly impose such security measures that the antisabotage plans would be useless.

It may be well at this point to review what had been happening along the coast. General de Lattre, restless because the American divisions had landed before his, wanted to get his forces into action. Four days after the landings, both de Lattre and Patch agreed that the French should move all out against Toulon and Marseille, while the American 3rd Division would proceed in the same direction just to the north.[4]

When he received Patch's order, de Lattre had available to him General Brosset's 1st Free French Division, General Magnan's 9th Colonial Infantry Division, and General de Monsabert's 3rd Algerian Infantry, all of which began an encircling movement against the French naval base at Toulon. Before he began his attack, de Lattre had received Sanguinetti, of the SAMPAN team, who had come through the German lines. De Lattre recalled the young officer as "something thin and feverish looking like a Corsican bandit," who told him about the German dispositions. The report impelled de Lattre to waste no time and to strike before German Admiral Ruhfus had deployed the 242nd Divison to points of maximum effectiveness.[5]

De Lattre analyzed the Toulon operation as consisting of three phases: the *investment* (August 21–22), in which Monsabert covered the north while General de Larminat coordinated actions of Monsabert and Magnan; second, the *dismantling* (August 22–23), during which the French regular forces broke through the outer belt; and third, the *final reduction* of the inner defenses, primarily the work of the 9th Colonial Infantry, ending with Admiral Ruhfus's surrender on the 27th.[6] It was during the "investment" that groups of the Resistance and members of the SAMPAN and GEDEON teams met the first *Bataillon de Choc* troops as they filtered into the city. Unfortunately, when he was carrying out a liaison mission to General de Linarès, Ensign Ayral, not properly identified, was killed in error by French soldiers. The remaining members of the team fought side by side with the FFI and with the regulars during the street fighting that followed. This effort, combined with artillery and bombardment from sea and air, brought the great naval base into allied hands.

While the fighting at Toulon continued, de Lattre fixed his attention on his next objective, Marseille, which with its outlying forts and suburbs, stretches along fifteen miles of coastline. He did not have to concern himself immediately with Sète, 100 miles west of Marseille, where the third antiscorch team, SCHOONER, had gone, because the Germans abandoned Sète on the 20th.[7]

General de Lattre did not wish to attack Marseille prematurely, wanting assurance that Toulon posed no threat to his flank and guarantees that sufficient fuel would be available. However, events caught up with him as a workers' strike and popular insurrection demanded the presence of the regular army.

Within Marseille, in spite of its population of almost a million, the Resistance was so divided, so disorganized, and so poorly armed that scarcely 500 FFI could provide a "fifth column" to hamper German defenses. Part of the disorganization had followed the arrest, in July, of Burdet, the regional military delegate, and Rossi, the regional FFI chief. The local Resistance, dominated by Communists and fellow-travelers, did not recognize either Widmer or Constans as replacements, with the consequence that the city had two rival FFI chiefs, Commandant Pierre Lamaison (VAUBAN), supported by COMAC and the Departmental Liberation Committee, and Jean Comte (LEVIS), head of the Bouche-du-Rhône *Groupes Francs*, who had contacts that might have enabled him to get more arms and explosives than the FTP. The rivalry produced a fundamental strategic difference, whether to foment a city-wide insurrection or, in line with a long-standing SOE policy, to concentrate on guerrilla attacks especially in the countryside. The insurrection, which would be dominated by leftist and FTP elements, could mean popular support, after liberation, of a local Communist government. Whether it would save German demolitions, as it did in Cannes and Nice, would depend on how rapidly the Germans evacuated the city. In the cases of Toulon and Marseille, where Hitler had ordered the garrisons to hold on to the last bullet, an insurrection would only increase security measures and reprisals. Nevertheless, it was Lamaison (VAUBAN) who was generally recognized. Comte sought out Constans, whom he found at Dieulefit, too late for an effective intervention.[8]

Parayre, of the Marseille antiscorch team CAIQUE, had learned that the German engineers responsible for destroying the port facilities were berthed in Hangar Three. He arranged for an attack only to find the engineers had been moved to more secure facilities. Meanwhile, in Parayre's words,

> I received a visit from VAUBAN, chief FFI Marseilles. . . . I asked him to hold off the insurrection planned for the night Sunday/Monday [20-21 Aug.] to avoid increased German security measures. . . . He agreed and asked me to wire General Cochet. However, access to the port . . . became practically impossible by the 21st. On the 22nd the insurrection began.

Although Parayre possessed plans of German defenses in the port, he considered an FFI attack certain to fail; it would be better to wait for the regulars, especially since General de Monsabert's troops were already in the outskirts.

With the insurrection in progress and the FFI calling for help, Monsabert could scarcely hold back. Taking advantage of "an opportunity," Colonel Chappuis, commander of the 7th Regiment of *Tirailleurs Algériens*, moved into the city on the 23rd, beginning an occupation that took another five days to complete. The German General Schaeffer, in spite of seeing his defenses crumble day by day, refused to give up. Finally, on the evening of the 27th, he agreed to a cease-fire and, on the next day, formally surrendered.[9]

For all practical purposes, however, the civil center of Marseille had been liberated by the 23rd. The *Commissaire de la République*, Raymond Aubrac, took over offices at the prefecture, and ensured the establishment of new prefects for the city and for the department.

In spite of the antiscorch operation, the Germans, with possession of the whole coastline and the harbor, were able to wreak great havoc—there was "an indescribable chaos of twisted ironwork, shattered concrete, and entangled cables." Without the efforts of the CAIQUE team, however, the damage would have been worse. By pouring cement into the primer ducts leading to preset charges, Parayre had thwarted the demolition of several quays. His people also prevented complete destruction of facilities at Port du Bouc, which, because it served as a pipeline terminal, was of crucial importance for Seventh Army operations. There, three tankers were sunk in such a way that they could be refloated.

The Germans had sunk over 75 ships in the channels, mined the basins, and sabotaged 257 cranes, but Marseille was so important to the Allies that an all-out effort began at once to make the harbor usable, to make the basins safe, and to get pipelines in operation. Engineers found that, in some cases, Liberty ships could pass around the sunken vessels; by September 30 they declared one basin to be free of mines and serviceable. Within three weeks of liberation, a Liberty ship was unloading directly alongside a Marseille quay.[10]

For the French, the liberation of Marseille brought forth an enormous emotional outpouring. Although Paris had been freed at the same time, Marseille had fallen in consequence of an entirely French attack, the second city (after Toulon) in France to recover its independence in this manner. Although already planning maneuvers far to the north, de Lattre returned on the 29th to participate in a victory parade that included de Gaulle's ministers for war and interior. There they listened to the *Marseillaise* in the city that had given the national anthem its name, and they watched

the unforgettable and poignant procession of all the makers of this second victory—the *tirailleurs*, the Moroccan Tabors, troopers, zouaves, and gunners—followed by the motley, fevered, bewildering mass of the FFI, between the two lines of a numberless crowd, frenzied, shouting with joy and enthusiasm, whom the guardians of order could not hold back.[11]

16

West: Across the Rhône—
The Ardèche

Although a super highway, constructed since the war, now carries north-south traffic along the Rhône River at incredible speeds, in 1944 the two lanes of the principal highway, N7, were strained to capacity during the retreat of General Wiese's Nineteenth Army. Day and night the German convoys streamed northward, two and even three abreast when one-way traffic would permit. For the Germans, N7 held an enormous strategic significance because their best divisions, the 198th, the 338th, and the powerful 11th Panzer, had all been deployed east of the Rhône to confront the attacking Allies.

On the western side of the river ran another road, N86, that would serve many of those German forces, some largely administrative, that had been stationed farther south and along the Pyrenees. Germans obliged to escape by this winding route would find N86 and its feeder roads unpleasantly hazardous to traverse due to the aggressive hostility of Maquis encamped in the mountainous Ardèche and Loire Departments. For 60 miles along the Rhône from Viviers to Serrières, N86 is never far from the wooded hills in which lurked bands of 50-100 guerrillas, whose constant ambushes and sabotage had made the Ardèche so inhospitable to German garrisons.

In 1944, the Ardèche possessed Resistance elements in common with other departments—active Maquis, a Departmental Committee of Liberation, the eternal quarrels between Left and Right—but it differed in one significant way from the departments east of the Rhône: It had no SOE circuit corresponding to Cammaert's JOCKEY circuit in the southeast.[1]

That SOE was not entrenched in the area does not mean that SPOC had not attempted to make contacts there. A three-man team had indeed established a landing zone, code named Tandem, near the small town of Devesset, located away from German concentrations in rugged country along the northwest departmental boundary. This would become headquarters for Allied teams, mostly American operational groups, cooperating in the ANVIL/DRAGOON campaign.[2]

SPOC also sent in an inter-allied mission code named PECTORAL, of which the ranking French member, Cdt. Jean-Paul Vaucheret (VANEL), had been named by de Gaulle as the departmental military delegate. A Canadian, Maj. Pierre Chassé, represented the Allied command. The team arrived on June 15, a week after Normandy D Day, in the midst of that hectic period in which all Resistance groups throughout France were attempting to carry out General Koenig's order for a national insurrection. In the Ardèche, as in the Vercors and the Ubaye Valley, the Germans, reacting vigorously, had dealt ruthlessly with demonstrations of independence. They attacked Le Cheylard, headquarters of the FFI, who quickly shifted into stronger defensive positions at Antraigues, north of Vals-les-Bains.[3]

Vaucheret, a strictly military career officer, strongly anti-Communist, quickly ran into difficulties in his attempt to unify the Maquis into an organized body of fighters. Unlike the areas east of the Rhône, where such officers as Lécuyer, Descour, Zeller, and de Lassus had been able to form an influential ORA segment, the Ardèche had no ORA and only a handful of regular army officers dispersed among the Resistance groups. Furthermore, the FTP was unusually strong, and Vaucheret, in an attempt to act not simply as military delegate but as FFI chief, antagonized many native leaders who had been ambushing Germans for months before he arrived. In the event, Col. Henri Provisor, FFI chief over the R-1 departments west of the Rhône, had to intervene. By the middle of July, he and Vaucheret had formulated a theoretical structure that recognized the able René Calloud as departmental FFI chief, together with a staff of AS and FTP officers. FFI headquarters remained in the hill country above Vals-les-Bains, with the PECTORAL mission nearby at Aizac. In time, the inter-allied PECTORAL mission grew to include about twenty persons, and altogether there were eleven Allied radio operators in the Ardèche with contacts to London and Algiers. Major Chassé was able to obtain a large number of parachuted supplies and occasionally to call in technical air support.[4]

The next military mission from SPOC to the Ardèche came in on June 28: Jedburgh team WILLYS, including the British Capt. J. C. Montague, a Frenchman, Capt. P. J. Granier, and a British wireless operator, Sgt. F. A. Cornick. Relations with the PECTORAL mission were not entirely satisfactory, since disputes developed as to whether the primary task should be gathering intelligence or carrying out sabotage operations. About three weeks later, on July 18, LOUISE, an OG of fifteen commanded by 1st Lt. W. H. McKensie and 1st Lt. Roy K. Rickerson, parachuted into Tandem at Devesset and, after making

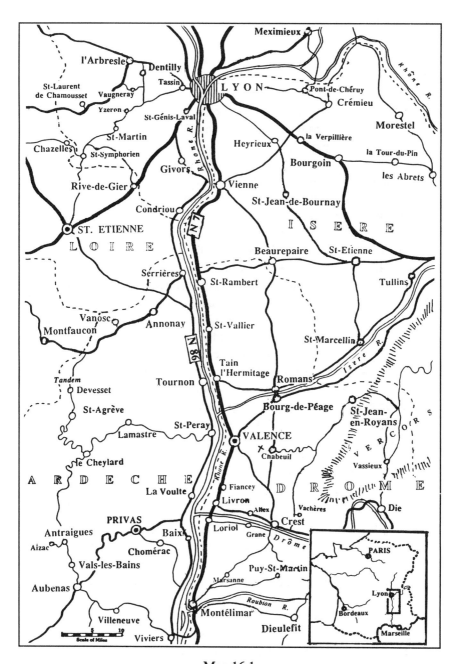

Map 16.1
THE RHÔNE VALLEY
Northern Parts of Ardèche and Drôme Departments

contact with PECTORAL, established its base of operations in a stone school-house near Aizac.[5]

The team soon saw action. They took orders from FFI chief Calloud, who assigned them to work with a *Groupe Franc* commanded by Sous-Lt. Fernand Crespy. With the OG and Jedburgh teams numbering eighteen, and the *maquisards* about twenty-five, the whole company of forty-three was typical of the many Resistance groups, mostly AS and FTP, under Calloud's command. Special Operations groups from outside comprised but a small part of the total clandestine effort, and, while this study concentrates on Allied missions, one should keep in mind that many guerrillas, with no outside contacts at all, kept up continued harassment of the occupier. The unique feature of the Allied missions lay in the fact that the agents were well trained, well armed, well supplied, and in touch by radio with Seventh Army strategic requirements.

High on the list of Allied priorities stood the need to limit German use of the Rhône valley—the roads, the railways, the bridges, and the river traffic. Air force bombings helped fill this requirement, but frequently with deplorable civilian casualties and unnecessary destruction of property. If the same results could be achieved through clandestine sabotage, such as Brooks' PIMENTO was accomplishing, the needless overkill could be avoided and the strategic requirements equally met. Such a situation led to OG LOUISE's first actions.

Seventh Army wanted a bridge over the Rhône not only destroyed, but dumped into the river so as to block navigation. Some of the FFI officers, like Calloud and Pierre Fournier, with engineering background, viewed the bridge at Viviers, about fifty miles north of Avignon, as a possibility. Because this was a suspension bridge, they were able, by cutting the cables on one side, to make it settle into the water. Fournier took charge of the operation, to which was assigned OG LOUISE and Crespy's company. The LOUISE report describes the result: "the bridge dropped flat across the river making it impossible for the barges and breaking all communication lines and power lines."

On July 26, LOUISE was joined by BETSY, a fifteen-man French-speaking OG that set up its base camp in the northern part of the Ardèche, at Vanosc, near Annonay, about halfway between Valence and Lyon. The team worked with local FFI companies and later, once the Allied landings forced a German retreat, harassed the withdrawing enemy along the western parts of the Rhône Valley. BETSY was commanded by Lt. Paul E. Boudreau and Lt. Leroy E. Barner. On August 10, when Vanosc was attacked by a German bomber, the OG lost one man (Sgt. C. A. Barnabe) killed and three wounded. Concern for their losses kept the OG men preoccupied at the time when the Ardèche liberated its prefectural seat, Privas.

In July, the possibility of liberating Privas, firmly held by German occupation forces, did not seem possible, but in August the prospects improved. Some German occupation troops had packed up and had begun to evacuate small towns. Calloud organized his Maquis formations so that, if the garrison at Privas moved out, he would be able to take over at once and make it possible for the Departmental Liberation Committee to replace the Vichy officials. By August 10, it had become clear that the German occupation troops were indeed preparing to withdraw. Two days later, they abandoned Privas, moving up the Rhône Valley to Tournon. Privas thus became one of the first prefectural cities to be liberated without assistance from Allied regular forces. Calloud deployed his companies around the town to safeguard it from a German return.

It is interesting to note that, while an event of outstanding political significance for the department had occurred on August 12, the journals of the American OGs contain no record that anything unusual took place during that week. In fact, some of the paratroopers had gone to the western edge of the department, where they were received with the usual Gallic enthusiasm as liberators. Others were busy assembling several 37-mm. guns that, in separate parachutes, had been dropped three days after Privas was liberated, on August 15, the same day Operation ANVIL/DRAGOON was launched on the Riviera beaches.

A conflict developed with regard to these 37-mm. cannon. The guns had been packed, unassembled, in containers and required considerable expertise to place them in working order, especially since some parts were damaged in landing. Vaucheret believed the guns should be made available to the FFI, not unreasonably considering that his *maquisards*, numbered in the thousands, possessed more combat potential than a handful of G.I.s. Not entirely convinced, but obeying the Frenchman's orders, McKensie began to train the French guerrillas on how to man the newly arrived weapon. With the long-awaited Allied landings now in process, the Ardèche guerrillas, as well as the Americans, believed the gun could soon be put to good use.

MORE OPERATIONAL GROUPS TO THE ARDÈCHE

The Americans in OSS were particularly anxious for the OGs, specially trained volunteer OSS paratroops, to be tested. Col. Russell Livermore, in charge of OG forces in the Mediterranean, from his command post in Corsica, urged Maj. Alfred Cox, the OG officer in SPOC, to get his men to the mainland. Uncommitted on the ANVIL/DRAGOON D Day, four OG teams, two Italian-speaking and two French-speaking, waited their turn. Cox had tried to send in one of the Italian groups, HELEN, led by Capt. Leslie Vanoncini, to the Larche area on August 11, and he had personally seen the men take off, but, prevented by an overcast sky from making the jump, the team returned to base. There they waited. As Vanoncini put it: "Day after day operations alerts would come up, only to be scrubbed later on in the day."[6]

From one point of view, an emphasis on the Ardèche did not make sense because the FFI had already taken over most of the towns when the German regular garrisons began to depart early in August. There were only isolated enemy groups still in the department, and most of these, with high concentrations of Russian and Polish troops—"Mongols" the French called them—were willing to surrender, indeed even to join the Resistance. However, with Hitler's retreat order of August 17, German contingents from the south began moving in north-bound convoys. Most of these had either crossed the Rhône to march up N7 or had avoided the mountainous Ardèche by traveling via Clermont toward Dijon and Besançon.[7] There still existed the possibility, however, that major forces would be using the west-bank highway N86, and this possibility became reality when on August 20 a new threat developed from the south.

Just as it appeared that most German garrisons had left, the Ardèche Department became the focus of heavy combat. Lieutenant McKensie, in charge of LOUISE and then at already-liberated Privas, learned on August 22 that a German column had been reported about thirty-five miles to the south. Furthermore, some elements of the German Nineteenth Army had crossed the Rhône at Montélimar and were pursuing their flight north in small groups along the west bank. The FFI chief, Commandant Calloud, alerted several AS groups, among them Lt. Charles Escudier's 51st and 52nd companies, which he ordered to set up a road-block at Baix, about midway between Montélimar and Loriol, but on the opposite bank. For several days, they tried to stop the Germans, but, exhausted and famished, the *maquisards* had to break off and fall back.[8]

The column reported to McKensie included forward elements of the *IV Luftwaffenfeldkorps*, commanded by General Petersen, which had been ordered to cover the French coast from Montpellier to the Spanish border. The corps, which had included three divisions, airport defensive units, and trainees, had already seen action, as the 198th, and parts of the 189th divisions, were fighting east of the Rhône. The remaining division (the 716th) and several thousand miscellaneous troops were streaming north by two routes, one along the Rhône and the other inland, toward the Ardèche by way of Montpellier, Alès, and Aubenas. The convoy extended for some 30–40 miles, its rear guard crossing the Gard River, west of Avignon, while its advance units probed the roads south of Aubenas. As some elements pushed through the area that Jed PACKARD surveyed, between Uzès and Alès, Capt. Aaron Bank tried to persuade de Lattre's staff to send a regular army force against them. The French, however,

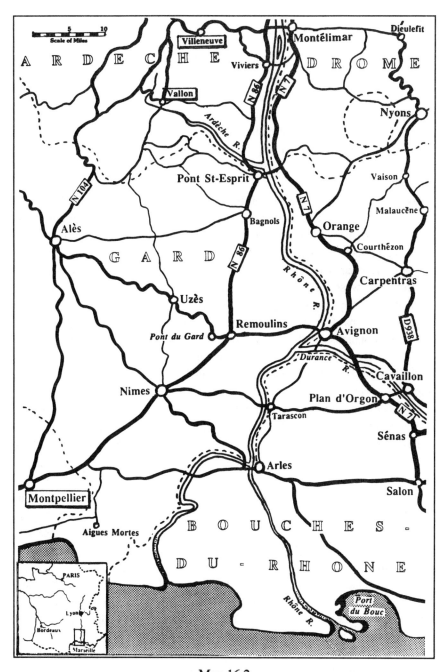

Map 16.2
THE LOWER RHÔNE VALLEY
German Retreat: Montpellier to Vallon and Villeneuve

short of gasoline and with only a few troops across the Rhône, were not yet in a position to take up the pursuit. Almost one hundred miles north, forward German elements reached St.-Peray, across the Rhône from Valence, on August 25, the day after Colonel Adams and Commandant de Lassus had made their premature attempt to seize Valence.[9]

Approximately halfway between the forward and rear guard units of Petersen's corps, the FFI had spotted several German convoy groups apparently headed for Aubenas, about ten miles beyond which lay Vaucheret's headquarters at Vals. Capt. Georges Picard (code named GEORGES), the FFI chief in whose sector the threat was developing, called upon Lieutenant Escudier, whose *maquisards* had just fallen back on Privas, to move over to Vals, and upon Lieutenant McKensie to block the fork about twenty miles farther south, where the Germans might choose the main road to Aubenas or a minor road to the east, leading to Villeneuve.

Other German troops, some of them disbanded garrison forces, were coming in from the west. They joined up with columns making their way north, producing perhaps another fifteen thousand men in addition to the elements of Petersen's corps. Commandant Calloud alerted many companies, AS and FTP, and they kept harassing the straggling Germans as best they could. Even though the Germans were not front-line combatants, they nevertheless possessed enough mortars and field guns to prevent the *maquisards* from completely blocking their path.[10]

McKensie set up his headquarters ten miles south of Aubenas and posted two sections of his LOUISE paratroopers, under Lieutenant Rickerson, a few miles farther south, each with one of two 37-mm. guns. There was only a little action during daylight, but throughout the night of August 24, a blacked-out German convoy took two hours to pass by. In the morning, the FFI reported that there were fifteen hundred Germans at Vallon, just northwest of the spectacular Ardèche River gorges. McKensie ordered the 37-mm. guns mounted above Vallon, commanding the town and its approaches. He was startled at the enemy numbers: "Instead of the reported 1500 Germans at Vallon, there were 10,000." Nor were they ready to surrender.

The Resistance forces around Vallon consisted mostly of FTP units under Capt. Ollier de Marichard, but they lacked the fire power to make a significant impression on the enemy columns. The 37-mm. guns of LOUISE provided the only real threat available to the Ardèche Maquis.

The OG knocked out three trucks, some half-tracks and guns, and killed possibly two hundred men. The enemy, having countered the fire, flanked the position and after a day-long fight forced McKensie, Rickerson, and their men, together with those FFI who stuck with them, to withdraw. The Germans captured the two 37-mm. guns. Escudier meanwhile had gone to Vals but, learning the Germans had gone farther east, withdrew toward Privas. He skirmished with Germans southwest of Privas and took eighty prisoners.[11]

On this same day, August 25, Major Alfred Cox, the OG officer at SPOC, together with the company's medical officer, Capt. John Hamblet, parachuted into Devesset with a six-man French-speaking group, LEHIGH, headed by Capt. Roger J. Morin.[12] Realizing that there had been some friction between McKensie and Vaucheret, Cox hoped to resolve the problem as well as develop better coordination of guerrilla activity. Vaucheret had come to Devesset, where he and Cox (who incidentally equalled him in rank) came to an understanding. Out of the discussion, Cox learned something of the French attitudes. Vaucheret told him that the department, with five thousand armed men, was essentially liberated except for the escape route by way of Privas and Route N86 along the Rhône. Cox and Vaucheret then drove to Vals, now FFI headquarters, where he met other members of the PECTORAL team, as well as Captain Montague (of Jedburgh team WILLYS) and Maj. Carl Nurk, a British officer of Russian ancestry,[13] sent in by SPOC to subvert the Poles, Cossacks, and Ukrainians—the "Mongols"—who made up a fraction of the German army of occupation. Later Cox met with McKensie and his men, who had to withdraw to a position south of Aubenas. He learned quickly about the recent operations and returned to Vals prepared to restructure his command by assigning OGs to specific sectors and by establishing a central reserve. He knew that two or possibly three more OGs would soon be coming in. He could not tell, however, how long the Germans would continue to move through the Ardèche or when units of the regular French army would arrive.

Cox would soon find out about Germans. He and his team, learning from the FFI that "a huge German column" (the head of Petersen's *IV Luftwaffen-feldkorps*) was headed for Tournon, on the Rhône's west bank, drove at once to a hilltop observation point. In Cox's words:

> Unfortunately we did not know that the column had left the Rhône to by-pass a blown bridge, and was headed west on the same road on which we were proceeding. We had good distance, about 40 or 50 yards between men, with two men on each side of the road. I had reached a point approximately 125 yards from a tunnel carrying an aqueduct over the road when the advance guard of the column—two open cars and a double line of foot troops—pushed through the tunnel. They deployed and opened fire immediately and machine guns opened up at almost the same moment from flank patrols, about 150 out in each flank.
>
> The fire was intense and too damned close for comfort, with mortar shells beginning to drop fairly close. We dropped into a ditch, lying in water

up to our chests, and covered ourselves with brushwood. The fire continued for quite some time and several flank patrols passed near us, but did not discover us.

Cox and his men finally made their way to a French farmhouse where the family, at the risk of their own lives, sheltered them until morning. Then, disguised in civilian clothes, they darted through a gap between the German convoys, took to the cover of adjacent hills, and ultimately found their way back to Devesset. Major Cox had very rapidly learned about the Maquis, the heroism of French civilians, the competence of the Germans, and Ardèche terrain. Cox estimated the enemy column, which took four days to pass through Tournan, as numbering 50,000. "Some of the equipment," he noted, "indicated that in addition to an infantry division many of the service units, Ordnance, Q. M., etc. from the south of France were included in the column. There was no armor, a few half-tracks and artillery, but in the main, foot troops and bicyclists."[14] Without heavy weapons, neither the OGs nor the FFI could directly confront the Germans, but they could observe and possibly take prisoners if they could find isolated groups or garrisons—especially those with a high proportion of disgruntled Slavs.

While Major Cox was observing the main German column passing through Tournon, and while the men of OG LOUISE busied themselves assembling a third recently dropped 37-mm. gun, the German column harassed at Vallon continued to press on toward Privas. Although weakened by lack of food and motorized transport, the column of possibly 7,000 still possessed artillery and around 500 vehicles, many of them horse-drawn. As they struggled northward, they were constantly attacked by over fifteen AS and FTP companies that Calloud had managed to deploy in the hills on either side of the German escape route. On August 29, some *maquisards* blew three bridges ten miles southwest of Privas. In the ravine-studded country, the lack of bridges caused a complete bottleneck for vehicles and heavy guns, many of which had to be abandoned in riverbeds. The Germans scattered, some to the hills where they were taken prisoner—over a thousand—by the *maquisards*. The principal column, numbering about 5,000, pressed on, seeking to by-pass Privas to the south, hoping to join the main convoys—such as Major Cox had encountered—working their way along N86.

By August 30, still hounded by the Maquis at their heels, this group reached Chomérac. Ahead of them lay more hazards, and having lost their heavy guns, they had no advantages over Resistance forces armed only with small-caliber weapons. Among the FFI groups east of Privas were George Maleval's 6th and 7th AS companies, together with some members of OG LOUISE and one

37-mm. cannon. (The newly arrived gun, however, with parts damaged in the drop, did not fire satisfactorily.)[15]

On this same day, LAFAYETTE, an Italian speaking OG commanded by Lt. Odilon J. Fontaine and Lt. Leonard Rinaldi, had dropped into Devesset and had been ordered by Major Cox to join LOUISE at the Maquis CP north of Privas. Learning from the Maquis that Germans had been reported a few miles east of Privas, Fontaine and Rickerson (of LOUISE), with an FFI patrol under Captain Maleval (MARGUERITE), drove out to investigate. They soon found a prisoner held by some FFI, and through him finally made contact with a German colonel who had five battalions scattered in the hills, including a "Mongol" company that wanted desperately to join the Allies.

This group represented a majority of the worn-out Germans, who were determined to make a last stand at Chomérac. The German colonel expressed willingness to negotiate if he could obtain the approval of his battalion commanders and if he would have a guarantee he was surrendering to the American army, equipped with artillery, not the Maquis.[16]

At the moment, the highest-ranking American officer in the area was Major Cox, who had gone to Devesset for a rendezvous with the newly parachuted OGs. An urgent phone call brought him quickly over the fifty miles of winding mountain roads that separate Devesset from Chomérac. The artillery was a different matter. The Americans could come up with nothing more formidable than a 37-mm. gun. However, word had come in that advance units of the regular French army had reached the Ardèche Department the day before. A resourceful French engineer, Raphael Evaldre, jumped on his bicycle and pedalled fifteen miles (downhill) until he encountered advance units of Combat Command Sudre.

When Major Cox arrived at Chomérac, he explained to the German colonel that his forces were surrounded. Finally, late in the afternoon, a French tank appeared and with a few shots persuaded the weary German officer to surrender. The OGs and FFI rounded up groups of enemy troops scattered among the hills, to a grand total of 3,824, including two colonels, six majors, and ten captains. Unable to cope with such numbers, the OGs stood by while the FFI rounded up the prisoners.

In most instances, the FFI abided by the Geneva Convention regarding prisoners, even though the Germans, when they caught "terrorists," invariably executed them, sometimes after abominable torture. Unknown to the Americans, who had guaranteed proper POW treatment, *maquisards* summarily executed some of the Germans. Reports reached the Americans that two colonels, a major, and 150 German prisoners had been killed. Lieutenant Escudier comments on this incident:

The prisoners were taken to Privas, Vals-les-Bains, Aubenas, and a number of other places. A German colonel was executed in the neighborhood of Privas, by Captain Maleval, known as "Marguerite," responsible for the Privas sector, under the orders of Commandant Calloud, FFI chief for Ardèche. This colonel was responsible for the massacre at Nîmes—they called him the "Butcher of Nîmes."

At Vals-les-Bains, 54 prisoners were executed by Commandant André Bourdin (code names: Richard, Dina) . . . the total was 54 Germans shot (150 is a fabrication). The Interallied Commission [i.e. PECTORAL] was opposed to these executions.[17]

The capture of over three thousand Germans proved to be the final operation for the two OG teams LOUISE and LAFAYETTE. With the prisoners in FFI custody, members of these groups finished up their duties, bade farewell to their FFI comrades-in-arms, and reported to Grenoble for debriefing. The remaining OGs prepared for the assault on Lyon.

Major Cox could only hope that the move on Lyon would open up more opportunities. A conscientious officer who loved action, Cox sincerely cared for his men, one of whom, Michael DeMarco of OG PAT, forty-seven years later at a reunion, could recall with affection his "flashing eyes and wide smile" as well as his "voice of command." Major Cox looked forward to one more guerrilla operation where his OGs, blending with their Maquis colleagues, would cooperate with them in one final action.

IV   From Grenoble
and Montélimar
to Lyon

17

North of Grenoble

When General Pflaum, commanding the German 157th Reserve Division, decided to abandon Grenoble, his troops had two possible escape routes, one to the northwest, toward Lyon, where they could join the main body of the Nineteenth Army, or to the northeast. Because Pflaum had been ordered to pull back to the Alps, the northeastern route, which led to the Mt.-Cenis pass and, farther north, to the Little St.-Bernard, offered the most reasonable possibilities for escape. Withdrawing along the broad mountain-lined Isère Valley out of Grenoble for thirty miles, the Germans faced a choice, as they entered the Savoie Department, of continuing to follow the Isère River past Albertville and into the Tarentaise, or of turning south, to work their way along the Arc Valley into the Maurienne, ultimately to reach Modane, where a ten-mile railway tunnel bores through the Alps to Italy. A few miles beyond Modane, Italy can be reached over the 6,000-foot Mt.-Cenis pass. As the retreat from Grenoble intensified, the Germans undertook to adapt the Modane tunnel roadbed, so that trucks could go through. They also used it to bring elements of the 90th Panzer Division from Italy into France. Whichever route they chose, the German convoys would confront harassment from the Maquis hidden in the mountains on either side of the road.

One of the first of the inter-allied missions, consisting of tough Pierre Fourcaud (French), H. H. A. Thackthwaite (British, representing SOE's RF section), and Capt. Peter Ortiz (an American marine) had been dropped in the area at the beginning of 1944. The members were attempting to assess Resistance strength in southeastern France, and they traveled through the Savoie, Isère, and Drôme Departments. Ortiz, known in the Resistance as Jean-Pierre, had visited the Drôme where he met L'HERMINE and de Lassus.

While the mission, withdrawn early in May, reported favorably on Resis-

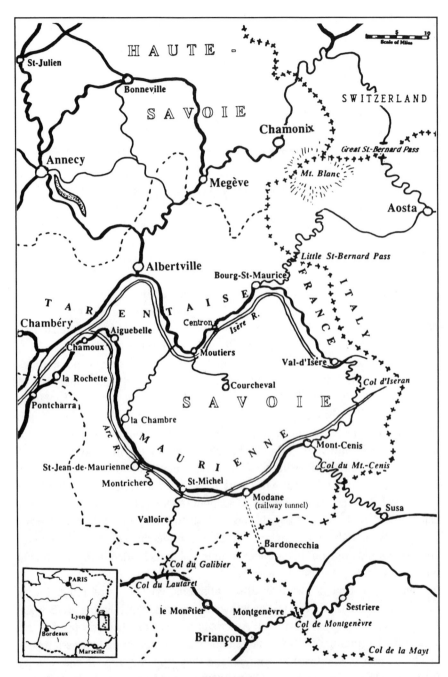

Map 17.1
MAURIENNE AND TARENTAISE

tance possibilities, some of the individuals they had encountered had been arrested or held in suspicion by the Gestapo. Among those were members of the Arcelin family, who had cooperated with the UNION mission as couriers, cipher clerks, and drivers. The mission also worked closely with Roger Lévy, code named INCIDENCE, who had been employed by the Ministry of Finances before he had been forced underground. When the UNION group left, Lévy maintained contact with London and kept in touch with the Savoie Resistance, as well as with SOE agents, Heslop (XAVIER) in the Ain and Jean-Pierre Rosenthal (CANTINIER) farther north in the Haute Savoie.[1]

After Thackthwaite and Ortiz reported back to London, Fourcaud was arrested. Thus, in July, with the southern France landings assured, no British or American SOE or OSS agent specifically had responsibility for the two important routes, the Maurienne and the Tarentaise, to Italy, nor was there any important contact with Colonel de Galbert (MATHIEU), FFI chief for Savoie. To correct this situation, London sent out another UNION mission, headed by Major Ortiz, accompanied by American Capt. Francis L. Coolidge and five U.S. Marine sergeants; two weeks later Algiers dispatched the PROGRESSION (UNION III) mission together with Jedburgh team EPHEDRINE.[2]

First to reach the field, Ortiz and his group landed near Beaufort (about halfway between Albertville and Mont Blanc) on August 1. One of the marines was killed in the jump, and one suffered a broken ankle.

It had appeared in July that German garrisons had been abandoning Savoie, but it soon became clear that the German command would not readily relinquish the routes from Grenoble to Italy. This was particularly true when, on August 15, word of the landings, several hundreds of miles away, reached the mountain passes. Ironically, just as the invasion began, Ortiz and several of his men were captured. Confronted by a superior German patrol, Ortiz had surrendered rather than permit the village of Centron, southwest of Bourg-St.-Maurice, to be destroyed. Thus, after August 16, leadership of the UNION team, and responsibility for its contacts with London and Algiers, devolved once more on INCIDENCE—Roger Lévy—together with Captain Coolidge, who though wounded had escaped.

Meanwhile, the missions from Algiers, PROGRESSION (British Maj. D. E. F. Green, Canadian Maj. C. B. Hunter, and radio operator Lieutenant Fournier) and Jedburgh EPHEDRINE (Capt. Rabeau and Corporal Bourgoin, both French), were slowly making their way north.[3]

By August 22, the day Grenoble was liberated, they reached Captain VILLON's Maquis camp at Montricher, in the heart of the Maurienne, between St.-Michel and St.-Jean. VILLON (code name for Captain Gerlotto, a regular French artillery officer) impressed Green and Hunter with "his firm and assured bearing" and his ability to muster five hundred to a thousand *maquisards*, who nevertheless possessed very limited amounts of arms and ammunition. No equipment had been parachuted to the area since April, and VILLON had no regular contact with Colonel MATHIEU at Chambéry, only thirty air miles away but very difficult of access because of the rugged terrain.

As the German garrison abandoned Grenoble, the Maurienne road toward Italy now saw a constant stream of convoys, trucks, armored cars, bicycles, and horse carts, working their way toward the passes. The German rear guard withdrew along the left bank of the Isère, leaving the right bank road, which leads to Chambéry and Albertville, relatively clear. Although there were pockets of resistance along the way, Colonel Meyer's 179th Infantry sent patrols as far as Chambéry and Albertville with small opposition.

The other road, leading to Aiguebelle and southeast to Modane and the Mont-Cenis pass proved to be another matter. The FFI, determined that the Germans should not get into the Maurienne, did everything in their power to block the ten-mile stretch between La Rochette (where the Americans had placed their most northerly road-block, about thirty miles from Grenoble) and Chamoux, to the east of which lies the opening to the narrow Arc River Valley and the road to Italy. The Germans, just as determined to hold the road open, laid down artillery barrages against which the embattled *maquisards* had little protection.

On August 26, the 179th Regiment extended its road-block closer to Chamoux and called up some batteries of the 160th Field Artillery, but unfortunately for the FFI, Truscott was more intent on getting the 45th Division north of Lyon, and on the next day, had both the 179th and the 180th get ready to shove northwest from Grenoble. Anticipating relief by French regular troops in the Savoie, Truscott did approve the 180th's 1st Battalion remaining at Grenoble until the French began to arrive. There is a pungent entry in the 180th S-2 Journal, authorizing guns and some infantrymen to Chamoux:[4] "In the valley up there is about a thousand Krauts raising hell, burning villages, etc. and we want to send a Battery of Artillery up there to shoot them up and then come back out."

However, the 180th could not remain beyond August 30, leaving the Maurienne and the Tarentaise to the FFI. From their command post at Montricher, the PROGRESSION and EPHEDRINE officers could see the smoke rising from burning villages, and they learned of horrid reprisals wreaked on the civilians. The strength of the Germans and lack of any Allied support, however, forced Captain VILLON to hold his people back so that the villages could be saved.

By August 30, the German rear guard had given up its holding operation at

Chamoux and at noon on the next day, had abandoned La Chambre, about ten miles from St.-Jean and the Maquis/Allied CP at Montricher. On September 2, the FFI, which now included an FTP battalion from the Haute-Savoie, and the STEPHANE company from Isère, planned to attack the German rear guard as it passed through St.-Jean. Rabeau recalled that the Maquis force was too small to make a serious impression on the Germans, but believed that "we did help to hasten their departure." Two days later, the Germans made their way through St.-Michel de Maurienne, while Major Hunter and the STEPHANE group forced the German garrison at the Fort du Télégraphe, just south of St.-Michel, to surrender.[5]

Since no American forces had come to help, it was hoped that the French regular army would soon make its appearance. In fact, advance units of General Linarès' 3rd Algerian Infantry had sped through Grenoble on September 1, and Colonel Bonjour, commanding a reconnaissance regiment of Algerian Spahis, had met Colonel Bibo at Chambéry on September 2, making arrangements to relieve the American troops in the Briançon area.

By this time, however, it was too late for regular forces to take any decisive measures in Savoie. Most of the Germans had reached Italy, and the few remaining were held in check by the FFI, which had liberated Savoie beyond Bourg-St.-Maurice in the Tarentaise, and up to St.-Michel in the Maurienne. On September 5, a battalion of the 5th *Tirailleurs Marocains* (of the 2nd Moroccan Division) brought some much-needed artillery to St.-Michel, and elements of the 3rd Algerian Division, in de Lattre's words, "cleaned up the Tarentaise." De Lattre had his eyes on the roads to Germany north of Switzerland, but General Béthouart, now commanding the French army's I Corps, would oversee much hard fighting in the Alps well into 1945. Also, many of the *maquisards*, with whom PROGRESSION, EPHEDRINE, and UNION had been in contact, would sign up with the regular army, serving France until the war's end as members of the 27th Alpine Division.[6]

ISÈRE DEPARTMENT: NORTH TO LYON

The situation to the northwest of Grenoble was similar to that in Savoie. On the first ten miles from Grenoble, following the Isère River, the road is dominated on either side by the great cliffs of the Chartreuse range to the north and the Vercors to the south, but beyond lies flat country with low rolling hills. The vast network of roads and numerous towns made a front line difficult to achieve. The American forces established road-blocks as far as the plain, but as of August 24, had no orders to move out of Grenoble toward Lyon or to the north. The American top commanders at this time were more concerned about the German Nineteenth Army withdrawing up the Rhône. (Colonel Adam's 143rd Infantry had left Grenoble, not to attack Lyon, but to go southwest, on the western side of the Vercors, to try to cut off the Germans at Valence.)

Consequently, it was left to Commandant Le Ray's FFI to prevent the Germans from retreating toward Lyon, to try to liberate towns where German garrisons remained, and to fend off any counterattacks toward Grenoble. On August 23 and 24, the FFI did heroic work throughout the area lying between the mountains and Lyon, 75 miles to the west. In hard fighting, they liberated Bourgoin, in the center of this area, and constantly harassed a German column despatched from Lyon to the point where it was forced to turn back at Voreppe, eight miles from Grenoble. When the 179th Regiment was ordered, on the 25th, to start reconnaissance toward Lyon, units found that the enemy had already been struck off balance by intensive guerrilla attacks. On the 26th, 45th Division recon found the road net clear as far as Bourgoin. Leaving the mopping up of the northeastern region to the Resistance, Meyer sent Philip Johnson's 3rd Battalion to Bourgoin on the 27th, where the Americans cooperated with Descour's *maquisards* to prevent the Germans from reoccupying the city. Johnson remained there for three days while the 1st and 2nd Battalions leapfrogged to positions farther north.[7]

The Americans moved so rapidly that there was scarcely time for Truscott to coordinate his strategy with that of the FFI. While Butler had met Colonel Constans as early as D + 5 (August 20), no general officer before August 24 had established contact with Constans' counterpart for R-1: Colonel Descour. With U.S. troops in Grenoble on the 22nd, accompanied by OSS and SOE agents, Descour and Huet soon learned about the Seventh Army, and they did their best to reach the appropriate authorities. On the 24th, coming down from Grenoble, Descour met the 45th Division commander, General Eagles, at Aspres.[8]

With the liberation of Bourgoin, Huet and Pecquet had made their way to that city (where Descour had established his command post), took note of the situation there, and then turned south to try to locate de Lassus and Constans, who might be able to facilitate an encounter with the American commanders. Crossing the Vercors Plateau, Huet and Pecquet reached de Lassus' head-quarters on August 28, just as Dahlquist's battle to cut off the retreating Nineteenth Army at Loriol was reaching its climax. From de Lassus' command post they could hear the artillery blasts ten miles to the west.

On the next day, the two officers saw Dahlquist and then, in the afternoon, met with General Truscott in his trailer parked at Aspres. Descour was also present and participated in the discussions with Truscott and his staff. Pecquet

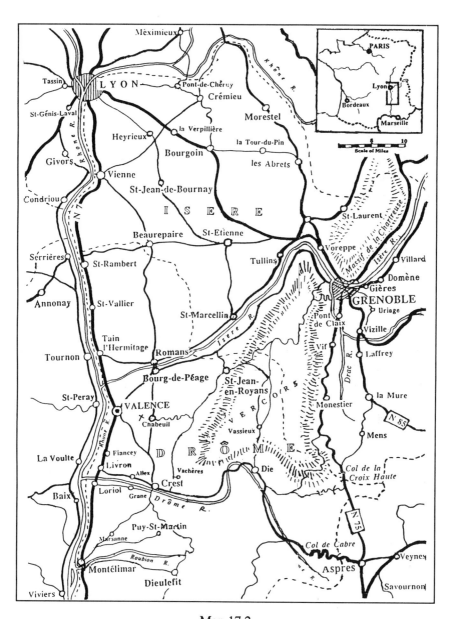

Map 17.2
GRENOBLE TO LYON

recalled Huet saying that, while the Americans were equipped to wage all-out war, the *maquisards* could assist by scouting, by working behind the lines, and by sabotage. Pecquet came away with the impression that the Americans had been convinced; in any case, Truscott promised to provide the FFI with gasoline and to turn over captured enemy weapons to them. Truscott's diary simply records that the general met with Descour, "a local FFI big wig," but there is no comment on overall strategy.[9]

The conference of Huet with Descour resulted in a tentative FFI plan to attack Lyon, based on the assumption that the Germans would try to defend the city. Carrying out instructions from Alban Vistel, Descour sent orders to his commanders to ready their forces in the outskirts and to the Resistance groups within Lyon to form up with them. The cooperation that developed between Americans and FFI around Lyon was complicated by internal French controversies over politics and tactics.

It was in the south, before 1943, in the Unoccupied Zone, that organized Resistance had begun. When the three southern Resistance groups, *Combat*, *Libération*, and *Franc-Tireur* had coalesced into the MUR, Lyon became the center for clandestine action in the south. When late in 1942 the Germans swept into the previously unoccupied Vichy-dominated area, Lyon provided them with a center for administration: It was here that the notorious Klaus Barbie concentrated his efforts to destroy Jews and Resistants; it was here that Jean Moulin, de Gaulle's choice to unify all Resistance movements, had been arrested and tortured; it was at Lyon where the stark Montluc prison, holding hundreds of political prisoners, represented for all Frenchmen a horrible symbol of Nazi persecution and cruelty.

The enthusiasm for liberating Lyon, manifested throughout the FFI ranks outside, pulsated as well in the hearts of those residents within the city who for two years had suffered under Nazi domination.[10] The popular opposition surfaced especially among workers, many of them Communists, whose ranks had been thinned by forced labor deportations. On the morning of August 24, even though the German garrison remained intact, workers and FTP guerrillas in the Villeurbanne section began an uprising. The action was premature: With thousands of German troops now streaming through Lyon, General Wiese could scarcely brook a movement that might jeopardize his use of the Rhône bridges. The insurrection was quickly and ruthlessly put down.[11]

The uprising in Lyon brought into focus a fundamental issue: Should an internal insurrection liberate a city, or should the citizens wait for regular Allied troops. Communists and leftists, supported by FTP guerrillas, saw the first alternative as a means of seizing political power before the armies arrived, whereas de Gaulle, with the backing of the FFI and de Lattre's army, exerted every effort to ensure order by means of authorities whose loyalty to his provisional government could not be questioned.

As far as Lyon was concerned, the issue divided itself neatly into east and west. Alban Vistel, recognized as the regional (R-1) FFI chief, exercised authority over his subordinates Henri Provisor, west of the Rhône, and Marcel Descour, on the east.[12] Provisor, whose forces were heavily FTP, advocated an insurrection within the city, while Descour, a regular army officer, already in touch with VI Corps commanders, preferred an attack from outside. There is a certain irony that a high OSS involvement—the OGs under Major Cox—should have been giving support to a command strongly influenced by the Left.

Vistel found himself on the fence, but he could not help but be impressed by the strength he observed building up in the east. As reports of Allied successes multiplied, many French citizens, previously uncommitted, left their homes to join the constantly swelling ranks. Vistel considered the Villeurbanne insurrection thoughtless and premature, and while he harbored some doubts about an outside FFI attack, he could not conceal his pride when he counted the numbers, perhaps three or four thousand, bivouacked within fifty miles of Lyon, increasing constantly as veterans and recruits poured in from south, east, and north.[13]

By the first of the month, thousands of FFI had encircled the city, but it had now become clear on both sides of Lyon that the Resistance attack should be geared to that of the regular Allied forces. On the western side, advance patrols of the French 1st Armored Division had reached St.-Etienne, fifty miles from Lyon, and on the eastern side, Dahlquist was on the outskirts prepared to move on the city if Truscott gave the order.

PLANNING THE LIBERATION OF LYON: THE ALLIED ARMY

While Vistel and all the French would have liked an immediate Allied attack on Lyon, Truscott had no desire to get bogged down inside a city unless he possessed clear indications that the Germans intended to make a stand there. With the last rear guard German units crossing the Drôme bottleneck on August 28, Truscott, while disappointed in his failure to destroy the Nineteenth Army, had to plan his next moves. He was operating under orders to advance north toward Dijon and to capture Lyon. By the same orders, Patch had directed de Lattre to advance along the west bank of the Rhône and assist in the capture of Lyon.

On August 29, when he received these orders, Truscott was not yet in a position to move on Lyon, which in any case he was reluctant to attack if it meant possession of a sack with the contents gone. He had held the 179th Regiment at Grenoble from the 23rd until the 27th while he shunted all the available gasoline and ammunition to Dahlquist during the Montélimar battle.

Truscott, however, had no intention of deploying the 45th Division against Lyon: If it should prove necessary to move into the city, he would use Dahlquist's 36th Division coming up along the Rhône. Furthermore, he had good information from Seventh Army G-2 and from French agents about the German defenses.

Some of Truscott's intelligence came from espionage sponsored by OSS. One of the members of the Strategic Services Section (SSS) team, Justin Greene, had been attached to the 36th Division since the landings. He had met Colonel Daviron (ORA chief in the Hautes Alpes) after Gap had been liberated, and the two had gone along to Grenoble on the following day. Once in Grenoble, Greene was able to round up a number of French agents who had been working for OSS, and obtain intelligence data from the Rhône to the Alps. Among the agents were two from Penny Farthing, Henry Hyde's most successful circuit. Greene infiltrated them into Lyon, where they obtained "the complete defense plan" of the city, which in due course was delivered to General Dahlquist as his division moved up to the outskirts. The General "was very happy and called the captain of the team in to compliment him on the material."[14]

The plan about an uprising in Lyon was transmitted to Patch's headquarters. It may have been discussed on August 29 when Patch went over his tactical plans with Gen. Maitland Wilson, General Devers, and others at St.-Tropez. Later in the same day, the group met with de Lattre. According to the Seventh Army history, regarding Lyon:[15]

General de Gaulle's military representative warned against "premature action." On 30 August the FFI at Lyon was given orders to be ready to establish contact with Allied columns, which were rapidly approaching the outskirts. The enemy was to be harassed but not actively engaged. An all-out attack was to take place only in cooperation with troops of the American and French armies.

Truscott received Patch's order during the afternoon of August 30. Subsequently, according to Truscott, Patch "ordered me that, for political reasons, it would be desirable to permit the French forces to enter Lyon first." This order, exactly what Truscott wanted, came at the crucial time when the VI Corps commander was galvanizing his forces for a strong thrust northward.[16]

Truscott could assume that the German Nineteenth Army, once through Lyon, would go straight north to Mâcon, Chalon-sur-Saône, then to Dijon or

Besançon, and ultimately to the Belfort Gap. In keeping with past experience, Truscott could also expect a flank protection by the 11th Panzer Division some 20 to 30 miles east of the main column. This would presumably mean defense of the main highway from Lyon to Bourg, with possible patrols to the east. Truscott could send his troops more safely along the Grenoble-Bourg road—the Route Napoléon, N85—to the east beyond reach of enemy patrols. Along this thoroughfare, he had General Eagles send Colonel Dulaney's 180th Regiment. To Dulaney's left, protecting the 180th's flank, would go Colonel Meyer's 179th.

General Wiese viewed the situation much the same as Truscott. He had to hold the Lyon-Bourg road as flank protection for his main body. He ordered von Wietersheim to prevent the Americans from crossing the Rhône or, assuming they may have in any case crossed farther east, to hold a line of defense along the Ain River, with destruction of all bridges.[17]

The tactical maneuvering consequent to the German and American decisions brought elements of the 11th Panzer and the 179th RCT into a confrontation that climaxed at Meximieux, a small town lying twenty miles northeast of Lyon, a few miles west of the Chazey bridge over the Ain.

In the midst of this confrontation fought several hundred *maquisards* of the Ain, Rhône, and Isère Departments. Certainly the FFI irregulars and American G.I.s had fought together from the first days of the landings—at Digne, Grenoble, Montélimar, and Bourgoin, along with hundreds of other skirmishes and ambushes—but the combats at Meximieux and its approaches were unique in the almost spontaneous way in which *maquisards* and Americans came to be fighting side by side. Unlike other battles, there had been no agreed-on strategy at higher staff levels, for indeed the 179th was pressing north, and the French guerrillas were moving southwest toward Lyon. Chance brought them together when the German Panzers struck.

18

End of DRAGOON: Meximieux and Lyon

Confident that Dahlquist's 36th Division could control the situation around Lyon, Truscott resumed the race northward. On August 29, he ordered the 45th Division to lead the advance. Colonel Meyer, commanding the 179th RCT, had his 2nd Battalion start for the Rhône, where advance patrols from Johnson's 3rd Battalion had found that the bridge between Pont-de-Chéruy and Loyettes stood intact and defended by guerrillas of Martin's Company. The FFI had repaired a small airport close by which served thereafter as a base for Piper Cub observation and liaison planes.[1] A jeep patrol sped up to Meximieux and encountered no enemy. On the next day, Capt. Fred Snyder drove his jeep just beyond Meximieux up to the old medieval fortress town of Pérouges, where he signed the "Golden Book" of the Hostellerie de Vieux Pérouges: "We are happy to be in France."[2]

Behind Snyder, on the 31st came the 1st Battalion, taking over at Meximieux, while the 2nd Battalion shoved ahead to Chalamont, seven miles farther on. Philip Johnson's 3rd Battalion remained behind at Loyettes, protecting the bridges over the Rhône and Ain, and safeguarding the line of supply.

Colonel Meyer and his deputy Col. Preston Murphy spent the night of August 31–September 1 at Meximieux, now occupied by Lt. Col. Michael Davison's somewhat depleted 1st Battalion. When the 2nd Batalllion passed through Meximieux, Colonel Grace had sent F company to reinforce an FFI road-block at La Valbonne. To replace company F, Davison had released B company to Grace's battalion. Since he had left company C to guard his rear, this left Davison with only companies A and D , Headquarters company, and two tank destroyers.

Colonel Meyer had outposts and artillery around Meximieux, but assuming the German threat, if any, would come from the west, he had not kept a guard

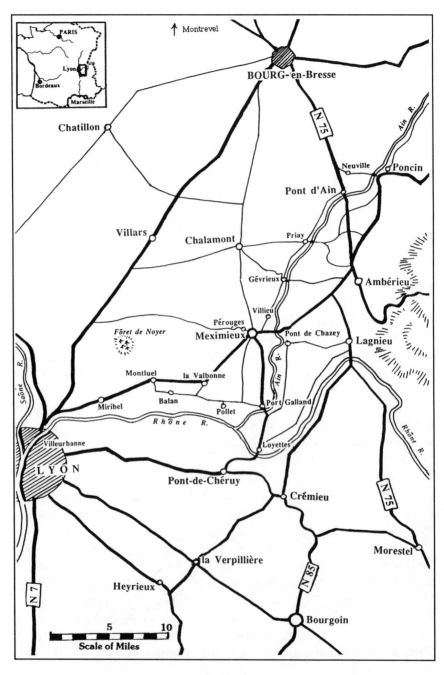

Map 18.1
THE BATTLE OF MEXIMIEUX

at the Chazey bridge, due east of Meximieux. During the night, German forces moved on the bridge, encountering only a small group of *maquisards* who unfortunately mistook them for Americans. Five of the guerrillas, members of the Martin company, were killed. Blowing the bridge shortly before dawn, the German troops then prepared to strike Meximieux from the northeast and east.[3]

No clear word had reached Colonel Meyer about the bridges at Pont d'Ain and Chazey, nor did reports from La Valbonne suggest a major enemy thrust. "My rest was quite complete," he recalled. "I found there was no news, everything was going as scheduled, so I mounted the jeep and in high spirits took off up north to watch the action of the [2nd] battalion which was 'up front'." When he heard firing behind him, he thought "a group of wandering or waiting Germans must have picked a scrap with some of Mike's [Lt. Col. Michael Davison] men." Meyer then learned from his executive officer, Colonel Murphy, that "there was a distant threat of tanks to the southwest. . . . Then the communications went out."

Not only were the Germans, elements of the 11th Panzer Division, taking the offensive at Pont d'Ain and Meximieux, but they were attacking to the south as well—the bridges at Pont-de-Chéruy, Loyettes, and Port Galland—protected by the 1st Battalion's company C and by the whole of Philip Johnson's 3rd Battalion, together with 160th Field Artillery batteries emplaced along the Ain River.

Around 9:00, about 150 Germans began an attack from the southwest toward the railroad station where Davison had his command post. The German infantrymen had support from tanks, but when a Panther was knocked out by 155-mm. artillery fire, the remaining tanks kept their distance. The S-2 journal reported "3 enemy tanks 800 yards southwest. Look like vultures awaiting the kill." With the tanks not joining in, Davison's men, with FFI *maquisards* alongside, repulsed the threat in a heavy fire-fight. By 1:00, the Germans had withdrawn—but only to regroup.

By 10 A.M., Murphy knew that he had to cope not with a group of "wandering" Germans, but with a full-fledged assault supported by formidable Mark IV and Mark V Panther tanks. Left in command at Meximieux, Murphy established his headquarters in an old convent. Unable to reach Colonel Meyer, he sent a message to Colonel Grace, ordering his 2nd Battalion back to Meximieux. Meyer did not learn of the order until noon but, with faith in Murphy's assessment, did not question it. Murphy also requested General Eagles, then at the 45th Division CP at Voiron, to divert some tank destroyers and antitank guns from the 157th Regiment, which he knew was moving rapidly north behind the 180th.

Murphy realized he would be confronted shortly with another attack. Although the morning thrusts from east and west had been turned back, Murphy now knew that a sizeable German force had surrounded Meximieux and had captured some outposts. Wounded men from company F and from Giraud's FFI section were coming into the convent, cared for in the basement by French and American doctors. The FFI group at Pérouges, where Captain Snyder had been posted with two tank destroyers, had been attacked. The tank destroyers, one out of gas, the other with its turret jammed, were abandoned. (Two Germans siphoned gas from one to the other and later drove it around town.) The Château north of Meximieux had come under attack.

Colonel Murphy, still without word from Meyer or the 2nd Battalion, repeated his appeal to General Eagles for reinforcements and pulled in his outlying positions for a defense of the town. Colonel Davison deployed the few forces he controlled as effectively as possible. His men—interspersed with maquisards—fought from roof tops, windows, behind walls, and in railway cars pulled up on a siding. He stationed his two tank destroyers near the City Hall back to back on Meximieux's main street, the Rue de Genève, where they commanded the two roads leading into town.

The German attack developed about 2:30 P.M., when six tanks, with infantrymen aboard, rumbled into town from the south, continued under heavy fire, which dispersed their riders, and turned into the main street heading for the City Hall. A shell from one tank struck the City Hall tower and killed the observer posted there. Davison later recalled what happened:

> The first tank, knocked out by the M-10 [tank destroyer], burst into flames and ran into the lobby of the Lion d'Or. Then the second was hit. The third and fourth got into high gear and charged the tank destroyer, scraping the paint as it went. But the other tank destroyer knocked it out. Number 4 tank went by the TD: Number 5 not sure. Meanwhile the tank destroyer was re-loaded and hit No. 4 and "D" Company hit No. 5 with a mortar, and blew it all to hell.

The hulks of these monsters, charred and smoking, remained as silent testimony of a German last effort to protect the Nineteenth Army retreat. Another tank, coming in from the east, was hit, turned tail, and rejoined others that stood guard but did not enter the town. Two great 105-mm. self-propelled guns had tried to set up positions south of town, only to be knocked out by bazookas.

By late in the afternoon of September 1, the Germans began to withdraw. General Wiese had given the order for all troops defending Lyon to pull out during the night of September 1-2, and he needed the 11th Panzer Division for a defensive ring around Bourg. Wiese had received only fragmentary reports about the fighting along the Ain River, but he had enough information to believe "that the Americans had given up the plan to proceed to Lyon and instead would shift their attack to the north, advancing from Ambérieu."[4]

Although many German tanks and infantrymen withdrew, a token force remained along the Ain River into the night, trying to pull a last-minute victory out of what had become a stalemate. With six smoldering hulks—tanks and self-propelled guns—left in the Meximieux area, the Germans, although unwilling to risk another strike against the American tank destroyers and artillery, left two tanks to support the riflemen closing in on stubbornly held positions.

The Germans kept hammering into the evening . They directed artillery fire at the Château, where a group of Americans and FFI, including the company of Chouchou (Marcel Vion), had been holding out during the day. While trying to repair his machine gun, Vion was killed by an exploding shell. The defenders repelled a series of attacks until finally the tank destroyer, abandoned at Pérouges and now manned by Germans, moved in and, with infantry surrounding the post, forced the garrison's surrender.

Late afternoon also saw the death of another Maquis officer, Lieutenant Giraud, whose group had fought at La Valbonne, and later, side by side with Americans, at the convent. He had gone on an exploratory patrol and died instantly from a direct hit near the square that now bears his name.

The final stage of the Meximieux battle was unique in the way French *maquisards* and G.I.s became completely brothers-in-arms as they defended themselves from a desperate assault on the convent. Neither tanks nor artillery could be brought to bear in the semi-darkness of hand-to-hand fighting. As reported by the FFI commander, Captain Clin:

> In front of this big building is a rather large courtyard. In accord with Colonel Murphy, . . . Colin [Captain Clin] transformed the convent into a fortress. The Maquis lads were at all the doors, all the windows. The order was to hold until reinforcements arrived, but not to waste ammunition. An enemy detachment climbed over the walls, slid into the courtyard and deployed in ditches. After heavy firing, the barrage stopped all of a sudden. The Germans let us know through prisoners that they demanded our surrender. They advised the "terrorists" not to obey their chiefs because they are all sleazy foreigners (*métèques*). Maybe they believed it, but they were quickly interrupted by a loud "*merde*." Gunfire sprayed from all the windows.
>
> One of our patrols sneaked into the courtyard, and moved up within a yard of the Germans, whose chief was knocked out by one of our lads. Ten minutes later, we had chased off all our assailants.
>
> A second attempt to climb over the wall was stopped cold by our

machine-guns. Colin sent out a strong reconnaissance detachment. He got word back: the Germans were withdrawing.[5]

By two o'clock in the morning of September 2, all the German forces were pulling back to the Lyon–Bourg road. Although the bridges at Chazey and Pont d'Ain had been destroyed, the 11th Panzer had failed to cut those at Loyettes or Poncin, and the way was clear for Truscott to keep moving on toward Bourg.

Meximieux stands as a unique monument, however, for FFI and American cooperation. Obviously, only American tank destroyers and artillery could oppose German tanks and self-propelled guns, but at the level of infantry combat, the *maquisards* fought side by side with the G.I.s and with equal valor. The French had possibly 300–400 deployed, numbers comparable to those of the Americans who were engaged. One estimate, for the final fight in the convent, has 150 Americans and 150 *maquisards*. In casualties, the French counted 39 killed, 40 wounded, and 12 prisoners; the Americans 11 killed, 30 wounded, and 50 prisoners.

The citizens of Meximieux keep alive the memory of American participation in this engagement. Colonels Murphy and Davison were made honorary citizens, and Colonel Davison (in 1972 a general in command of U.S. forces in NATO) is commemorated by "Place Davison," named in his honor.

THE LIBERATION OF LYON

Following the advice of the regular army commands, both east and west Resistance groups postponed the date for attacking Lyon from September 1 to September 2, and then to September 3. On the morning of the 2nd, however, Lyon's streets showed no signs of German occupancy; during the night, the rear guard had blown all but one of the many bridges over the Rhône, and a good many over the Saône. Had the Resistance armies been so ordered, they might have entered early on the second, to be confronted only by some scattered *Milice* fire and by a few Germans left behind.[6]

General Dahlquist, whose command post was then several miles south of Lyon, learned about the German withdrawal that same morning. With his entire 36th Division advancing to the outskirts, he could have pressed on and entered the city. The southeast part of Lyon forms a quadrant bounded on west and north by the Rhône, which makes its right angle turn in the city's heart. Outside the arc, about four miles from the center, perimetered by what is now the Boulevard Laurent-Bonneray, advance patrols mapped out bivouac areas for the half-tracks, trucks, and armored cars that would be moving in around noon.

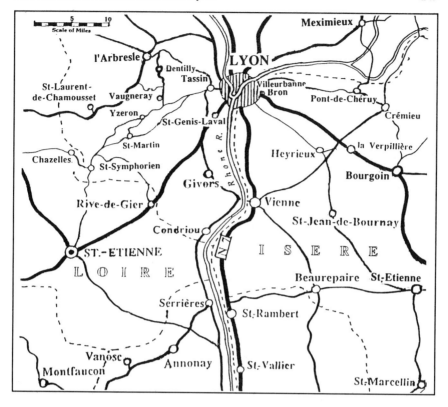

Map 18.2
APPROACHES TO LYON

One 142nd Regiment patrol, under Lt. James R. Crocker, guided by Tony Brooks (of SOE's PIMENTO circuit), reached the city's center around 11:30 and reported the Germans had left, but had blown up the dozen Rhône bridges that separate the eastern half from the "peninsula." One of Crocker's guns, aiming at snipers, set the roof of the Hôtel Dieu on fire. German artillery, he reported, still protected the rear guard, menacing the French and Resistance elements to the west.[7]

Truscott saw no reason for American troops to enter Lyon. The only problem for the VI Corps would occur if Lyon, an administrative and rail center, would become so entangled in local riots that logistic support would be impaired.

Dahlquist, however, had received no orders to move, either into or away from Lyon. A patrol, returning from the city around 5:00 in the afternoon, confirmed that no enemy forces remained in the section east of the river. By this time Truscott had informed Dahlquist definitely that he should not enter Lyon but could send some engineers to examine the bridges, as well as some light forces to reinforce the FFI.

Shortly before dark, Lt. Weldon M. Green, of the 142nd Regiment, led a company of infantry and tanks as an honor guard (and as a protecting show of force) for the new administration.[8] Alban Vistel had taken over the prefecture and notified Yves Farge, *Commissaire de la République*, that he should openly assume his new responsibilities. The Lyonnais populace was in the streets, shouting and rejoicing. Nevertheless, although the eastern sector was clear, and many of Descour's men held key positions, the official date for the FFI attack remained the same: dawn of the following day, September 3.[9]

Meanwhile, the Allied special forces were receiving reinforcements from the pool of OGs, Jedburghs, and other agents remaining in Algiers. In the week prior to the attack on Lyon, almost forty people were dropped by parachute into the Ardèche Department: one individual, two operational groups, and two Jedburgh teams, all coming into the drop zone near Devesset in the early hours of August 30.

Air force Lt. Paul C. Sheeline, unconnected with any field unit, had been sent to help resolve the reported friction between Vaucheret and OG LOUISE. Sheeline met both Vaucheret and Major Cox when he landed, and quickly obtained assurances that the problem had already been resolved. Vaucheret asked Sheeline to remain on his personal staff in a liaison capacity.[10]

After a few hours' sleep, Sheeline accompanied Vaucheret to Henri Provisor's CP at Yzeron, west of Lyon, where he learned that the FFI leaders, in planning the assault on Lyon, wanted the participation of as many OGs as possible. Major Cox believed that, while some of his men would be needed to help with the German prisoners, he could send Lieutenant McKensie and a crew to Lyon with one of the 37-mm. guns, as well as the other OGs.

Landing at the same time as Sheeline, OGs LAFAYETTE and HELEN, and Jedburghs SCION and MASQUE hoped they could serve some useful purpose before their value would be lost.[11] One of the OGs, LAFAYETTE, reinforced LOUISE; the other, HELEN, was immediately assigned to the projected assault on Lyon. Led by Captain Vanoncini, the team marched to St.-Etienne, southwest of Lyon, where it joined the Maquis battalion commander, Captain GEORGES [Georges Picard], and his next in command, Charles Escudier.

Of the two Jedburgh teams, SCION was Franco-British (Maj. O. P. Grenfell and Sergeant Cain with French Captain Revard), and MASQUE Franco-American, Capt. N. Guillot and Sergeant Poche (U.S. Army in spite of their French-sounding names), and French Captain de Gramont. These teams landed far too late to carry out the instruction and leadership expected of the Jedburghs, and simply became attached, more or less as observers, to Commandant Vaucheret's staff.

These units did not comprise all the special forces in the area. Another Jedburgh team, JUDE, had been sent to the field from England on August 15, along with part of a French SAS (Special Air Service) unit. The team consisted of British Capt. W. L. O. Evans and Sgt. A. E. Holdham, together with French Capt. J. Lavisme. They had been attached to Colonel Basset's (MARY) FFI force north of Lyon and accompanied his forces when the city was liberated.

In addition to the Jedburghs, OGs and inter-allied missions, there was a scattering of downed airmen and isolated G.I.s who had joined up. Among these must be counted Stephen Weiss and seven companions who had become separated from their unit during the attack on Valence. They had been taken in tow by the Resistance, ferried across the Rhône, and attached to Binoche's sector for several days before joining an OG.[12]

In the course of September 2, the Maquis forces, the OGs, the Jedburghs, and French regular troops moved into position, mostly in the hill country directly west and northwest of Lyon. Since this deployment was of course west of the Saône River, the French could readily occupy the heights commanded by the great Fourvière basilica, but they would still have to cross the Saône to reach the "peninsula," where the City Hall (Hôtel de Ville) was located, and again, cross the Rhône to reach the prefecture.

On the morning of September 3, section after section of Maquis fighters poured into Tassin and the entire western section of Lyon bordering on the Saône River. Only a few isolated German positions remained, but there were still pro-German members of the hated *Milice*, sniping at the oncoming guerrillas from windows and roof tops.

The Jedburghs and the American OGs advanced toward Lyon alongside their French comrades. The Jedburghs MASQUE and SCION joined the Ardèche FFI commander Calloud at Dentilly, northwest of Lyon. HELEN and BETSY came up just south of the FFI CP at Yzeron, along with McKensie and the gun crew from LOUISE. Lieutenant Sheeline went back to Devesset in an attempt to shepherd another OG, WILLIAMS, just landed, toward Lyon. Unfortunately, with no transport available, he had to leave this section, which only reached Lyon the day after its liberation. Major Cox and the LEHIGH group joined Captain Vanoncini's section (HELEN), which was traveling with Lieutenant Escudier's company from Privas.

Although the Germans had left the city, some danger remained from the *Milice*, whose sniping provided a macabre counterpoint to the general happy rejoicing. As Major Cox, describing the actions of HELEN and LEHIGH, recalled it:[13]

Somehow or other we got out in front of the attacking Maquis who were still forming up, and had to fight our way through wildly cheering crowds to get to where we wanted. We reached the Cathedral overlooking the city just about as the first Maquis and French Army units arrived at the river bank below us, and for half an hour enjoyed the spectacle. . . .

The Germans had blown all RHONE bridges (although one still was usable for foot traffic), and all but two SAONE bridges. When the French Armored Cars began to cross on our bridge, we dashed across on the other, and aided them in hunting down the Milice.

It would be interesting to record something of the mad hysteria that sprang up in LYON. The Milice were hunted down and killed with mad displays of hate. The actual battle casualties consisted of one or two Maquis and one or two civilians, but for the next two or three days, simply pointing a finger at a person and yelling "Milice" was enough to have him torn limb from limb. . . . The FFI as quickly as possible regained some semblance of control, and the sporadic firing gradually died away.

In the course of the day, both Major Cox and Lieutenant Sheeline were able to locate 36th Division headquarters and confer with General Dahlquist's staff. The general himself sneaked into the city for a quick look-see. He wrote his wife:[14]

I went in . . . unofficially because I was not supposed to be there even though my patrols had been in the night before. The reception was tremendous. When they found I am a "General" which none of them believe (I guess I do not look the part) they really let loose.

General Dahlquist, however, could not tarry. On that day, Truscott was already laying siege to Bourg-en-Bresse, forty miles to the north. He needed the Texas Division for pursuit, not for the good life in France's third city. By September 4, the men of the 36th Division had put Lyon behind them and were entering Bourg.

With the date September 3, the liberation of southeastern France, objective of Operation ANVIL/DRAGOON, comes to an end. The basic directive did not consider actions beyond Grenoble and Lyon, and the jurisdiction of SPOC over special operations extended no farther. Except for those involved in combats along the Italian frontier, the OGs, the Jedburghs, the inter-allied and liaison missions, and 4-SFU could consider their work completed, and their activities overrun. For many of the Maquis, the war also was finished, but for others, the liberation of the southeast meant joining the French regular army or becoming immersed in local politics. In any case, the heroic days were over.

19

Conclusion

Inevitably, in concluding a study on the French Resistance, one must ask: How helpful were the Maquis? Was there a solid and effective relationship among the FFI, the special forces, and the Allied regulars?

To a direct question, a direct answer: The Maquis brought substantial assistance to the regular forces. Comments from Allied units, even though they rarely identify individual persons or groups, bear consistent witness to Resistance cooperation and aid, just as German statements reiterate the repugnance and fear that governed the occupiers' attitude toward the "terrorists."

"The Maquis scour the hills . . . bring in prisoners . . . patrol at night . . . they work in close collaboration with the regular Allied forces." So ran the comment of a war correspondent with the 45th Division.[1] The 180th Infantry Operational Report for August 1944 acknowledges FFI aid "from the first day." The Combat Team "received information in every town," "reports of enemy strength were accurate," a cut-off platoon "escaped with the aid of the French who cared for them and guided them back." "The continual harassing by the Maquis of the German supply lines and communications weakened the enemy to the extent that he was unable to put up an organized resistance."[2] A report from an officer of the 142nd Infantry echoes this refrain: "The FFI have been a constant and thorough help in giving us valuable information, in posting lookouts on high ground around us, and in actually fighting and capturing the enemy. They deserve a great deal of our gratitude and respect."[3] Occasionally one finds that a good word for special agents crops up: The 117th Reconnaissance Squadron reported that "strong support was received from the local Maquis who were well organized in this vicinity by the OSS. Their splendid assistance although ill-equipped was indeed an inspiration to the American forces. . . . Their deeds will live forever in the memory of the Squadron."[4] At higher levels, officers also expressed their appreciation of Resistance help. General Butler is generous in recalling how his Task Force benefited from FFI actions:[5]

> These stalwart sons of France, and sons of the Blue Devils....proved invaluable to us. They reinforced the meager infantry in critical situations and guarded over our life line to the rear. . . . It is only fair to state that without the Maquis our mission would have been far more difficult, if indeed not possible.

The VI Corps commander, General Truscott, echoes these sentiments:[6]

> The Maquis were well provided with arms and explosives by the Allies, and Allied officers with communications had parachuted in to assist them in coordinating their operations. We had expected a good deal of assistance from them and we were not disappointed. Their knowledge of the country, of enemy dispositions and movements, was invaluable, and their fighting ability was extraordinary.

Unarmed, the *maquisards* could of course help the Allies with information and guide service, but the assistance they could provide as soldiers depended on what kind of weapons and training they had. Some of their arms came from hidden French army supplies, but the most effective ones, the Sten and Bren automatic guns, the bazookas and P.I.A.T.s, the plastic explosives, reached them in the cylindrical containers, over 20,000 of them in southern France, parachuted by the Allies to hundreds of prearranged drop zones. To southern France, more than 3,000 tons of supplies, as well as 500 persons—organizers and instructors—arrived by parachute. When the program reached its highest efficiency in mid-1944, more and more material reached the Maquis: For example, on the night of August 12, eleven aircraft took off from Algiers, flew to their assigned pinpoints, and dropped 67,000 pounds of ammunition and supplies, 18 "Joes," and 225,000 pamphlets. Any estimate of Resistance success must assign credit to those outside France—the British, American, and French organizers in SOE, OSS, and BCRA, the directors and packers in the supply depots, the pilots and crews of aircraft, the communication experts and radio operators—all of whom contributed to the end result: harassing and driving out the Nazi occupiers.[7]

Several specific actions highlight the value of FFI assistance. A prime example has to be the destruction of the bridge over the Drôme River between Livron and Loriol. There the retreating Germans confronted a devastating road-block, with men and equipment backed up for miles. Had Truscott's VI Corps been able to concentrate more fire power at the Drôme, the Americans might literally have destroyed the Nineteenth Army, stymied and forced to a last-ditch fight by reason of Maquis sabotage. Even then, although most of General Wiese's troops managed to escape, the Allies were able to wreak enormous havoc, as anyone who in August 1944 witnessed the wreckage could testify.

Another service worth special emphasis must be the argumentation of Gen. Henri Zeller, who persuaded Patch to accept the merits of a thrust toward Grenoble. Zeller arrived in Naples in early August when Seventh Army operational plans gave major attention to reaching Toulon, Marseille, and the Rhône, with no more than flank protection to the north and east. Zeller served as the influential catalyst in getting those plans altered; General Wilson, at Patch's request, modified the ANVIL/DRAGOON order to permit a march toward Sisteron. When Task Force Butler and VI Corps elements drove quickly to Sisteron, Aspres, and Gap, they took Pflaum's 157th Division by surprise and caused it to abandon Grenoble on August 22. With Pflaum's withdrawal, Wiese's Nineteenth Army lost a buffer against an attack from the east and, had it not been for the extraordinary mobility of the 11th Panzer Division, would have found its flank dangerously exposed.

The FFI played a significant role in areas that the Seventh Army by-passed. Along the Alpine frontier, more FFI than regular troops kept harassing the Germans until elements of de Lattre's French First Army appeared on the scene. In that vast mountainous area south of Lake Geneva—the Haute-Savoie, Savoie, and eastern Ain Departments—the Seventh Army left the Maquis to cope with the Germans as best they could. Also, to the west, once Seventh Army joined Patton's Third Army, thousands of Germans found themselves trapped, confronted not with regular troops, but with the FFI. Any account of Maquis contributions must examine the Alps and southwestern France, although this study, limited to the cooperation of Maquis and Seventh Army, makes no attempt to chronicle Resistance activity in regions where the guerrillas fought essentially on their own.

Examples and testimony can be repeated to make a conclusive case: The French Resistance seriously hampered the German forces and provided effective assistance to the Allied forces of ANVIL/DRAGOON. This is not to say that in all situations complete harmony governed relations between the regulars and the guerrillas. There were instances in which the Allied commanders, not comprehending the capabilities of the insurgents, called upon the *maquisards* to serve as if they were a well-trained infantry. Such situations caused unnecessary casualties and occasional hard feelings. On the other hand, many of the underground fighters, imbued with an implacable compulsion to kill Germans, complained when they were assigned to minor roles, such as the guarding of prisoners.

While most of the French within the ANVIL/DRAGOON area hailed the Americans as welcome liberators, enthusiasm for all aspects of Yankee tactics was not unanimous. Many French civilians believed that Allied bombers missed more bridges and hit more towns than was necessary. Criticism of badly aimed air raids came consistently from Communists, but all French people deplored wanton destruction that served no purpose. Even the guerrillas, much as they admired American tanks and howitzers, sometimes expressed shock at the overkill tactics whereby shelling might destroy a town in an effort to oust a handful of enemy defenders.

The foregoing problems, however, were minor when viewed in terms of the overall accomplishments of regular troops supported by thousands of *maquisards*. Particularly impressive was the way in which much of the cooperation had to be improvised. The G.I.'s had received virtually no briefing on French guerrillas, and were agreeably surprised at the difference between the French and the Italian civilians they had encountered south of Rome. As one Yankee soldier told a Frenchman in Digne: "If the Italians had supported us the way the French have, the war would already be over."[8] The cartoonist Bill Mauldin, who had been with the 45th Division in Italy and followed it to France, recalled: "The French were honestly and sincerely glad to see the Americans come, and the farther north we worked the more hospitable the people became. I had the feeling we were regarded truly as liberators, and not as walking bread baskets. It was a far cry from Italy."[9] With little information about Seventh Army strategy, the Maquis could sense the general direction of the Allied offensive and rallied round, "out of the woodwork," to render what assistance they could. They provided immediate on-the-spot information about German positions, even though their estimates of enemy numbers tended to be exaggerated. Advance units, such as Task Force Butler, urgently needed tactical intelligence and could not wait for army's G-2 to factor in the information from air surveys and ULTRA messages. Butler's decision to occupy Digne and Gap, providing him with flank protection, was clearly influenced by Maquis arguments.

Could this mutual assistance between Maquis and regulars have been less improvised and better organized? Indeed it could have been, but only with direction at the highest levels, and with an organization less cumbersome than the one that existed. Even so, if the ANVIL decision had been made earlier and the advance not so rapid, many of the problems might have sorted themselves out. Symptomatic of the entire operation's complexity stands the organization diagram, referred to in Chapter 5, wherein General Cochet attempted to outline the relationships: to the French chief of staff, under the minister of war, in de Gaulle's provisional government; to Soustelle's DGSS and the "Service Action" within it; to General Maitland Wilson and sections of AFHQ; to SPOC; to

4-SFU; to General Patch's Seventh Army; to General de Lattre's Army B; to the military delegates in southern France as well as to the *chefs* FFI. This simplification leaves out, of course, the complicated divisions within each office—for example, relations between SOE and OSS within SPOC, or other activities such as communication and codes, intelligence and counterintelligence, scheduling of aircraft. With three nationalities involved, together with air, naval, and ground forces, in a complex amphibious operation, no improvement in coordination could have been made in the short time available for planning and execution.

Normally a major operation requires months of preparation, and, if the campaign is to progress smoothly, it needs to correspond approximately to the planners' time schedule. ANVIL, however, was not normal: The final decision came only on July 2, six weeks before the landings. To be sure, planning for ANVIL had proceeded since the Teheran Conference where, late in 1943, the Big Three agreed on a landing in southern France, but this planning could not, for security reasons, bring the French Resistance into top-level decisions. To include the French would have required, on the Allied military side, a directive at the highest echelon—specifically the Combined Chiefs of Staff—but the Combined Chiefs could not take initiative without the approval of Churchill and Roosevelt, and the American president refused to recognize de Gaulle's National Committee as the French provisional government. Roosevelt's unbending position prevented a clear cut early acceptance of Gaullist officers as the legal and official representatives of France. Churchill, while supporting SOE and the Resistance in southeastern France, so strongly opposed ANVIL that he forced a postponement until scarcely a month remained before the troops were scheduled to land.

Suppose Roosevelt, Churchill, and the Combined Chiefs of Staff had unanimously and enthusiastically concurred that ANVIL must coincide with OVERLORD in late May or early June, and that the Big Three had recognized de Gaulle as heading a French provisional government. Assume also that the Italian campaign proceeded on schedule and that no Anzio prevented an early release of landing craft for ANVIL. Under such conditions, the Allies would have supported Gaullist delegates and liberation plans. Would there then have been in France a unified military organization, more effective than the FFI structure headed by General Koenig? If this hypothetical Allied recognition had come in, say, February or March 1944, would the FFI have been, in June, a stronger and more effective force? An affirmative answer would have required a unification of Resistance movements as well as a massive introduction of weapons, instructors, and qualified officers to mold the FFI into a cohesive force. It is unlikely that these conditions could have been met.

Even if we assume that the Combined Chiefs of Staff agreed to send significant amounts of aid to the Resistance, we are still faced with a formidable problem: The Supreme Command would have to divert material, officers, and aircraft from other programs. If planes capable of dropping supplies were to be used, they would have to be acquired from missions already going to Greece, Yugoslavia, and Italy. Note the actual situation in 1943 to 1945:[10]

	Number of Sorties	Gross tonnage
Greece	2,064	4,205
Yugoslavia	11,632	16,469
Italy	4,280	5,907
	17,976	26,581

Compare these figures with those for southern France:

S. France	1,713	2,878

When one considers that, in spite of Churchill's personal efforts to intensify aid to southeastern France, the actual assistance authorized by the Combined Chiefs of Staff was so far below the quotas for the Balkans and Italy that it would have taken enormous pressures at the very highest levels to alter the priorities.[11]

Granted that political and practical considerations militated against sending significant aid to the Resistance, there is still another element that must be factored in: How many Allied officers in 1944 were sold on guerrilla warfare? Consider not simply the Marshalls and Alanbrookes, or even the Eisenhowers, Montgomerys and de Lattres, but the generals who commanded corps and divisions, the colonels and majors who were close to the firing line. No courses in commando operations then graced the curriculum of Sandhurst, West Point, and St.-Cyr. Such courses did exist in 1944, but many were sponsored by SOE and OSS, organizations frequently viewed with mistrust by regular officers. During World War II, no television series romanticized the Green Berets.

Clearly, the regular military staffs were willing to obtain whatever help they could from guerrillas, but no planning officer would have dared place such reliance on Resistance support that he would have based an operation on it.[12] Planning officers in 1944 did not think in FFI terms; they thought about air support, artillery, tanks, mobility, and logistics, while the *maquisard* talked of surprise attacks, ambushes, sabotage, living off the land, and knowledge of seldom-used mountain passes. Colonel Zeller was surprised, in Naples two weeks before the landing, how little French regular officers understood conditions inside France.

While the FFI, if recognized earlier and more strongly supported, could have been somewhat more effective in the ANVIL/DRAGOON campaign, Resistance forces could not have been the decisive element. But any attempt to evaluate the relative effectiveness of the Resistance in southeastern France runs into an insurmountable road-block: Hitler's retreat order of August 16 produced a unique situation. With the Germans abandoning their hold on the south, the Seventh Army advanced way ahead of schedule. Based on assumptions valid for Salerno and Normandy, the ANVIL planners assumed a beachhead build-up of several weeks, then a breakthrough, and finally possession of Grenoble and Lyon in three months. In actual fact, the Allies reached Grenoble in one week and were almost to the Rhine before three weeks had passed.

If the planners' timetable had prevailed, the historian, facing a completely different situation, might have reached different conclusions. The Jedburghs, the OGs, and other missions, all of whom complained that they were sent in too late, would have had several months with the FFI before they were overrun. There would have been time to work with the Maquis, to coordinate operations with regular forces, and to promote fifth-column-type activities to hamper German defenses. The 4-SFU group, with its mission of facilitating cooperation with the FFI, would have had a month to organize and get all its personnel and transport ashore. As it was, the first agents on land found the units they were to accompany already 100 miles ahead of them. The full complement of 4-SFU reached the beach after the Seventh Army had left the Mediterranean Theater. If cooperation with the Resistance appeared to be helter-skelter and improvised, it was in part due to a rapidly moving retreat-and-pursuit situation.

While the liberation of Digne, Gap, Grenoble, and Lyon came easily, in areas where the Germans decided to fight, the conflicts reached different proportions. In the two port cities, Toulon and Marseille, the Resistance had not in the years of enemy occupation made any dents in the German defenses and, while the Maquis hindered truck movements in the cities proper, it took de Lattre's French First Army, with howitzers and armor, along with naval bombardment, to force a surrender. Along the Rhône, where General Wiese was able to deploy three divisions, all of the formidable array of artillery and air bombardment the Allies could concentrate on a fifteen-mile stretch did not prevent the Germans from breaking through. Also, defenses along the Italian frontier, which the Germans were determined to hold, kept the Americans and French at bay until well into 1945.

Thus, southeastern France does not provide the conditions on which a complete and fair assessment of Allied–Resistance cooperation can be based. However, if one is willing to forgo an exact and quantitative analysis, one can affirm that, without help from the French Resistance, the Allied task would have been extremely more difficult. Conversely, the regular armies boosted Maquis morale and helped them accomplish tasks otherwise impossible. This was a symbiotic relationship, and the Allied forces gratefully pay tribute to the French Resistance for the incalculable benefits they reaped from their hidden ally.

Appendix: Special Operations in Southeastern France

OPERATIONAL GROUPS (OGs)

Company "B," 2671st Special Reconnaissance Battalion (OSS), under command of Maj. Alfred T. Cox. OGs normally comprised thirteen men and two officers. All were American. (Dates are given American style: month/day/year.)

	Leaders	Arrived in Field	Area
ALICE (Signal Plan HYDROGEN)	Lt. R. N. Bernard Lt. D. J. Meeks	8/8/44	Drôme
BETSY (Signal Plan OXYGEN)	Lt. P. E. Boudreau Lt. L. E. Barner	7/26/44	Ardèche
EMILY (Signal Plan HELIUM)	Lt. A. P. Frizzell Lt. O. M. Huguet	6/9/44	Lot
HELEN (Signal Plan BISMUTH)	Capt. L. Vanoncini Lt. V. Ralph	8/30/44	Ardèche
JUSTINE (Signal Plan MAGNESIUM/ BARIUM)	Lt. V. G. Hoppers Lt. C. L. Myers	6/29/44	Vercors

LAFAYETTE (Signal Plan SODIUM)	Lt. O. J. Fontaine Lt. L. L. Rinaldi	8/30/44	Ardèche

*LEHIGH
(Signal Plan
SIMONE)
	Maj. A. T. Cox
	  (Commanding Officer,
	    Co. "B")
	Capt. J. Hamblet
	  (Medical Officer, Co. "B")
	Capt. R. Morin
		8/25/44	Ardèche

LOUISE (Signal Plan STRONTIUM)	Lt. W. H. McKensie III Lt. R. K. Rickerson	7/18/44	Ardèche
NANCY (Signal Plan ALUMINUM)	Capt. A. Lorbeer Lt. W. F. Viviani	8/13/44	Hautes-Alpes
PAT (Signal Plan NITROGEN)	Lt. C. E. La Gueux Lt. M. A. De Marco	8/7/44	Tarn
PEG (Signal Plan PLATINUM)	Lt. G. H. Weeks Lt. P. Swank	8/12/44	Aude
RUTH (Signal Plan ARSENIC)	Lt. M. C. Brandes Lt. C. O. Strand, Jr.	6/4/44	Basses-Alpes
WILLIAMS (Signal Plan MERCURY)	Lt. H. L. Herres Lt. C. P. Davis	9/2/44	Ardèche

*LEHIGH consisted of only five men plus the three officers.

JEDBURGH TEAMS

(Abbreviations: Am=American; Br=British; Can=Canadian; Fr=French; S. Afr.=South African.)

	Leaders	Arrived in Field	Area
CHLOROFORM	Capt. J. Martin (Fr) (Nom-de-guerre: Martino) Lt. H. D. McIntosh (Am) Lt. J. Sassi (Fr) (Nom-de-guerre: Nicole)	6/30/44	Drôme, then Hautes-Alpes
CINNAMON	Lt. F. N. Ferandon (Fr) Capt. R. Harcourt (Br) Lt. J. G. Maurin (Fr)	8/14/44	Var
CITROEN	Capt. J. E. Smallwood (Br) Capt. R. Alcée (Fr) Sgt. F. A. Bailey (Br)	8/14/44	Vaucluse
DODGE (Joined VEGANINE)	Capt. C. E. Manierre (Am) Sgt. L. T. Durocher (Can)	6/26/44	Drôme
EPHEDRINE	Lt. L. Rabeau (Fr) Lt. L. E. Swank (Am) Cpt. J. Bourgoin (Fr)	8/13/44	Savoie
GRAHAM	Maj. M. G. M. Crosby (Br) Capt. P. Gouvet (Fr) M/Sgt. W. H. Adams (Am)	8/13/44	Basses-Alpes
MINARET	Maj. L. Hartley-Sharpe (Br) Sgt. J. W. Ellis (Br)	8/14/44	Gard
MONOCLE	Capt. J. Tosel (Fr) Lt. R. H. Foster (Am) M/Sgt. R. C. Anderson (Am)	8/14/44	Drôme
NOVOCAINE	Lt. C. J. Gennerich (Am) Lt. J. Y. Le Lann (Fr) T/Sgt. W. T. Thompson (Am)	8/7/44	Hautes-Alpes

PACKARD	Capt. A. Bank (Am) Lt. C. Boineau (Fr) Lt. F. Montfort (Fr)	7/31/44	Gard
SCEPTRE	Lt. W. C. Hanna (Am) Lt. F. Tevenac (Fr) M/Sgt. H. W. Palmer (Am)	8/14/44	Hautes-Alpes
VEGANINE	Maj. H. N. Marten (Br) Capt. C. L. Vuchot (Fr) (Nom-de-guerre: Noir) Sgt. D. Gardner (Br)	6/9/44	Drôme
WILLYS	Capt. P. J. Granier (Fr) Capt. J. C. Montague (Br) Sgt. F. A. Cornick (Br)	6/29/44	Ardèche

The above-listed teams operated in the ANVIL/DRAGOON area. Other Jedburgh teams also operated in southern France: ALAN, AMMONIA, BUGATTI, CHRYSLER, COLLODION, JEREMY, JOHN, JUDE, MARK, MARTIN, MASQUE, MILES, QUININE, SCION, and TIMOTHY.

INTER-ALLIED AND SPECIAL MISSIONS

	Leaders	Arrived in Field	Area
BASSES-ALPES (Also known as Maquis Mission MICHEL)	Capt. H. Chanay (MICHEL) (Fr) Capt. A. Hay (EDGARD) (Br) Lt. M. Lancesseur (VICTOR) (Fr) Lt. M. d'Errecalde (LUCAS) (Am) D. Ferracci (ROBERT) (Fr) Marie Bauer (SOUTANE) (Fr) A. Appere (ANTOINE) (Fr) L. Paucaud (ADRIEN) (Fr) Dr. H. Rosencher (Fr)	4/10/44 Agents came in from March to June)	Basses-Alpes

BASSES-ALPES	Cdt. C. Sorenson (CHASUBLE) (Fr)	8/4/44	Basses-Alpes
	Maj. H. Gunn (BAMBUS) (Br)		
	Capt. J. (Kerdrel) Halsey (LUTRIN) (Br)		
	Capt. J. Fournier (CALICE) (Fr)		
	Maj. X. Fielding (CATHEDRALE) (Br)	8/11/44	
	Capt. J. Lezzard (EGLISE) (S. Afr)		
	Capt. Y. F. Hautière (VESTIAIRE) (Fr)		
	Sgt. L. Fernandez (RUDOLPHE) (Br)		
EUCALYPTUS	Maj. D. Longe (Br)	6/29/44	Vercors
	Maj. J. Houseman (Br)		
	Lt. A. Pecquet (Am) (Nom-de-guerre: Paray)		
HAUTES-ALPES	Cdt. J. Pelletier (CONFESSIONAL) (Fr)	8/7/44	Hautes-Alpes
	Maj. R. W. B. Purvis (MANIPULE) (Br)		
	Capt. J. C. A. Roper (RETABLE) (Br)		
	Lt. M. Volpe (ROSSINI) (Am)		
ISOTROPE	Cdt. J. Baldensperger (ISOTROPE) (Fr)	6/9/44	Lozère
	Maj. D. Hamson (ETOLE) (Br)		
	Capt. G. Pezant (ROCHET) (Fr)		
	QM L. Barthou (PELICAN) (Fr)		
	S/Lt. P. Fournier (PERDRIX) (Fr)		
	Maj. W. Jordan (PINTADE) (Br)	6/29/44	
	Capt. M. Castaing (RADEAU) (Fr)	7/7/44	

PECTORAL	Cdt. J. P. Vaucheret (VANEL) (Fr) Maj. Chassé (TRANSEPT) (Can) Capt. Williams (Fr)	6/13/44	Ardèche
TOPLINK	Maj. L. Hamilton (CROSSE) (Br) (Nom-de-guerre for L. Blanchaert of Belgian origin) Capt. P. O'Regan (CHAPE) (Br) Lt. S. Kalifa (PARADISIER) (Br) Lt. M. Morpurgo (MICHELANGE) (Am)	8/1/44 8/11/44	Hautes-Alpes
UNION I	Capt. P. Fourcaud (SPHERE) (Fr) Capt. P. Ortiz (CHAMBELLAN) (Am) Maj. H. H. A. Thackthwaite (PROCUREUR) (Br)	1/6/44	Savoie, Drôme, Isère
UNION II	Capt. F. Coolidge (AIMANT) (Am) Capt. P. Ortiz (CHAMBELLAN) (Am) Mission included five U.S. Marine sergeants: R. E. LaSalle, F. J. Brunner, J. Bodner, C. Perry, and J. Risler Joseph Arcelin (Fr)	8/1/44	Savoie
UNION III	Maj. D. E. F. Green (PROGRESSION) (Br) Maj. C. B. Hunter (DALMATIQUE) (Can) Lt. Fournier (AUTRUCHE) (Fr)	8/13/44	Savoie

VAUCLUSE	Cdt. C. de Mangoux (AMICT) (Fr)	7/12/44	Vaucluse
	Maj. J. Goldsmith (ORFROI) (Br)		
	Capt. P. Labelle (NARTEX) (Can)		
	Capt. R. C. Bourcart (HORS BORD) (Fr)		
	Lt. R. Hébert (CORVETTE) (Fr)		
	S/Lt. P. E. Morand (BECCASSINE) (Fr)		

LEADERS OF SOE CIRCUITS IN R-1 AND R-2, ACTIVE IN 1944

	Principal Members	Area
JOCKEY	Lt. Col. F. Cammaerts (ROGER) (Br)	R-1 and R-2
	Christine Granville (PAULINE) (Br)	
	(Nom-de-guerre for Krystyna	
	Skarbek, of Polish origin)	
GARDENER	Lt. Col. R. Boiteux (FIRMIN) (Br)	Bouches du Rhône
	Capt. G. A. Cohen (Br)	
MARKSMAN	Lt. Col. R. Heslop (XAVIER) (Br)	Ain, Savoie
	J.-P. Rosenthal (CANTINIER) (Fr)	
	Capt. Denis Johnson (GAEL) (Am)	
	(With three nationalities represented, similar to an inter-allied mission.)	
PIMENTO	Maj. A. Brooks (ALPHONSE) (Br)	Lyon, Montauban,
	Lt. R. Caza (EMMANUEL) (Can)	Toulouse, Rhône
		Valley, RR System
		of southern France

FRENCH COUNTERSCORCH TEAMS
(Groupe de parachutistes de la Marine)

Leaders	Arrived in Field	Area
Capt. de Corvette L. P. A. Allain (LOUGRE) (Dropped in the Var with Lt. G. Jones, 8/12/44)		

CAIQUE	Eng. Off. (Nav.) Parayre (CAIQUE) Eng. Off. Granry (COTRE) Eng. Off. Lavigne (SLOOP)	7/18/44	Marseille
SAMPAN	Lt. (Nav.) de la Ménardière (SAMPAN) Lt. Midoux (JONQUE) Lt. Sanguinetti (CANOT) Maître Turluer (PERROQUET)	6/14/44	Toulon
GEDEON	Ens. Ayral Ens. Moore (Br) Maître Badaud	8/12/44	Toulon
SCHOONER	Eng. Off. Kervarec	8/20/44	Sète

FRENCH SPECIAL FORCES

Bataillon de Choc (15 men, similar to OG)	Lt. Corley Asp. R. Muelle	8/2/44	Drôme
Equipes d'encadrement (Recruiting Teams)	Capt. D. Hennequin (HEPP) Lt. Beaumont (BATUT)	8/1/44 8/4/44	Drôme Drôme

SPECIAL PROJECT OPERATIONS CENTER (SPOC)

Commanding Officers
Lt. Col. John Anstey (Br)
Lt. Col. William B. Davis (Am)

Staff
Maj. Stewart L. McKenney (Am) (Exec. Off.)
Maj. Matthew Hodgart (Br) (Planning Off.)
Capt. A. R. Moore (Br)
Capt. James H. W. Thompson (Am)

French Representation
Lt. Col. Jean Constans
Cdt. Guillaume Widmer

French Country Section

      Lt. Comdr. F. Brooks Richards (Br)
      Capt. Gerard de Piolenc (Am)

      Maj. John Goldsmith (Br) (in field 7/19 to 8/11/44)
      Capt. Alfred J. Ayes (Br)
      Capt. Val Barbier (Br)
      Captain Fontaine (Am)
      Capt. Robert Searle (Br)*
      Capt. Peter Storrs (Br)
      Lt. Emile Bonnet (Am)
      Lt. Brinckerhoff (Am)
      Lt. Geoffrey Jones (Am) (in field after 8/10/44)
      Lt. Jackie Porter (Br) (FANY)**

Intelligence and War Room

      Lt. Col. Kenneth Baker (Am)*
      Capt. John Follett (Br)
      Capt. Merowit (Am)

Air Operations

      Lt. Col. Joseph W. Brooks (Am)
      Squad. Ldr. Jack (Br)
      Maj. Ray Wooler (Can) (Parachutes)
      Capt. Benjamin H. Cowburn (Br) (temp. duty)

Jedburghs

      Maj. James Champion (Br) (until 8/5/44)
      Maj. Neil Marten (Br) (after 8/6/44)
      Lt. Peg Todd (Br) (FANY)**

Operational Groups (OGs)

      Lt. Col. Alfred G. Cox (Am)

Signals (Communications)

      Maj. Bill Corbett (Br)
      Lt. Colley (Br)
      Lt. Lang (Am)
      Lt. Carl R. Thompson (Am)

*Colonel Baker and Searle (promoted to major) shared command of SPOC
Advanced Base at Avignon after 9/11/44.
**First Aid Nursing Yeomanry (British women's auxiliary).

Special Forces Unit No. 4 (4-SFU)

    Col. William G. Bartlett (Am) (Commanding)
    Lt. Col. E. S. N. Head (Br) (Deputy)
    Maj. James H. W. Thompson (Am) (Exec. Off.)
    Maj. John Oughton (Br)
    Maj. Douglas G. Bonner (Am)
    Maj. Val Barbier (Br) (Promoted and transferred from French
                          Country Section)
    Capt. C. C. Gregory (Br)
    Capt. A. R. Borden (Am)
    Capt. Stephen Hastings (Br)
    Capt. John Hoar (Am)
    Capt. William S. Coleman (Am)
    Capt. Robert H. Mutrux (Am)
    Capt. Ralph Banbury (Br)
    Capt. Henry Leger (Am)
    Lt. Harvey Bathurst (Br)
    Lt. William H. Woolverton (Am)
    Lt. Wilson (Br)
    Lt. Raymond de Vos (Am)
    Lt. Pons (Fr)
    Lt. Marc Rainaud (Fr)
    Mr. Donald King (Am)

Strategic Service Section (SSS)

Company "A," 2677th Regiment (OSS), attached to US Seventh Army for contacts
with OSS/SI agents in southern France. The 2677th Regiment was commanded
by Col. Edward J. F. Glavin. List includes senior officers (captain and above) and
civilians.

    Lt. Col. Edward W. Gamble, commanding
    Lt. Col. Peter S. Mero (communications)
    Maj. Richard Crosby (deputy)
    Maj. Nathan Wentworth
    Lt. Comdr. Warwick Potter
    Mr. Henry Hyde
    Mr. Frank Schoonmaker
    Mr. DeWitt Clinton
    Capt. Henry Leger (assigned in field to 4-SFU)
    Capt. Leslie Atlass
    Capt. John Millas

Capt. Justin Greene
Capt. Alan P. Stuyvesant (assigned to First Airborne Task Force)
Capt. John Dodge
Capt. Roger Goiran

FRENCH FORCES OF THE INTERIOR LEADERS
IN SOUTHEASTERN FRANCE (ANVIL/DRAGOON AREA)

(Note: Because the clandestine nature of the Resistance involved constant shifting of personnel and allegiances, this list should not be considered as a rigid "Table of Organization." It is a simplification that omits personnel of factions, such as the FTP and COMAC, that in some instances disputed the FFI chain of command.)

Military Delegate, South	Maurice Bourgès-Maunoury (POLYGONE)
Military Delegate, Operations South	Gen. Gabriel Cochet
C-in-C Southeastern France	Henri Zeller (FAISCEAU)

Regional Officials, R-1

Commissaire de la République	Yves Farge
Military Delegate (DMR)	P. Leistenschneider (CARRE)
Chief, FFI	Alban Vistel (MAGNY)
Chief, FFI East	Marcel Descour (BAYARD)
Chief, FFI North	H. Jaboulay (BELLEROCHE)
Chief, FFI West	Henri Provisor (DARCIEL)
Chief, FFI Vercors	François Huet (HERVIEU)
Deputy	R. Bousquet (CHABERT)
Chief, FFI Central Alps	Drouot (L'HERMINE)
FFI Departmental Chiefs	
Ain and upper Jura	H. Romans-Petit
Ardèche	René Calloud
Drôme	J. P. de Lassus St.-Geniès (LEGRAND)
Haute-Savoie	Joseph Lambroschini (NIZIER)
Isère	Alain Le Ray (BASTIDE)
Loire	Jean Marey (HERVE)
Rhône	Raymond Basset (MARY)
Savoie	de Galbert (MATHIEU)

Regional Officials, R-2

Commissaire de la République	Raymond Aubrac
Military Delegate	Guillaume Widmer (CLOITRE)
Chief, FFI	Jean Constans (SAINT-SAUVEUR)
Landing Officer (SAP)	Camille Rayon (ARCHIDUC)
FFI Departmental Chiefs	
Alpes-Maritimes	Jacques Lécuyer (SAPIN)
Basses-Alpes	Georges Bonnaire (NOEL)
Bouches-du-Rhône	Pierre Lamaison (VAUBAN)
Gard	Magnant (BOMBYX)
Hautes-Alpes	Paul Héraud (DUMONT) (until Aug. 9)
	Etienne Moreaud (DUMAS)
Var	Salvatori (SAVARY)
	Lelaquet (VERNIE) (after Aug. 23)
Vaucluse	Philippe Beyne (D'ARTAGNAN)

Notes

Archives Nationales French National Archives, Paris

FRUS   Foreign Relations of the United States. Volumes pub-
                lished by the Department of State.

NARA   National   Archives   and   Records   Administration,
                Washington, D.C. RG = Record Group. E = Entry.

PRO   Public Record Office, Kew, London. WO = War Office.
                FO = Foreign Office. PREM = Premier. DEFE =
                Defense.

SOE Archives   Archives of the Special Operations Executive, Foreign &
                Commonwealth Office, London. As these archives are
                not open to the public, the citation refers to material
                provided to the researcher in writing on request.

Reports of Jedburgh teams and Operational Groups (OGs) are identified by the
mission's code name (e.g., CHLOROFORM Report). Unless otherwise indicated, these reports are located in NARA: RG226, E 154, Box 156. (Duplicates
in E 190, Box 741, and E 143, Boxes 10 and 11.) U.S. Army reports and
histories, Washington National Records Center, Suitland, Maryland, supervised
by NARA's Military Reference Branch.

CHAPTER 1:   INTRODUCTION

1.   The pros and cons of ANVIL have been dealt with in detail: See Alan F. Wilt, *The French Riviera Campaign of August 1944* (Carbondale, Ill., 1981), 1-24; Maurice Matloff, "The ANVIL Decision," in K. R. Greenfield (ed.), *Command Decisions* (New York, 1959); A. L. Funk, *"Considérations stratégiques sur l'invasion du sud de la France,"* in Henri Michel (ed.), *La guerre en Méditerrannée* (Paris, 1971), 439-65; F. H. Hinsley, et al., *British Intelligence in the Second World War*, III, Part 2 (New York, 1988), 316-18.

2.   United States Seventh Army, *Report of Operations in France and Germany, 1944-1945* (Heidelberg, 1946), I, 1-14. Forrest Pogue, *George C. Marshall: Organizer of Victory* (New York, 1973), 373-77. *The Conferences at Washington and Quebec, 1943* (Foreign Relations of the United States [hereafter FRUS], Washington, D. C., 1970), 898, 945, 1025, 1038.

3.   Charles de Gaulle, *Mémoires de guerre* (Paris, 1956), II (Politique); English ed. (New York, 1959) section "Politics." Arthur L. Funk, *Charles de Gaulle: The Crucial Years* (Norman, Oklahoma, 1959), 177-236; Marcel Vigneras, *Rearming the French* (Washington, D.C., 1957), 86-129.

4.   A. de Dainville, *L'ORA: La Résistance de l'armée* (Paris, 1974).

5.   Henri Michel, *Histoire de la Résistance* (Paris, 1950), is the classic while his *The Shadow War: Resistance in Europe 1939-1945* (London, 1972) covers a wider field. On the MUR: John F. Sweets, *The Politics of Resistance in France, 1940-1944* (DeKalb, Ill., 1976). See also H. R. Kedward, *Resistance in Vichy France* (Oxford, 1978) and the massive 5-volume study, in French: Henri Noguères, *Histoire de la Résistance en France* (Paris, 1974-81).

6.   Charles Tillon, *Les F.T.P.: la guérilla en France* (Paris, 1972).

7.   For details on the BCRA, see Passy (André Dewavrin), *Souvenirs* (vol.I, *Deuxième bureau à Londres*, vol. II, *10 Duke Street, Londres*, vol. III, *Missions secrètes en France* [Monte Carlo, 1947]); Jacques Soustelle, *Envers et contre tout*, 2 vols. (Paris, 1950); as well as de Gaulle's memoirs.

8.   On SOE see M. R. D. Foot, *SOE: An Outline History of the Special Operations Executive* (London, 1984), and for operations in France, the same author's authoritative *SOE in France* (London, 1966); Marcel Ruby, *F Section SOE: The Buckmaster Networks* (London, 1988).

9.   A. L. Funk, "Churchill, Eisenhower, and the French Resistance," *Military Affairs* (Feb., 1981), 31-33; David Stafford, *Britain and European Resistance, 1940-1945: A Survey of the Special Operations Executive, with Documents* (London, 1980), 150-52.

10. Forrest Pogue, *The Supreme Command* (Washington D.C., 1954), 152-54; Foot, *SOE in France*, 31-32,236; PRO, WO 204/1834; NARA, RG 226, E

168, Box 81. For SHAEF plan of March 17, 44, *The Papers of Dwight D. Eisenhower*, A. D. Chandler and S. E. Ambrose (eds.), *The War Years*, III (Baltimore, 1970), 1771. For SOE policy, see Chiefs of Staff directive, March 20, 1943 (PRO, CAB 80/68) published as Document 7 in Stafford, *Britain and European Resistance*, 248-57; Foot, *SOE in France*, 233-35.

11. "L'Etat Major des Forces Françaises de l'Intérieur," in *Les réseaux ACTION de la France Combattante* (Paris, 1986), 259-70; *The French Forces of the Interior* (Library of Congress, Washington, D.C.), cited hereafter as *FFI History*; communications to author of Paul van der Stricht and Henri Ziegler. An ardent flier, Colonel Ziegler later became head of Air France.

12. Funk, *Charles de Gaulle*, 233-76; Julian G. Hurstfield, *America and the French Nation, 1939-1945* (Chapel Hill and London, 1986), 207-19; Foot, *SOE in France*, 360-64, 385,435; Pogue, *Supreme Command*, 236-37; PRO, WO 219/2330.

CHAPTER 2:   RESISTANCE IN SOUTHEASTERN FRANCE

1. For books in English on the French Resistance, see Henri Michel, *The Shadow War* (London, 1972), David Schoenbrun, *Soldiers of the Night* (New York, 1980), Henri Frenay, *The Night Will End* (New York, 1975), Martin Blumenson, *The Vildé Affair* (Boston, 1977), Robert Aron, *France Reborn* (New York, 1964), John Sweets, *The Politics of Resistance in France* (DeKalb, Ill., 1976), Frida Knight, *The French Resistance* (London, 1975), and H. R. Kedward, *Resistance in Vichy France* (New York, 1978). In French, the standard works are Henri Michel, *Histoire de la Résistance* (Paris, 1950), Henri Noguères, *Histoire de la Résistance*, 5 vols. (Paris, 1974-81).

2. Lucien Micoud, *Nous étions 150 maquisards* (Valence, 1982), 197-201. (A U.S. atlas reveals neither a town nor county called "Madison" in Pennsylvania.)

3. The Drôme Resistance is well documented: In 1989 appeared Jean Abonnenc's *Pour l'amour de la France: Drôme-Vercors 1940-1944*, published in Valence by the "Fédération des unités combattantes de la Résistance et des F.F.I. de la Drôme." Besides the Micoud book cited above, there are other memoirs: General de Lassus Saint-Geniès (Drôme FFI chief) and Pierre de Saint-Prix (Resistance prefect) collaborated on *Combats pour le Vercors et pour la liberté* (2d ed., Valence, 1984), Cdt. P. Pons, *De la Résistance à la libération* (Romans, 1962), René Ladet, *Ils ont refusé de subir: La Résistance en Drôme* (Crest, 1987). Additional material is available in the 72 AJ 39 files, *Archives Nationales*, Paris.

4. Père Richard Duchamblo, *Maquisards et Gestapo*, Cahier 16 (Gap, 1949), 3, 25–32. The writer has interviewed Henry McIntosh (of Jedburgh team CHLOROFORM), General de Lassus, and Francis Cammaerts, all of whom knew L'HERMINE.

5. De Lassus, *Combats pour le Vercors*, 27–28. In the appendix of *Pour l'amour de la France*, there is a Table of Organization for FFI units as of Aug. 20, 1944, with commentary on changes in previous months. The northern sector had three battalions, comprising five or six companies each; in the center, under Captain Benezech (ANTOINE), were eleven companies, and in the south, dominated by the FTP, were some twelve companies. Of special interest to this study is the 4th AS Battalion, under Captain Bernard, whose five companies fought with the Americans in the Battle of Montélmar. For more details, see the section "Resumé-Unités militaires de la Résistance en Drôme," in Ladet, *Ils ont refusé de subir*, 352–74.

6. Charles de Gaulle, *War Memoirs* (1 vol. ed., New York, 1967), 618. Between June 1943 and May 1944, the French Resistance sabotaged 1822 locomotives. After the Normandy landings, during June, July, and August, 658 sabotage operations were executed and 820 locomotives were damaged (*FFI History*, 1352). Annex F of the *FFI History* (1352–81) lists specific acts of sabotage by region. Sabotage data is found in PRO: WO 204/1965, 2348; also in "OSS Aid to the French Resistance, Operations in southern France, SO-RF Section Missions: Sabotage," NARA: RG 226, E 190, Box 741. The French "Comité d'Histoire de la deuxième guerre mondiale," and the Institut d'Histoire du Temps Présent, Paris, have published many departmental maps showing sabotage.

7. *Pour l'amour de la France*, 142. Details on sabotage, 132–56. See also: "Coupures et attentats sur les voies ferrées sur le territoire du département de la Drôme," *Archives Nationales*, 72 AJ 39.

8. Report of the Supreme Commander to the Combined Chiefs of Staff on the Operations in Europe (Washington, D.C., 1946), 53.

9. Operation UNION I Report, SO-RF Missions (NARA: RG 226, E 190, Box 741); *Archives Nationales*, 72 AJ 545; Edward Hymoff, *The OSS in World War II*, rev. ed. (New York, 1986), 246–49 (Anecdotes about Ortiz); de Lassus, *Combats pour le Vercors*, 26–27.

10. Material on Cammaerts comes from many interviews and considerable correspondence over several years. Mr. Cammaerts has read and commented on the sections relating to his activities. Cammaerts is featured in several journalistic accounts, notably E. H. Cookridge, *They Came from the Sky* (New York, 1967), 73–151, and Madeleine Masson, *Christine* (London, 1975). Cookridge's account, while readable and detailed, owes much of its color to a

fanciful imagination. Accurate information can be found in Foot's *SOE in France*, 81-82, 253-56, 392-94, 412, and in Cammaert's own account (in French) of his activities in the Drôme (*Pour l'amour de la France*, 80-86). Official accounts: SOE Archives, London; *Archives nationales*, Paris, 72 AJ 39, 85; War Diary in *Covert Warfare*, Vol. 5 (New York, 1989); NARA: RG 226, E 190, Boxes 132, 139.

11. Pons, *De la Résistance à la libération*, 23-31. Interview and correspondence of author with Pierre Raynaud.

12. Cookridge, *They Came from the Sky*, 96-97; for Cammaerts' contacts in Basses Alpes: Jean Garcin, *De l'armistice à la Libération dans les Alpes de Haute-Provence* (Digne, 1983), 126-27.

13. Ibid., 238; Richard Duchamblo, *Maquisards et Gestapo*, Cahier No. 7 (Gap, 1947). Richard Duchamblo, *Histoires de notre ville* (Gap, 1991), 7-16. As Moreaud was an engineer employed by the electric utility company *Energie Alpine*, he knew the vulnerable points of transmission lines.

14. Cammaerts to the author.

15. JOCKEY Report, *Archives Nationales*, 72 AJ 39.

16. Foot, *SOE in France*, 82; see also JOCKEY report, July 1944: "Among last deliveries from Algiers results appalling both in Vercors and south Drôme. Half material broken or useless." (NARA: RG 226, E 190, Box 132, Folder 710). Ray Wooler, who supervised parachute packing for MASSINGHAM, explained the situation thus: "The trouble was not careless packing by the Spanish Republicans we used in this work, but the fact that we had to use parachutes made in Egypt of Egyptian cotton for lack of parachute silk in the Middle East. These parachutes were far more prone to failure than the silk ones, but they were all we had and it was that or nothing, until silk became available in the required quantities from US sources." (Information provided the writer by Sir Brooks Richards.)

17. Excerpts from "Special Operations Executive Directive for 1943," Chiefs of Staff Memorandum of March 20, 1943, in David Stafford, *Britain and European Resistance, 1940–1945* (London, 1980), 250-51.

18. On the CDLs, see Hilary Footit and John Simmonds, *France 1943–1945* (New York, 1988), 363-69.

19. De Gaulle, *Memoirs*, 491-94, 591; Charles-Louis Foulon, *Le pouvoir en province à la libération* (Paris, 1975), 277; *Les réseaux ACTION de la France Combattante*, published for the "Amicale" by France Empire (Paris, 1986), 98-102.

20. Dossier Zeller, 72 AJ 66 (*Archives Nationales*); see also 72 AJ 449. Interview of author with General Zeller, Mar. 21, 1969. COMAC (the military Committee of Action within the CNR) approved Zeller's appointment at the

request of Fourcaud, head of the UNION mission; the appointment was confirmed by General Revers, head of the ORA.

21. De Gaulle, *Memoirs*, 489–91, 632–33; for detailed material on the CNR, see René Hostache, *Le Conseil National de la Résistance* (Paris, 1958).

22. Foulon, *Pouvoir en province*, 116, 122–31, 232–36, 280.

CHAPTER 3: SPECIAL OPERATIONS
IN SOUTHEASTERN FRANCE

1. Douglas Dodds-Parker, *Setting Europe Ablaze* (London, 1983), 117.

2. Anthony Cave Brown, *The Last Hero: Wild Bill Donovan* (New York, 1982), 297–340; Thomas F. Troy, *Donovan and the CIA* (Frederick, Md., 1981), 162–208; R. Harris Smith, *OSS: The Secret History of America's First Central Intelligence Agency* (Berkeley, California, 1972), 69–72; Bradley F. Smith, *The Shadow Warriors* (New York, 1983), 178–80, 227–28; W. F. Craven and J. L. Cate, *The Army Air Forces in World War II* (Chicago, 1951), 499–506; Fabrizio Calvi, *OSS: La guerre secrète en France* (Paris, 1990), 85–95, 139–79; Max Corvo, *The O.S.S. in Italy* (Westport, Conn., 1990), 41–82; *The War Report of the OSS*, edited by Kermit Roosevelt (New York, 1976).

3. OSS Historical File (NARA: RG 226, E 99, Box 30, Folder 144). By the beginning of 1944, SOE supported de Gaulle rather than Giraud; SOE's final operation with a Giraudist agent was Lt. Marcel Sobra's HERCULE mission, Jan.–May 1944. OSS continued to maintain contacts with Giraudist services for a longer time.

4. Jacques Soustelle, *Envers et contre tout*, II, *D'Alger à Paris* (Paris, 1950), 285–96, 323–28, 351–52, 388–91; Noguères, *Histoire de la Résistance*, V, 354–55.

5. Communication of General Constans to author, Feb. 15, 1985. Communication of Sir Brooks Richards to author, July 7, 1988.

6. Report on SPOC dated July 12, 1944 (NARA: RG 226, E 190, Box 132). SPOC was subordinated to General Wilson's Supreme Mediterranean Command and, thus, came administratively under AFHQ: Lt. Gen. Sir James A. H. Gammell (British), chief of staff, Maj. Gen. Lowell Rooks (U.S.), deputy chief of staff. More closely associated with SPOC, for policy and administration, were the officers heading the AFHQ Special Operations Section in G-3: Maj. Gen. Daniel Noce (U.S.) and Brig. Gen. B. F. Coffey (U.S).

7. In an earlier book, the current writer referred to the fact that arms promised the Algerian insurgents never arrived (*The Politics of TORCH* [Lawrence, Kansas, 1974], 155). It is now known that Brooks Richards was

sent by SOE, and that failure to deliver them derived from a confusion over signals ("Operation TORCH and its Political Aftermath," special issue of *Franco-British Studies*, No. 7, Spring 1989, 38-45). For details of Richard's role in Tunisia: Carleton Coon, *A North African Story, 1941-1942* (Ipswich, Mass., 1980); Henri Rosencher, *Le sel, la cendre, et la flamme* (Privately printed, 1985), 151-52, 163-99, 232-33. After SPOC closed, Richards remained for four years at the Embassy in Paris. He continued in the foreign service with various appointments. He served as minister to Bonn (1969-71), ambassador to Saigon (1972-74), and ambassador to Greece (1974-78). He was deputy secretary in the Cabinet Office (1978-80) and subsequently security coordinator in Northern Ireland.

8. On Jedburghs: AFHQ History of Special Operations (PRO: WO/2030 B); for southern France: "Report on Jedburghs" by Maj. H. N. Marten (NARA: RG 226, E 154, Box 56, Folder 945). For popular accounts: S. Alsop and T. Branden, *Sub Rosa: The O.S.S. and American Espionage* (New York, 1946); E. H. Cookridge, *They Came from the Sky* (New York, 1967).

9. "Report on O.G.'s in southern France," prepared by Maj. Alfred T. Cox, Sept. 20, 1944 (NARA: RG 226, E 190, Box 741). For recollections of an OG commander operating in France: Serge Obolensky, *One Man in His Time* (New York, 1958).

10. Report on SPOC (see n. 6); Fernand Rude, who was able to examine virtually all the messages sent by a single operator from the Vercors, estimates that several hundred were sent in a 50-day period ("Le dialogue Vercors-Alger," *Revue d'histoire de la deuxième guerre mondiale*, XLIX [Jan. 1963], 79-110). A summary of messages in 1944 from the field to London shows: Jan.: 620; May: 1,674, July: 3,472 (*Les réseaux ACTION*, 235).

11. Foot, *SOE in France*, Appendix C (Supply), 470-77; Craven and Cate, *Army Air Forces in World War II*, III, 496-506; John Ehrman, *History of the Second World War: Grand Strategy*, V (London, 1956), 325-26; Forrest Pogue, *The Supreme Command*, 156; Maj. H.G. Warren, *Special Operations: AAF Aid to European Resistance Movements* (Washington, D.C.: U.S. Air Historical Office, 1947); Hugh Verity, *We Landed by Moonlight* (London, 1978), and the corrected and augmented French edition: *Nous atterrissions de nuit* (Paris, 1989); PRO: WO 204/1959.

12. Marten Report; Cox Report. Officially the OGs trained for southern France were Company "B," 2671st Special Reconnaissance Battalion, under the overall command of Col. Russell Livermore. (Company "A" was "Italian," and Company "C" "Balkans.") NARA: RG 226, E 143, Box 11.

13. Constans' desk diary, entry of 22 May 1944, communicated to author by General Constans.

14. Since Cochet had served briefly as director of the *Services Spéciaux* (Oct.–Nov. 1943) and had been replaced by Soustelle, a basis of friction already existed (Soustelle, *Envers et contre tout*, II, 289–92, 321). The antagonism is confirmed in a letter from Maj. S. L. McKinney to Colonel Haskell, July 11, 1944 (NARA: RG 226, E 190, Box 139, Folder 838). Soustelle considered General Cochet uncooperative and given to grandiose, unworkable staff organization.

15. "Note du général Constans à l'attention de Monsieur Rude, 1962," in *Grenoble et le Vercors*, Pierre Bolle (ed.) (Lyon, 1985), 291–94.

16. Cave Brown, *Last Hero*, 503–05; B. Smith, *Shadow Warriors*, 187, 248.

17. Report of OSS Activities with 7th Army, Oct. 14, 1944 (NARA: RG 226, E 99, Folder 145, Box 30).

18. Reports on 4-SFU (NARA: RG 226, E 158, Box 5, Folder 67); Headquarters 7th Army report (PRO: WO 204/1962).

19. Report of OSS Activities, 17.

CHAPTER 4: IMPACT OF THE NORMANDY LANDINGS

1. Harry C. Butcher, *My Three Years with Eisenhower* (New York, 1946), 540–41; AFHQ History of Special Operations, Sec. VII, Annex E (PRO: WO 204/2030 B).

2. The Vercors has become a symbol of French Resistance and has been described in many books: Paul Dreyfus, *Vercors, citadelle de liberté* (Paris, 1969); Pierre Tanant, *Vercors, haut-lieu de France* (Paris, 1947); H. Noguères, *Histoire de la Résistance*, vol. V; Pierre Bolle (ed.), *Grenoble et le Vercors* (Lyon, 1985); Gen. de Lassus, *Combats pour le Vercors et pour la liberté* (Valence, 1984). In English, a journalistic account is Michael Pearson, *Tears of Glory* (New York, 1978) and a chapter in Robert Aron, *France Reborn* (New York, 1964), 182–208.

3. Madeleine Baudoin, *Histoire des Groupes Francs (M.U.R.) des Bouches-du-Rhône* (Paris, 1962), 137, 144–45. Rossi was arrested and executed in 1944, but Lécuyer survived the war, continued his military career, and wrote memoirs, *Méfiez-vous du toréador* (Toulon, 1987). He summarizes his early Resistance activities (16–60) and discusses in detail his relations with Rossi. He found Rossi "sympathetic, intelligent, active, and energetic" and emphasizes that his differences and reservations applied not to the man but to the "system" (38). The author interviewed General Lécuyer in 1984.

4. SOE Archives; Lécuyer, *Méfiez-vous du toréador*, 294–336. Several of Lécuyer's lieutenants were assigned to the mission. A Polish physician, Dr.

Henri Rosencher, also came in with the mission and has described the boat voyage from Corsica to the French coast, and the landing on May 25 in his memoirs, *Le sel, la cendre, et la flamme, 252–56.*

5. Lécuyer, *Méfiez-vous du toréador*, 44.

6. Garcin, *Libération dans les Alpes de Haute-Provence*, 17–18; Lécuyer, *Méfiez-vous du toréador*, 44–48.

7. *Journal de Marche de la Résistance en Ubaye*, published by the Amicale des Maquisards et Résistants, Secteur Ubaye (Digne, *n.d.*), 8–11 (hereafter cited as *Ubaye Journal de Marche*). Henri Béraud, *La seconde guerre mondiale dans les Hautes-Alpes et l'Ubaye* (Gap, 1990), 103–06; Lécuyer, *Méfiez-vous du toréador*, 47–48, 55–56, 296–97; Garcin, *Libération dans les Alpes de Haute-Provence*, 289–329. The Ubaye actions are based on these works, together with SOE records and interview of Cammaerts and Lécuyer.

8. Ibid., 322–23.

9. The FFI command's radio operator transmitting to Algiers was Lt. Robert Bennes (BOB), and to London Sous-Lt. Argentin (TITIN). Cammaerts' JOCKEY circuit was served by Auguste Floiras (ALBERT) and by Lieutenant Sereni (ANTOINE). The transmissions to Algiers went to SPOC, and the ones involving the French went to Colonel Constans, who would reply when the concerns were essentially French. Rude, "Le dialogue Vercors-Alger," *Revue d'histoire de la deuxième guerre mondiale*, XLIX (Jan., 1963), 79–110.

10. Craven and Cate, *Army Air Forces*, III, 503–04; Marcel Vigneras, *Rearming the French* (Washington, D. C., 1957), 301–03; FRUS, 1944, III, 692–93; Cave Brown, *Last Hero*, 561–62; PRO: WO 204/1164; interview of author with Joseph Haskell.

11. JUSTINE, VEGANINE, CHLOROFORM Reports; Pecquet report on EUCALYPTUS (NARA: RG 226, E 190, Box 740).

12. JOCKEY Report, in *War Diary, OSS London*, III, 460–61 (NARA: Microfilm M 1623, Roll 6).

13. Garcin, *Libération dans les Alpes de Haute-Provence*, 340–45.

14. Duchamblo, *Maquisards et Gestapo*, 7th Cahier, 18th Cahier.

15. Cammaerts to author.

16. Christine's adventurous life has been recounted in detail by the British writer Madeleine Masson: *Christine: A Search for Christine Granville* (London, 1975). For her arrival in France as Cammaert's assistant, see pages 151–52, 159–60, 179–87. After the war, she settled in London, worked for a while as a steamship stewardess, and in 1952 was murdered by a jealous would-be lover.

17. Craven and Cate, *Army Air Forces*, III, 503–04; Gilles Lévy, *14 Juillet 1944: L'Opération "Cadillac"* (St.-Leonard, France, 1989); Dreyfus, *Vercors*, 169.

18. JUSTINE Report.

19. Dreyfus, *Vercors*, 262.

20. Wilt, *French Riviera Campaign*, 43.

CHAPTER 5: PREPARATIONS FOR ANVIL/DRAGOON

1. On ANVIL planning: U.S. Seventh Army, *Report of Operations*, I, 1–70; Wilt, *French Riviera Campaign*, 46–80; L. K. Truscott, *Command Missions* (New York, 1954), 381–409.

2. Cochet's "Southern Zone of Operations" was defined as R-2 and R-3 plus Ardèche, Drôme, Tarn, Haute-Garonne, Ariège, and part of Isère. It comprised only a part of the area covered by Bourgès-Maunoury, military delegate for Southern France (*Archives Nationales*, 72 AJ 237).

3. On Cochet and the Allied Command: NARA: RG 226, E 190, Box 139, Folder 834; RG 226, E 110, Box 2, Folder 23; PRO: WO 204/1164, 1959, 1961, 5653, 5739; *Archives Nationales*: Cochet papers (72 AJ 441–49).

4. PRO: WO 204/1494.

5. Ibid., 1959, 1449.

6. *Archives Nationales*, 72 AJ 446.

7. PRO: WO 204/5653.

8. NARA: RG 226, E 99, Box 34; E 190, Box 139; PRO: WO 204/1959; AFHQ History of Special Operations, WO 204/2030 B.

9. On July 26, Seventh Army sent SPOC a revised list of targets, and a modified plan was developed by SPOC on August 1, further modified later by General Cochet regarding use of the Route Napoleon (NARA: RG 407, E 427, Box 2641).

10. Lawrence Wylie's well-known study, *Village in the Vaucluse* (New York, 1964), describes life in Peyrane (Roussillon) about 30 miles from landing zone Spitfire. While nearby towns saw atrocities and German reprisals, "at Peyrane nothing of the kind occurred. No one was arrested. No one was killed."

11. Noguères, *Histoire de la Résistance*, V, 111, 327–28. The men were betrayed by a French agent, generally identified as Seignon de Poissel (code named NOEL), who was directed by the notorious Gestapo (properly Section IV of the *Sicherheitspolizei*) agent Ernest Dunker (Delage). See Lucien Gaillard, *Marseille sous l'occupation* (Rennes, 1982) 56–61; Pierre Roumel, "La verité sur le massacre de Signes," *Marseille-Magazine* (July, 1957); Jean Vial,

Souvenirs d' un Résistant (Aix-en-Provence, 1976), 212–21; Baudoin, *Groupes francs des Bouches-du-Rhône*, 59–60, 131–33, 146, 254–55. On the American OSS agent, d'Errecalde: NARA: RG 226, E 190, Box 128, Folder 684.

12. Unlike some delegates, Burdet had no deputy, although his courier, Marguerite Petitjean (BINETTE) was extremely capable—"a sort of sub-chief of mission" according to Lécuyer (*Méfiez-vous du toréador*, 39. See also Margaret Rossiter, *Women in the Resistance* [New York, 1985], 171). Although disappointed at his dismissal, Burdet had no alternative but to withdraw from active participation in the Resistance. He later became manager of the Stafford Hotel in London. For details on the financing of Burdet's mission, see Baudoin, *Groupes francs des Bouches-du-Rhône*, 60, 264–66.

13. Remainder of section "Arrangements in R-2" based on Lécuyer, *Méfiez-vous du toréador*, 64–67; Garcin, *Libération dans les Alpes de Haute-Provence*, 345 (on Bonnaire, 30, 40, 71, 90, 172); interviews of Lécuyer, Garcin, Cammaerts.

14. Communication of General Constans to author.

15. Jedburgh GRAHAM Report.

16. Details of Zeller's mission from: General Zeller, "Rapport sur ses missions à Alger et à Naples" (*Archives Nationales*, 72 AJ 66, 44).

17. Sir Brooks Richards confirms this conversation (communication to author). He believes that Zeller, unfamiliar with British naval insignia, confused "Lt. Commander" with "Captain."

18. This section based on Truscott, *Command Missions*, 401–08; Gen. Frederic B. Butler, "Task Force Butler," *Armored Cavalry Journal* (Jan.-Feb., 1948), 13–14; Report of Task Force Butler, Sept. 6, 1944 (NARA: RG 407, E 427, Box 3825).

19. De Lattre, *French First Army*, 58.

20. NARA: RG 407, E 427, Box 2641.

21. PRO: WO 204/1959.

CHAPTER 6: EVE OF THE LANDINGS

1. Report on Jedburghs-zone sud, Avignon, Oct. 6, 1944 (NARA: RG 226, E 154, Box 56, Folder 945); Major A.T. Cox, Report on OGs, Grenoble, Sept. 20, 1944 (NARA: RG 226, E 190, Box 741).

2. AFHQ History of Special Operations, Annex E (PRO: WO 204/2030B); WO 204/1958; WO 219/2370; Wilson to de Gaulle, Aug. 4, 1944 (WO 204/1959); SPOC Body Operations for July and August 1944 (NARA: RG 226, E 97, Box 45); Canfield to Haskell, July 28, 1944:

Critical morale situation here regarding 10 Jedburghs. . . . Absolutely essential that first class US briefing officer . . . come immediately to assist CHAMPION, bringing briefs and radio equipment and above all clear cut decision as to LONDON's intentions for use of Jedburghs. Recommend strongly that SPOC be authorized to employ these teams in AFHQ Zone in support ANVIL unless LONDON already has definite plan for their early dispatch.

(NARA, RG 226, E 190, Box 139, Folder 832.) On Jedburgh effectiveness, Baker to Davis, Nov. 15, 1944 (NARA, RG 226, E 190, Box 135, Folder 757.

3. On national differences, note that the Allied Command emphasized that "SPOC's directive is the support of ANVIL." Yet Colonel Constans (in a note to the historian F. Rude) asserted: "The primordial mission of SPOC was and remained *aid to the Resistance*" (Bolle [ed.], *Grenoble et le Vercors*, 293).

4. SOE Archives; Jedburgh PACKARD report; correspondence with Colonel Bank. ISOTROPE included Cdt. Jean Albert Baldensperger, with British representative Maj. Denys Hamson (ETOLE), French Capt. Georges Pezant (ROCHET), and, as wireless operator, QM Louis Berthou (PELICAN), dropped June 8/9, 1944, and joined on June 28/29 by New Zealand Maj. William Jordan (PINTADE) and French wireless operator Sous-Lt. Pierre Fournier (PERDRIX). Jordan, who broke a leg on landing, has written memoirs, *Conquest without Victory* (London: 1969), which provide extensive details of the mission (pp. 215–55). Aaron Bank, leader of Jedburgh PACKARD, has published memoirs: *From OSS to Green Berets* (Novato, Calif.: 1986). Written without records, Bank's account is a vivid story of Jedburgh operation but not accurate on details. The official report names his two French team members as Capt. C. Boineau and Lieutenant Montfort, but Bank refers to them as Henri Denis and Jean. His principal FFI contact he calls Raymond, perhaps Michel Bruguier (AUDIBERT), leader of the *Corps Franc de la Libération* in the Gard, or Commandant Magnat (BOMBYX), FFI chief of staff, Gard. Both are mentioned in his official report, but Raymond is not mentioned.

5. OG Ruth report; Oxent Miesseroff, *Le charme discret des maquis de Barrème*, (Paris, 1978), 81. Interview of author with Mills Brandes.

6. OG ALICE report.

7. De Lassus, *Combats pour le Vercors*, 86–87.

8. OG ALICE report. The official Drôme history states 280 dead, 200 wounded, 480 buildings destroyed, but the strategic bridge untouched (*Pour l'amour de la France*, 383–87).

9. Interview of author with Havard Gunn.

10. "Plan for the Use of Resistance in Support of Operation ANVIL," July 15, 1944, p. 15 (PRO: WO 204/1959).

11. Activities of Cammaerts, Christine, Hamilton, etc., based on reports in SOE Archives; O'Regan papers, in Liddell Hart collection, King's College, London. Christine's biographer, Madeleine Masson, seems to have confused the trip to Italy with a later expedition to Larche (*Christine*, 200). On Italian partisans, see Charles F. Delzell, *Mussolini's Enemies* (Princeton, 1961), 379–81, 419–22. On the Alpine campaign, see Henri Béraud, *La seconde guerre mondiale dans les Hautes-Alpes* (Gap, 1990), 116–200.

12. SOE Archives.

13. Ibid.

14. Ibid. Jed NOVOCAINE Report; interview with John Roper; Garcin, *Libération dans les Alpes de Haute-Provence*, 147, 387–88.

15. Ibid. 217–22; PRO: WO 204/1502, 1958, 2293; Baudoin, *Groupes Francs du Bouches-du-Rhône*, 252–53; Lécuyer, *Méfiez-vous du toréador*, 44–45; Duchamblo, *Maquisards et Gestapo*, 7th Cahier, p. 20.

16. Ibid., p. 26.

17. Jed NOVOCAINE Report; Roper report (SOE Archives).

18. Halsey Report; Gunn Report (SOE Archives); Lécuyer, *Méfiez-vous du toréador*, 68–69, 253–54; Fournier Report (Digne Archives). Cammaerts' reports to SPOC, July 13, 17, Aug. 5 (NARA: RG 226, E 190, Box 140, Folder 844); On July 27, Cammaerts reported "Christine intends to see Poles at Gap" (SOE Archives); note of A. Vincent-Beaume (*Archives Nationales*, 72 AJ 39).

19. Jed GRAHAM Report.

20. Information to writer from General Constans, including photocopy of orders in French signed by de Gaulle. This order expanded R-2 to the north to include most of the Drôme department and all of the Vercors.

21. Hugh Verity, *We Landed by Moonlight* (London, 1978), 188. Report of Roger Vencell, Widmer's radio operator, Sept. 25, 1944 (NARA, RG 226, E 110, Box 4, Folder 77).

22. Although de Gaulle himself named Constans as FFI chief, inside France the National Council of the Resistance, which frequently contested de Gaulle's authority, opposed the appointment and requested Cochet to recall Constans. Constans never received any countermanding order. Noguères, *Résistance*, V, 435; Maurice Kriegel-Valrimont, *La Libération: les archives du COMAC* (Paris, 1964), 233; correspondence with General Constans.

23. Xan Fielding, *Hide and Seek* (London, 1954), 234.

24. Ibid., 236–37. Fielding may have described a stop at Manosque (or Forcalquier) where Cammaerts met Widmer. OG NANCY Report; communication of Cammaerts.

25. When Constans learned that Héraud had wished Moreaud to succeed him, he gave Robert Bidault, from Gap, a blank order to be filled in with the approval of the Hautes-Alpes leaders (Duchamblo, *Maquisards et Gestapo*, 7th Cahier, 22–24; Roper Report and interview with John Roper).

26. Christine never spoke very much about her role in bringing about Cammaerts' release, but she did write a report and her biographer has pieced together most of the relevant information (Masson, *Christine*, 201–09). Fielding provides a detailed account of the imprisonment in his memoirs (*Hide and Seek*, 237–51), alluding frequently to his fear and guilt that he, lacking the *savoir-faire* of his colleagues, had brought them into the predicament. Cookridge (*They Came from the Sky*, 133–48), having interviewed Cammaerts, gives a long and dramatic account, liberally peppered by a fertile imagination. Garcin, *Libération dans les Alpes de Haute-Provence*, 400–402, as a resident of Digne and a meticulous chronicler, adds some details from the French side. One of Lécuyer's lieutenants, Tilly, provided safe-conduct for Schenk and Waem (Lécuyer, *Méfiez-vous du toréador*, 234). Their later fate is mentioned by Douglas Dodds-Parker (*Setting Europe Ablaze*, 168–69). The writer's discussions with Cammaerts have not evoked information that significantly expands on what has been published.

CHAPTER 7: THE LANDINGS

1. *La Résistance dans le Var, 1940-1944* (Victor Masson [ed.] for the Association des Mouvements Unis de la Résistance et des Maquis du Var, Draguignan, 1983), 13–73.

2. *Archives Nationales*, 72 AJ 200 B; Eric Sevareid, *Not So Wild a Dream* (New York, 1978), 435.

3. *Résistance dans le Var*, 96. This figure must be related to the fact that SPOC averaged 19 sorties a night in R-1 and R-2 (NARA: RG 226, E 190, Box 132).

4. For details of the airborne operation, see Gerard M. Devlin, *Paratrooper!* (New York, 1979), 439–57; William B. Breuer, *Operation Dragoon* (Novato, California, 1987), 129–63; Charles La Chaussee, *Northwest for France* (unpublished manuscript, Military History Institute, Carlisle Barracks, Pennsylvania); PRO WO 204/1818 and 1645.

5. NARA: RG 226, E 190, Box 133, Folder 723. The activities of Jones (who later became president of the Veterans of OSS) are described, not with complete accuracy, in R. H. Adleman and G. Walton, *The Champagne Campaign* (Boston, 1969). Inaccuracies have been here corrected by conversations

with Mr. Jones and by materials he has provided the writer.

6.   Allain Report, "Rapport de mission particulière de l'équipe LOUGRE," Oct. 30, 1944 (Service historique de la Marine, Vincennes, courtesy of Admiral Chastel and Sir Brooks Richards).

7.   Geoffrey Jones, "The Liberation of the French Riviera," May 1980 (8-page unpublished account, courtesy of Mr. Jones); Jones' report on mission RABELAIS (NARA: RG 226, E 110, Box 3, Folder 49).

8.   According to a "Rapport du Capitaine Bialque concernant le comporte-ment de la Commune de FAYENCE" (Archives Nationales, 72 AJ 199), there was an AS group in Fayence organized by Adjutant-Chief Pignault, which included among others, M. Farraut, *garde-champêtre*, who saved Pignault's life when he was being sought by the Gestapo.   Referring to the day of the Allied landings, the report says:

> A 8 heures des F.F.I. et F.T.P.F. ainsi que ceux de la S.A.P. passèrent à l'attaque, en ceinturant le poste d'observation fortifié de la ROCHE, occupé depuis plusieurs mois par les Allemands qui riposté [*sic*] avec leurs armes automatiques. . . . Cette première attaque de nos forces (résistance) n'eut qu'un sensible résultat, mais il y eut, hélas, des blessés.

Queried in 1989 about the radar, the Cercle d'Etudes et de Recherches sur l'histoire de Fayence obtained the testimony of M. Farraut, who stated:

> Le radar allemand était placé à la Roque, sur l'emplacement des anciens reservoirs d'eau de Fayence. Le radar a été détruit par des explosifs introduits sous le poste allemand par des résistants qui y étaient parvenus en remontant depuis l'aval des reservoirs par les conduites d'alimentation d'eau.

9.   Jedburgh SCEPTRE Report.

10.   Jacques Robichon, in *Le débarquement en Provence* (Paris, 1962), identifies the gendarmes (179-80). See also Adleman and Walton, *Champagne Campaign*, 131-33; Edward Hymoff, *The OSS in World War II* (rev. ed., New York, 1972), 344-57.

11.   Devlin, *Paratrooper!*, 449; Robichon, *Débarquement en Provence*, 261-65; *Résistance dans le Var*, 137-39; U.S. Seventh Army *Operations*, I, 114, 123, 149; Breuer, *Dragoon*, 152-158; Patch Diary, Aug. 17, 1944 (Center of Military History, Washington, D. C.).

12.   Jedburgh SCEPTRE Report; *Paratroopers' Odyssey: A History of the 517th Parachute Combat Team*, Clark L. Archer (ed.), (Hudson, Florida, 1985), 62-63, 69-71.

13.   Allain and Jones Reports (see notes 6 and 7); Report of O.S.S. Activities with Seventh Army (SI unit), Oct. 14, 1944 (NARA: RG 226, E 99, Folder 145, Box 30), 6-7; Report of Dyas, part of OG RUTH report. Another member of

the SI team, Marine Lt. Walter W. Taylor, did not long survive the landings. Assigned to the 36th Division, he and a French agent attempted to obtain information in Grasse, but ran into a nearby German road-block. The agent was killed and Taylor taken prisoner. He ended up in the same POW camp where Ortiz (UNION II) was interned. Both he and Ortiz survived the war. (Hymoff, *OSS in World War II* [rev. ed.], 314-16; Frank and Shaw, *Marine Corps in World War II*, 748.)

14. Actions of the First Airborne Task Force, in NARA: 99/06 (FABTF) 0.3; in PRO: WO 204/1625, 1645, 1818.

15. *Résistance dans le Var*, 137.

16. Ibid., 43; Jean-Marie Guillon, "La libération du Var: Résistance et nouveaux pouvoirs," *Les Cahiers de l'IHTP* (No. 15, June 1990), 15-16. Guillon's article represents part of a doctoral thesis, *La Résistance dans le Var: Essaie d'histoire politique* (Aix-en-Provence, 1989). On Henri Michel's career, see A. L. Funk, "Henri Michel, 1907-1986," *Military Affairs* (Jan. 1987), 14-26.

17. Patch Diary, Aug. 17, 18, 1944.

18. Gunn report (SOE Archives); correspondence and interview with Mr. Havard Gunn; Lécuyer, *Méfiez-vous du toréador*, 68-73; 132-33 (account of Lieutenant Gautier); J.-L. Panicacci, "Le Comité départemental de Libération dans les Alpes-Maritimes, 1944-1947," *Revue d'histoire de la deuxième guerre mondiale* (July 1982), 77-84; Garcin, *Libération dans les Alpes de Haute-Provence*, 408-10.

CHAPTER 8: TASK FORCE BUTLER
AND THE LIBERATION OF DIGNE

1. Truscott, *Command Missions*, 413-20; Wilt, *French Riviera Campaign*, 81-87.

2. Task Force Butler: NARA: RG 407, E 427, Box 3825; Frederic B. Butler, "Task Force Butler," *Armored Cavalry Journal* (Jan.-Feb. 1948), 13-14. 117th Cavalry History of Operations: NARA: RG 407, CAVS-117-0.7, Boxes 18282 to 18292. The writer has interviewed Colonel Hodge and Col. Harold J. Samsel (Operations officer in 1944) and received from them supplementary documentation: Colonel Hodge's typed unpublished memoirs; reports of operations; articles by Colonel Samsel ("Shades of Jeb Stuart," "Knights of the Yellow Cord"); and a volume edited by Colonel Samsel: *The Battle of Montrevel*, brought out in 1986 for members of the 117th Cavalry Association.

3. On the Enigma coding machine and the operation at Bletchley, see Peter Calvocoressi, *Top Secret Ultra* (London, 1980); on the situation in southern France, Ralph Bennett, *Ultra in the West* (New York, 1980), 158-160; Thomas Parrish, *The Ultra Americans* (New York, 1986), 180, 257-58; Alexander S. Cochran, Jr., "Protecting the Ultimate Advantage" (interview of Donald Bussey), *Military History* (June, 1985), 42-47. In France, Truscott did not receive ULTRA messages but, since he had had access to them in Italy, he knew about this source of intelligence.

4. Message of Aug. 17, 1944 (XL 6753), message of Aug. 18, 1944 (XL 6919), PRO: DEFE 3/121. F. H. Hinsley, et al., *British Intelligence in the Second World War*, Vol. 3, Pt. II (New York, 1988), 274, 334.

5. De Lattre, *Première Armée Française*, 130, 135-37.

6. Adleman and Walton, *Champagne Campaign*, 165-67. Devers saw Patch at various times on Aug. 18 and 19, but Patch's Diary only records that Devers "offered General Patch all available aid in pushing the advance."

7. Patch Field Order in Seventh U.S. Army *Operations*, III, Appendix. Bussey's memorandum to Colonel [Telford] Taylor, "Ultra and the Seventh Army," May 12, 1945 (NARA: RG 457, SRH-022). Published in French in *Revue d'histoire de la deuxième guerre mondiale* (Jan., 1984), 59-63.

8. "Task Force Butler," *Armored Cavalry Journal* (Jan.-Feb., 1948), 13; *The Complete Official History of the 59th Armored Field Artillery Battalion*, compiled by Charles G. Castor (Decorah, IA: 1990), 107-14.

9. Colonel Hodge to author.

10. 117th Cavalry History of Operations. Interview of author with Colonel Piddington.

11. Garcin, *Libération dans les Alpes de Haute-Provence*, 412, reproduces NOEL's handwritten order.

12. Ibid. Interview of author with Justin Boeuf.

13. *Armored Cavalry Journal* (Jan.-Feb. 1948), 17. Butler refers to Lt. Brandes as a Captain. Brandes told the writer he wore captain's insignia, under instructions, in anticipation of an already authorized promotion.

14. OG RUTH Report.

15. Material on SSS from OSS Report (NARA: RG 226, E 99, Folder 145). On 4-SFU: NARA: RG 226, E 158, Boxes 2-5; E 190, Box 129, Folder 696; Box 139, Folders 838-39; PRO: WO 204/1962.

16. NARA: RG 226, E 99, Folder 145, Box 30.

17. Garcin, *Alpes de Haute-Provence*, 414.

18. Testimony of Gen. Jean Fournier, Jan. 15, 1987, provided to writer by Guy Reymond, Communal Archives, Digne. Fournier was accompanied by Sous-Lieutenant Cheylus from Lécuyer's staff (Lécuyer, *Toréador*, 354).

19. Schuberth to General Huhnermann, Aug. 18, 1944, Task Force Butler records (NARA, RG 407, 206-TF-0.7, Box 3825). Interviewed by author, Colonel Hodge spoke contemptuously of Schuberth, hurried out of the hotel in his underclothes.

20. Details on liberation of Digne in Garcin, *Alpes de Haute-Provence*, 414–23; newspaper accounts in Communal Archives, Digne; comments to writer of Padraig O'Dea and William Magee (members of Troop B, 117th Cavalry); "Interrogation and papers of General Schuberth," Task Force Butler records (NARA, RG 407, 206-TF-07 Box 3825); 117th Cavalry message log (NARA, RG 94, CAVS 117-07, Box 181291); Louis Gazagnaire, *Le peuple héros de la Résistance* (Paris, 1971), 206–20; Guy Reymond, *Histoire de la libération de Digne* (in press).

21. "Compte rendu sur les circonstances de la libération de Château-Arnoux," written by Jean Rey, former mayor, Sept. 15, 1944 (Communal Archives, Digne); communication of Piddington to writer. Thomas Piddington visited Château-Arnoux in June, 1984, where he met the gendarme, Max Bossert, who had guided him 40 years earlier. The writer interviewed them both at that time.

22. Comments of James Gentle (on tape, in possession of Digne archivist Guy Reymond).

23. Butler, "Task Force Butler," *Armored Cavalry Journal* (Jan.-Feb. 1948), 15.

24. 117th Cavalry History, August 19, 1944 (NARA: RG 94, CAVS 117-0.7, Box 18283).

CHAPTER 9: LIBERATION OF GAP AND GRENOBLE

1. Most of the information on the French side regarding Gap comes from Richard Duchamblo, *Maquisards et Gestapo*, published in Gap between 1945 and 1951 in nineteen "cahiers" of about fifty pages each. Abbé Duchamblo published a collection of his writings as *Histoires de notre ville* (Gap: 1991), of which pp. 7–26 relate to World War II. The writer had the pleasure of meeting Père Duchamblo and his publisher, M. Guiboud Ribaud, in Gap, Sept., 1984. See also Henri Béraud, *La seconde guerre mondiale dans les Hautes-Alpes et l'Ubaye* (Gap, 1990), 117–20. Information about L'HERMINE is in part derived from interviews with Dr. Henry McIntosh (of Jedburgh Team CHLOROFORM).

2. Jedburgh CHLOROFORM Report; Duchamblo, *Maquisards*, Cahier 16, p. 8; Jedburgh NOVOCAINE Report.

3. The meeting took place at St.-Etienne-en-Dévoluy, in the mountains (a winter ski resort) between Gap and the Col de la Croix Haute, and included L'HERMINE, Colonel Daviron (the ORA head), Pelletier (inter-allied mission), Commandant Terrason-Duvernon (regular *Chasseurs Alpins* officer), Martin and McIntosh (Jedburgh CHLOROFORM); and local FFI chiefs Tortal, Genty, Woussen, and Céard, but not Moreaud or Bertrand, who were delayed. Duchamblo describes these activities in great detail in *Maquisards*, Cahier 16, pp. 17-20. Captain Hermann was acting commander of the 555 Feldkommandantur, attached to General Pflaum's 157th Reserve Division (Interrogation Report, No. 2, 21 Aug. 1944, Task Force Butler Journal).

4. Butler, "Task Force Butler," *Armored Cavalry Journal* (Mar.-Apr. 1948), 32-33; Task Force Butler Report; Jedburgh CHLOROFORM Report; 117th Cavalry History; Duchamblo, *Maquisards*, Cahier 16, p. 21, Cahier 15, pp. 28-30.

5. Butler, "Task Force Butler," 33 (Butler misspells Constans' code name "Saint Savour"); Leger 4-SFU Report (NARA: RG 226, E 99, Box 30, Folder 145); correspondence of writer with General Constans; Butler to Truscott, 0015, Aug. 21, 1944 (Task Force Butler Journal).

6. Cammaerts to writer, Dec. 9, 1983. For a colorful account of this incident, Cookridge, *They Came from the Sky*, 149-50.

7. Thomas C. Piddington, "Town of Gap, France: Operation during World War II," typed unpublished manuscript in possession of the writer. Duchamblo devotes Cahiers 16 to 19 of *Maquisards* to the liberation of Gap. He interviewed many of the people involved. Coverage of the Gap-Col Bayard operations is from these sources, together with interviews of Piddington and of Etienne Moreaud. A war correspondent, Newbold Noyes, Jr., was at Gap and wrote an account for the Washington *Star*, Aug. 26, 1944.

8. The Gestapo agent, Willi Schmidt, his deputy, Hans Stahl, and a French traitor, André Vallet, were executed at the Caserne Desmichels on Aug. 21, 1944. Duchamblo asserts that Stahl may have been a double agent (Cahier 19, pp. 19-20). The captured Germans included members of the 157th Reserve GR *Restverband*, as well as customs officers, border police, and medical units.

9. Cammaerts to the writer.

10. Some Poles, under a Lieutenant Buisky, had already joined the Maquis, and others continually tried to desert (Duchamblo, Cahier 17, p. 8; Cahier 18, pp. 3-11; Cahier 19, p. 20). Both Piddington and Cammaerts agree on their efforts to employ the Poles: Cammaerts has a vivid memory of Christine addressing Polish prisoners who tore off their *Wehrmacht* uniforms in their enthusiasm to join the Allies. Cammaerts and Christine drove to Aspres to try to obtain Butler's authorization, but he refused to see them.

11. By error, Major Gentle, whose mini-task force had completed the liberation of Digne, also showed up in Gap. Ordered to report to a bivouac area near Aspres, he had made a wrong turn and was in Gap when General Butler arrived. Butler temporarily relieved him of his command (Gentle to writer, Sept. 19, 1984, including Gentle's report to Colonel Adams, Aug. 23, 1944).

12. Report of McNeill Force, Appendix, Task Force Butler Journal; 117 Cavalry History; Jedburgh CHLOROFORM Report; "Combats de St. Firmin-Chauffayer," Duchamblo, *Maquisards*, Cahier 19, pp. 20-25.

13. G-2 History, Seventh Army Operations in Europe, Aug. 15-31, 1944 (U.S. Army Military History Institute, Carlisle Barracks, Pennsylvania), 5 (Aug. 20, 21, 1944); Truscott, *Command Missions*, 415-26.

14. Dahlquist left to Adams the deployment of his two battalions (Vincent M. Lockart, *T-Patch to Victory* [Canyon, Tex., 1981] 22-23). Adams considered that the "movement required me to make one of the most difficult tactical decisions of my career."

15. "OKW War Diary," *World War II Military Studies* (New York, Garland, 1979), X, 102-06; G-2 History, Seventh Army; Foreign Military Studies, Pflaum (NARA: A 946); Col. J. Defrasne, "L'occupation allemande dans le sud-est de la France" (mimeographed), Service historique de l'Armée, Vincennes, France, 6.

16. XL 6919, 7246, 1793 (PRO: DEFE 3/122); Ralph Bennett, *Ultra in the West* (New York, 1980), 159-60; Charles von Luttichau, "German Operations in Southern France," MS R-99, R-111 (Center of Military History, Dept. of the Army, Washington, D.C).

17. Lanvin (André Lespiau), *Liberté provisoire* (Grenoble, 1973), 209-17; Paul and Suzanne Silvestre, *Chronique des maquis de l'Isère* (Grenoble, 1978), 294-98.

18. Col. J. Defrasne, "L'occupation allemande dans le sud-est de la France," 30-35; Le Ray, Preface to Silvestre, *Chronique des Maquis de l'Isère*, 21-22; comments of General Le Ray in *Grenoble et le Vercors*, Pierre Bolle (ed.) (Lyon, 1985), 113-14, 127-28; Jean-Pierre Bernier, *Maquis Rhône-Alpes* (Paris, 1987), 90-93, 101-03. On the Drôme contingents, *Pour l'amour de la France*, 404-06; "Aperçu sur les conditions de la progression alliée du 18 au 21 août 1944 entre Aspres-sur-Buech et Grenoble et sur le rôle joué par les forces FFI des secteurs de l'Isère," a six-page typewritten account given the author by General Le Ray in 1984.

19. Silvestre, *Maquis de l'Isère*, 325-31, covers these events in minute detail. Pierre Flaureau, "Le Comité de Libération de l'Isère," in *Grenoble et le Vercors*, 83-96.

20. 143rd Infantry Journal, NARA, 336, INF (143)-0.3.

21. "Grenoble French Applaud Newsman as Liberator," by Edd Johnson, Chicago *Sun*, Aug. 25, 1944.

22. Lanvin, *Liberté provisoire*, 234–35.

23. Ibid., 236–38, 383–84; 143rd Infantry Journal.

24. Interview of General Adams, May 5, 1975 (Oral History Program, Military History Institute, Carlisle Barracks, Pennsylvania).

25. Meyer Papers, Archives of 45th Division Museum, Oklahoma City, Okla.

26. Meyer Papers; interview with Col. Harlos Hatter.

27. Johnson is mentioned by name in Silvestre, *Maquis de l'Isère*, 331, and in Bernier, *Maquis Rhône-Alpes*, 103. Clearly, Johnson loved France and the French reciprocated. At age 48, he was older than most battalion commanders; he had served in World War I and then, after the Armistice, had remained for a year in France, a sojourn that gained him language resources that permitted direct communication with Resistance leaders. In 1951, the French government made him *chevalier* of the Legion of Honor, praising him for his "devout and loyal remembrance of France, his second country," for his decisive part in liberating Grenoble, for his energetic and daring entry into action at Bourgoin— "great friend of France, he has been for the population of the Isère Department a veritable symbol." After the war, Johnson returned many times to Grenoble, where a plaque commemorates his and his colleagues' accomplishments. He died in 1985. Citations, newspaper clippings, and text of memorial service have been provided the author by Mrs. Virginia Johnson and Mr. Dion Johnson.

28. Paray (Pecquet) report, part of EUCALYPTUS Mission report (NARA: RG 226, E 190, Box 740; also RG 226, E 168, Box 1030); interview with André Pecquet (June 9, 1988) and correspondence. The S-2 log of the 179th RCT shows Paray logged in at 1217, 23 Aug. 1944.

29. Interview with General Davison; on "Le Barbier," see Silvestre, *Maquis de l'Isère*, 167–68, 205, 246, 313, 330.

30. 179th Infantry, S-2 Journal, Aug. 23, 24, 1944; Warren Munsell, *The Story of a Regiment: A History of the 179th Regimental Combat Team*, 75; Report of Henri Zeller (*Archives Nationales*, 72 AJ 66); Huet radio speech, April 20, 1954 (part of Zeller commentary); 45th Div. Archives; Capitaine Poitau, "Guérilla en montagne," *Revue d'histoire de la dexuième guerre mondiale*, XLIX (Jan. 1963), 36–37 (as STEPHANE, Etienne Poitau headed one of the principal guerrilla groups in Isère); Silvestre, *Maquis de l'Isère*, 333. The German unit that surrendered was the 7th Engineer Battalion of the 157th Division. It was trying to move south of Grenoble to set up a road-block (G-2 Periodic Report, 45th Division, Aug. 26, 1944).

CHAPTER 10: THE 3RD DIVISION TO THE RHÔNE

1. Jörg Staiger, *Rückzug durchs Rhônetal* (Neckargemünd, 1965), 41-57; Truscott, *Command Missions*, 421-23; Seventh U.S. Army *Operations*, I, 172-74; Seventh U.S. Army G-2 History, Part I (Aug. 15-31, 1944), U.S. Army Military History Institute, Carlisle, Penn.; Charles von Luttichau, "German Operations in Southern France and Alsace," Chapter 13, MS R-111, Center of Military History.

2. Jedburgh CINNAMON Report. Activities of CINNAMON and the Var Resistance based on "Compte rendu des opérations du FFI du Var," 72 AJ 200 (*Archives Nationales*); Masson, *Résistance dans le Var*, 70-93, 133-35. American actions based on Seventh U.S. Army *Operations*, 174-76; regimental journals.

3. Gouzy to HQ, 179th regiment, 0950, 8/20/44, recorded in 179th Regiment S-2 journal, 1330, Aug. 20, 1944.

4. Vaucluse actions largely based on Claude Arnoux, *Maquis Ventoux* (Avignon, 1974). This study benefits from extensive use of German sources.

5. SOE Archives: "The Vaucluse Mission"; Antoine Benoit, "Le Groupe Franc de Saint-Christol," *Proceedings of the Colloque international d'histoire militaire* (Montpellier, 1974), 473-80.

6. John Goldsmith, *Accidental Agent* (New York, 1971). His mission is described in pages 134-78, but his account, filled with exaggerations and errors, must be read with care.

7. Arnoux, *Maquis Ventoux*, 174-79, 190-98; *Archives Nationales*, 72 AJ 39; SOE Archives; "Rapport sur l'activité . . . ORA en Vaucluse," Hoover Institution, Stanford, Calif.

8. Arnoux, *Maquis Ventoux*, 194-99; Garcin, *Libération dans les Alpes de Haute-Provence*, 406.

9. CITROEN and MONOCLE Reports. De Lassus, *Combats pour le Vercors*, 85-87.

10. Jedburgh GRAHAM Report; SOE Records; Garcin, *Alpes de Haute-Provence*, 402, 408, 421, photograph on p. 148 (figure in kilts is Crosby, not Gunn).

11. Jedburgh CITROEN Report; Arnoux, *Maquis Ventoux*, 189; "Rapport sur l'activité . . . ORA en Vaucluse" (Hoover Institution); Dainville, *ORA*, 293; Antoine Benoit, "Le Groupe Franc de Saint-Christol"; interview of writer with Louis Malarte.

12. 157th Infantry Regiment, Summary of Operations, August 1944 (NARA); 45th Division Situation Reports.

13. Staiger, *Rückzug*, 57-61 (map, p. 63).

14. Arnoux, *Maquis Ventoux*, 203-06.

15. Truscott, *Command Missions*, 424-26.

16. Staiger, *Rückzug*, 62; Von Luttuchau, "German Operations," Chapter 13, 4-6.

17. Jedburgh CITROEN Report. Claude Arnoux admits there were Gaullist-FTP differences, but adds: "let us not forget that the Vaucluse was one of those rare departments where a unity of command was realized" (*Maquis Ventoux*, 220).

CHAPTER 11: TASK FORCE BUTLER TO THE RHÔNE

1. The official Drôme history, *Pour l'amour de la France*, describes the bombings in detail and summarizes French casualties: 550 killed, 713 wounded, 1,221 buildings destroyed (382-89).   The unhit railway bridge had been rendered unusable by the Resistance two months earlier (OG ALICE Report); the rails had been removed.

2. Destruction of the Loriol-Livron bridge is celebrated in the Drôme Department as one of the most daring acts of the FFI, and is well documented. Henri Faure has produced a mimeographed account, "Compte rendu de l'opération 'Pont de Livron' (nuit du 16 au 17 août 1944), établi à la suite d'une Réunion, en 1970, des 17 survivants." See also *Pour l'amour de la France*, 378-82; de Lassus, *Combats pour le Vercors*, 86; *Les réseaux ACTION de la France Combattante*, 276-81.

In his *T-Patch to Victory* (Canyon, Texas, 1981), 31-32, Vincent Lockhart recounts from the testimony of Charles Hodge (commanding officer of the 117th Cavalry) that Hodge's squadron blew the bridge when they reached the area on August 21. Although until his death General Hodge insisted that his version was correct, there is no question but that the bridge had been blown earlier. Under date of August 21, the official journal of the 117th Squadron reads: "When reaching Crest, Troop 'C' arrived at Livron and found that the bridge south of there had been blown." Colonel Lockhart agrees that Hodge was in error when he described the bridge blowing. It is possible that Hodge confused the incident with another: the bridge over the Roubion at Charols was blown by the 36th Division on 25 August. As Hodge's CP was only three miles from Charols at that time, he could have witnessed the destruction of a smaller bridge over a smaller river.

3. Butler, "Task Force Butler," *Armored Cavalry Journal* (Mar.-Apr., 1948), 34. On 17 August, Jean Abonnenc, of the Drôme Secret Army, had sent a messenger to the Americans, pointing out that the road was free of Germans

(de Lassus, *Combats pour le Vercors*, 127). On August 21, Butler conferred with Constans (SAINT SAUVEUR), who assured him the FFI controlled areas leading to the Rhône (VI Corps War Room Journal, NARA: RG 407, E 427, Box 3605).

4.   Paul Pons, *De la Résistance à la Libération* (Romans, 1964), 214–16, 232; interview of author with Father Lucien Fraisse.

5.   Bernard's FFI 4th Battalion included the 7th Company (BONFILS), the 8th Company (RIGAUD), the 13th Company (DIDIO), the 14th Company (APOSTAL), and the 17th Company (VERNIER [VALLIERE]) into which had been incorporated CAILLET's 9th Company. The battalion also included Lt. RIVE's *Corps franc*. René Ladet, *Ils ont refusé de subir: La Résistance en Drôme* (Portes-lès-Valence, 1987), 364; 117th Cavalry History of Operations (NARA: RG 407, CAVS-117. O.1, Box 18284); Lockhart, *T-Patch to Victory*, 33; Drôme 4th Battalion report, Drôme A No. 2 V, *Archives National*, 72 AJ 120–21.

6.   Account of the Montélimar battle, if not otherwise indicated, based on reports of VI Corps; 36th and 45th Divisions; Task Force Butler; General Truscott's memoirs (*Command Missions*); U.S. Seventh Army *Operations*, Vol. I; Lockhart, *T-Patch to Victory*; Wilt, *French Riviera Campaign*. For French participation: the Drôme history: *Pour l'amour de la France*, 419–65; Pons, *De la Résistance à la Libération*; Ladet, *Ils ont refusé de subir*; de Lassus, *Combats pour le Vercors*; Lucien Micoud, *Nous étions 150 maquisards* (Valence, 1982); *Archives Nationales*: 72 AJ 120–21. For German actions: OKW War Diary in *World War II German Military Studies* (New York, Garland, 1979), X, 106–08; Charles von Luttichau, "German Operations in Southern France" (MS # R-111, Center of Military History); Army Group G War Diary (English translation, NARA: RG 242); Jörg Staiger, *Rückszug durchs Rhônethal*. Author interviews with General de Lassus, Albert Fié.

7.   Abbé Vignon, "Evénements à St.-Vallier-sur-Rhône," *Le Semeur* (Nos. 61–64, Sept. 1944–Jan. 1945).

8.   Pons, *De la Résistance*, 219–20; Micoud, *150 maquisards*, 163–65.

9.   Pons, *De la Résistance*, 223. For an illuminating account of how the Americans appeared to the French, see Henri Audra's reaction quoted in *Pour l'amour de la France*, 398–401.

10.   Pons, *De la Résistance*, 224–29; de Lassus, *Combats pour le Vercors*, 90–92. Bulletin No. 13 (Jan. 1991) of the *Amicale Pons* (*10 ème compagnie, Réseau Buckmaster-Roger*) includes several eye-witness accounts of the Fiancey action.

11.   Butler to Dahlquist, 1100, Aug. 22, 1944 (Task Force Butler Records).

12.   Lockhart, *T-Patch for Victory*, 32.

13. Interview of Col. Piddington by author. One of Piddington's platoon leaders, Lt. Kenneth J. Cronin, recalls hearing that a German command car was coming down from the north. His reaction: "I couldn't figure out how it approached from that direction since some of our people were supposed to be in Puy" ("Montelimar to Montrevel," by Maj. K. J. Cronin, in Col. Harold J. Samsel [ed.], *The Battle of Montrevel* [privately printed for the 117th Cavalry Association, 1986], Chap. IV). Just south of Puy-St.-Martin, Capt. Dominique Hepp, the paratrooper whom de Lassus had appointed deputy commander for south Drôme, accompanied an American patrol that was captured. When the Germans were fired on by an American tank destroyer, Hepp and a companion escaped, but the Americans remained, relying on their Geneva Convention status. Their bodies were recovered next day (testimony of Hepp, in *Pour l'amour de la France*, 425). See also de Lassus, *Combats pour le Vercors*, 91, 124-25.

14. 4th Battalion report (*Archives Nationales*, 72 AJ 120-21).

15. Truscott, *Command Missions*, 425; Truscott Diary (Marshall Library, Lexington, Virg.).

16. Lockhart, *T-Patch to Victory*, 63-68.

CHAPTER 12: MONTÉLIMAR AND VALENCE

1. De Lassus, *Combats pour le Vercors*, 94.

2, Ibid., 95.

3. American side of the attack on Valence from 143rd Regiment records and diary (NARA: RG 407, E 427, Boxes 9997 and 1857); interview of author with General Adams. French side from memoirs of de Lassus, Pons, and Micoud, cited above; records of 5th Co. FFI (Sabatier), *Archives Nationales*, 72 AJ 121; *Pour l'amour de la France*, 436-45.

4. Pons, *De la Résistance*, 233.

5. NOIR Report (NARA: RG 226, E 154, Box 56), 22. This 22-page report is much more detailed than the VEGANINE Jedburgh report and provides in great detail NOIR's reactions to local conditions. On German reactions, Foreign Military Studies: NARA, A 868 (Blaskowitz), A 881 (Drews).

6. OG ALICE report.

7. Weiss account in Lockhart, *T-Patch to Victory*, 74-91.

8. De Lassus, *Combats pour le Vercors*, 97. De Lassus believed that Adams needed Patch's approval but agrees that Dahlquist, not Patch, made the decision.

9.   A copy of Wiese's Operation Order of August 24 is located in the Drôme archives and has been published, in French, in *Pour l'amour de la France*, 409–11. See also von Luttichau, "German Operations in Southern France," in Center of Military History; Dahlquist's letter to his wife in U.S. Army Military History Archives, Carlisle Barracks, Penn., and also cited by Wilt, *French Riviera Campaign*, 141. Hinsley, *British Intelligence*, Vol. 3, Pt. II, 276.

10.   Truscott, *Command Missions*, 431. If a tough, experienced officer like Truscott was willing to keep Dahlquist in charge of the largest battle in the southern France campaign, it is difficult to accept the evaluation of the journalist Eric Sevareid, who met Dahlquist about this time, that the general "was obviously a man who was losing his nerve" (*Not So Wild a Dream* [New York, 1978], 444). It is true that Dahlquist, having been dressed down several times by Truscott, had some personal misgivings about his actions. Three days after his meeting with the VI Corps commander, he wrote his wife, "I have a very classic military role and a great opportunity. I feel I fumbled it badly and should have done a great deal better." Perhaps he could have acted with more vigor, but General Dahlquist, according to those who knew him, was a courageous man, always in the front lines, and dedicated to his professional obligations. It is not likely that any commander, regardless of his brilliance, could have overcome the logistic problems and brought more firepower to the Rhône. For a detailed analysis of the Sevareid comment, see Lockhart, *T-Patch to Victory*, 43–44.

11.   *Pour l'amour de la France*, 427–28; de Lassus, *Combats pour le Vercors*, 126–27.

12.   Von Luttichau, "German Operations in Southern France," 28–31. Although the 11th Panzer had lost many tanks, it had suffered only 747 casualties out of 14,000 men. The division obtained replacement tanks from Germany. See also Staiger, *Rückszug durchs Rhônetal*, 90–98.

13.   Pons, *De la Résistance*, 249–63; *Pour l'amour de la France*, 455–60; Micoud, *Nous étions 150 maquisards*, 177–89.

14.   *Combats pour le Vercors*, 106.

CHAPTER 13: EAST: THE DAUPHINÉ ALPS

1.   Truscott, *Command Missions*, 391–94.
2.   "Report of O.S.S. Activities with 7th Army, 14 Oct. 44" (NARA: RG 226, E 99, Box 30, Folder 145, p. 14).
3.   Report of Jed EPHEDRINE.

4.   Officially, PROGRESSION was a continuation of the UNION mission and is sometimes referred to as UNION III. The five Frenchmen were Lt. Fournier, Lt. Flicourt (MARABOUT), radio operator, and instructors: Sous-Lt. Hook (EGRAPPOIR), Lt. Carrière, and Lt. Appui. (SOE Archives; *Archives Nationales*, 72 AJ 545.)

5.   Report of OG NANCY.

6.   *Journal de Marche...en Ubaye*, 34; Béraud, *La seconde guerre mondiale dans les Hautes-Alpes*, 120–25.

7.   John Halsey report (SOE Archives).

8.   Based on Halsey's report; *Journal de Marche...en Ubaye*, 35–36; Garcin, *Libération dans les Alpes de Haute-Provence*, 410, 413, 419 (n. 121). In his report, Halsey mentions that Christine was present. Because Christine had been occupied with Cammaert's release on Aug. 17, and accompanied him to see Butler on the 20th, she would have had a full schedule if she went to Larche and back. Cammaerts' recollection:

> When I saw Christine after getting out of prison, she had already been to Larche. I don't think she went to Larche on 18/19 though that would have been possible since our base was Seyne-les-Alpes and she wasn't with me on those two days. On the motor bike Seyne–Larche is only a couple of hours.

9.   The following account based on Roper's report (SOE Archives) and interview with Roper, Mar. 3, 1988.

10.   Report of OG NANCY.

11.   Actions of 142nd RCT throughout from S-3 Journal, NARA. Jedburgh and OG actions from their reports; BLOs, SOE Archives.

12.   *Command Missions*, 427.

13.   The FFI units were led by Frison, Nortier, Ambrosi (district chief), and Sallot des Noyers, later joined by Begoud and Céard. The groups came under the overall command of Daviron (for East Alps) and L'HERMINE (for Central Alps). Records under A III (Hautes-Alpes) and "Journal de Marche du Cie AMBROSI," A II 6 (Hautes-Alpes), in *Archives Nationales*.

14.   Purvis and Roper reports, SOE Archives. Interview with John Roper. Aerial reconnaissance did not reveal enemy columns at Larche (VI Corps War Room Journal, Aug. 23, 1944).

15.   Halsey Report, SOE Archives.

16.   XL 7493 (Aug. 22, 1944), XL 7584 (Aug. 23, 1944) (PRO: DEFE 3/122).

17.   *Command Missions*, 429–30. While he acknowledges the help of Resistance units, Truscott says little about them. Among his papers is a nine-page, single-spaced G-2 summary, "The Maquis of France," dated July 28,

1944 (Truscott Papers, Box 13, Marshall Library, Lexington, VA). One wonders if he had read it.

18. Halsey Report, SOE Archives.

19. Actions in the Larche area based on Cronin communication in Col. Harold J. Samsel, *The Battle of Montrevel* (privately printed, 1986). Cronin recalled Halsey as "Jack Darcy," but from the context, it is clear that he refers to Halsey. Also: 117th Cavalry Reconnaissance Squadron reports and journal (NARA: RG 407, Box 3825); interviews with Col. Thomas Piddington; Report of Jedburgh CHLOROFORM (McIntosh, Martin); interviews with Henry Mc-Intosh and Jacques Martin; Halsey report; *Journal de Marche...en Ubaye*, 37–52; Béraud, *La seconde guerre mondiale dans les Hautes-Alpes*, 123–27.

20. Garcin, *Libération dans les Alpes de Haute-Provence*, 426–27.

21. *Journal de Marche...en Ubaye*, 53–78. It was not until Aug. 30 that the ABTF journal reported "Advance echelon of 550th CT closed on Barcelonnette and established base of operations there," five days after Patch had ordered Frederick to assume responsibility for the Larche pass.

22. Unit Journal, Provisional Flank Protective Force (NARA: RG 206, PFPF-07). See also U.S. Seventh Army *Operations*, I, 241–48.

23. Interview of author with Colonel Piddington, who has read this section.

24. The Céard company, under the general orders of Captain Frison, took up positions at the Fort des Têtes on Aug. 29 (Duchamblo, *Maquisards et Gestapo*, Cahier 15, 30–31). Céard had guided units of Task Force Butler to Col de la Croix Haute a week earlier.

25. "Evénements que se sont déroulés à Briançon (*Archives Nationales*, 72 AJ Hautes Alpes [A II 3]); Béraud, *La seconde guerre mondiale dans les Hautes-Alpes*, 123–27.

26. Ibid.; Jedburgh NOVOCAINE report; Purvis and Roper reports (SOE Archives). Patch knew through ULTRA as early as August 22 that the 90th Panzer Grenadier Division was being ordered to the Franco-Italian frontier (Hinsley, *British Intelligence*, Vol. III, Pt. 2, 334).

27. Colonel Bonjour commanded the RSAR (*Régiment de Spahis Algériens de Reconnaissance*) of the 3rd Algerian Infantry Division. In the latter days of August, his regiment, of about 6000 men, had swung behind the U.S. 45th Division and had occupied Aix-les-Bains and areas to the northeast of Albertville, the northern limit of Bibo's responsibility (De Lattre, *French First Army*, 131).

28. For Troop A, this would mean one long drive. On September 1, VI Corps had ordered the 117th Reconnaissance Squadron to patrol in the area of Meximieux, where the 179th Infantry was holding off attacks of the 11th Panzer. Meximieux is about 250 miles from Briançon, and the roads are in many places

curving and steep. Throughout the 2nd, Piddington's troop drove through the rain to rejoin the squadron, which had been ordered to seize and hold Montrevel, northwest of Bourg-en-Bresse, another 40 miles beyond Meximieux. On September 3, Piddington and part of Troop A joined Troop B in a day-long fruitless attempt to keep Montrevel from being occupied by elements of the 11th Panzer. Piddington was captured and spent the rest of the war in German prison camps. See A. L. Funk, "Mandate for Surrender," *World War II* (Mar. 1990), 27–33.

CHAPTER 14: EAST: CANNES AND NICE

1. PRO: DEFE 3/122: XL 7198, 1320 Aug. 20, 1944; XL 7246, 2202 Aug. 20, 1944.
2. Robert D. Burhans, *The First Special Service Force: A War History of the North Americans, 1942–1944* (Washington, D.C., 1947); Patch Field Order No. 2, Aug. 19, 1944.
3. First Airborne Task Force, Summary of Operations (NARA: 99/06-(FABTF)-0.3, Box 1746) (hereafter cited as FABTF Operations); S-3 Journal, 141st Infantry; Masson, *Résistance dans le Var*, 141.
4. Jones report (NARA: RG 226, E 110, Box 3, Folder 49).
5. Lécuyer, *Méfiez-vous du toréador*, 73–74, 132–33.
6. Ibid., 235. The HOCHCORN Battalion is one of the few FFI units identified by name in American records (see Burhans, *Special Services Force*, 282). The group is referred to by various spellings: Hochcorn, Hochscorn, Hochgorn. Perhaps it is the Norman name "Hauchecorne."
7. Gunn report (SOE Archives); Lécuyer, *Méfiez-vous du toréador*, 70.
8. The first patrols of the 550th went north on Aug. 26, but not until the 28th was a Combat Team organized. The first elements, badly informed on road conditions, detoured by way of Digne, and reached Barcelonnette late on Aug. 29. Not until the 31st did the battalion take up positions (FABTF Operations; *Journal de Marche de la Résistance en Ubaye*, 51–55).
9. Lécuyer, *Méfiez-vous du toréador*, 71.
10. FABTF Operations; Burhans, *Special Service Force*, 273–76; *Paratroopers' Odyssey: A History of the 517th Parachute Combat Team*, 72–73; Jones report.
11. FABTF Operations; *Archives Nationales*, 72 AJ 97; Adleman and Walton, *Champagne Campaign*, 170–72; Peter Leslie, *The Liberation of the Riviera: The Resistance of the Nazis in the South of France and the Story of its Heroic Leader, Ange-Marie Miniconi* (New York, 1980), 200–43. While

Leslie's volume is an excellent, detailed, journalistic account of the FTP in Cannes, its title makes claims hardly substantiated by its contents: a study of a local Resistance leader who commanded three companies, about 650 people.

12. Gunn report (SOE Archives).

13. Lécuyer, *Méfiez-vous du toréador*, 133–34.

14. OG RUTH report; *Paratroopers' Odyssey*, 72–73.

15. Jones to author. For a colorful but inaccurate account of this incident, see Adleman and Walton, *Champagne Campaign*, 154–60. The authors erroneously refer to the 148th Division order as applying to the entire German Nineteenth Army. (For text, see NARA: US Seventh Army, 107-2.9 "Captured documents.")

16. J. L. Panicacci, "Le Comité Départemental de Libération dans les Alpes-Maritimes, "*Revue d'histoire de la deuxième guerre mondiale*, July, 1982, 78–90; Joseph Girard, "Organisation et les opérations à caractère militaire des Forces Françaises de l'Intérieur dans les Alpes-Maritimes," *Revue d'histoire de la deuxième guerre mondiale* (Jan. 1972), 73–94.

17. Burhans, *Special Service Force*, 282; comments of Pierre Gautier (MALHERBE) in Lécuyer, *Méfiez-vous du toréador*, 134–35.

18. FABTF G-2 Reports and Journal, Annex #2, SSS Subsection, Administrative Report, Oct. 1, 1944 (NARA: RG 407, 99/06 [FABTF]-0.3; 4-SFU order to CG ABTF, Sept. 3, 1944); Gunn report, Halsey report (SOE Archives); interview of author with Havard Gunn. With the closing of Gunn's section, efforts to equip the FFI in southern France no longer were supervised by SPOC, 4-SFU, or inter-allied missions, but devolved on General Devers, commanding Sixth Army Group (Vigneras, *Rearming the French*, 324–25).

19. Jones, "The Liberation of the French Riviera" (8-page typed summary written in 1980, copy provided author by Geoffrey Jones); correspondence, Jones to author, Sept. 14, 1982; SSS Administrative Report, Oct. 1, 1944 (see previous note) and Oct. 22, 1944; interview of author with Emile Adès, interpreter with mission MICHEL.

20. Chief of staff ABTF to CG, Seventh Army, Sept. 27, 1944 (NARA: RG 407, 99/06 [FABTF]-0.3); Commendation of CG, Forty-fourth A.A.A. Brigade, Mar. 14, 1945 (NARA: RG 226, E 110, Box 3, Folder 49).

21. Lécuyer, *Méfiez-vous du toréador*, 78–81; Jean Delmas, "L'amalgame: Forces Françaises de l'Intérieur, lère Armée," in *Les armées françaises pendant la seconde guerre mondiale* (Paris, 1986), 415–25.

CHAPTER 15: WEST: TOULON AND MARSEILLE

1. GARDENER Circuit (SOE Archives); Foot, *SOE in France*, 215, 379. On Méker, Madeleine Baudoin, *Histoire des Groupes Francs (M.U.R.) des Bouches du Rhône* (Paris, 1962), 7, 161, 173-77. Interview with Francis Cammaerts.

2. Antiscorch operations based on records from the *Service historique de la Marine* (Château de Vincennes, Paris): "Rapport de mission particulière de l'équipe LOUGRE, Oct. 30, 1944;" "Compte rendu de la mission SAMPAN, Sept. 10, 1944;" "Rapport particulier de la mission GEDEON, Oct. 30, 1944;" "Rapport particulier de la mission CAIQUE, Sept. 10, 1944;" "Rapport de mission [SCHOONER], Sept. 27, 1944." Also interview with Lt. Cmdr. Brooks Richards of the SPOC French desk, and letter of Aug. 8, 1989.

3. Victor Masson, *La Résistance dans le Var* (Hyères, 1983), 93-95.

4. In his memoirs (*French First Army*, 74-75) de Lattre gives the impression that he had to persuade Patch for authorization to attack earlier than planned: "It was *after midday* [August 19] when, by sheer insistence, I succeeded in overcoming the opposition of the cautious. General Patch gave me a free hand." It is worth noting that Patch's Field Order No. 2, issued *at noon*, August 19, ordered the French II Corps to "capture and secure TOULON without delay." Truscott, in his memoirs (*Command Missions*, 241) writes: "Patch was concerned about de Lattre's delay in beginning the attack on Toulon. . . . Patch was urging de Lattre to begin operations but de Lattre insisted . . . on the full-scale attack he had planned."

5. De Lattre, *French First Army*, 74. In the French ed. (*Histoire de la première Armée française*, 105-06) de Lattre provides a graceful acknowledgement of FFI value. This is omitted in the English version.

6. De Lattre, *French First Army*, 76.

7. Although they withdrew on August 20, the Germans had already begun sabotage operations in Sète. The SCHOONER team, headed by engineer Kervarec, had blocked a swing bridge (by removing a machinery part), preventing a vessel from being used as a block ship. They also sunk, so that it could be refloated, a massive 135-ton floating crane that was later used to move concrete blocks in the channel. Kervarec's report on the Sète installations right after the Germans left points out that some damage resulted from an Allied air strike on June 25. Allain (with Lt. W.H. Woolverton of 4-SFU) visited Sète on August 30 and reported: "Docks fair condition. Railway operating. Harbor can be used soon as mines cleared. Counter scorch team did superb job" (4-SFU sitcom, Sept. 1, 1944, NARA: RG 226, E 190, Box 132).

8. Baudoin (*Groupes Francs du Bouches du Rhône*, 159–210) analyzes these differences in great detail.

9. For details regarding the liberation of Marseille, see (in English) de Lattre, *French First Army*, 99–115; Robert Aron, *France Reborn* (New York, 1964); US Seventh Army *Operations*, I, 162–69; (in French) Noguères, *Histoire de la Résistance*, V, 441–53; Lucien Gaillard, *Marseille sous l'occupation* (Rennes, 1982), 94–119.

10. De Lattre, *French First Army*, 115; Marcel Vigneras, *Rearming the French*, 324–35; Roland C. Ruppenthal, *Logistical Support of the Armies* (Washington, D.C., 1953), II, 116–24.

11. De Lattre, *French First Army*, 114.

CHAPTER 16: WEST: ACROSS THE RHÔNE—THE ARDÈCHE

1. Cammaerts had a few contacts in the Ardèche, and Tony Brooks's PIMENTO, concentrating on railways and Rhône bridges, was familiar with the area.

2. Ducros, *Montagnes ardéchoises*, III, 200–01, 391. The agents were Pierre Casanova, Henri Rozan, and Marcel-Jean Michel.

3. Ibid., 68–69, 90–91. Vaucheret was caught in a poplar tree, one member had the misfortune to land in a ditch of liquid manure, while Chassé was greeted by a little girl: *"cher officier, tombé du ciel"* (Dear officer, fallen from heaven).

4. Ibid., 183–96.

5. The following account is based on reports of Jedburgh WILLYS, OGs LOUISE and BETSY, and Ducros, *Montagnes ardéchoises*, III, 211–12, 270–307.

6. OG HELEN Report; Report on OGs, Sept. 20, 1944, by Maj. Alfred T. Cox (NARA: RG 226, E 146, Box 230).

7. On the retreat of Germans from southwest France, a topic that lies outside the scope of the present study, see David Wingeate Pike, "Les forces allemandes dans le sud-ouest de la France," *Guerres mondiales et conflits contemporains*, 152 (Oct. 1988), 3–24; Noguères, *Résistance*, V, 716–36; Robert Aron, *Libération*, 548–72.

8. Ducros, *Montagnes ardéchoises*, III, 332–35; Escudier papers in possession of author.

9. Pike, *Guerres mondiales* (Oct. 1988), 6; Jedburgh PACKARD Report; OG LOUISE Report; Staiger, *Rückzug durchs Rhônetal*, 50–52. ULTRA had information on August 26 that the Field Corps was going to Lyon (Hinsley, *British Intelligence*, III, Pt. 2, 273–77).

10. Ducros, *Montagnes ardéchoises*, III, 340–44. Ducros identifies over twenty skirmishes between August 22 and 25.

11. Ibid., 345–47; OG LOUISE Report; Escudier papers.

12. OG LEHIGH Report. Interview with Dr. John Hamblet (Sept. 6, 1991).

13. Nurk, born in 1904 in Esthonia of Russian parents, formerly a white hunter in East Africa, was parachuted into the Ardèche on August 25 (SOE Archives).

14. OG LEHIGH Report; Ducros, *Montagnes ardéchoises*, III, 390.

15. Ducros (ibid., 395–98) enumerates FTP 3rd and 5th Battalions, FTP Companies 7103, 7107, 7108, 7110, 7111, 7116, 7118, 7124, the *Groupe Franc Dury*, AS companies 6, 7 (Maleval), 23 (Anselin), 51, 52 (Escudier), 53, 54 (Rouyer), and others. Escudier took as prisoners a group of "Mongols" (*Turkmènes*) who had captured peasants as hostages. Altogether 1,750, of which the majority belonged to the SS Legion of Azerbaijan, assembled at Privas. The FFI picked up four 77-mm. guns; twelve guns of 37- to 47-mm.; thirty 20-mm., fifteen heavy machine guns, dozens of mortars (some 105-mm.), 380 vehicles, and 600 horses.

16. Ibid., 399–400; reports of LOUISE, LAFAYETTE.

17. Escudier to author.

CHAPTER 17: NORTH OF GRENOBLE

1. On the heroic women of the Arcelin family, see Margaret Rossiter, *Women in the Resistance* (New York, 1985), 85, 177. Situation in Savoie, *Archives Nationales*, 72 AJ 86, 72 AJ 545; Foot, *SOE in France*, 357–58, 403; Bernier, *Maquis Rhône-Alpes*, 111–15.

2. On UNION II, *Archives Nationales*, 72 AJ 86; B. M. Frank and H. I. Shaw, *History of U. S. Marine Corps Operations*, V (Washington, D.C., 1968), 747. The five sergeants were John P. Bodner, Frederick J. Brunner, Jack Risler, Robert E. La Salle (injured on landing), and Charles R. Perry (killed on landing).

3. PROGRESSION information from SOE Archives; EPHEDRINE Report; Hymoff, *OSS in World War II* (rev. ed.), 312–14.

4. 180th Regiment Journal (NARA).

5. PROGRESSION Report; Bernier, *Maquis Rhône-Alpes*, 114.

6. De Lattre, *French First Army*, 130–32. EPHEDRINE reported to 4-SFU in Grenoble on Sept. 8, 1944. PROGRESSION continued to work with the FFI until the French 2nd Moroccan Infantry Division arrived and requested further orders from London. Receiving no instructions, the mission left the Savoie on Oct. 2, 1944, and proceeded to England via Lyon and Paris.

7. Silvestre, *Maquis de l'Isère*, 339-41; Marcel Ruby, *La Résistance à Lyon* (Lyon 1979), II, 803-05; Alban Vistel, *La nuit sans ombre* (Paris, 1970), 501-11. General Eagles phoned Truscott on Aug. 26: "I have Meyer at Grenoble and he is in a huddle with the head of the Maquis . . . . I have been asking the Maquis for the last two days to cut all those roads that cross the Grenoble-Lyon road so that the Boche can't get out. Meyer will work them over again on that" (VI Corps War Room Journal). A grateful French government later awarded Colonel Johnson the Legion of Honor. The citation (with slight errors of dates) reads in part:

> At the request of the French Forces of the Interior his battalion moved to BOURGOIN the 24th of August at the farthest point of the Allied advance. The city had been liberated the day before and his energetic and daring entry into action permitted the conquered ground to be held. The moral and material assistance given to the troops of Commandant CHABERT [René Bousquet] permitted the intensive guerrilla action which terminated in the taking of Lyon the 2nd of September. (Citation courtesy of the Johnson family.)

8. Justin Greene of OSS and Colonel Cusenier, FFI, had accompanied Colonel Adams to Grenoble. Alban Vistel states that on Aug. 25 Descour reported to him that the evening before he had made contact with the general commanding the 5th [*sic*] American division (*La nuit sans ombre*, 509). This presumably refers to the 45th division.

9. Pecquet (Paray) to author; Truscott diary (George Marshall Library and Archives, Lexington, Virginia).

10. For details and documentation on what liberation meant politically to the French, see Hillary Footit and John Simmonds, *France 1943-1945* (New York, 1988), especially 40-57; John Sweets, *The Politics of Resistance in France, 1940-1944*, 196-210. The French side of Lyon's liberation is covered in detail in Fernand Rude, *Libération de Lyon et de sa région* (Paris, 1974); Marcel Ruby, *La Résistance à Lyon*, 2 vols. (Lyon, 1979); Henri Noguères, *Histoire de la Résistance*, V, 631-93.

11. For reprisals carried out by the Germans in the Lyon area, see Robert Aron, *Libération*, 526-32; Ted Morgan, *An Uncertain Hour: The French, the Germans, the Jews, the Klaus Barbie Trial, and the City of Lyon, 1940-1945* (New York, 1990), 251-322; Hinsley, *British Intelligence*, III, Pt. 2, 375-76.

12. The French clandestine command structure, on paper, was complicated but did not always function according to the organization plan. In the Lyon area, three men dominated the hierarchy: Yves Farge, regional commissioner of the Republic, Jacques Maillet, delegate of the [provisional] French government, and Bourgès-Maunoury, FFI chief for the Southern Zone. Bourgès

worked closely with Marcel Degliame, a Communist, who was not only FFI inspector general for the Southern Zone, but also a member of the Directing Committee for the MLN (*Mouvement de Libération Nationale*), formerly the MUR. These men operated from clandestine headquarters in Lyon, or from a command post at St.-Laurent-de-Chamousset in the hilly country twenty-five miles west of the city. There they maintained contact with London (General Koenig's FFI headquarters) and with the National Resistance Council in Paris. The R-1 military delegate, Paul Leistenschneider (CARRE), maintained liaison with Alban Vistel, the Regional FFI chief.

13. Vistel, *Nuit sans ombre*, 511–18.

14. SSS Report, 25; Report of Justin Greene (NARA, RG 226, E158, Box 6, Folder 75).

15. U.S. Seventh Army, *Report of Operations*, I, 254. In a telephone conversation at 0930, Aug. 28, Patch told Truscott: "Don't put any of your troops anywhere within the city of Lyon" (NARA: RG 407, E 427, Box 3605).

16. Truscott, *Command Missions*, 434.

17. Charles von Luttichau, "German Operations in Southern France" (MS R-112, U.S. Army Center of Military History, Washington, D.C.), Chap. XIV, 19–22; Staiger, *Rückszug durchs Rhônetal*, 98–100.

CHAPTER 18: END OF DRAGOON: MEXIMIEUX AND LYON

1. Fol and Rudigoz, *La bataille de Meximieux*, 28. Operations at Meximieux and the Ain, unless otherwise noted, are based on reports of the 45th Division, 179th and 180th Regiments (NARA), and Warren P. Munsell, Jr., *The Story of a Regiment: A History of the 179th Regimental Combat Team*, Part 5. The book of Fol and Rudigoz, cited above, is an extremely detailed account, based on testimonies by witnesses enhanced by careful research. The present writer used materials at the 45th Division Museum and Archives in Oklahoma City, Oklahoma, and interviewed Col. Harlos Hatter, in 1944 179th RCT Supply Officer. At the Museum are the papers of Col. Harold Meyer, CO of the 179th, among which are included a long account of the action at Meximieux written several months later while Meyer was hospitalized. The account of Gen. Michael Davison, in 1944 CO of the 1st Battalion, had been recorded in an official U.S. Army interview deposited in the archives of the Military History Research Collection at Carlisle Barracks, Pennsylvania. The writer has also corresponded with and interviewed General Davison. Both Davison and Meyer have read this section.

2. Seen by the writer at Pérouges in 1982.

3. Staiger, *Rückzug durchs Rhônetal*, 98–99.

4. Luttichau, "German Operations in Southern France," Chapt. XIV, 22.

5. H. Romans-Petit, *Les obstinés* (Lille, 1945), 253–54.

6. Noguères, *Résistance*, V, 696–93.

7. 142nd Regiment, S-3 journal (NARA). Anthony Brooks, interview and correspondence.

8. Ibid.

9. De Lattre, *French First Army*, 124–26; Ducros, *Montagnes ardéchoises*, III, 400–06.

10. Sheeline Report (NARA, RG 226, E 190, Box 128).

11. Following details based on OG and Jedburgh reports in NARA.

12. Weiss's account of his work with the Resistance has been printed in Lockhart, *T-Patch to Victory*, 83–91. See also Ducros, *Montagnes ardéchoises*, III, 351–52, 385–86.

13. De Lattre, *French First Army*, 127–28; OG LEHIGH Report. For details of an American patrol into Lyon, see *MacGibbon's Mule Barn* (Portland, Oregon, privately printed, 1976), 18–21.

14. Dahlquist Papers, Military Research Collection, Carlisle Barracks, Pennsylvania.

CHAPTER 19: CONCLUSION

1. Bill Harr, *Combat Boots* (New York, 1953), 20–21.

2. 180th Infantry, Operations Report, August 1944, 241, 243.

3. Report of Capt. Dewey Mann, 142nd Infantry, August 1944.

4. 117th Cavalry Reconnaissance Squadron, History, Entry for Aug. 26, 1944.

5. "Task Force Butler," *Armored Cavalry Journal* (Jan.–Feb., 1948), 15.

6. *Command Missions*, 420.

7. Appendix C, Foot, *SOE in France*. See also *Special Operations: AAF Aid to the Resistance Movements, 1943–1945*, 66–75. (I am assuming that roughly one-third of the supplies went to southern France.)

8. Ernest Borrely, in *Le Provençal*, Sept. 16, 1944.

9. Bill Mauldin, *Up Front* (New York, 1945), 204.

10. *Special Operations: AAF Aid*, 231 (Appendix 15).

11. On the occasion of de Gaulle's visit to Washington in July 1944, Donovan presented what his biographer calls the "longest report of his career so far," a memorandum on "Performance and Potential of the French Resistance," which argued strongly for more support (Cave Brown, *The Last Hero*,

361–64). A similar argument, at the same time, was made by General Caffey to General Noce (Asst. Chief of Staff, G-3, Special Operations, AFHQ) June 30, 1944 (PRO, WO 204/1164). All these arguments came too late to have any significant impact.

12. In early OVERLORD planning by COSSAC, the point was made that "assistance of the [Resistance] groups . . . should be treated as a bonus rather than an essential part of the plan" (cited in Ehrmann, *Grand Strategy*, V, 324–25).

Glossary

ABTF	Airborne Task Force.
Aeronavale	French Navy Air Force.
AFHQ	Allied Force Headquarters (Algiers).
AMGOT	Allied Military Government of Occupied Territory.
ANVIL	Code-name for Southern France Landings, later changed to DRAGOON.
AS	Armée Secrète (Gaullist Secret Army).
Asp.	*Aspirant* (French officer candidate).
BBC	British Broadcasting Company.
BCRA	*Bureau Central de Renseignements et d'Action* (Gaullist intelligence service first established in London).
Black Devils	First Special Service Force.
BLO	British Liaison Officer.
Blue Devils	Refers to the French Chasseurs Alpins, who wear a blue uniform and characteristic floppy beret.
BOA	*Bureau d'Opérations Aériennes* (Service for arranging clandestine air operations in northern France).
BRAL	*Bureau de Renseignements et d'Action Londres* (BCRA service remaining in London after de Gaulle moved to Algiers).
Capitaine de Corvette	French Navy equivalent of Lieut. Commander.

CC	Combat Command.
CCS	Combined Chiefs of Staff.
Cdt.	Commandant (French Army equivalent of major).
CDL	*Comité Départemental de Libération* (Departmental Liberation Committee).
CFL	*Corps Francs de la Libération* (name of MUR military groups unified in 1944).
CFLN	*Comité Français de la Libération Nationale* (French Committee of National Liberation. See FCNL).
CG	Commanding General.
CNR	*Conseil National de la Résistance* (National Resistance Council, acting inside occupied France).
CO	Commanding Officer.
COMAC	*Comité d'Action Militaire* (Military Action Committee of the CNR. Not to be confused with the *Comité d'Action Militaire en France*, attached to the DGSS).
Corps Franc	Commando-type military groups.
CP	Command Post.
CT	Combat Team (see RCT).
D Day	Commencement date of operaton: June 6, 1944 for the Normandy (OVERLORD) landings; Aug. 15, 1944 for the southern France (ANVIL/DRAGOON) landings.
Dauphiné	French region, with Grenoble as capital, between the Rhône River and the Alps.
DGSS	*Direction Générale des Services Spéciaux* (Gaullist Special Services Executive, headed by Jacques Soustelle).
DM	*Délégué Militaire* (Military Delegate).
DMOS	*Délégué Militaire Opérations Sud* (Military Delegate for Southern Operations, position held by Gen. Gabriel Cochet).
DMR	*Délégué Militaire Régional* (Regional Military Delegate).
DRAGOON	Code name which replaced ANVIL, the southern France landings, on July 1, 1944.
EMFFI	*Etat Major des Forces Françaises de l'Intérieur* (General Staff, French Forces of the Interior).

Eng. Off.	Engineer Officer, Navy (equivalent of French *Ingénieur Mécanicien Principal*).
F section	SOE branch controlling non-Gaullist agents.
FABTF	First Airborne Task Force.
FANY	First Aid Nursing Yeomanry (British women's auxiliary service).
FCNL	French Committee of National Liberation (Exterior Resistance executive body, dominated after March 1944 by de Gaulle. English for CFLN).
FFI	*Forces Françaises de l'Intérieur* (French Forces of the Interior, Resistance military forces unified under command of General Koenig).
FN	*Front National* (Communist-dominated Resistance organization).
4-SFU	See SFU.
FTP(F)	*Francs-Tireurs et Partisans (Français)* (Communist-dominated military Resistance units).
G-2	Military designation of intelligence section (French equivalent is *Deuxième Bureau*).
G-3	Military designation of operations section.
GARDENER	SOE F-section circuit controlled by R. R. Boiteux, in Marseille area.
Groupes francs	Military units of the MUR specializing in sabotage and raids.
H Hour	Time for commencement of an operation.
HQ	Headquarters.
JCS	U. S. Joint Chiefs of Staff.
JOCKEY	SOE F-section circuit controlled by F. Cammaerts, in southeastern France.
LO	Liaison Officer.
Maître	French equivalent of Chief Petty Officer (Navy).
MASSINGHAM	SOE base at Guyotville, west of Algiers.
Maquis	Clandestine Resistance group, many of which had arms and undertook guerrilla operations. An individual member of a Maquis was a *maquisard*.

Maurienne	Region in Savoie through which the Arc River flows.
MI6	British Military Intelligence.
Milice	Vichy police force, headed by Joseph Darnand, that employed Gestapo-like tactics against the Resistance.
MLN	*Mouvement de Libération Nationale* (A federation of the MUR with several northern Resistance groups).
MUR	*Mouvements Unis de la Résistance* (a consolidation of three southern Resistance groups: *Combat, Libération,* and *Franc-Tireur*).
NARA	National Archives and Records Administration (Washington, D. C.).
NCO	Non-Commissioned Officer (Navy).
OG	Operational Group (OSS paratroopers, normally consisting of 28 men and 2 officers).
ORA	*Organisation de Résistance de l'Armée* (Army Resistance organization of which the nucleus was the Armistice Army, disbanded by the Germans in 1942).
OSS	Office of Strategic Services.
OVERLORD	Code name for cross-channel attack.
PC	*Poste de Commandement* (Command Post).
P.I.A.T.	Projector, Infantry, Anti-Tank (British rocket projector similar to a Bazooka).
PIMENTO	SOE F-section circuit controlled by A. Brooke, in Rhône valley and adjacent areas.
PRO	Public Record Office (British archives).
Provence	French region, with Aix-en-Provence as capital, along the Mediterranean between the Rhône River and the Alps.
Queyras	Mountainous area east of Gap, between the Larche and Montgenèvre passes.
PWE	Political Warfare Executive (British).
R-1, R-2	Resistance Regions (see map: "Southeastern France").
RAF	Royal Air Force.
RCT	Regimental Combat Team.
Recce	Reconnaissance (British usage).
Recon	Reconnaissance.

RF section	SOE branch cooperating with Gaullist BCRA.
RIA	*Régiment d'Infanterie Alpine* (Alpine Infantry Regiment).
Route Napoléon	The route (N 85) from Cannes to Grenoble, followed by Napoleon on his escape from Elba.
RSAR	*Régiment de Spahis Algériens de Reconnaissance* (Algerian Cavalry Reconnaissance Regiment).
SACMED	Supreme Allied Commander, Mediterranean Theater (in 1944 Gen. Sir Henry Maitland Wilson).
SAP	*Section d'atterrissage et de parachutage* (Section for Landings and Parachuting in southern France).
SAS	Special Air Service (airborne commandos).
Savoie	French region, with Chambéry as capital, south of Switzerland.
Secret Army	Gaullist military forces: the *Armée secrète*, or AS.
SFHQ	Special Force Headquarters (staff of SOE/SO affiliated with SHAEF in London).
SFU	Special Force Unit. (SFU No. 4 was SPOC's field unit serving as liaison between the FFI and the Seventh Army.)
SHAEF	Supreme Headquarters, Allied Expeditionary Force. (Eisenhower's headquarters for OVERLORD.)
SI	Secret Intelligence Branch, OSS.
SIPO	*Sicherheitspolizei* (German secret police).
SO	Special Operations Branch, OSS.
SOE/SO	Joint SOE and SO (of OSS) office in London (later became SFHQ).
Sous/Lt.	French equivalent of second lieutenant.
Spitfire	Landing strip on the Vaucluse Plateau, ten miles north of Apt.
SPOC	Special Project Operations Center (Algiers).
SSS	Strategic Service Section (OSS/SI unit attached to Seventh Army).
STO	*Service du Travail Obligatoire* (Compulsory Labor Service).
Tarentaise	Region in Savoie through which the Isère River runs.

TD	Tank Destroyer.
Texas Division	The 36th Division.
TF	Task Force.
Thunderbird Division	The 45th (Oklahoma) Division.
T-Patch	Sobriquet for the 36th (Texas) Division.
ULTRA	Code name for German messages deciphered at Bletchley Park, England.
USAAF	United States Army Air Force.
W/T	Wireless Telegraphy. British W/T operator equivalent to US radio operator.
Y Day	Readiness date. (For OVERLORD, June 1, 1944.)

Selected Bibliography

ARCHIVES

United States

National Archives and Records Administration (NARA), Washington, D.C. At the Suitland National Records Center are records of military units, of which regimental histories and communication logs have been especially useful. During the 1980's, in Record Group 226, NARA acquired large holdings of OSS records, essential for this study.

Center of Military History, Washington, D.C. Holdings include materials useful for U.S. Army official historians, such as the diary of General Patch, and in-house studies such as the history of the German Nineteenth Army by Charles von Luttichau.

Forty-Fifth Division Museum, Oklahoma City, Oklahoma. Holds miscellaneous materials relating to the 45th Division, including the papers of Col. Harold Meyers.

George C. Marshall Library, Lexington, Virginia. Holds papers of Gen. Lucian Truscott.

Hoover Institution, Stanford, California. Collection on French Resistance includes materials on COMAC, the ORA, and Resistance areas.

Military History Research Collection, Carlisle Barracks, Pennsylvania. Papers of Gen. William J. Donovan, and large collection of unit histories. Especially useful are oral interviews of retiring officers.

Great Britain

Public Record Office (PRO), Kew Gardens, London. Records of War Office (WO), Cabinet (CAB), Foreign Office (FO), Premier (PREM), and Defense, including ULTRA (DEFE).

Foreign and Commonwealth Office, London. Holds SOE records, which are not
   open to the general public. The archivist/adviser, however, may provide
   information regarding the contents of files to qualified researchers.

France

Archives Nationales, Paris. The 72 AJ series, "Fonds relatifs à l'histoire de la
   deuxième guerre mondiale," contains an enormous body of materials on the
   Resistance. Many of these records were originally compiled by the *Comité
   français d'histoire de la deuxième guerre mondiale*, and for many years could
   be examined at the Committee's offices in Paris. They were later transferred
   to the *Institut d'histoire du temps présent*, and more recently moved to the
   Archives Nationales.
Service historique de l'Armée de Terre, Château de Vincennes, Paris. Holds
   papers of many military Resistance leaders and has an excellent library.

INTERVIEWS

Having worked in the field of French-American wartime relations for forty
years, I have had the good fortune to make many sojourns in France, including
three trips by car through the Southeast. Both there and in Paris, I have been able
to meet and interview members of the Resistance, some through the good offices
of Francis Cammaerts. In England Michael Foot has been instrumental in enabling
me to meet British agents, many of them members of the Special Forces Club.
Living in the United States, I have been able, over the years, to travel to New York,
Washington, D.C., Pennsylvania, Florida, Oklahoma, and Texas, to interview
Americans who participated in ANVIL/DRAGOON. In the following list, an
asterisk indicates correspondence only.

French Resistance: Jean Abbonenc,* Emile Adès, Antoine Benoit, Justin Boeuf,
   Richard Duchamblo, Pierre Escot, Charles Escudier,* Lucien Fié, Pierre Four-
   caud, Lucien Fraisse, M. Guiboud-Ribaud, Louis Malarte, Raymond Mollard,
   Etienne Moreaud.
French Army Resistance: Jean Constans,* J.-P. de Lassus St.-Geniès, Jacques
   Lécuyer, Alain LeRay, Gilles Lévy,* Louis Terrason-Duvernon, Henri Zeller,
   Henri Ziegler.
Jedburghs: Aaron Bank,* Jacques Martin (Martino), Henry McIntosh, Jean Sassi
   (Nicole), John Smallwood.
SOE: Anthony Brooks, Francis Cammaerts, Sir William Deakin, Sir Douglas
   Dodds-Parker, Havard Gunn, Pierre Raynaud, Sir Brooks Richards, John
   Roper.
Royal Air Force: Hugh Verity.

U.S. Army: Paul Adams, Theodore Andrews, Donald Bussey, Michael Davison, James Gentle,* Harlos Hatter, Charles Hodge, John Kinzer, Raymond Lynch, Willliam Mecabe, Harold Meyer,* Padraig O'Day,* Thomas Piddington, William Quinn, Harold Samsel, Stephen Weiss.

OSS: Franklin Canfield, William Casey, Joseph Haskell, Henry Hyde, Denis Johnson, Geoffrey Jones, André Pecquet (Paray), Paul Sheeline, William Woolverton.*

OGs: Mills Brandes, Michael De Marco, John Hamblet, Harry Herres, Arnold Lorbeer,* Leonard Rinaldi.

DOCUMENTS, MEMOIRS, AND SPECIAL STUDIES

Abonnenc, Jean. *Pour l'amour de la France: Drôme-Vercors 1940–1944*. Valence: Editions Peuple Libre, 1989.

AFHQ History of Special Operations, Mediterranean Theatre, 1942-1945. Section VII: "Resistance in France." PRO: WO/2030B; NARA: Modern Military Reference.

Amicale des Réseaux Action. *Les Réseaux Action de la France Combattante 1940–1944*. Paris: France-Empire, 1986.

Arnoux, Claude. *Maquis Ventoux*. Avignon: Les Presses Universelles, 1974.

Bank, Aaron. *From OSS to Green Berets*. Novato, Calif.: Presidio, 1986.

Baudoin, Madeleine. *Histoire des Groupes Francs (MUR) des Bouches-du-Rhône*. Paris: Presses Universitaires de France, 1962.

Béraud, Henri. *La seconde guerre mondiale dans les Hautes-Alpes et l'Ubaye*. Gap: Société d'Etudes des Hautes-Alpes, 1990.

Buckmaster, Maurice. *Specially Employed: The Story of British Aid to French Patriots of the Resistance*. London: Batchworth, 1952.

Burhans, Lt. Col. Robert D. *The First Special Service Force: A War History of the North Americans, 1942–1944*. Washington, D.C.: Infantry Journal Press, 1947.

Butcher, Harry C. *My Three Years with Eisenhower*. New York: Simon & Schuster, 1946.

Butler, Brig. Gen. Frederic B. "Task Force Butler," *Armored Cavalry Journal* (Jan.-Feb., Mar.-Apr. 1948).

Castor, C. G. (comp.). *The Complete Official History of the 59th Armored Field Artillery Battalion*. Decorah, Iowa (privately printed), 1990.

Cave Brown, Anthony (ed.). *The Secret War Report of the OSS*. New York: Berkley, 1976. See also *War Report of the OSS*.

Champlain, Helène de. *The Secret War of Helène de Champlain*. New York: W. H. Allen, 1980.

Chandler, A. D. Jr., and S. E. Ambrose (eds.). *The Papers of Dwight D. Eisenhower. The War Years.* 5 vols. Baltimore, MD: Johns Hopkins University Press, 1970.

Churchill, Winston. *The Second World War.* Vol. 5, *Closing the Ring*; Vol. 6, *Triumph and Tragedy.* Boston: Houghton Mifflin, 1951; 1953.

Covert Warfare. Edited by John Mendelsohn. Vols. 3, 4, 5. New York: Garland, 1989.

D'Astier de la Vigerie, Emmanuel. *Les dieux et les hommes.* Paris: Julliard, 1952.

De Gaulle, Charles. Mémoires de guerre. 3 vols. Paris: Plon, 1954–59. English ed.: *The Complete War Memoirs of Charles de Gaulle.* 3 vols. New York: Simon & Schuster, 1955–60.

De Lassus Saint-Geniès, Gen. J.-P., and Pierre de Saint-Prix. *Combats pour le Vercors et la liberté.* 2nd ed. Valence: Editions Peuple Libre, 1984.

De Lattre de Tassigny, Maréchal Jean. *Histoire de la Première Armée Française.* Paris: Plon, 1949. English ed.: *The History of the French First Army.* London: Allen & Unwin, 1952.

Dodds-Parker, Douglas. *Setting Europe Ablaze.* Windlesham: Springwood, 1983.

Duchamblo, Abbé Richard. *Maquisards et Gestapo.* Gap: Imprimerie Ribaud Frères, 1945–51.

Ducros, L.-F. *Montagnes ardéchoises dans la guerre.* 3 vols. Romans: Dauphiné Vivarais, 1977–82.

Farge, Yves. *Rebelles soldats et citoyens.* Paris: Grasset, 1946.

Fielding, Xan. *Hide and Seek.* London: Secker & Warburg, 1954.

The French Forces of the Interior: Their Organization and Participation in the Liberation of France. French Resistance Unit of the U.S. Army Historical Section (Maj. R. A. Bourne Patterson [SOE], Capt. H. S. Griffiths [OSS], Capt. L. Galimand [FFI], and Capt. M. Vigneras [FFI]), 1945. Microfilm available at Library of Congress, Washington, D. C.

Garcin, Jean. *De l'armistice à la libération dans les Alpes de Haute-Provence.* Digne: Vial, 1983.

Gazagnaire, Louis. *Le peuple héroes de la Résistance: Témoignages de patriote de Provencier.* Paris: Editions Sociales, 1971.

Ginette, Lt. *Le temps des fauves.* Paris: La Pensée Universelle, 1972.

Goldsmith, John. *Accidental Agent.* New York: Scribner's, 1971.

Guillon, Jean-Marie. "La libération du Var: Résistance et nouveaux pouvoirs," *Les Cahiers de l'IHTP*, No. 15 (June 1990).

Hamson, D. O. H. *We Fell Among Greeks.* London: Jonathon Cape, 1946.

Harr, Bill. *Combat Boots: Tales of Fighting Men.* New York: Exposition Press, 1952.

Jordan, W. S. *Conquest Without Victory.* London: Hodder & Stoughton, 1969.

Journal de marche de la Résistance en Ubaye. Amicale des Maquisards et Résistants, Secteur Ubaye. Barcelonnette: Imprimerie Départementale, n. d.

Kriegel-Valrimont, Maurice. *La Libération: les archives du COMAC (Mai-Août 1944).* Paris: Les Editions de Minuit, 1964.

Ladet, René. *Ils ont refusé de subir.* Crest: Imprimerie Véziant, 1987.

La libération de la France. (Proceedings of Conference of October, 1974.) Edited by Henri Michel. Paris: CNRS, 1974.

Lanvin, Lt. Col. *Liberté provisoire: Le Secteur I (Grenoble) au maquis dans l'Oisans.* Grenoble: Imprimerie des Deux Ponts, 1973.

La Picirella, J. *My Diary of the Vercors.* Vaulx-en-Velin: Imprimerie H. M., 1980.

Lécuyer, Jacques. See SAPIN.

Lemonnier, Adm. A. G. *Cap sur la Provence.* Paris: France-Empire, 1954.

Martin, Yves. *L'Ain dans la guerre, 1939-1945.* Bourg: Editions Horvath, 1989.

Masson, Victor. *La Résistance dans le Var.* Hyères: Alphonse Denis, 1983.

Micoud, Lucien. *Nous étions 150 maquisards.* Valence: Editions Peuple Libre, 1982.

Nal, Commandant Louis. *La bataille de Grenoble* (Mémoires posthumes présentées par Joseph Perrin). Paris: Editions des Deux Miroirs, 1964.

Nelson, Guy. *Thunderbird: A History of the 45th Division.* Oklahoma City, Okla.: 45th Division Association, 1970.

Obolensky, Serge. *One Man in His Time.* New York: McDowell, 1958.

OKW War Diary, April-Dec. 1944. *World War II German Military Studies* (edited by Donald Detwiler), Vol. 10. New York: Garland, 1979.

OSS/London: Special Operations Branch and Secret Intelligence War Diaries. Microfilm of OSS documents in National Archives. Frederick, Maryland: University Publications of America.

Paillole, Paul. *Services spéciaux, 1939–1945.* Paris: Laffont, 1975.

Panicacci, Jean-Louis. *Les Alpes-Maritimes de 1939 à 1945: un département dans la tourmente.* Nice, 1989.

Paratroopers' Odyssey: A History of the 517th Parachute Combat Team. Edited by Clark L. Archer. Hudson, Fla.: 517th Parachute RCT Association, 1985.

Passy, Col. [André Dewavrin]. *Souvenirs.* 3 vols. Monte Carlo and Paris: Solar, 1947-51.

Pons, Commandant Paul. *De la Résistance à la Libération.* Romans: P. Pons, 1962.

Romans-Petit, Henri. *Les Obstinés.* Lille: Editions Janicot, 1945.

Rosencher, Henri. *Le sel, la cendre, et la flamme.* Paris (privately printed), 1985.

Ruby Marcel. *La Résistance à Lyon.* 2 vols. Lyon: Editions L'Hermes, 1979.

Rude, Fernand. "Le dialogue Vercors-Alger," *Revue d'histoire de la deuxième guerre mondiale,* No. 49 (Jan. 1963).

_____. *La libération de Lyon et de sa région.* Paris: Hachette, 1974.

SACMED. Report by the Supreme Commander Mediterranean to the Combined Chiefs of Staff on the Operations in Southern France, August 1944. London: HMSO, 1946.

Samsel, Col. Harold J. (ed.). *The Battle of Montrevel.* Princeton, N.J. (privately printed), 1986.

Sapin (Jacques Lécuyer) et quelques autres. *Méfiez-vous du toréador.* Toulon: AGPM, 1987.

Sevareid, Eric. *Not So Wild a Dream.* New York: Atheneum, 1978.

Silvestre, Paul and Suzanne. *Chronique des Maquis de l'Isère, 1943–1944.* Grenoble: Editions des 4 Seigneurs, 1978.

Soustelle, Jacques. *Envers et contre tout.* 2 vols. Paris: Laffont, 1947–50.

Special Operations: AAF Aid to European Resistance Movements. Compiled by Harris G. Warren. U.S. Army Air Force, 1947. (Reprinted ed.: Manhattan, Kansas: MA/AH Publishing.)

Tanant, Pierre. *Vercors, haut-lieu de France.* Paris: Arthaud, 1966.

Truscott, Lt. Gen. Lucien K. *Command Missions.* New York: Dutton, 1954.

United States Seventh Army. *Report of Operations in France and Germany.* 3 vols. Heidelberg: Aloys Graf, 1946.

Verity, Hugh. *We Landed by Moonlight.* London: Ian Allan, 1978. Updated version in French: *Nous atterrissions de nuit.* Paris: Editions France-Empire, 1982.

Vial, Jean. *Souvenirs d'un Résistant: Un de l'Armée Secrète Bas-Alpine.* Aix-en-Provence: Imprimerie la Mualatière, 1976.

Vistel, Alban. *La nuit sans ombre.* Paris: Fayard, 1970.

Vomécourt, Philippe. *An Army of Amateurs.* Garden City, N.Y.: Doubleday, 1961.

War Report of the OSS. Kermit Roosevelt and staff, History Project, Strategic Services Unit (eds.). Washington, D. C.: War Department, 1947. Published in 2 vols., New York: Walker, 1976.

Wilson, Field Marshal Lord (Henry Maitland). *Eight Years Overseas.* London: Hutchinson, 1950.

Zeller, Henri. "De la chute du Vercors à la libération de Grenoble," *Revue historique de l'Armée,* No. 4 (1969).

SECONDARY STUDIES

Adleman, Robert R., and George Walton. *The Champagne Campaign.* Boston: Little Brown, 1969.

Aglion, Raoul. *Roosevelt and de Gaulle.* New York: Free Press, 1988.

Alsop, Stewart, and Thomas Braden. *Sub Rosa: The O.S.S. and American Espionage.* New York: Reynal & Hitchcock, 1946.

Ambrose, Stephen E. *The Supreme Commander: The War Years of General Dwight D. Eisenhower.* Garden City: Doubleday, 1970.

Amouroux, Henri. *La vie des Français sous l'occupation.* Paris: Laffont, 1961.

Les armées françaises pendant la seconde guerre mondiale. (Proceedings of Conference of May 1985.) Paris: Atelier d'Impression de l'Armée de Terre, 1986.

Aron, Robert. *Histoire de la libération de la France.* Paris: Fayard, 1959. English ed.: *France Reborn.* New York: Scribner's, 1964.

Azeau, Henri. *La lutte pour les Alpes: les deux Savoies.* Paris: Presses de la Cité, 1968.

Bennett, Ralph. *Ultra and Mediterranean Strategy.* New York: Morrow, 1989.
_____. *Ultra in the West.* New York: Scribner's, 1980.

Bernier, Jean-Pierre. *Maquis Rhône-Alpes.* Paris: Lavauzelle, 1987.

Blumenthal, Henry. *Illusion and Reality in Franco-American Diplomacy, 1914–1945.* Baton Rouge, Louisiana: Louisiana State University Press, 1986.

Bolle, Pierre (ed.). *Grenoble et le Vercors de la Résistance à la Libération.* (Proceedings of Conference of November, 1975.) Lyon: La Manufacture, 1985.

Breuer, William R. *Operation Dragoon.* Novato, California: Presidio, 1987.

Brown, Anthony Cave. See Cave Brown.

Calvi, Fabrizio. *OSS: La guerre secrète en France.* Paris: Hachette, 1990.

Calvocoressi, Peter. *Top Secret Ultra.* London: Cassell, 1980.

Cave Brown, Anthony. *The Last Hero: Wild Bill Donovan.* New York: Times Books, 1982.

Clarke, Jeffrey. *From the Riviera to the Rhine.* U.S. Army in World War II. Washington, D. C: U.S. Government Printing Office, 1992.

Cochran, Alexander S., Jr. "Protecting the Ultimate Advantage," *Military History* (June 1985).

Cookridge, E. H. [Edward Spiro]. *Set Europe Ablaze.* New York: Crowell, 1967.
_____. *They Came From the Sky.* New York: Crowell, 1967.

Costes, Col. Louis. *La Résistance au pays d'Apt.* Apt: Vioud et Coumes, 1974.

Craven, W. F., and J. L. Cate. *The Army Air Forces in World War II.* 3 vols. Chicago: University of Chicago Press, 1951.

Dainville, Col. A. de. *L'ORA: La Résistance de l'Armée.* Paris: Lavauzelle, 1974.

Defrasne, Col. J. "Un réseau de renseignements de l'ORA dans le Sud-est de la France," *Revue historique de l'Armée,* No. 4 (1969).

Devlin, Gerard M. *Paratrooper!* New York: St. Martin's, 1979.

Dreyfus, Paul. *Vercors, citadelle de la liberté.* Paris: Arthoud, 1969.

Dunlop, Richard. *Donovan: America's Master Spy.* New York: Rand McNally, 1982.

Durand, Paul. *La S. N. C. F. pendant la guerre.* Paris: Presses Universitaires de France, 1968.

Duroselle, Jean-Baptiste. *L'Abîme, 1939–1945.* Paris: Imprimerie Nationale, 1982.

Ehrlich, Blake. *Resistance: France 1940–1945.* Boston: Little Brown, 1965.

Ehrman, John. *Grand Strategy*: vol. 5 of the *Grand Strategy* series, J. R. M. Butler (ed.). London: HMSO, 1956.

Eisenhower, David. *Eisenhower at War, 1943–1945*. New York: Vintage, 1987.

Even, Commandant. "La retraite allemande des Côtes de Provence à Lyon," *Revue historique de l'Armée*, No. 3 (Aug., 1959).

Fol, V., and R.-C. Rudigoz. *La bataille de Meximieux*. Trévoux: Périodiques Spécialisées, 1979.

Foot, M. R. D. *SOE: An Outline History of the Special Operations Executive*. London: BBC, 1984.

_____. *SOE in France*. London: HMSO, 1966.

Footit, Hillary, and John Simmonds. *France 1943–1945*. New York: Holmes & Meier, 1988.

Foulon, Charles-Louis. *Le pouvoir en province à la libération: les Commissaires de la République*. Paris: Armand Colin, 1975.

Funk, Arthur L. *Charles de Gaulle: The Crucial Years, 1943–1944*. Norman, Okla.: University of Oklahoma Press, 1959.

_____. "Considérations stratégiques sur l'invasion du sud de la France," *La guerre en Méditerrannée 1939–1945* (Proceedings of Conference of April 1969, edited by Henri Michel). Paris: CNRS, 1971.

Girard, J. "La participation des FFI des Alpes-Maritimes à la libération," *Cahiers de la Méditerrannée*, No. 12 (1976).

La guerre en Méditerrannée, 1934–1945 (Proceedings of Conference of April, 1969). Edited by Henri Michel. Paris: CNRS, 1971.

Guiral, Pierre. *Libération de Marseille*. Paris: Hachette-Littérature, 1974.

Haestrup, Jorgen. *European Resistance Movements*, 1939–1945. Westport, Conn.: Meckler, 1981.

Heroes of the Resistance. By the Editors of the Army Times. New York: Army Times, 1967.

Hinsley, F. H., et al. *British Intelligence in the Second World War: Its Influence on Strategy and Operations*. 5 vols. New York: Cambridge University Press, 1979–90.

Hostache, René. *De Gaulle 1944: victoire de la légimité*. Paris: Plon, 1978.

_____. *Le Conseil National de la Résistance*. Paris: Presses Universitaires de France, 1958.

Howard, Michael. *Strategic Deception*. Vol. 5 of *British Intelligence in the Second World War*. New York: Cambridge University Press, 1990.

Howarth, Patrick (ed.). *Special Operations*. London: Routledge & Kegan Paul, 1955.

Hurstfield, Julian G. *America and the French Nation, 1939–1945*. Chapel Hill, North Carolina: University of North Carolina Press, 1986.

Huston, James A. *Out of the Blue: US Army Airborne Operations in World War II*. West Lafayette, Ind.: Purdue University Press, 1972.

Hymoff, Edward. *OSS in World War II.* 2nd ed. New York: Richardson & Steirman, 1986.

Jankowski, Paul. *Communism and Collaboration: Simon Sabiani and Politics in Marseille, 1919–1944.* New Haven, Conn.: Yale University Press, 1989.

Judt, Tony (ed.). *Resistance and Revolution in Mediterranean Europe, 1939–1948.* New York: Routledge, 1989.

Kedward, H. Roderick. *Occupied France: Collaboration and Resistance, 1940–1944.* Oxford: Blackwell, 1985.

_____. *Resistance in Vichy France.* 2nd ed. New York: Oxford University Press, 1978.

Lacouture, Jean. *De Gaulle.* 3 vols. Paris: Editions du Seuil, 1984–89.

Leslie, Peter. *The Liberation of the Riviera: The Resistance to the Nazis in the South of France and the Story of Its Heroic Leader, Ange-Marie Miniconi.* New York: Wyndham, 1980.

Lewin, Ronald. *Ultra Goes to War.* New York: McGraw-Hill, 1978.

Lockhart, Col. Vincent M. *T-Patch to Victory: The 36th "Texas" Division.* Canyon, Texas: Staked Plains Press, 1981.

Lorain, Pierre. *Clandestine Operations: The Arms and Techniques of the Resistance.* English adaptation by David Kahn. New York: Macmillan, 1983.

Masson, Madeleine. *Christine: A Search for Christine Granville.* London: Hamish Hamilton, 1975.

Matloff, Maurice. "Was the Invasion of Southern France a Blunder?" *U.S. Naval Institute Proceedings* (July 1958).

Michel, Henri. *La guerre de l'ombre.* Paris: Grasset, 1970. English ed.: *The Shadow War: Resistance in Europe, 1939–1945.* London: Andre Deutsch, 1972.

_____. *Histoire de la Résistance.* Paris: Presses Universitaires de France, 1950.

Montfort, Col. M. "Les combats entre Montélimar et Valence du 21 au 30 août 1944," *Revue Militaire Suisse,* No. 5 (May 1966).

Morgan, Ted. *An Uncertain Hour.* New York: Arbor House/Morrow, 1990.

Morgan, William J. *The OSS and I.* New York: Norton, 1957.

Noguères, Henri. *Histoire de la Résistance en France.* 5 vols. Paris: Laffont, 1974–81.

Novick, Peter. *The Resistance versus Vichy: The Purge of Collaborators in Liberated France.* New York: Columbia University Press, 1968.

Parrish, Thomas. *The Ultra Americans.* New York: Stein & Day, 1986.

Paxton, Robert. *Parades and Politics at Vichy.* Princeton, New Jersey: Princeton University Press, 1966.

_____. *Vichy France: Old Guard and New Order.* 2nd ed. New York: Knopf, 1982.

Pearson, Michael. *Tears of Glory* (Vercors). Garden City, New York: Double-Day, 1978.

Pogue, Forrest. *The Supreme Command.* The U.S. Army in World War II. Washington, D. C.: U.S. Government Printing Office, 1954.

"La Provence pendant la guerre," *Revue d'histoire de la deuxième guerre mondiale* (Special issue), No. 113 (Jan. 1979).

Revue historique de l'Armée, No. 4, 1969. (Special issue commemorating the 25th anniversary of French liberation.)

Robichon, Jacques. *Le débarquement en Provence.* Paris: Laffont, 1962. English ed.: *The Second D-Day.* New York: Walker, 1962.

Rossiter, Margaret. *Women in the Resistance.* New York: Praeger, 1985.

Ruby, Marcel. *F Section, SOE: The Buckmaster Networks.* London: Leo Cooper, 1988.

Schoenbrun, David. *Soldiers of the Night: The Story of the French Resistance.* New York: Dutton, 1980.

Simmonds, John. See Footit.

Smith, Bradley F. *The Shadow Warriors: OSS and the Origins of the CIA.* New York: Basic Books, 1983.

Smith, R. Harris. *OSS: The Secret History of America's First Central Intelligence Agency.* Berkeley: University of California Press, 1972.

Stafford, David. *Britain and European Resistance.* London: Macmillan, 1980.

Staiger, Jörg. *Rückzug durchs Rhônetal.* Neckargemund: Vowinkel, 1965.

Sweets, John. *Choices in Vichy France: The French under Nazi Occupation.* New York: Oxford University Press, 1986.

_____. *The Politics of Resistance in France, 1940–1944.* De Kalb, Illinois: Northern Illinois University Press, 1976.

Tillon, Charles. *Les F.T.P.* Paris: Beauval, 1962.

Troy, Thomas. *Donovan and the CIA.* Frederick, Md.: UPA, 1981.

Vernet, J. *Le réarmement et la réorganisation de l'armée de terre française, 1943–1946.* Vincennes: Service historique de l'armée, 1980.

Vigneras, Marcel. *Rearming the French.* U.S. Army in World War II. Washington, D. C.: U.S. Government Printing Office, 1957.

Wilt, Alan F. *The French Riviera Campaign of August 1944.* Carbondale, Illinois: Southern Illinois University Press, 1981.

Wright, Gordon. "Reflections on the French Resistance," *Political Science Quarterly* (Sept. 1962).

Wyant, William K. *"Sandy" Patch.* New York: Praeger, 1991.

Wylie, Laurence. *Village in the Vaucluse.* New York: Harper & Row, 1957.

Index

About the Author

ARTHUR LAYTON FUNK is Professor Emeritus of History at the University of Florida. He is a recognized expert on American-French relations in World War II and the author of *Charles De Gaulle: The Crucial Years, 1943-44* (1959); *The Politics of TORCH* (1974); and *De Yalta à Potsdam* (1982).